La Corda d'Oro

3
Story & Art by Yuki Kure

Characters

Kahoko Hino
(General Education School, 2nd year)

The heroine. She knows nothing about music, but she still finds herself participating in the music competition equipped with a magic violin.

Len Tsukimori
(Music School, 2nd year)

A violin major and a cold perfectionist from a musical family of unquestionable talent.

Ryotaro Tsuchiura
(General Education, 2nd year)

A member of the soccer team who seems to be looking after Kahoko as a fellow Gen Ed student.

Keiichi Shimizu
(Music school, 1st year)

A student of the cello who walks to the beat of his own drum and is often lost in the world of music. He is also often asleep.

Kazuki Hihara
(Music school, 3rd year)

An energetic and friendly trumpet major and a fan of anything fun.

Azuma Yunoki
(Music school, 3rd year)

A flute major and the son of a graceful and kind traditional flower arrangement master. He even has a dedicated fan club called the "Yunoki Guard."

Hiroto Kanazawa
(Music teacher)

The contest coordinator whose lazy demeanor suggests he is avoiding any hassle.

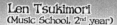

MATSURI HINO burst onto the manga scene with her title
Kono Yume ga Sametara (When This Dream Is Over), which was published
in *LaLa DX* magazine. Hino was a manga artist a mere nine months after
she decided to become one.

With the success of her popular series *Captive Hearts* and *MeruPuri*, Hino
has established herself as a major player in the world of shojo manga.
Vampire Knight is currently serialized in *LaLa* and *Shojo Beat* magazines.

Hino enjoys creative activities and has commented that she would
have been either an architect or an apprentice to traditional
Japanese craft masters if she had not become a manga artist.

Captive Hearts
Vol. 3

The Shojo Beat Manga Edition

STORY & ART BY
MATSURI HINO

Translation & Adaptation/Andria Cheng
Touch-up Art & Lettering/Sabrina Heep
Design/Amy Martin
Editor/Amy Yu

Editor in Chief, Books/Alvin Lu
Editor in Chief, Magazines/Marc Weidenbaum
VP, Publishing Licensing/Rika Inouye
VP, Sales & Product Marketing/Gonzalo Ferreyra
VP, Creative/Linda Espinosa
Publisher/Hyoe Narita

Toraware no Minoue by Matsuri Hino
© Matsuri Hino 1997
All rights reserved.
First published in Japan in 2001 by HAKUSENSHA, Inc., Tokyo.
English language translation rights arranged with Hakusensha, Inc., Tokyo.
The stories, characters and incidents mentioned in this publication are entirely fictional.

Printed in Canada

Published by VIZ Media, LLC
P.O. Box 77010
San Francisco, CA 94107

Shojo Beat Manga Edition
10 9 8 7 6 5 4 3 2 1
First printing, March 2009

store.viz.com

NOTES CONT.

Page 55, panel 7 – **Meiji Era**
Period in time that designates the reign of the Meiji Emperor from approximately 1868 to 1912.

Page 73, panel 2 – **Danna**
An old-fashioned word for "master." The girls call Kuronekomaru this because he is a patron.

Page 76, panel 4 – **Neesan**
Neesan is an informal way to say "elder sister," but this term can be used to address women that are not related to you by blood.

Page 106, panel 4 – **Oniisama**
Oniisan is a formal way to say "older brother," and swapping the *-san* honorific with *-sama* adds more respect. Rui is not literally calling Megumi her older brother. Rather, she feels close to him and respects him greatly.

Page 135, panel 6 – **Awa Odori**
A traditional folk dance that is synonymous with the Awa Dance Festival in Tokushima City. Tokushima used to be called Awa in ancient times, and *odori* means "dance."

Captivated by the story but confused by some of the terms? Here are some cultural notes to help you out!

HONORIFICS

Chan – an informal version of *san* used to address children and females.

Kun – an informal honorific used primarily for males; it can be used by people of more senior status addressing those junior to them or by anyone in addressing male children.

San – the most common honorific title; it is used to address people outside one's immediate family and close circle of friends.

Sama – the formal version of *san*; this honorific title is used primarily in addressing persons much higher in rank than oneself.

NOTES

Page 7, panel 3 – *LaLa*
Captive Hearts was originally serialized in *LaLa*, a Japanese *shojo manga* (girls' comics) magazine published monthly by Hakusensha.

Page 7, panel 3 – **Aomori Nebuta Festival**
The Aomori Nebuta Festival takes place in early August every year in the city of Aomori. Over twenty large floats called *nebuta* are pulled by people in the streets. The *nebuta* designs are usually patterned after Japanese historical figures or themes, often showcasing fierce-looking Kabuki characters or warriors.

Page 18, panel 1 – **Muromachi Era**
A period of Japanese history that ran from approximately 1336 to 1573. The era ended when the last shogun, Ashikaga Yoshiaki, was driven out of the capital Kyoto by Oda Nobunaga.

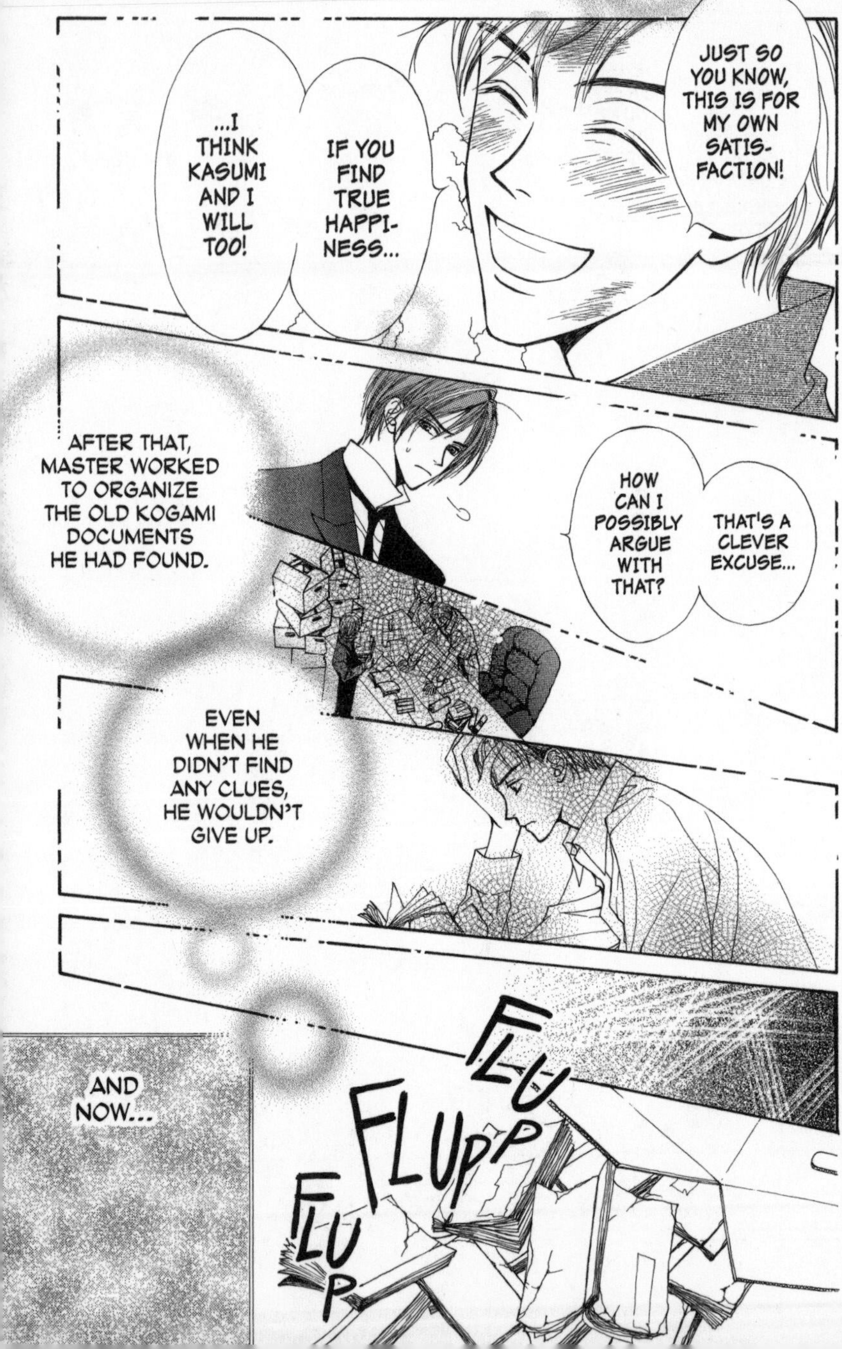
JUST SO YOU KNOW, THIS IS FOR MY OWN SATIS-FACTION!
IF YOU FIND TRUE HAPPI-NESS...
...I THINK KASUMI AND I WILL TOO!
THAT'S A CLEVER EXCUSE...
HOW CAN I POSSIBLY ARGUE WITH THAT?
AFTER THAT, MASTER WORKED TO ORGANIZE THE OLD KOGAMI DOCUMENTS HE HAD FOUND.
EVEN WHEN HE DIDN'T FIND ANY CLUES, HE WOULDN'T GIVE UP.
FLUP
FLUPP
FLUP
AND NOW...

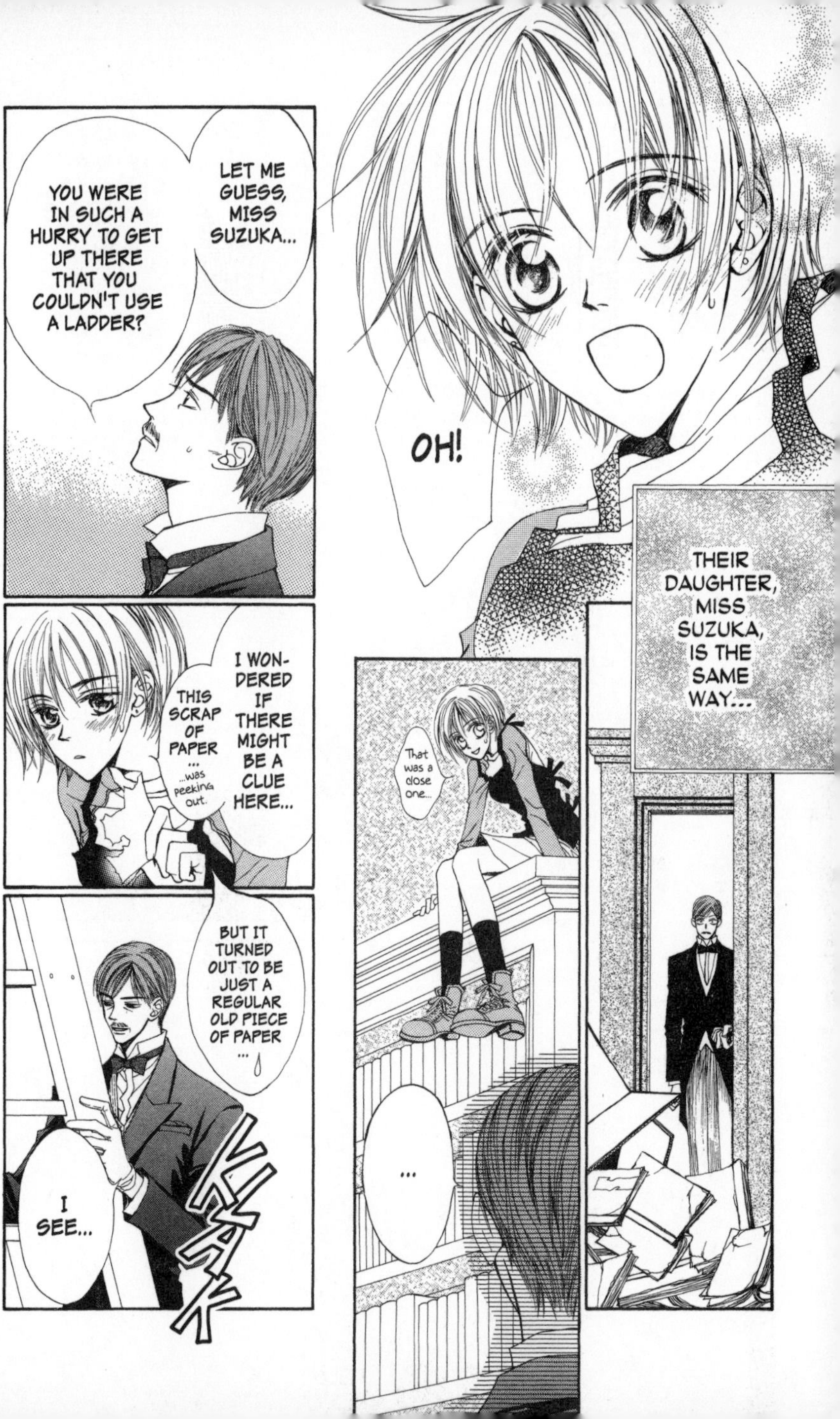
OH!
THEIR DAUGHTER, MISS SUZUKA, IS THE SAME WAY...
That was a close one...
...
LET ME GUESS, MISS SUZUKA...
YOU WERE IN SUCH A HURRY TO GET UP THERE THAT YOU COULDN'T USE A LADDER?
I WONDERED IF THERE MIGHT BE A CLUE HERE...
THIS SCRAP OF PAPER ...
...was peeking out.
BUT IT TURNED OUT TO BE JUST A REGULAR OLD PIECE OF PAPER ...
I SEE...

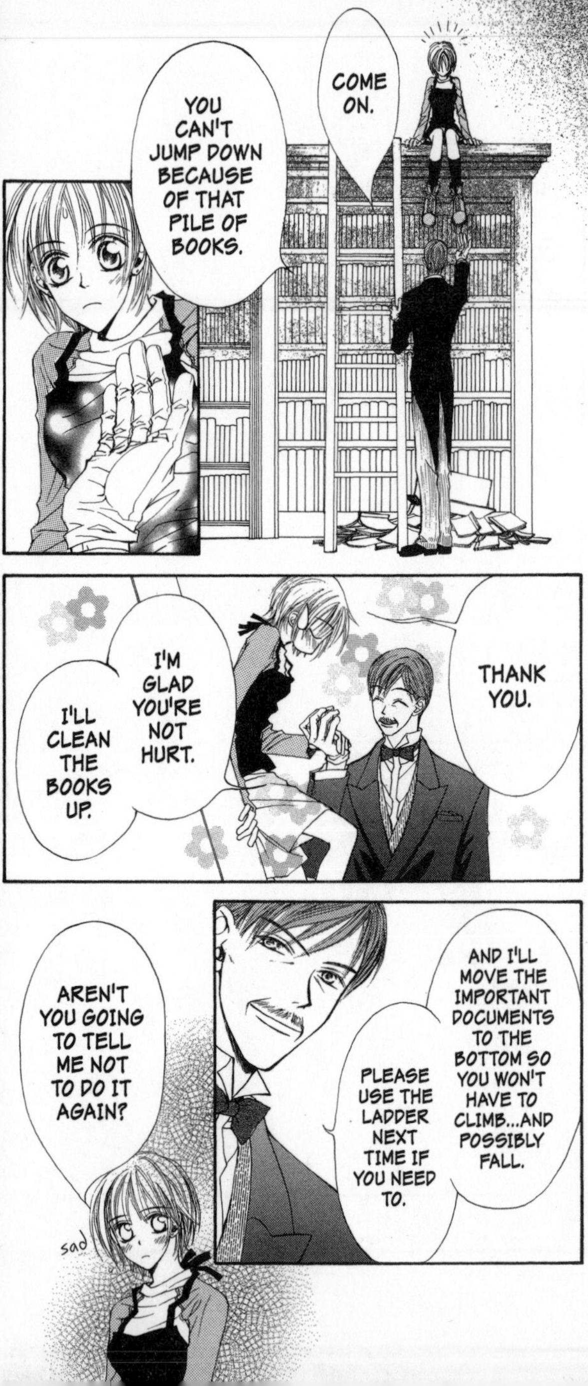
COME ON.
YOU CAN'T JUMP DOWN BECAUSE OF THAT PILE OF BOOKS.
THANK YOU.
I'M GLAD YOU'RE NOT HURT.
I'LL CLEAN THE BOOKS UP.
AND I'LL MOVE THE IMPORTANT DOCUMENTS TO THE BOTTOM SO YOU WON'T HAVE TO CLIMB...AND POSSIBLY FALL.
PLEASE USE THE LADDER NEXT TIME IF YOU NEED TO.
AREN'T YOU GOING TO TELL ME NOT TO DO IT AGAIN?
sad

Even though this space is supposed to be for me to write in, I'm usually too shy and can't think of anything.

But I know it's better if I write something, so I'll do my best.

Because of your support, this silly manga has reached its third volume. It feels like it's gone by so fast!

Today I was lectured by my acupuncturist to put out my manga faster! Am I really that slow? I think this is as fast as I can work.

But I'll do my best. As long as I'm not putting too much stress on my body.

sheepish laugh

↓ To be continued...

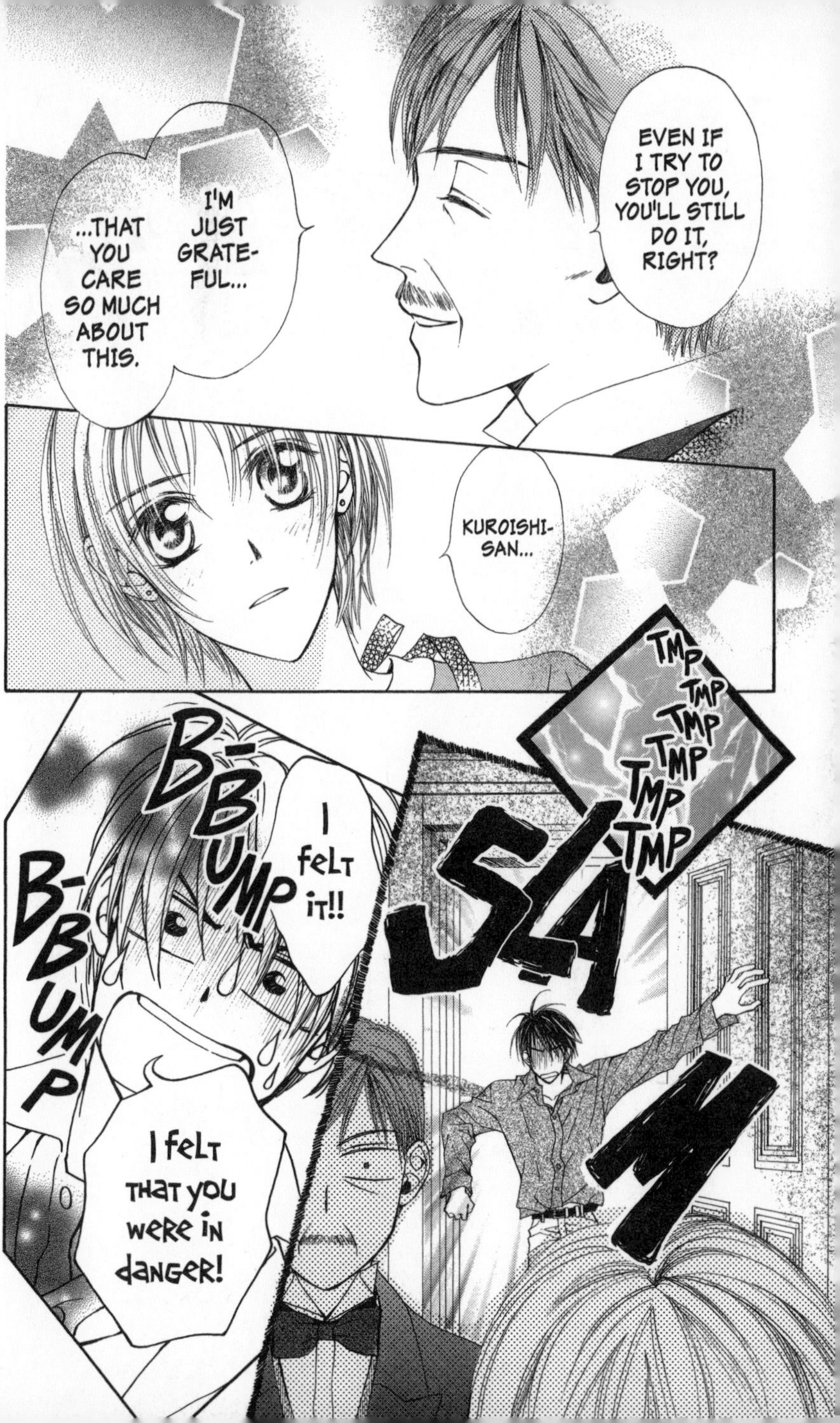
EVEN IF I TRY TO STOP YOU, YOU'LL STILL DO IT, RIGHT?
I'M JUST GRATE-FUL...
...THAT YOU CARE SO MUCH ABOUT THIS.
KUROISHI-SAN...
TMP TMP TMP TMP TMP TMP
SLAM
B-BUMP
I felt it!!
B-BUMP
I felt that you were in danger!

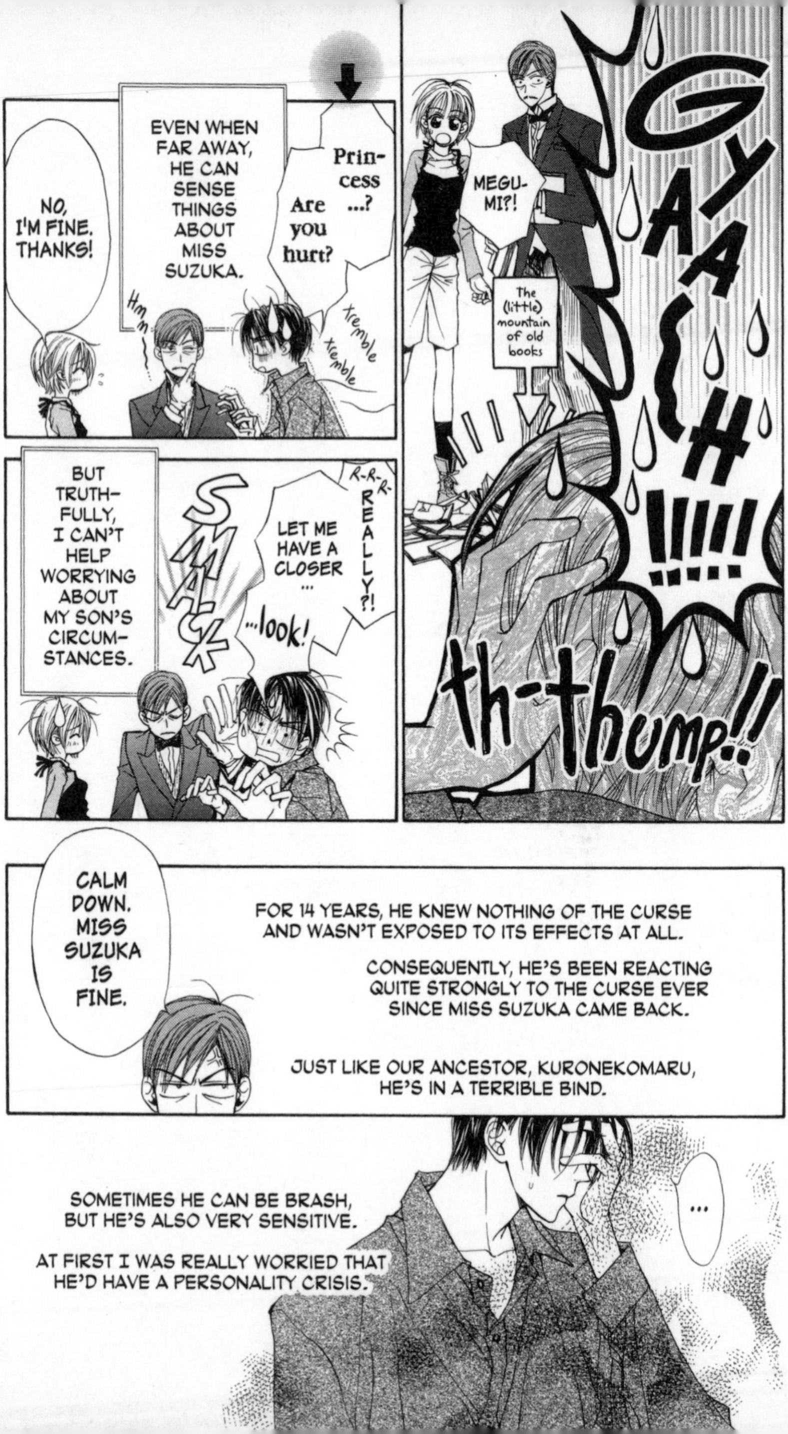
GYAAAHH!!!!!
MEGUMI?!
The (little) mountain of old books
th-thump!!
Princess...? Are you hurt?
EVEN WHEN FAR AWAY, HE CAN SENSE THINGS ABOUT MISS SUZUKA.
NO, I'M FINE. THANKS!
Hmm...
xtremble xtremble
R-R-R-REALLY?!
LET ME HAVE A CLOSER ... ...look!
SMACK
BUT TRUTHFULLY, I CAN'T HELP WORRYING ABOUT MY SON'S CIRCUMSTANCES.
FOR 14 YEARS, HE KNEW NOTHING OF THE CURSE AND WASN'T EXPOSED TO ITS EFFECTS AT ALL.
CONSEQUENTLY, HE'S BEEN REACTING QUITE STRONGLY TO THE CURSE EVER SINCE MISS SUZUKA CAME BACK.
JUST LIKE OUR ANCESTOR, KURONEKOMARU, HE'S IN A TERRIBLE BIND.
CALM DOWN. MISS SUZUKA IS FINE.
...
SOMETIMES HE CAN BE BRASH, BUT HE'S ALSO VERY SENSITIVE.
AT FIRST I WAS REALLY WORRIED THAT HE'D HAVE A PERSONALITY CRISIS.

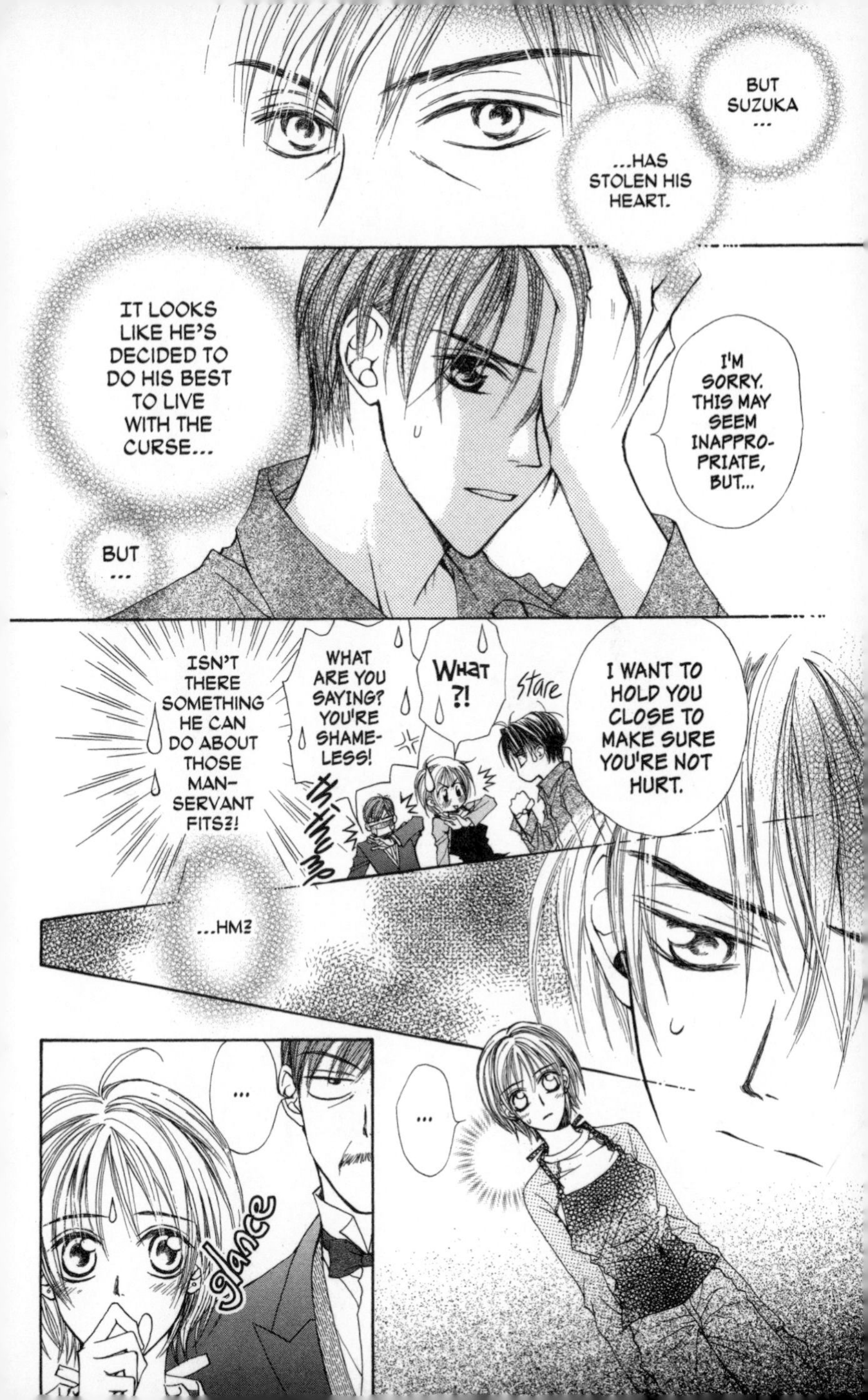
BUT SUZUKA ...
...HAS STOLEN HIS HEART.
I'M SORRY. THIS MAY SEEM INAPPROPRIATE, BUT...
IT LOOKS LIKE HE'S DECIDED TO DO HIS BEST TO LIVE WITH THE CURSE...
BUT ...
I WANT TO HOLD YOU CLOSE TO MAKE SURE YOU'RE NOT HURT.
stare
WHAT ?!
WHAT ARE YOU SAYING? YOU'RE SHAMELESS!
ISN'T THERE SOMETHING HE CAN DO ABOUT THOSE MAN-SERVANT FITS?!
thump
...HM?
...
...
glance

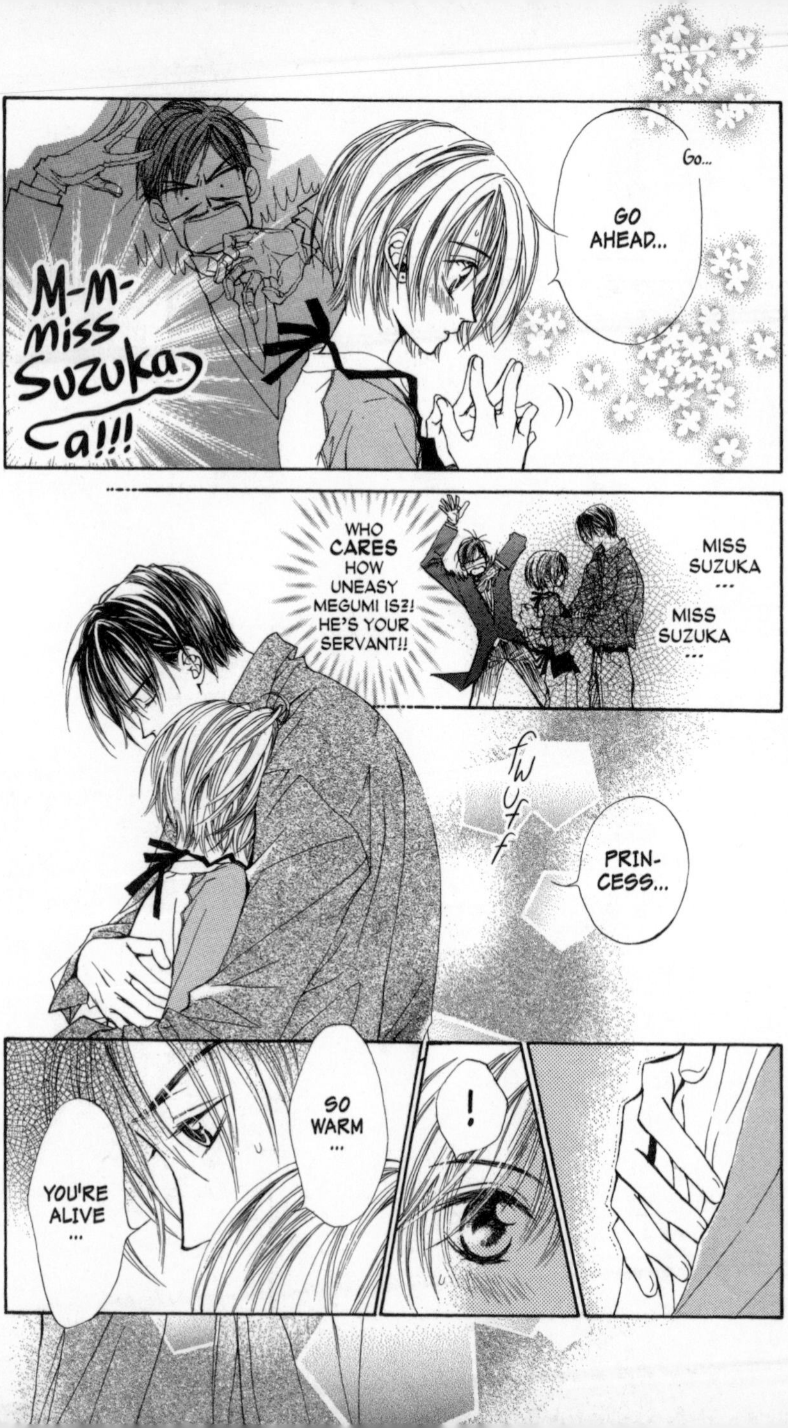
Go...
GO AHEAD...
M-M-Miss Suzuka a!!!
MISS SUZUKA ...
MISS SUZUKA ...
WHO CARES HOW UNEASY MEGUMI IS?! HE'S YOUR SERVANT!!
FWUFF
PRIN-CESS...
!
SO WARM ...
YOU'RE ALIVE ...

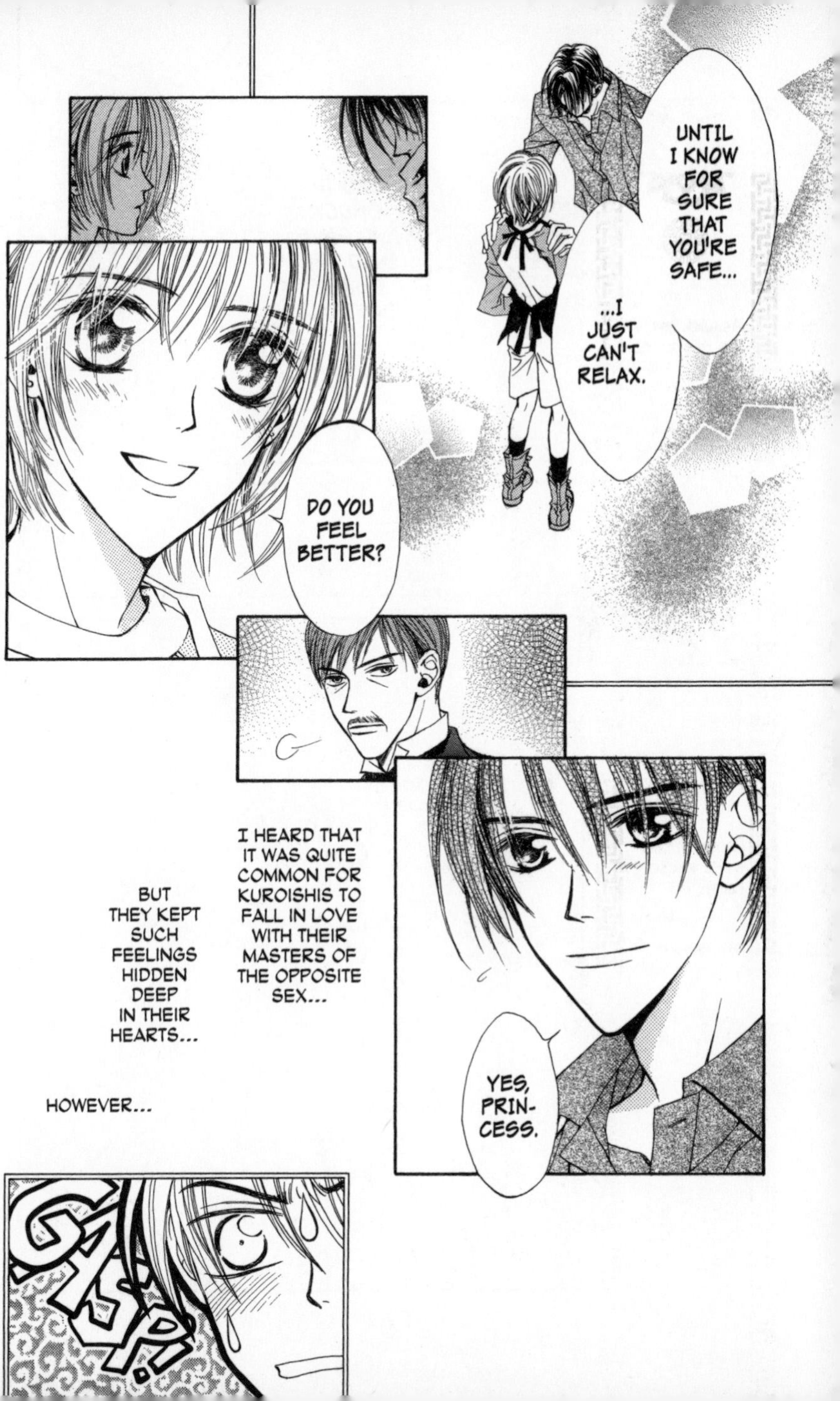
UNTIL I KNOW FOR SURE THAT YOU'RE SAFE...
...I JUST CAN'T RELAX.
DO YOU FEEL BETTER?
YES, PRINCESS.
I HEARD THAT IT WAS QUITE COMMON FOR KUROISHIS TO FALL IN LOVE WITH THEIR MASTERS OF THE OPPOSITE SEX...
BUT THEY KEPT SUCH FEELINGS HIDDEN DEEP IN THEIR HEARTS...
HOWEVER...
GASP!

SHOOK!!!!
I WANTED TO SAVOR SUZUKA'S TOUCH LONGER!
BUT I WAS IN SHOCK AND GAVE INTO THE CURSE INSTEAD!
GRR...
TWITCH
Whaaat?!!
WHAAM
THIS IS UNPRECEDENTED!!
WASN'T THERE SOMETHING IN THE BASEMENT YOU WANTED TO SEE, MISS SUZUKA?
STOMP
LET'S LEAVE MEGUMI TO TAKE CARE OF THE BOOKS HERE.
OH...
THANKS, MEGUMI ...
Yes, sir...
Yes...
Yes...

As with any job, there are various inconvenient things that come with mine, but I like being a manga artist. I'm very thankful to all of my readers...

Even when I hear something as simple as "I read it!" I get so shy and happy and thankful at the same time.

↓ ↓

I ask myself:

↓

"Doesn't this make you so happy?"

↓ ↓

My answer:

↓

"Yeaaah! Super happy!!"

(laugh)

↓ To be continued...

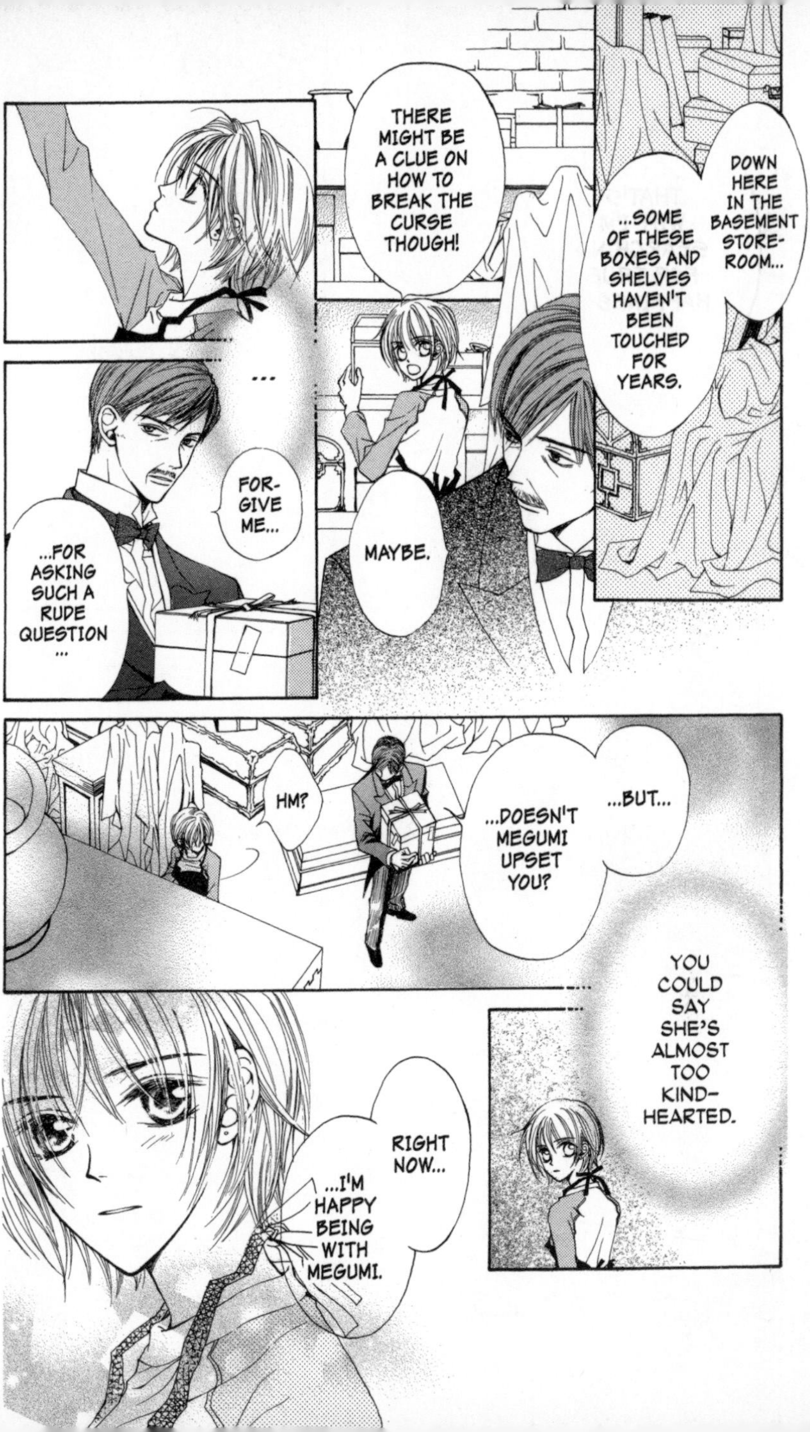
DOWN HERE IN THE BASEMENT STORE-ROOM...
...SOME OF THESE BOXES AND SHELVES HAVEN'T BEEN TOUCHED FOR YEARS.
THERE MIGHT BE A CLUE ON HOW TO BREAK THE CURSE THOUGH!
MAYBE.
...
FOR-GIVE ME...
...FOR ASKING SUCH A RUDE QUESTION...
...BUT...
...DOESN'T MEGUMI UPSET YOU?
HM?
YOU COULD SAY SHE'S ALMOST TOO KIND-HEARTED.
RIGHT NOW...
...I'M HAPPY BEING WITH MEGUMI.

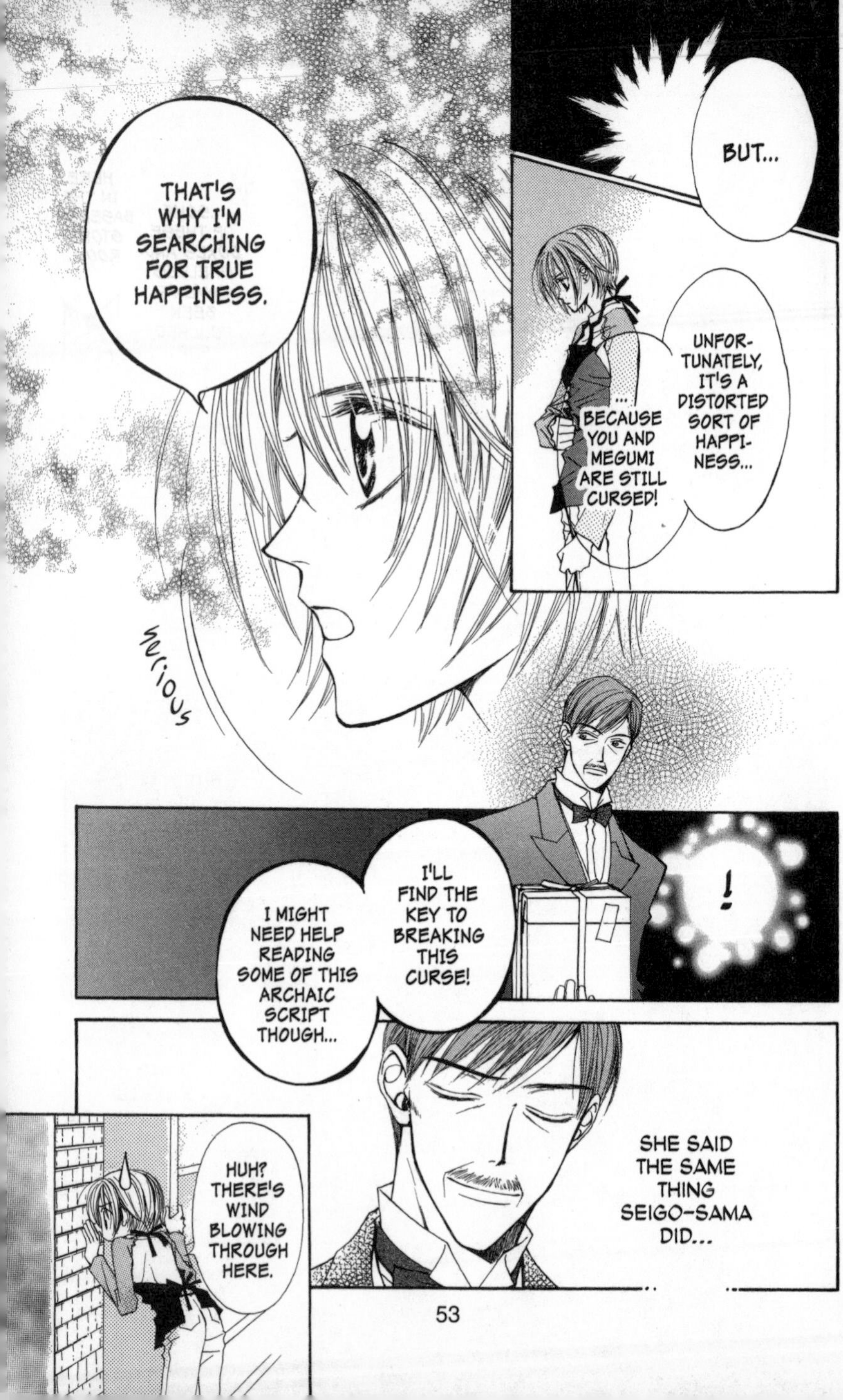
BUT...
UNFORTUNATELY, IT'S A DISTORTED SORT OF HAPPINESS...
...BECAUSE YOU AND MEGUMI ARE STILL CURSED!
THAT'S WHY I'M SEARCHING FOR TRUE HAPPINESS.
serious
!
I'LL FIND THE KEY TO BREAKING THIS CURSE!
I MIGHT NEED HELP READING SOME OF THIS ARCHAIC SCRIPT THOUGH...
SHE SAID THE SAME THING SEIGO-SAMA DID...
HUH? THERE'S WIND BLOWING THROUGH HERE.

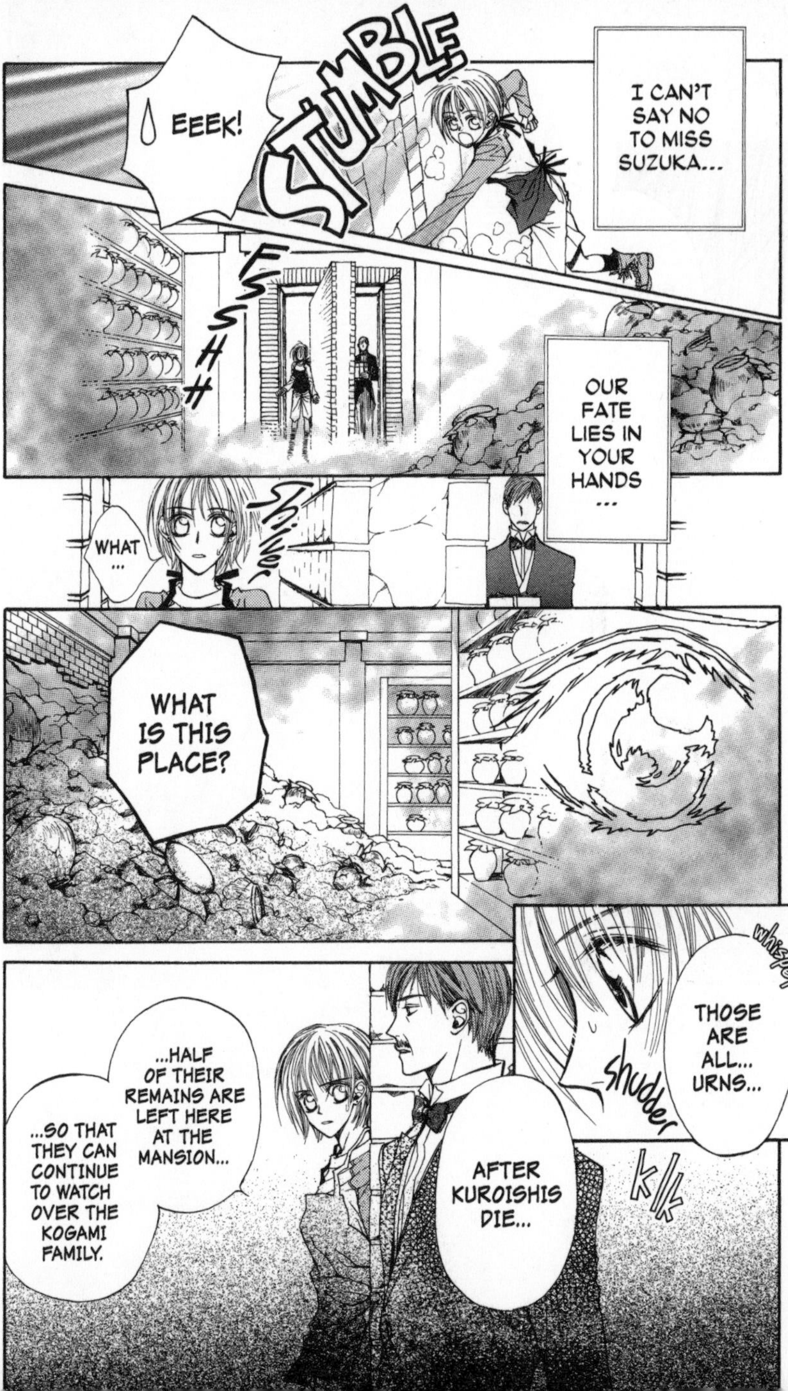
I CAN'T SAY NO TO MISS SUZUKA...
STUMBLE
EEEK!
OUR FATE LIES IN YOUR HANDS...
FSSHH
Shiver
WHAT...
WHAT IS THIS PLACE?
whisper
THOSE ARE ALL... URNS...
shudder
klk
AFTER KUROISHIS DIE...
...HALF OF THEIR REMAINS ARE LEFT HERE AT THE MANSION...
...SO THAT THEY CAN CONTINUE TO WATCH OVER THE KOGAMI FAMILY.

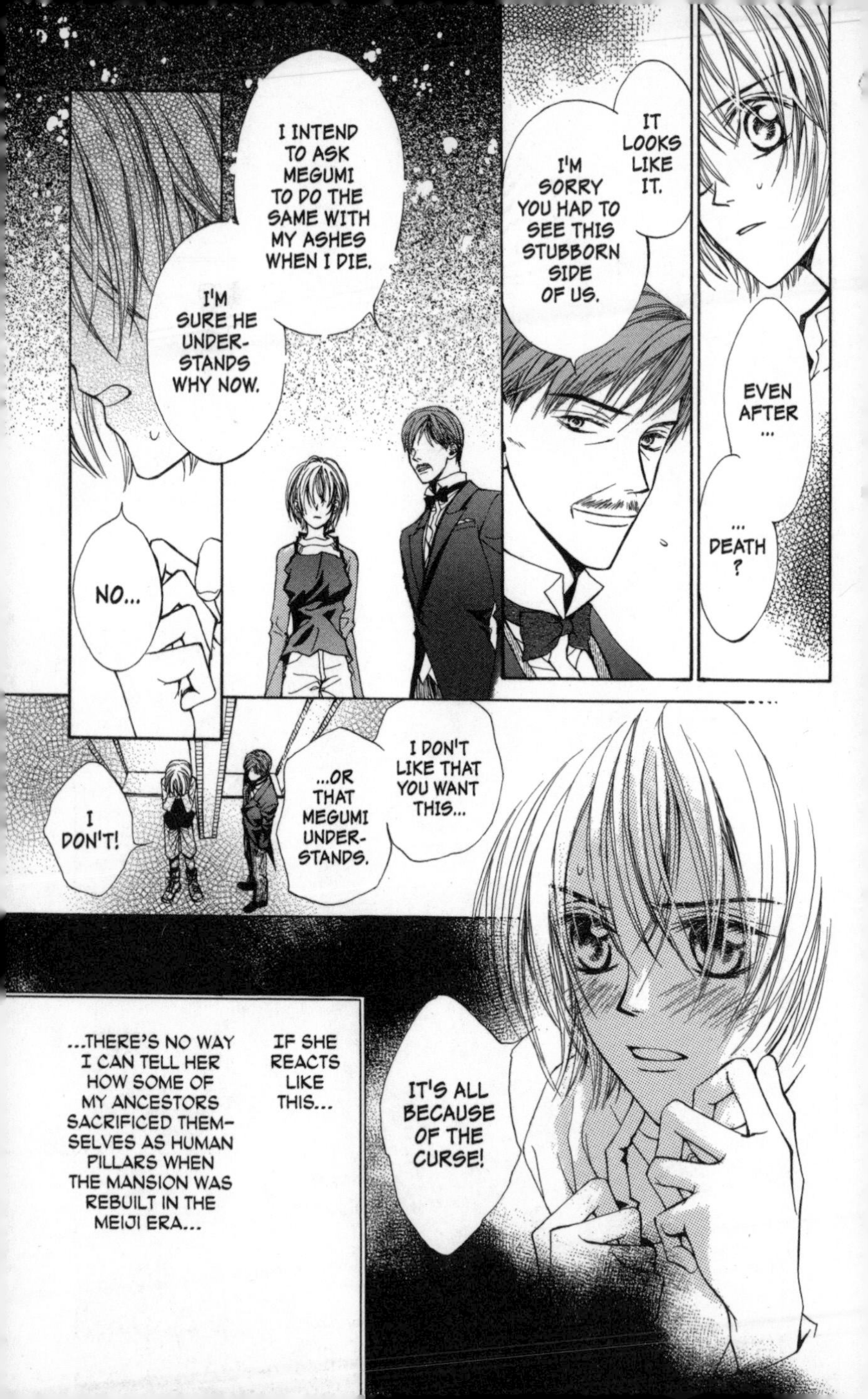
EVEN AFTER...
...DEATH?
IT LOOKS LIKE IT.
I'M SORRY YOU HAD TO SEE THIS STUBBORN SIDE OF US.
I INTEND TO ASK MEGUMI TO DO THE SAME WITH MY ASHES WHEN I DIE.
I'M SURE HE UNDERSTANDS WHY NOW.
NO...
I DON'T LIKE THAT YOU WANT THIS...
...OR THAT MEGUMI UNDERSTANDS.
I DON'T!
IT'S ALL BECAUSE OF THE CURSE!
IF SHE REACTS LIKE THIS...
...THERE'S NO WAY I CAN TELL HER HOW SOME OF MY ANCESTORS SACRIFICED THEMSELVES AS HUMAN PILLARS WHEN THE MANSION WAS REBUILT IN THE MEIJI ERA...

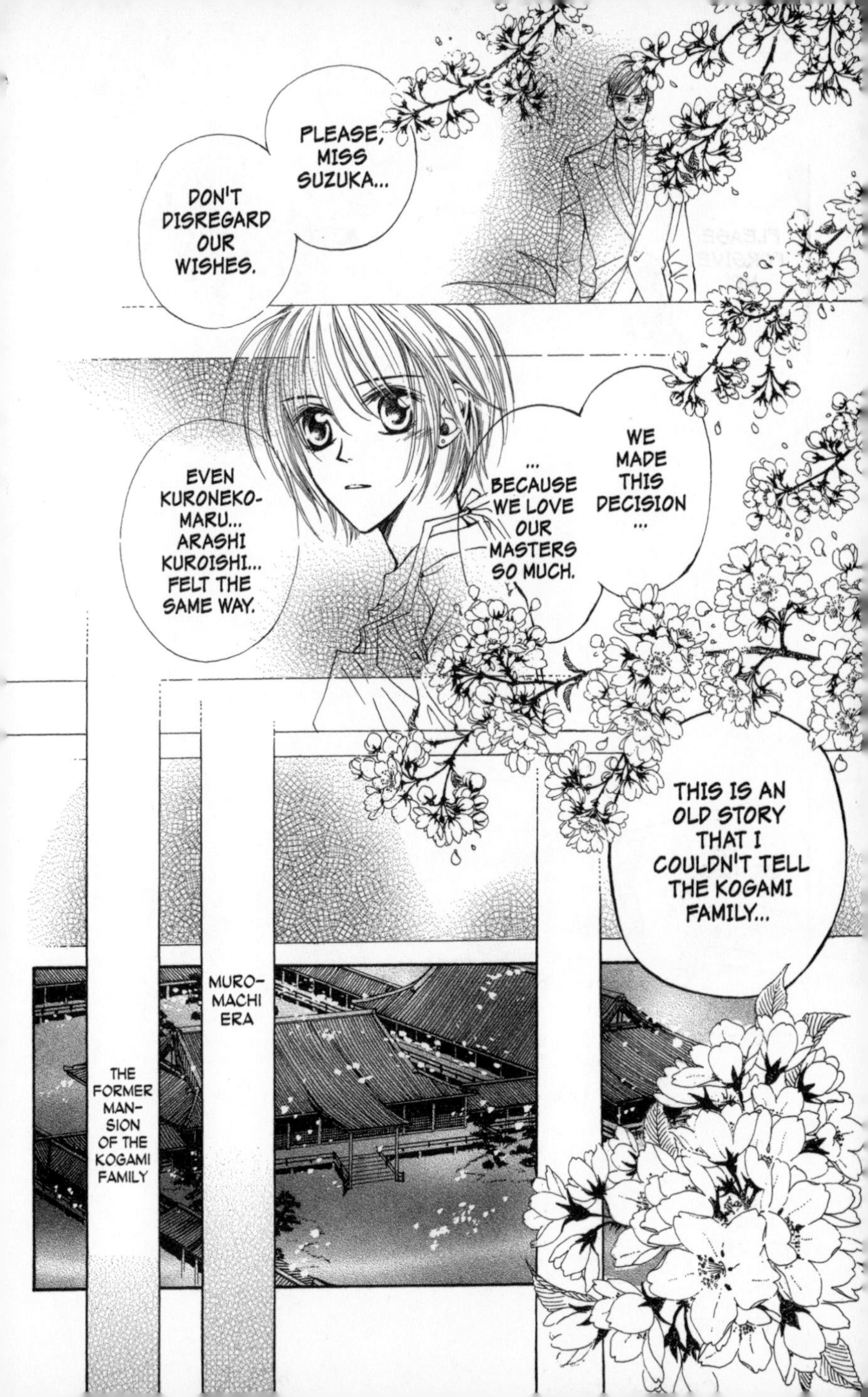
PLEASE, MISS SUZUKA...
DON'T DISREGARD OUR WISHES.
WE MADE THIS DECISION...
...BECAUSE WE LOVE OUR MASTERS SO MUCH.
EVEN KURONEKO-MARU... ARASHI KUROISHI... FELT THE SAME WAY.
THIS IS AN OLD STORY THAT I COULDN'T TELL THE KOGAMI FAMILY...
MURO-MACHI ERA
THE FORMER MAN-SION OF THE KOGAMI FAMILY

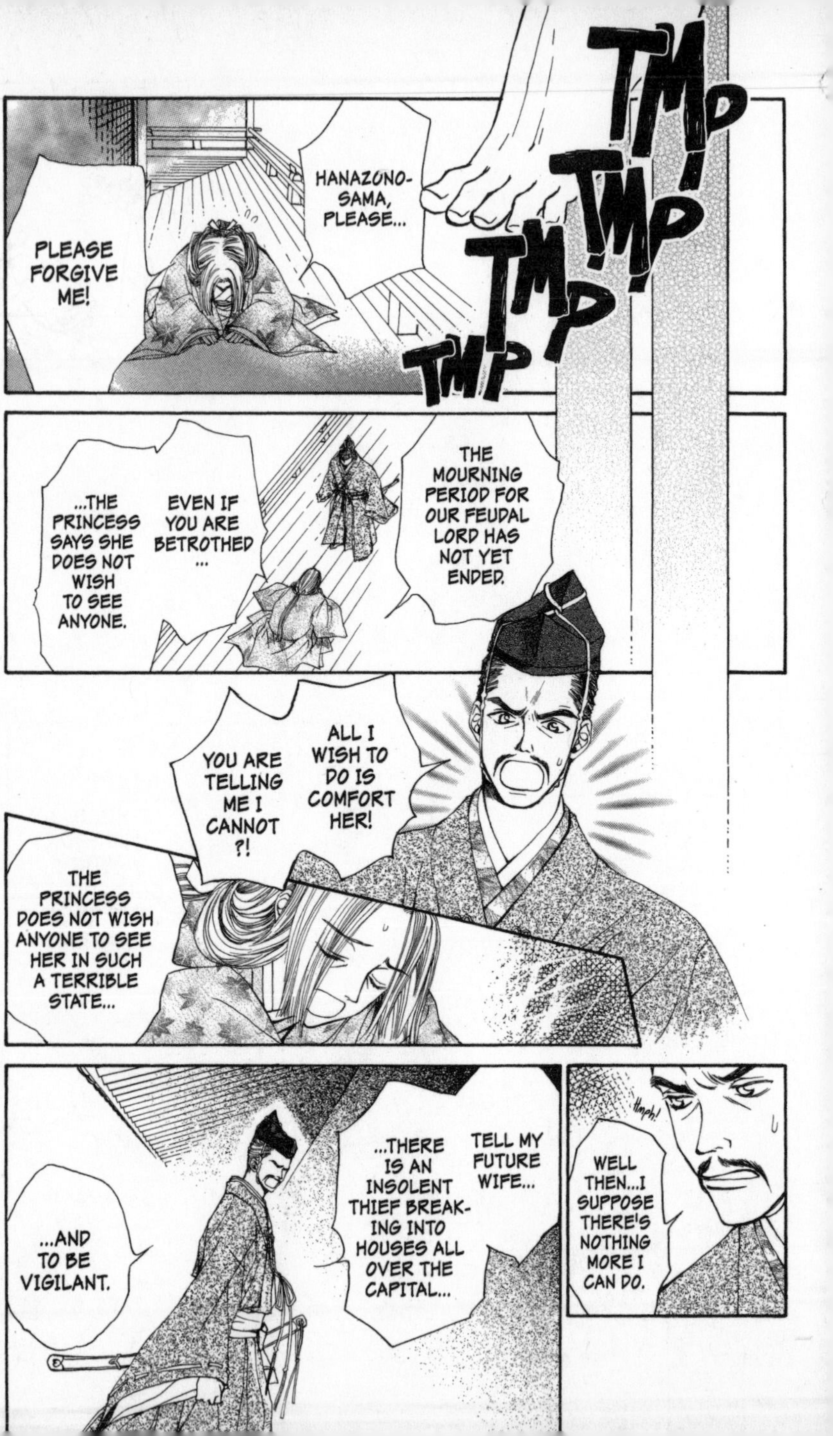
TMP TMP TMP TMP
HANAZONO-SAMA, PLEASE...
PLEASE FORGIVE ME!
THE MOURNING PERIOD FOR OUR FEUDAL LORD HAS NOT YET ENDED.
EVEN IF YOU ARE BETROTHED...
...THE PRINCESS SAYS SHE DOES NOT WISH TO SEE ANYONE.
ALL I WISH TO DO IS COMFORT HER!
YOU ARE TELLING ME I CANNOT?!
THE PRINCESS DOES NOT WISH ANYONE TO SEE HER IN SUCH A TERRIBLE STATE...
Hmph!
WELL THEN...I SUPPOSE THERE'S NOTHING MORE I CAN DO.
TELL MY FUTURE WIFE...
...THERE IS AN INSOLENT THIEF BREAK-ING INTO HOUSES ALL OVER THE CAPITAL...
...AND TO BE VIGILANT.

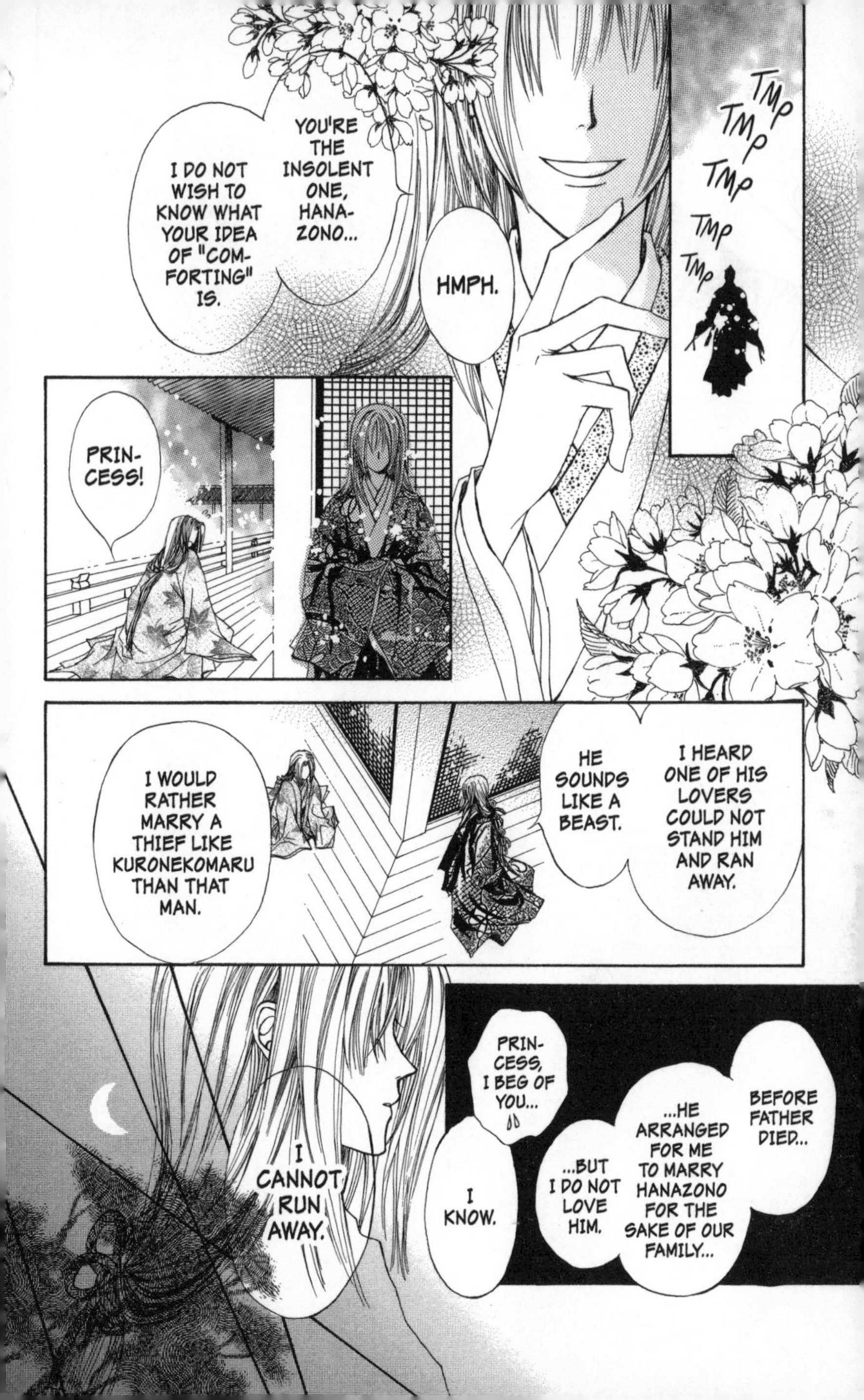
TMP TMP TMP TMP TMP
YOU'RE THE INSOLENT ONE, HANA-ZONO...
I DO NOT WISH TO KNOW WHAT YOUR IDEA OF "COM-FORTING" IS.
HMPH.
PRIN-CESS!
I HEARD ONE OF HIS LOVERS COULD NOT STAND HIM AND RAN AWAY.
HE SOUNDS LIKE A BEAST.
I WOULD RATHER MARRY A THIEF LIKE KURONEKOMARU THAN THAT MAN.
BEFORE FATHER DIED...
...HE ARRANGED FOR ME TO MARRY HANAZONO FOR THE SAKE OF OUR FAMILY...
PRIN-CESS, I BEG OF YOU...
...BUT I DO NOT LOVE HIM.
I KNOW.
I CANNOT RUN AWAY.

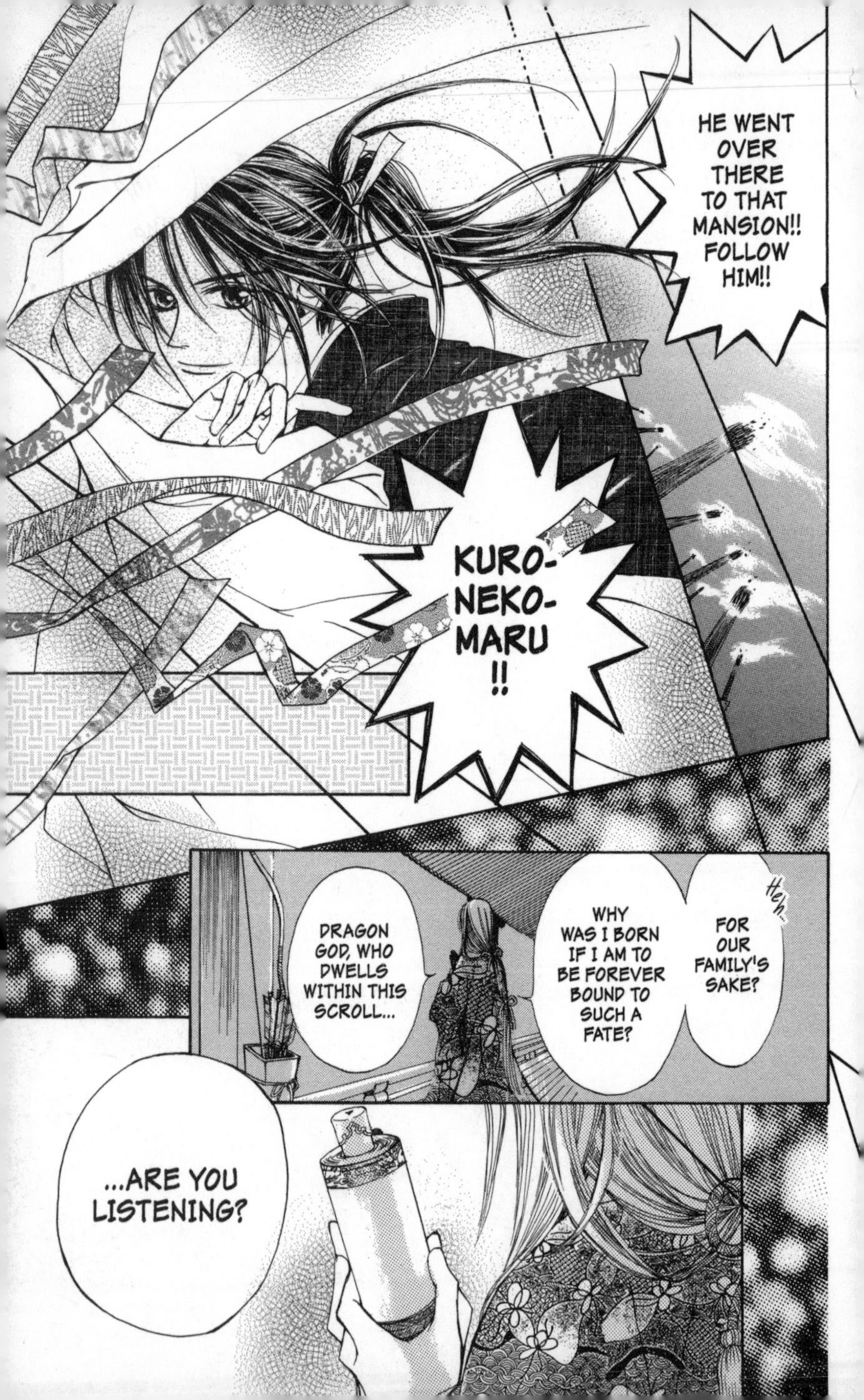
HE WENT OVER THERE TO THAT MANSION!! FOLLOW HIM!!
KURO-NEKO-MARU!!
Heh...
FOR OUR FAMILY'S SAKE?
WHY WAS I BORN IF I AM TO BE FOREVER BOUND TO SUCH A FATE?
DRAGON GOD, WHO DWELLS WITHIN THIS SCROLL...
...ARE YOU LISTENING?

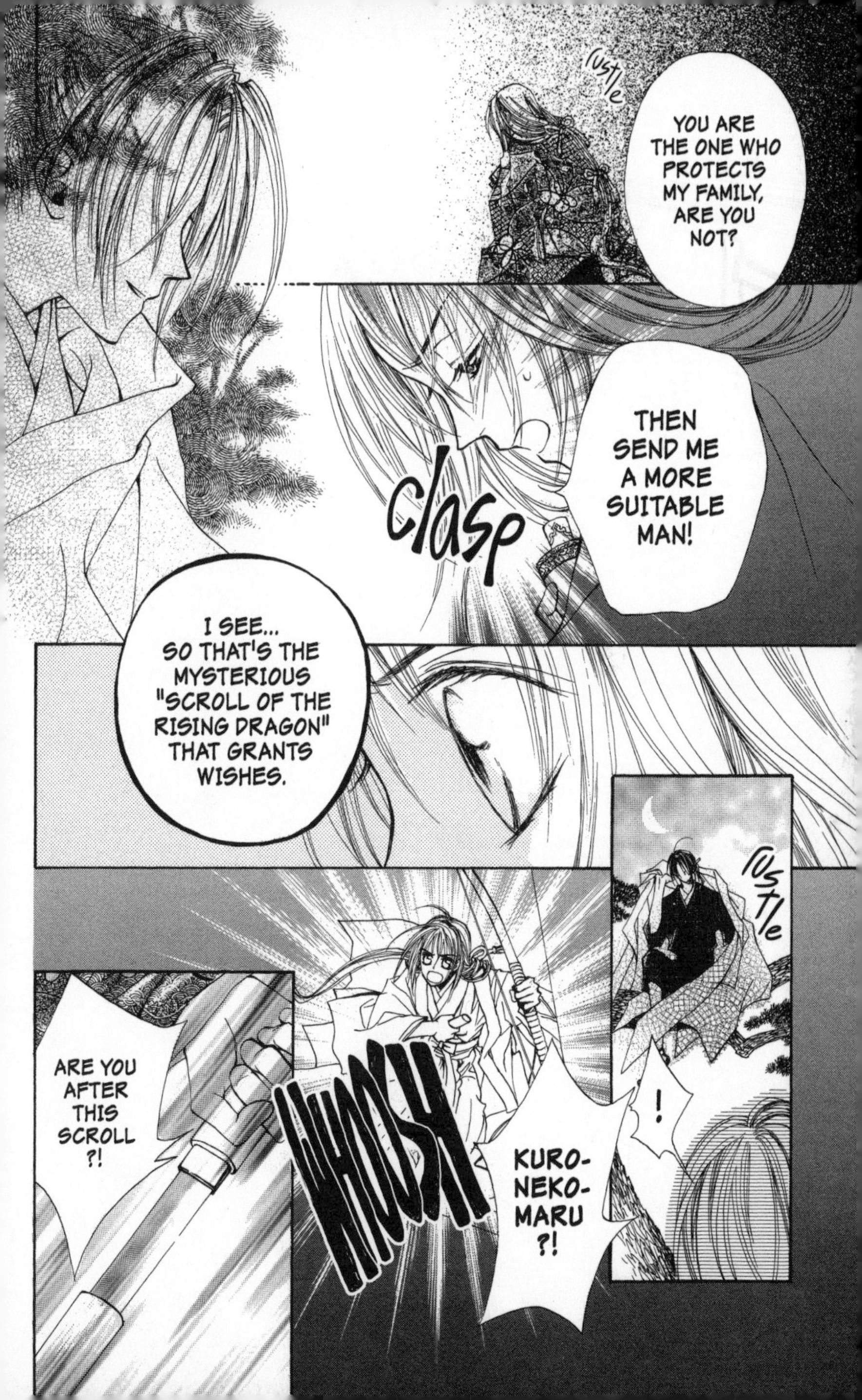
rustle
YOU ARE THE ONE WHO PROTECTS MY FAMILY, ARE YOU NOT?
clasp
THEN SEND ME A MORE SUITABLE MAN!
I SEE... SO THAT'S THE MYSTERIOUS "SCROLL OF THE RISING DRAGON" THAT GRANTS WISHES.
rustle
!
KURO-NEKO-MARU?!
WHOOSH
ARE YOU AFTER THIS SCROLL?!

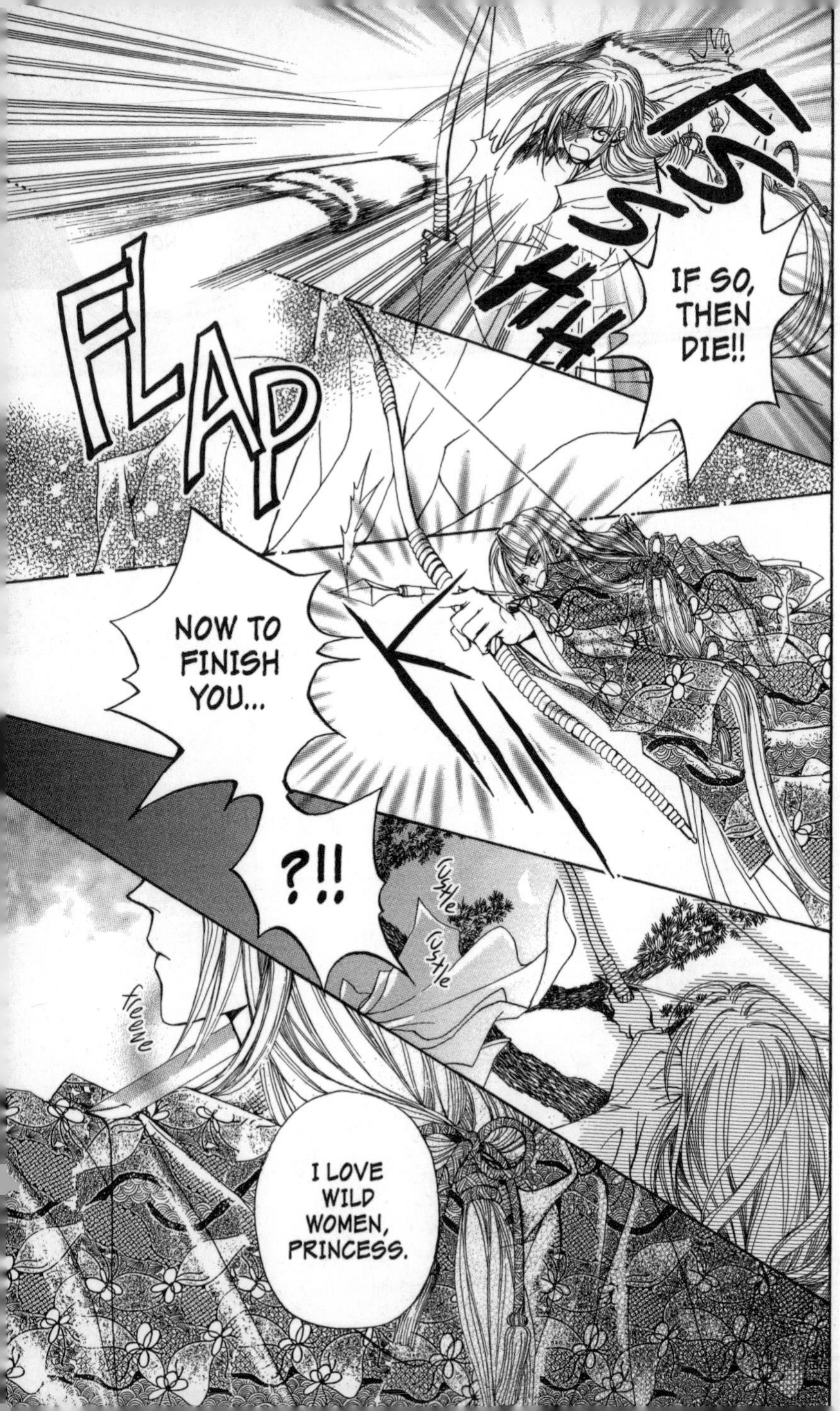
FSSHH
IF SO, THEN DIE!!
FLAP
NOW TO FINISH YOU...
?!!
rustle
rustle
I LOVE WILD WOMEN, PRINCESS.

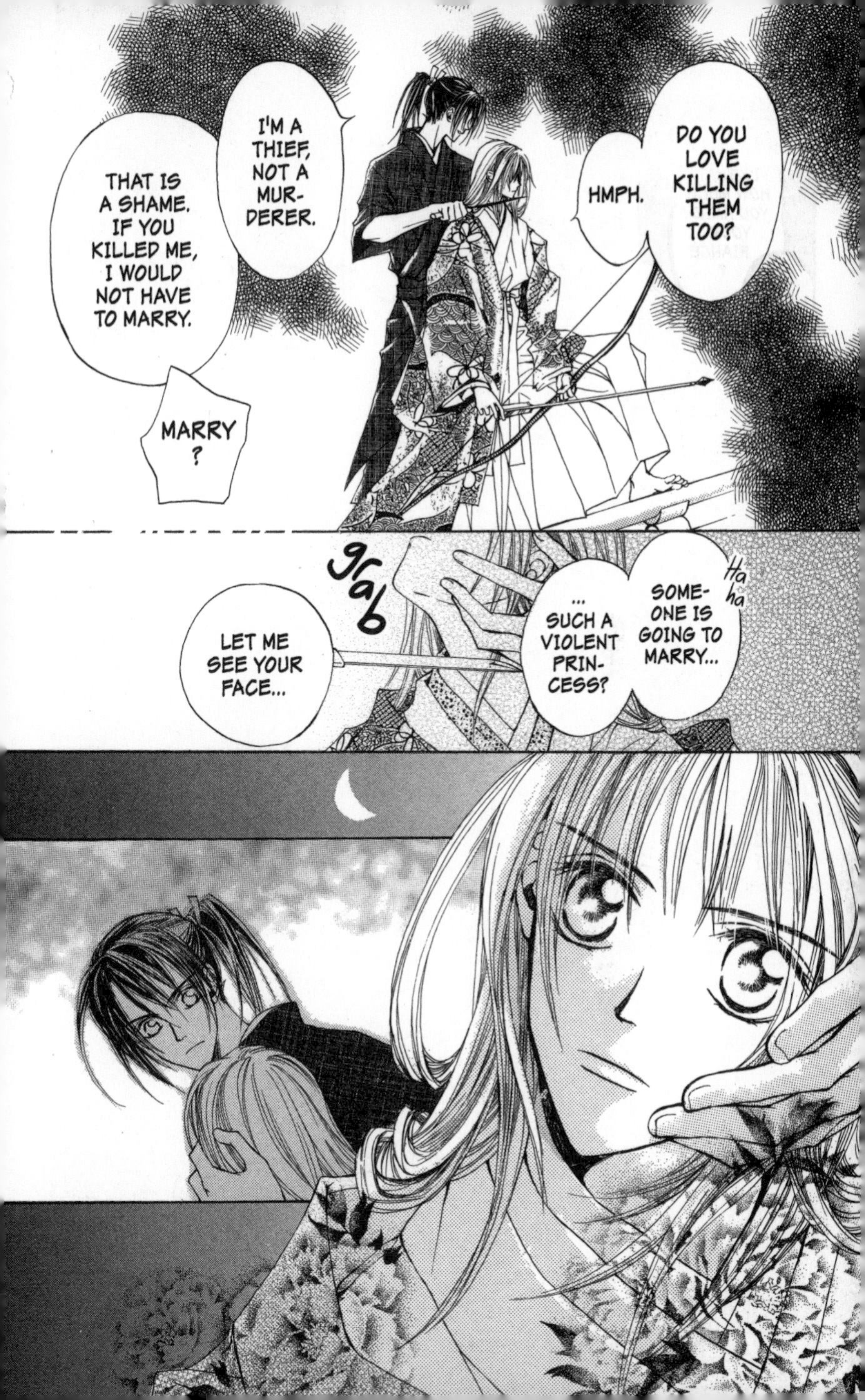
DO YOU LOVE KILLING THEM TOO?
HMPH.
I'M A THIEF, NOT A MUR-DERER.
THAT IS A SHAME. IF YOU KILLED ME, I WOULD NOT HAVE TO MARRY.
MARRY?
Ha ha
SOME-ONE IS GOING TO MARRY...
... SUCH A VIOLENT PRIN-CESS?
grab
LET ME SEE YOUR FACE...

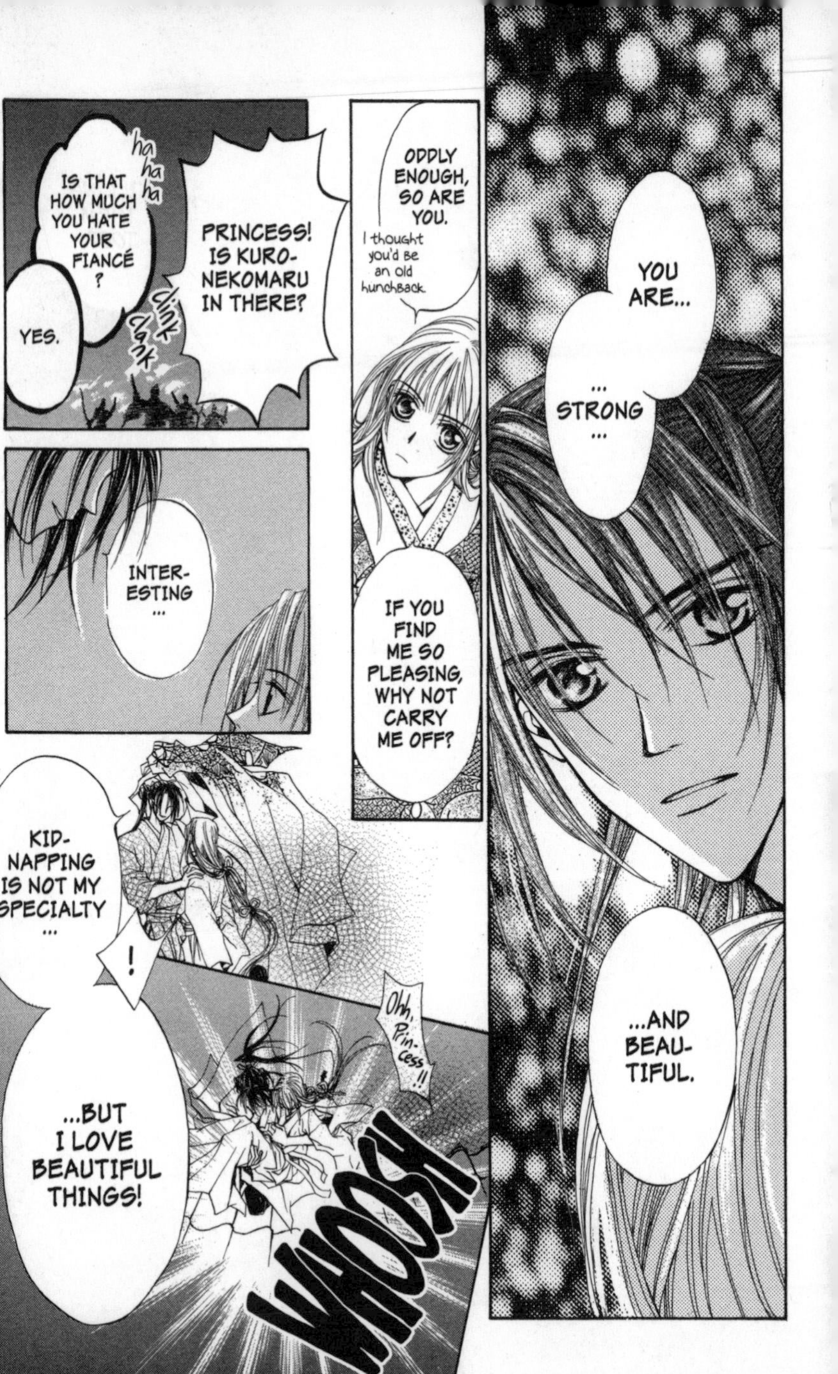
YOU ARE...
...STRONG...
...AND BEAUTIFUL.
ODDLY ENOUGH, SO ARE YOU.
I thought you'd be an old hunchback.
IF YOU FIND ME SO PLEASING, WHY NOT CARRY ME OFF?
PRINCESS! IS KURO-NEKOMARU IN THERE?
ha ha ha
IS THAT HOW MUCH YOU HATE YOUR FIANCÉ?
YES.
clink clank
INTER-ESTING...
KID-NAPPING IS NOT MY SPECIALTY...
!
...BUT I LOVE BEAUTIFUL THINGS!
Ohh, Prin-cess!!
WHOOSH

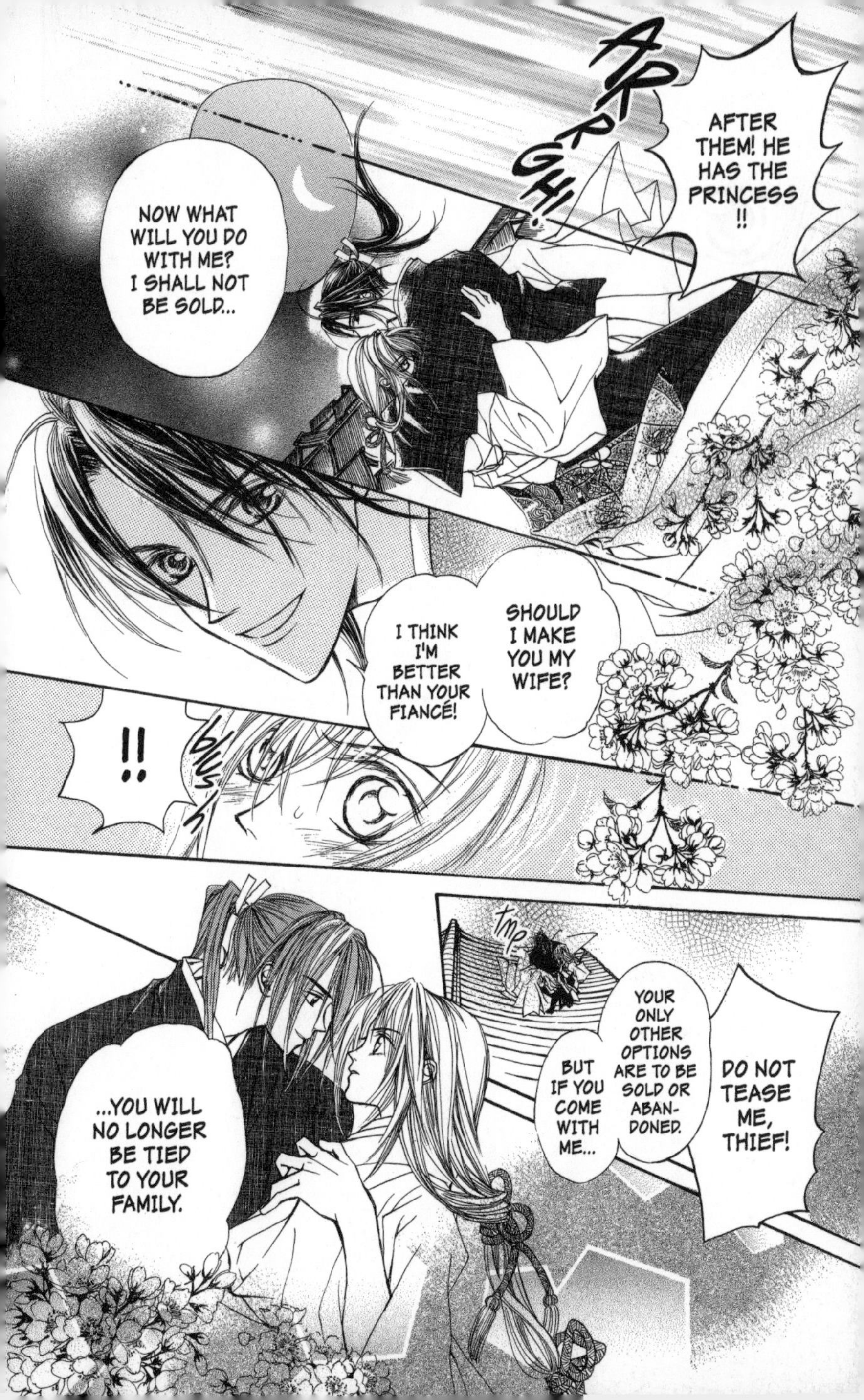
AFTER THEM! HE HAS THE PRINCESS !!
ARRGH!!
NOW WHAT WILL YOU DO WITH ME? I SHALL NOT BE SOLD...
SHOULD I MAKE YOU MY WIFE?
I THINK I'M BETTER THAN YOUR FIANCÉ!
!!
blush
tmp
DO NOT TEASE ME, THIEF!
YOUR ONLY OTHER OPTIONS ARE TO BE SOLD OR ABAN-DONED.
BUT IF YOU COME WITH ME...
...YOU WILL NO LONGER BE TIED TO YOUR FAMILY.

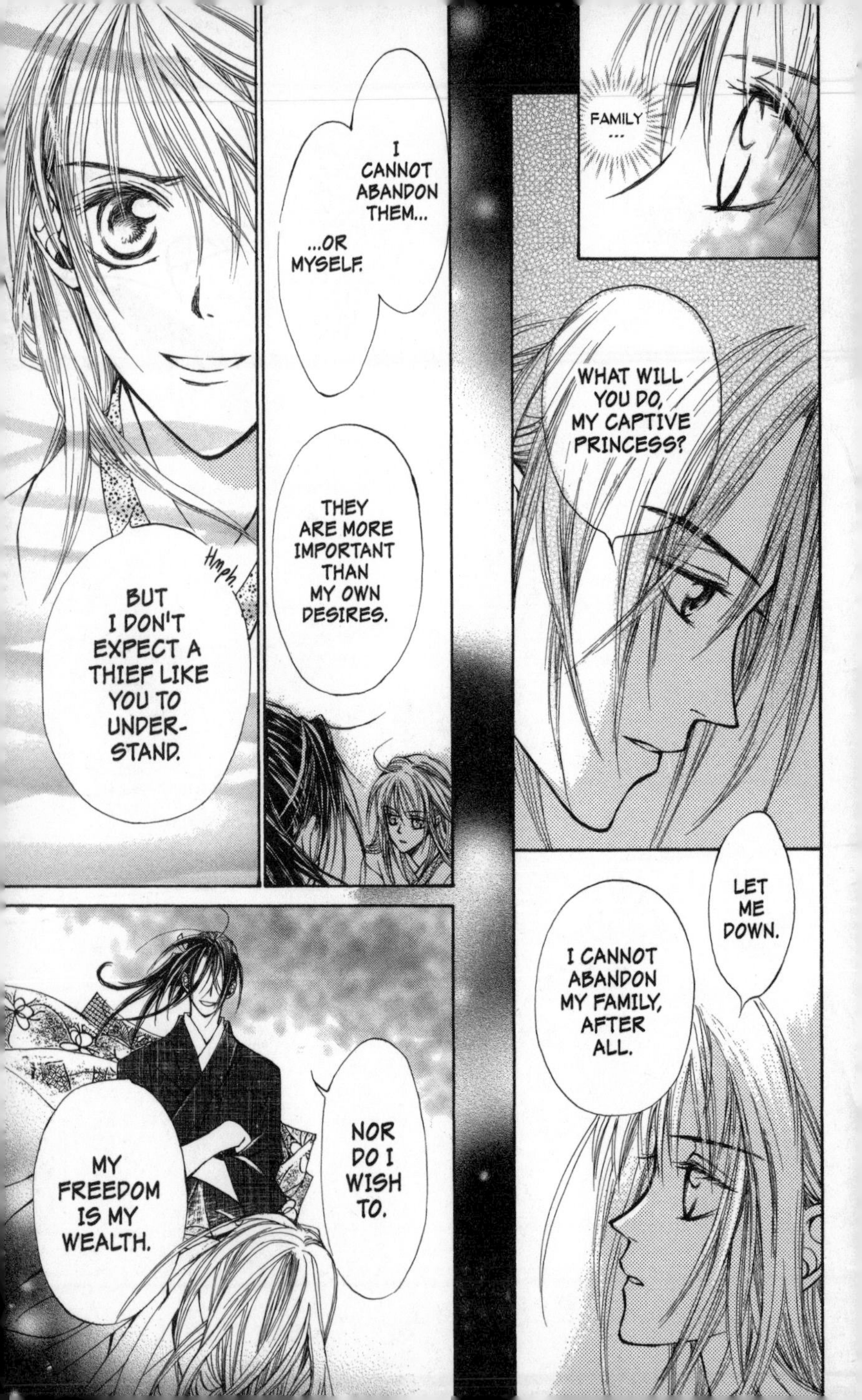
FAMILY...
WHAT WILL YOU DO, MY CAPTIVE PRINCESS?
LET ME DOWN.
I CANNOT ABANDON MY FAMILY, AFTER ALL.
I CANNOT ABANDON THEM...
...OR MYSELF.
THEY ARE MORE IMPORTANT THAN MY OWN DESIRES.
Hmph.
BUT I DON'T EXPECT A THIEF LIKE YOU TO UNDERSTAND.
NOR DO I WISH TO.
MY FREEDOM IS MY WEALTH.

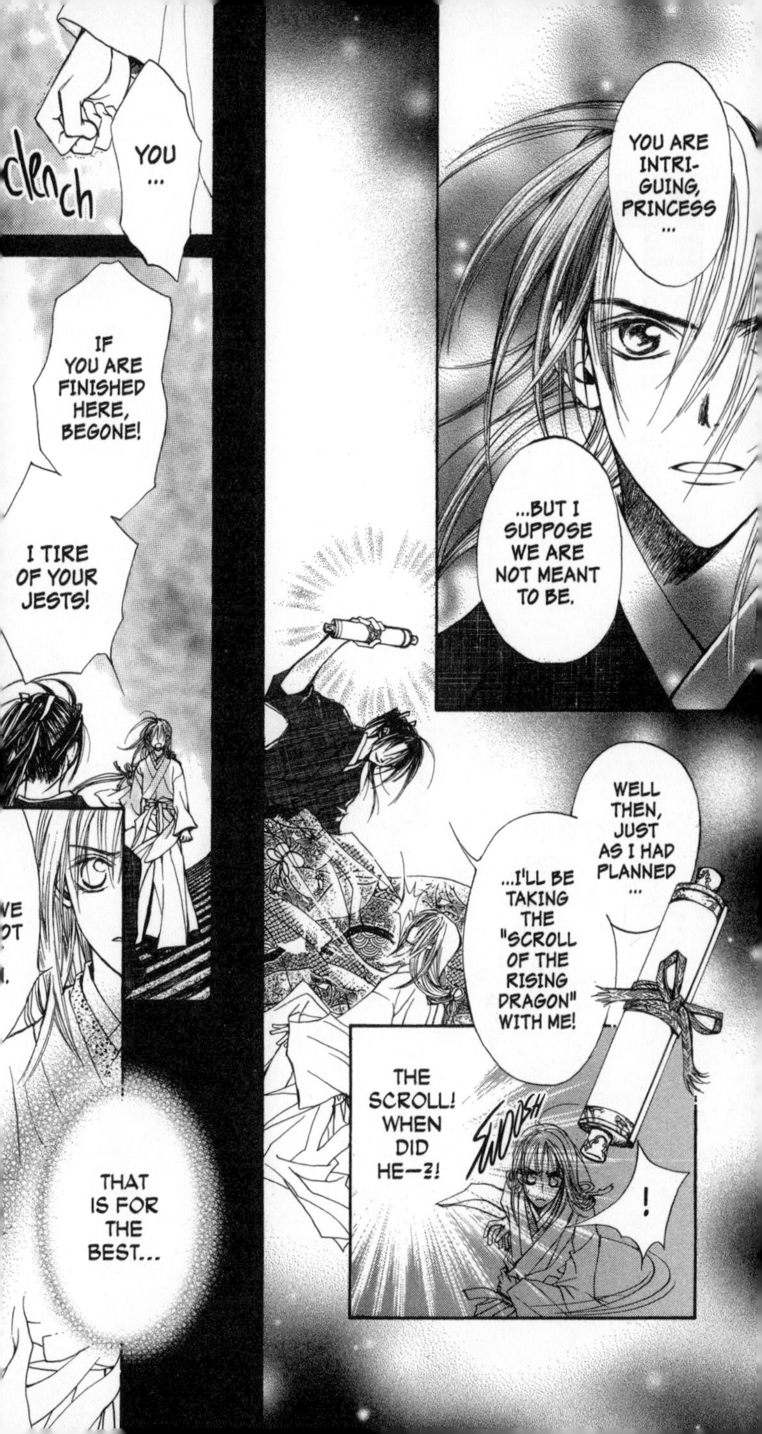
YOU ARE INTRI-GUING, PRINCESS...
...BUT I SUPPOSE WE ARE NOT MEANT TO BE.
WELL THEN, JUST AS I HAD PLANNED...
...I'LL BE TAKING THE "SCROLL OF THE RISING DRAGON" WITH ME!
!
SWOOSH
THE SCROLL! WHEN DID HE—?!
YOU...
clench
IF YOU ARE FINISHED HERE, BEGONE!
I TIRE OF YOUR JESTS!
THAT IS FOR THE BEST...

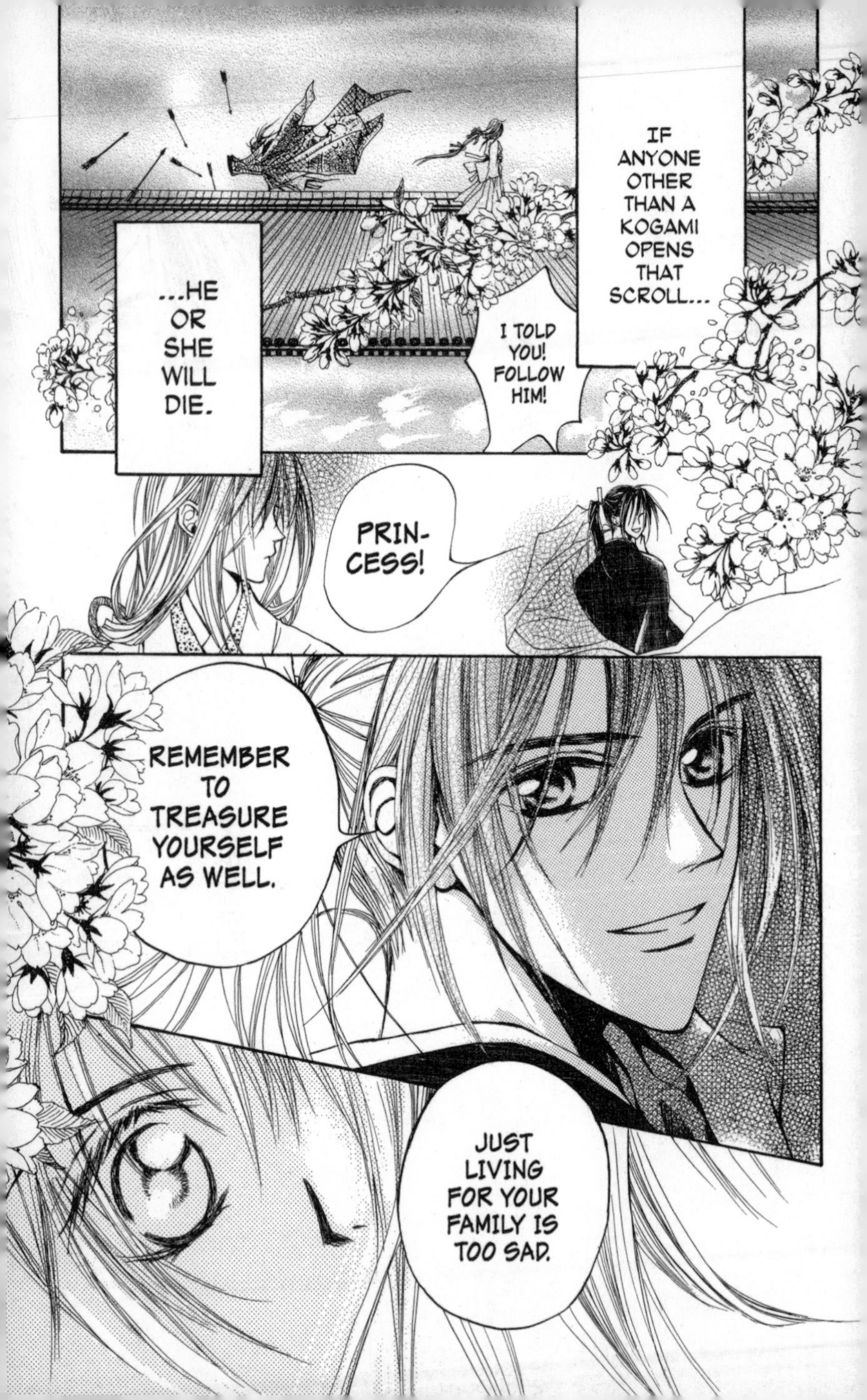
IF ANYONE OTHER THAN A KOGAMI OPENS THAT SCROLL...
I TOLD YOU! FOLLOW HIM!
...HE OR SHE WILL DIE.
PRIN-CESS!
REMEMBER TO TREASURE YOURSELF AS WELL.
JUST LIVING FOR YOUR FAMILY IS TOO SAD.

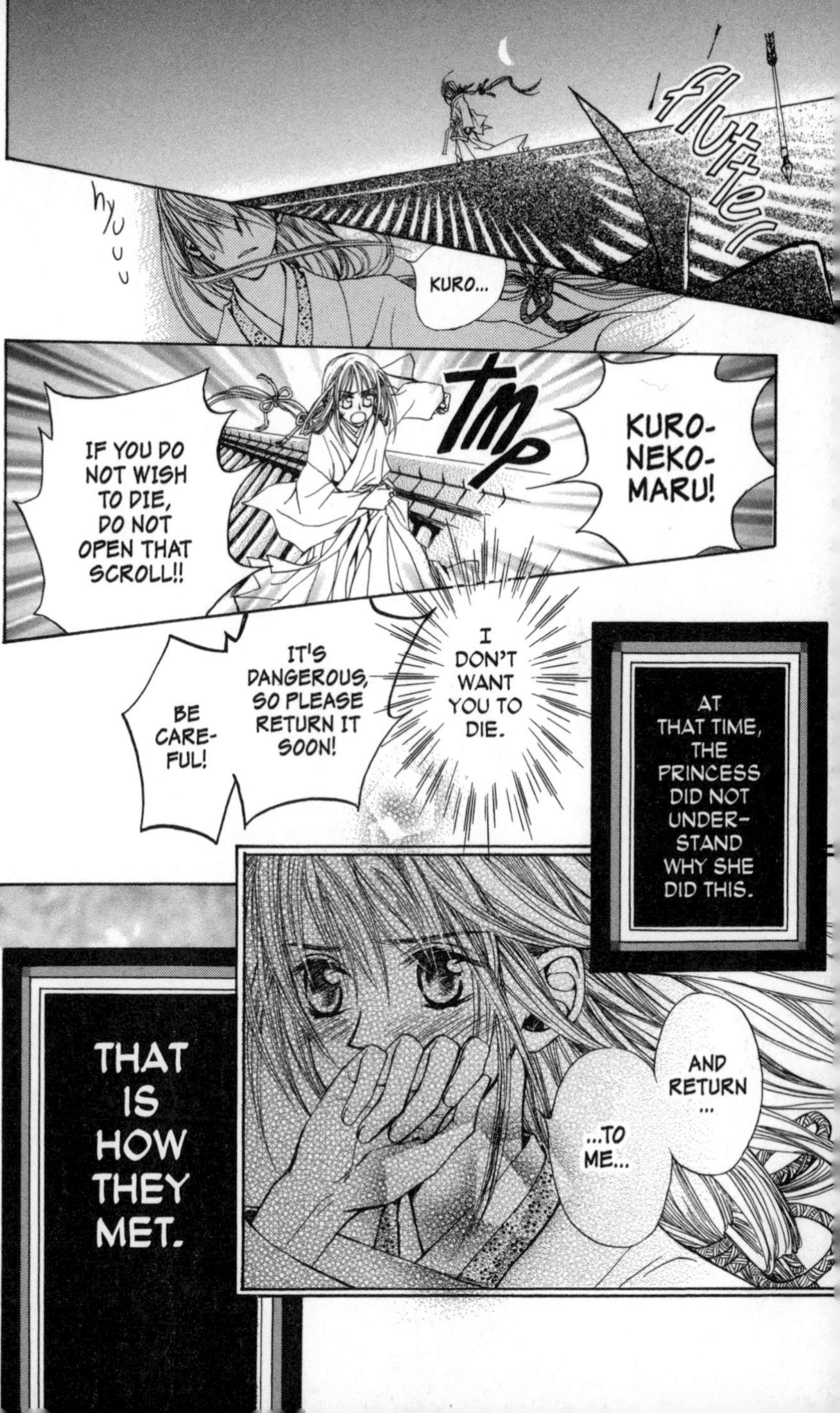
flutter
KURO...
hyuuu
KURO-NEKO-MARU!
tmp
IF YOU DO NOT WISH TO DIE, DO NOT OPEN THAT SCROLL!!
AT THAT TIME, THE PRINCESS DID NOT UNDER-STAND WHY SHE DID THIS.
I DON'T WANT YOU TO DIE.
IT'S DANGEROUS, SO PLEASE RETURN IT SOON!
BE CARE-FUL!
AND RETURN...
...TO ME...
THAT IS HOW THEY MET.

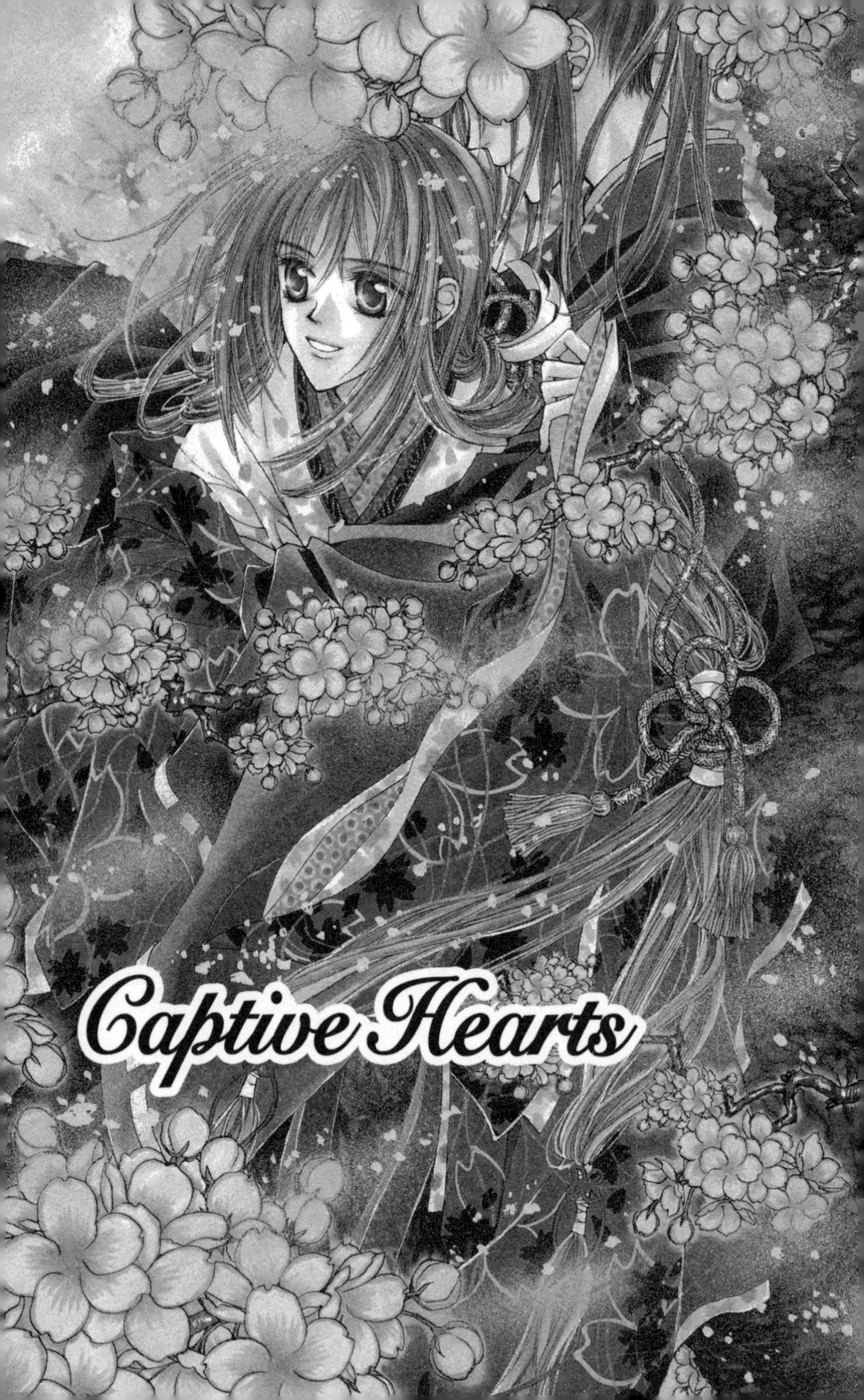
Captive Hearts

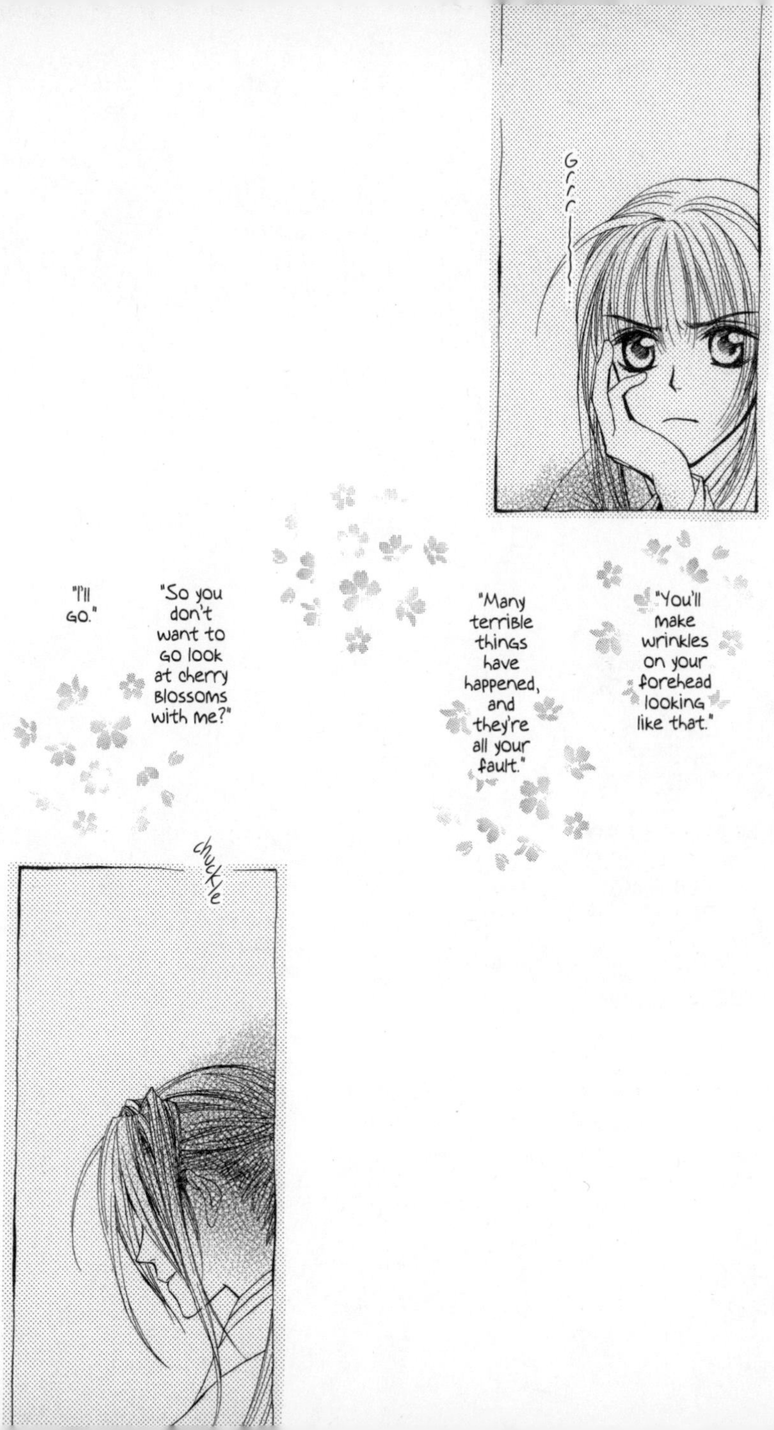
Grrr......
"You'll make wrinkles on your forehead looking like that."
"Many terrible things have happened, and they're all your fault."
"So you don't want to go look at cherry blossoms with me?"
"I'll go."
chuckle

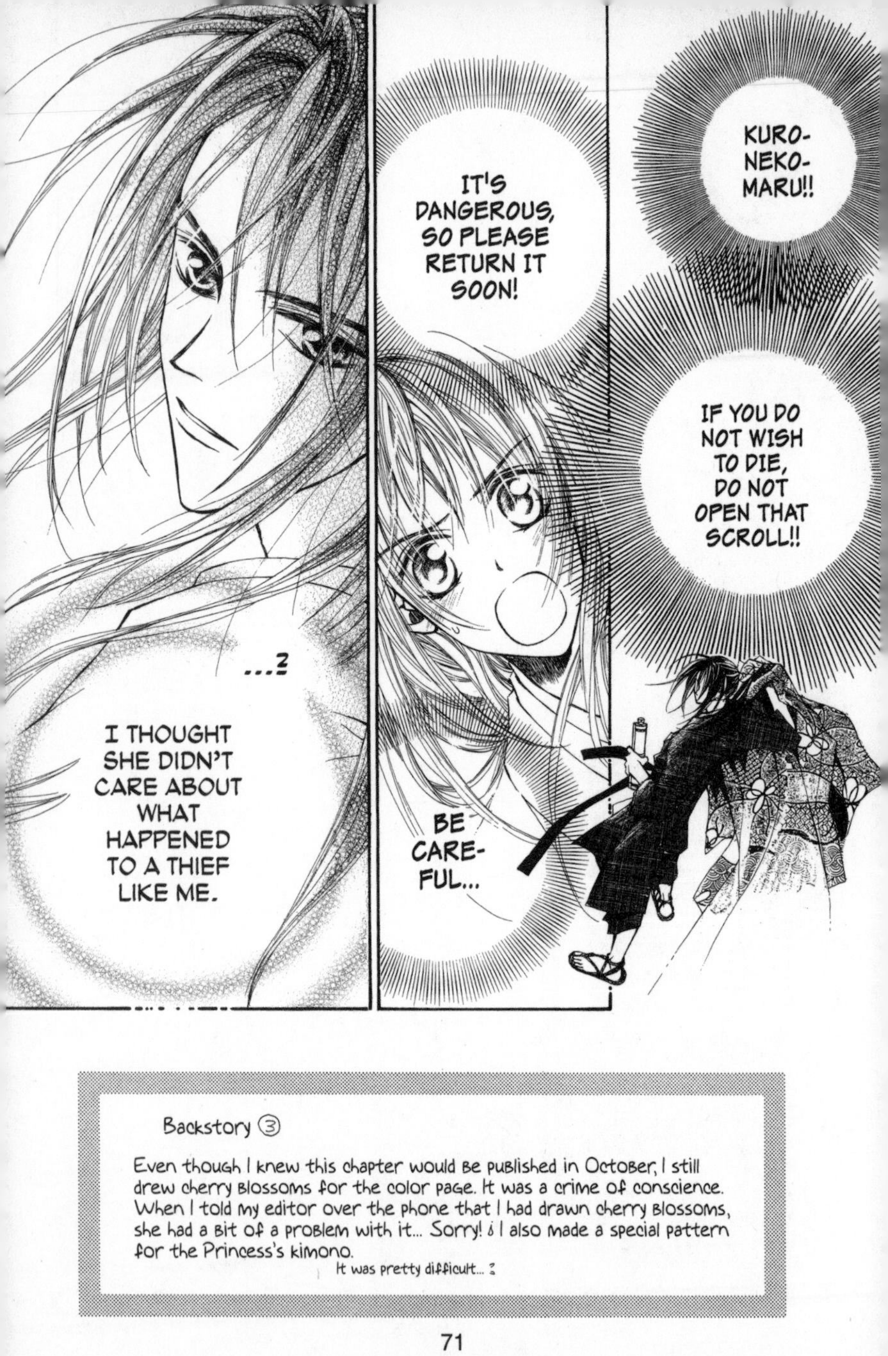
KURO-NEKO-MARU!!
IF YOU DO NOT WISH TO DIE, DO NOT OPEN THAT SCROLL!!
IT'S DANGEROUS, SO PLEASE RETURN IT SOON!
BE CARE-FUL...
...?
I THOUGHT SHE DIDN'T CARE ABOUT WHAT HAPPENED TO A THIEF LIKE ME.

Backstory ③

Even though I knew this chapter would be published in October, I still drew cherry blossoms for the color page. It was a crime of conscience. When I told my editor over the phone that I had drawn cherry blossoms, she had a bit of a problem with it... Sorry! I also made a special pattern for the Princess's kimono.

It was pretty difficult...

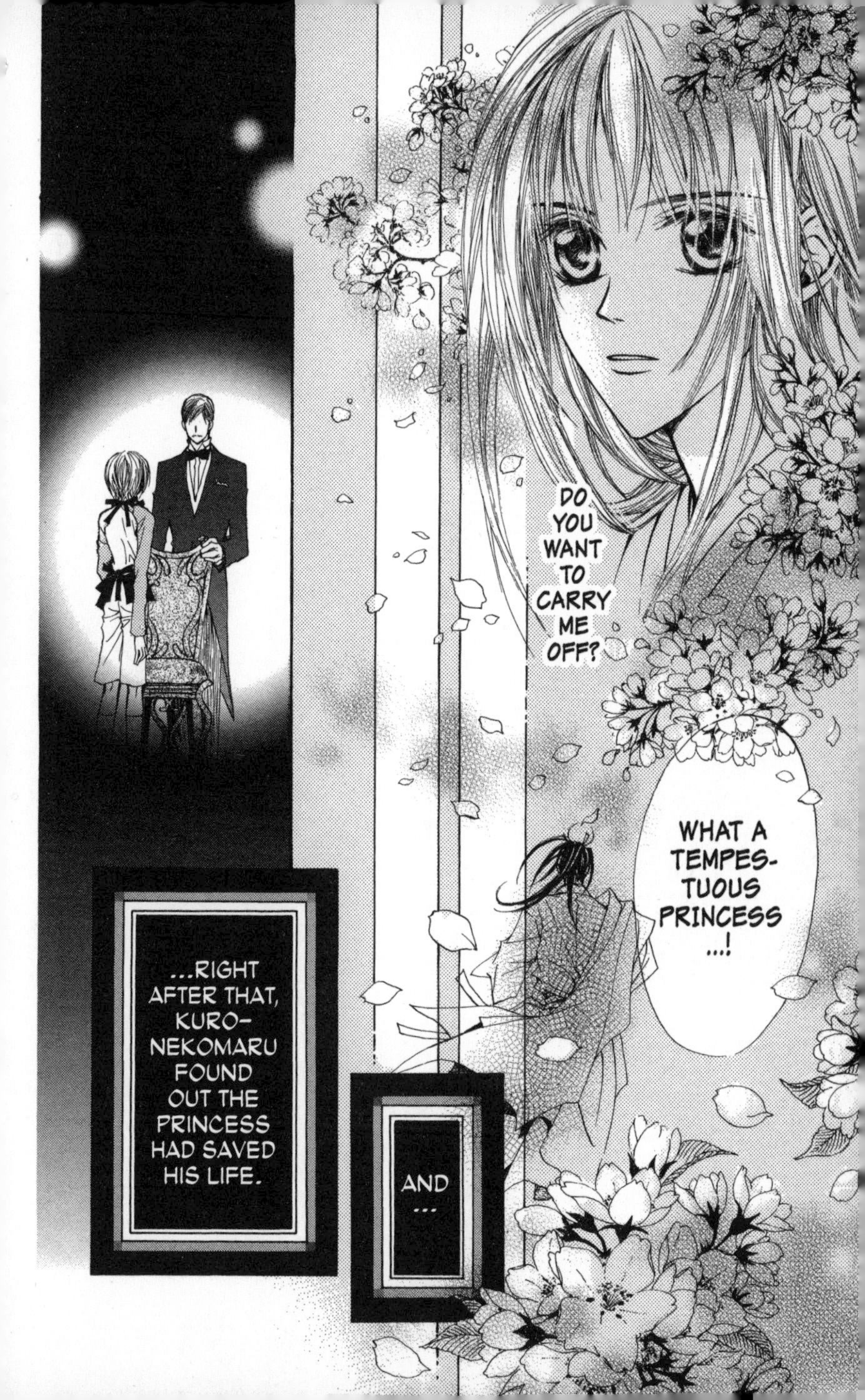
DO YOU WANT TO CARRY ME OFF?
WHAT A TEMPES-TUOUS PRINCESS ...!
...RIGHT AFTER THAT, KURO-NEKOMARU FOUND OUT THE PRINCESS HAD SAVED HIS LIFE.
AND ...

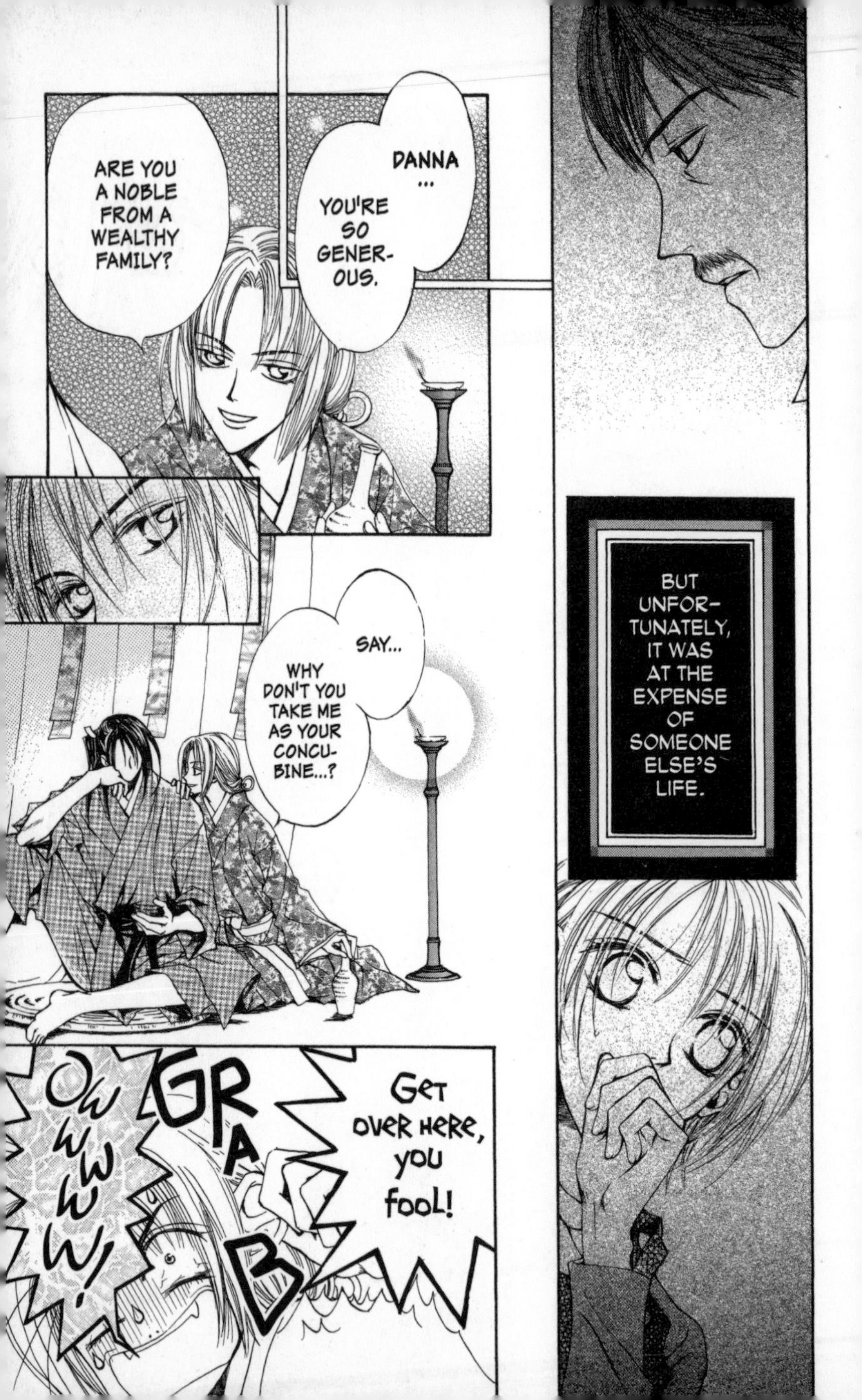
BUT UNFORTUNATELY, IT WAS AT THE EXPENSE OF SOMEONE ELSE'S LIFE.
DANNA ... YOU'RE SO GENEROUS.
ARE YOU A NOBLE FROM A WEALTHY FAMILY?
SAY... WHY DON'T YOU TAKE ME AS YOUR CONCUBINE...?
Get over here, you fool!
GRAB
OWWWWW!

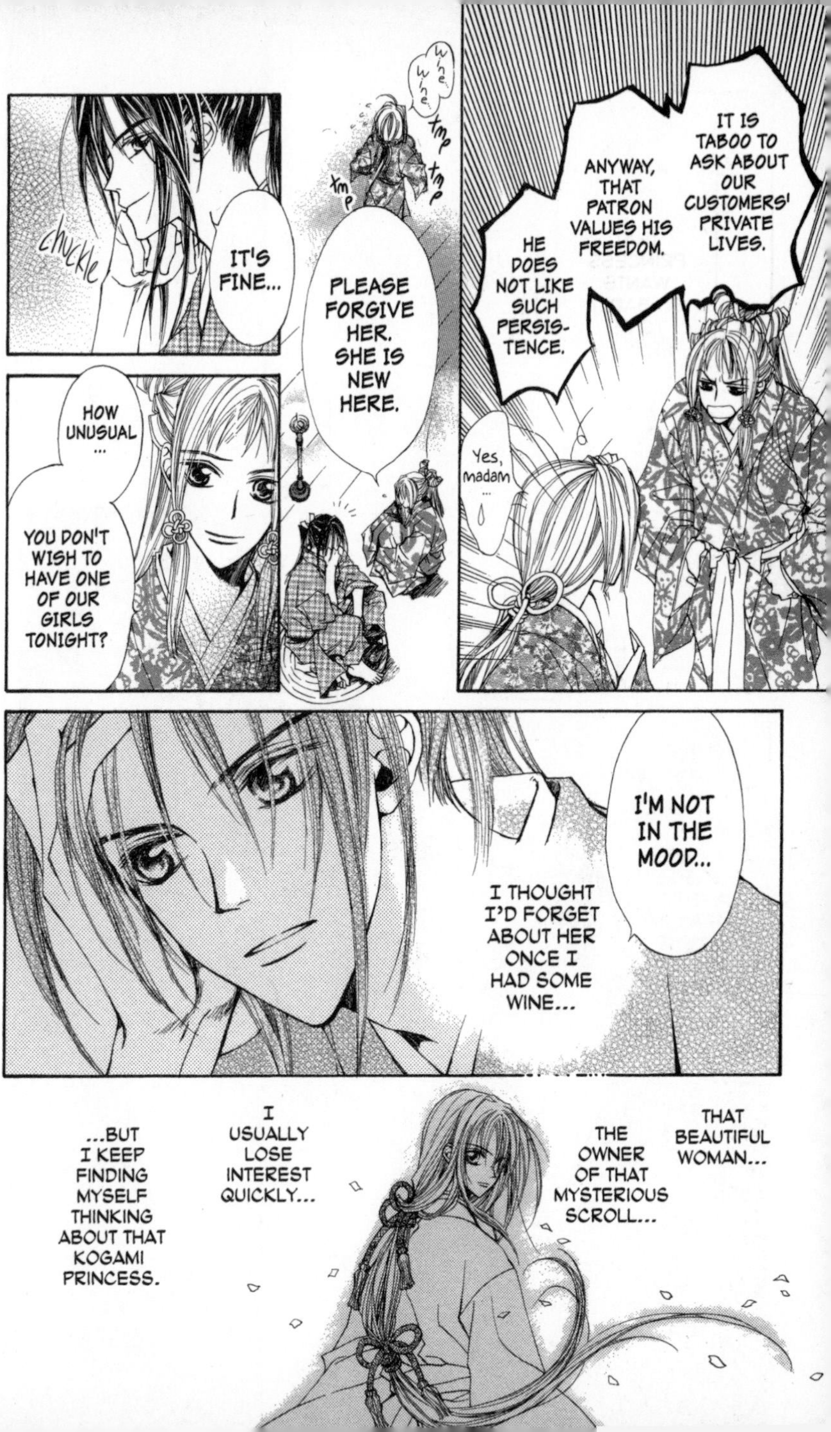
IT IS TABOO TO ASK ABOUT OUR CUSTOMERS' PRIVATE LIVES.
ANYWAY, THAT PATRON VALUES HIS FREEDOM.
HE DOES NOT LIKE SUCH PERSISTENCE.
Yes, madam...
Wine... Wine...
tmp tmp tmp
PLEASE FORGIVE HER. SHE IS NEW HERE.
IT'S FINE...
chuckle
HOW UNUSUAL...
YOU DON'T WISH TO HAVE ONE OF OUR GIRLS TONIGHT?
I'M NOT IN THE MOOD...
I THOUGHT I'D FORGET ABOUT HER ONCE I HAD SOME WINE...
THAT BEAUTIFUL WOMAN...
THE OWNER OF THAT MYSTERIOUS SCROLL...
I USUALLY LOSE INTEREST QUICKLY...
...BUT I KEEP FINDING MYSELF THINKING ABOUT THAT KOGAMI PRINCESS.

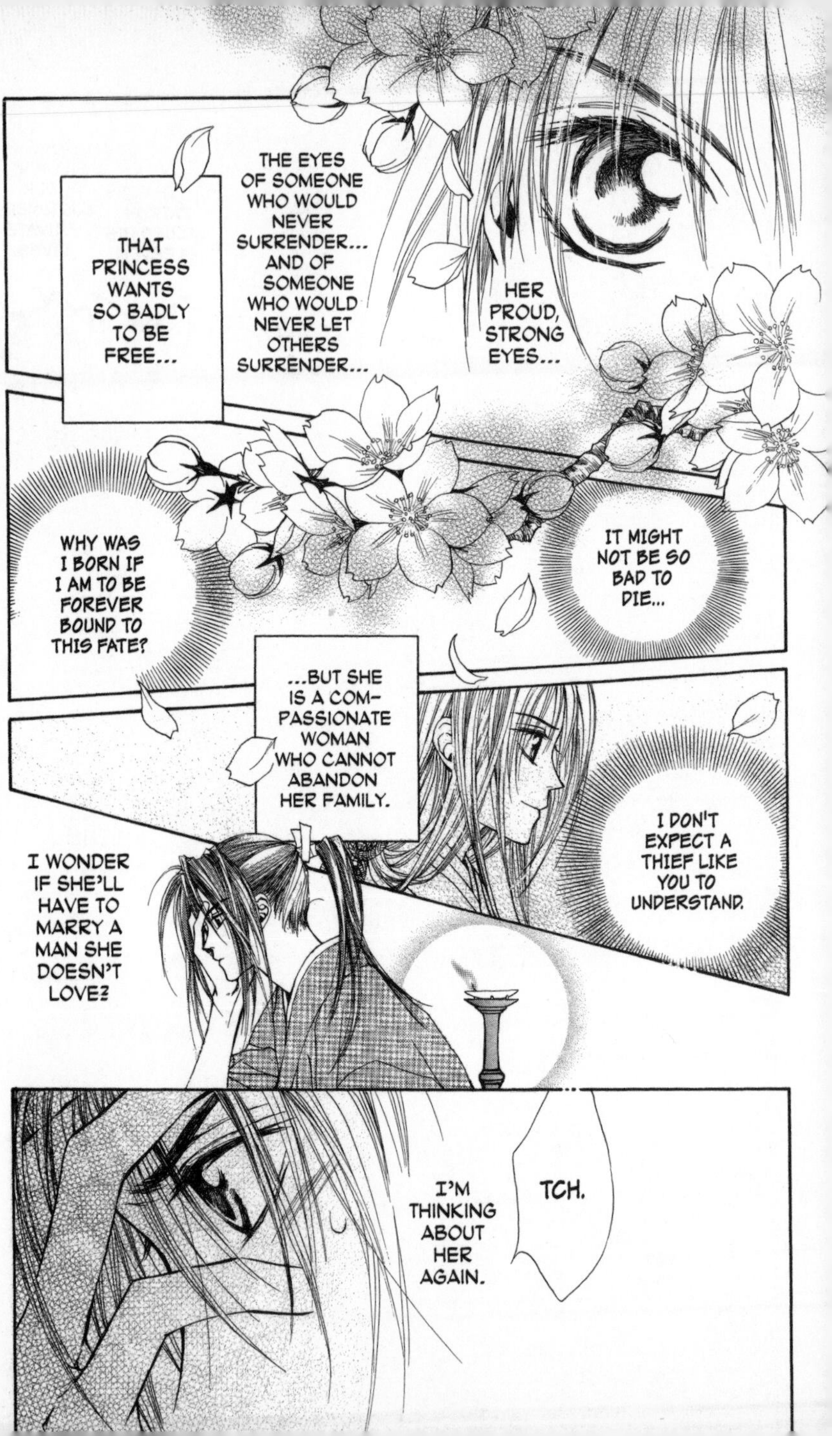
HER PROUD, STRONG EYES...
THE EYES OF SOMEONE WHO WOULD NEVER SURRENDER... AND OF SOMEONE WHO WOULD NEVER LET OTHERS SURRENDER...
THAT PRINCESS WANTS SO BADLY TO BE FREE...
IT MIGHT NOT BE SO BAD TO DIE...
WHY WAS I BORN IF I AM TO BE FOREVER BOUND TO THIS FATE?
I DON'T EXPECT A THIEF LIKE YOU TO UNDERSTAND.
...BUT SHE IS A COMPASSIONATE WOMAN WHO CANNOT ABANDON HER FAMILY.
I WONDER IF SHE'LL HAVE TO MARRY A MAN SHE DOESN'T LOVE?
TCH.
I'M THINKING ABOUT HER AGAIN.

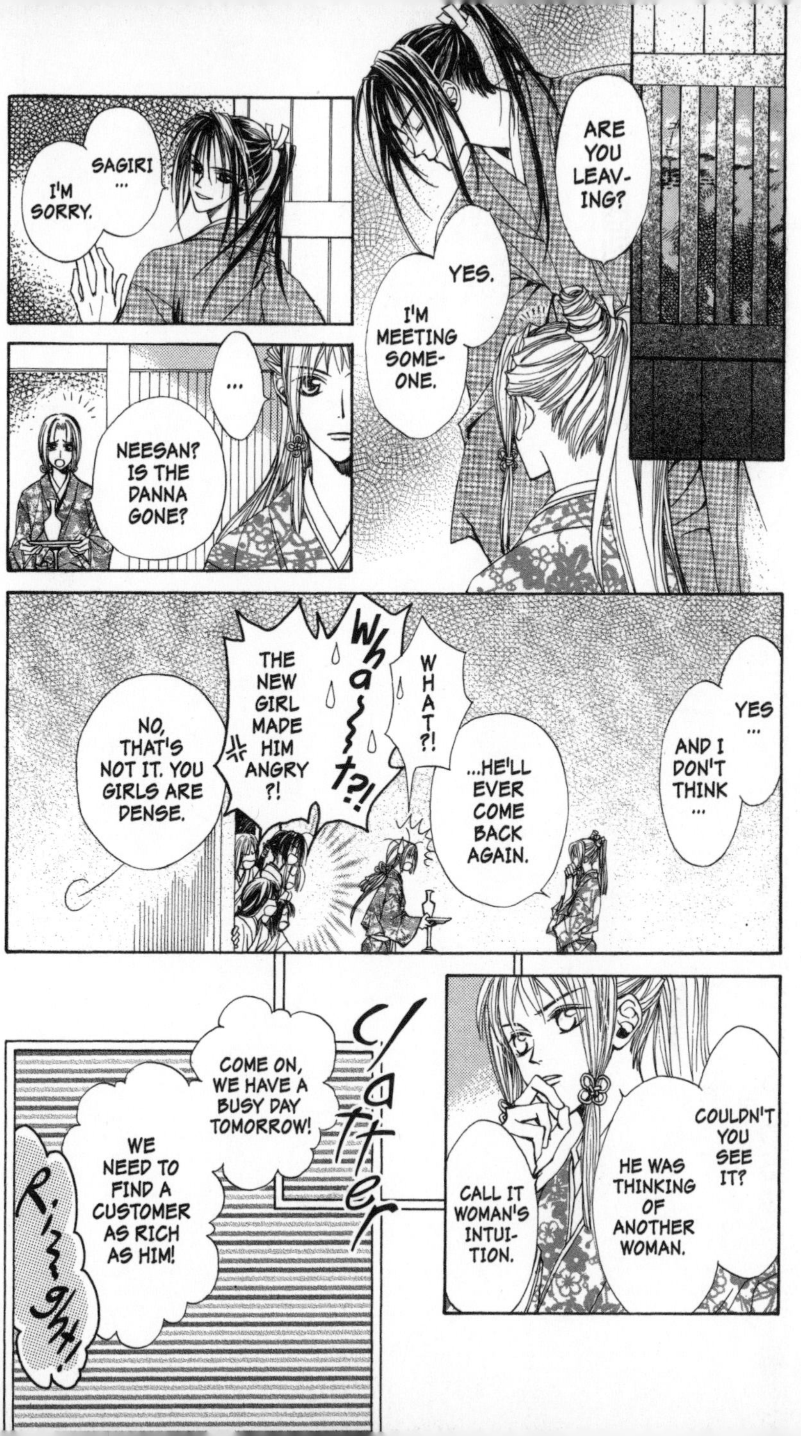
ARE YOU LEAVING?
YES.
I'M MEETING SOMEONE.
SAGIRI...
I'M SORRY.
...
NEESAN? IS THE DANNA GONE?
YES... AND I DON'T THINK...
...HE'LL EVER COME BACK AGAIN.
WHAT?!
Whaaat?!
THE NEW GIRL MADE HIM ANGRY?!
NO, THAT'S NOT IT. YOU GIRLS ARE DENSE.
COULDN'T YOU SEE IT?
HE WAS THINKING OF ANOTHER WOMAN.
CALL IT WOMAN'S INTUITION.
Clatter
COME ON, WE HAVE A BUSY DAY TOMORROW!
WE NEED TO FIND A CUSTOMER AS RICH AS HIM!
Right!

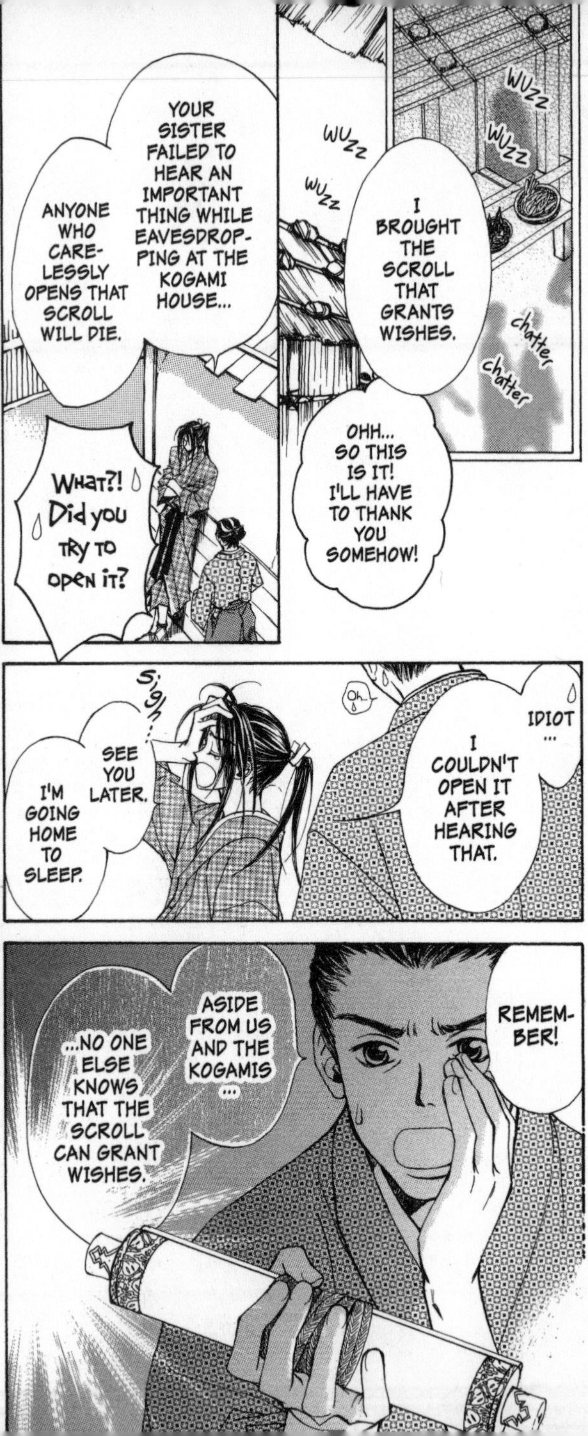
WUZZ
WUZZ
WUZZ
WUZZ
I BROUGHT THE SCROLL THAT GRANTS WISHES.
chatter
chatter
OHH... SO THIS IS IT! I'LL HAVE TO THANK YOU SOMEHOW!
YOUR SISTER FAILED TO HEAR AN IMPORTANT THING WHILE EAVESDROPPING AT THE KOGAMI HOUSE...
ANYONE WHO CARELESSLY OPENS THAT SCROLL WILL DIE.
WHAT?! Did you TRY TO open it?
IDIOT...
I COULDN'T OPEN IT AFTER HEARING THAT.
Oh...
Sigh...
SEE YOU LATER.
I'M GOING HOME TO SLEEP.
REMEMBER!
ASIDE FROM US AND THE KOGAMIS...
...NO ONE ELSE KNOWS THAT THE SCROLL CAN GRANT WISHES.

4

A terrible thing happened to my body.

The Muromachi Era story began in the first volume, but I never would have thought the manga would continue long enough for me to finish it! Back then, I thought "This is how the princess and Kuronekomaru met..." and "This is kinda sad..." when I was thinking of the story.

And then...!!

To be continued...

4

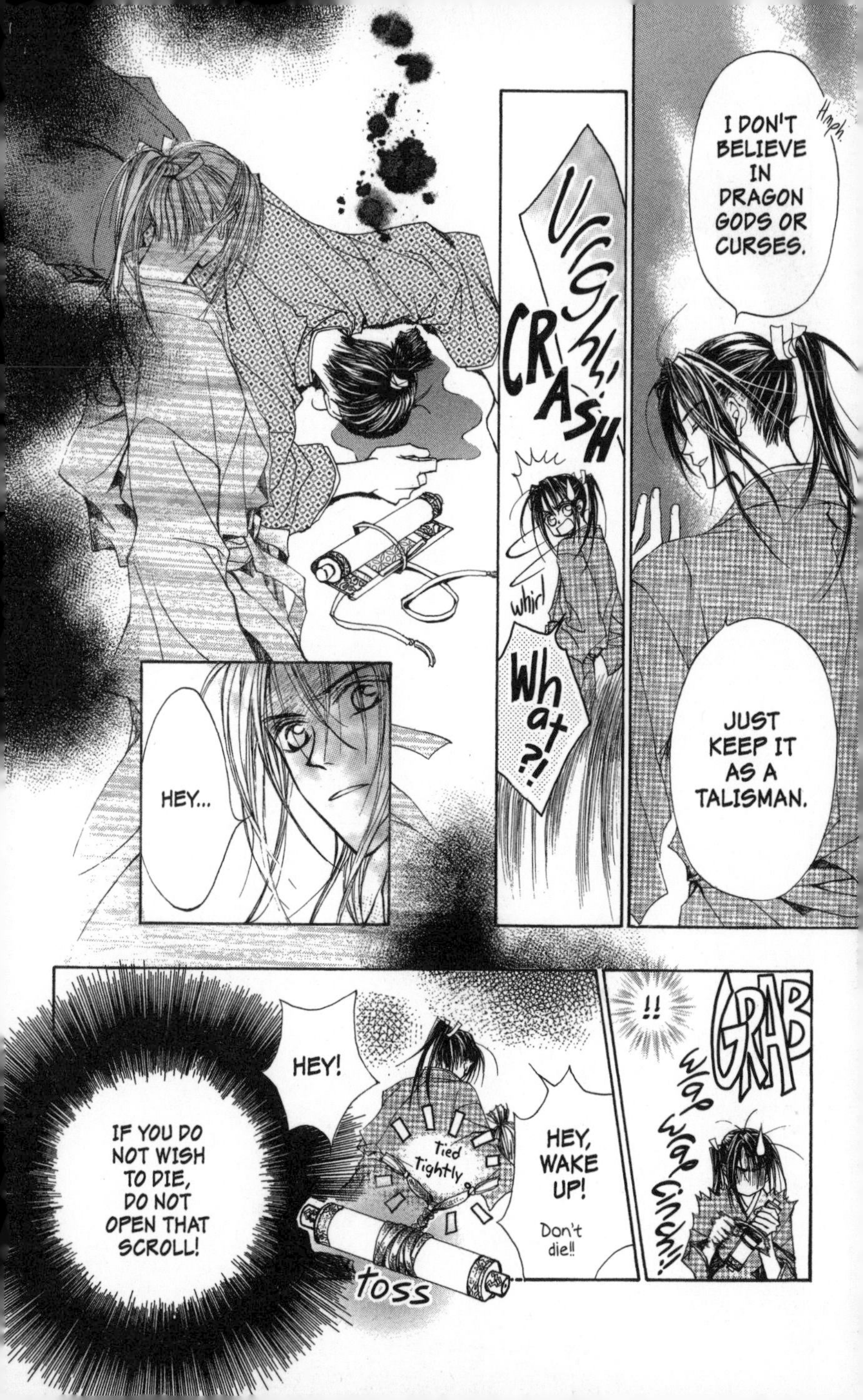
Hmph.
I DON'T BELIEVE IN DRAGON GODS OR CURSES.
JUST KEEP IT AS A TALISMAN.
URGHHH!
CRASH
whirl
What?!
HEY...
!!
GRAB
wrap wrap cinch!!
HEY, WAKE UP!
Don't die!!
Tied tightly
HEY!
IF YOU DO NOT WISH TO DIE, DO NOT OPEN THAT SCROLL!
toss

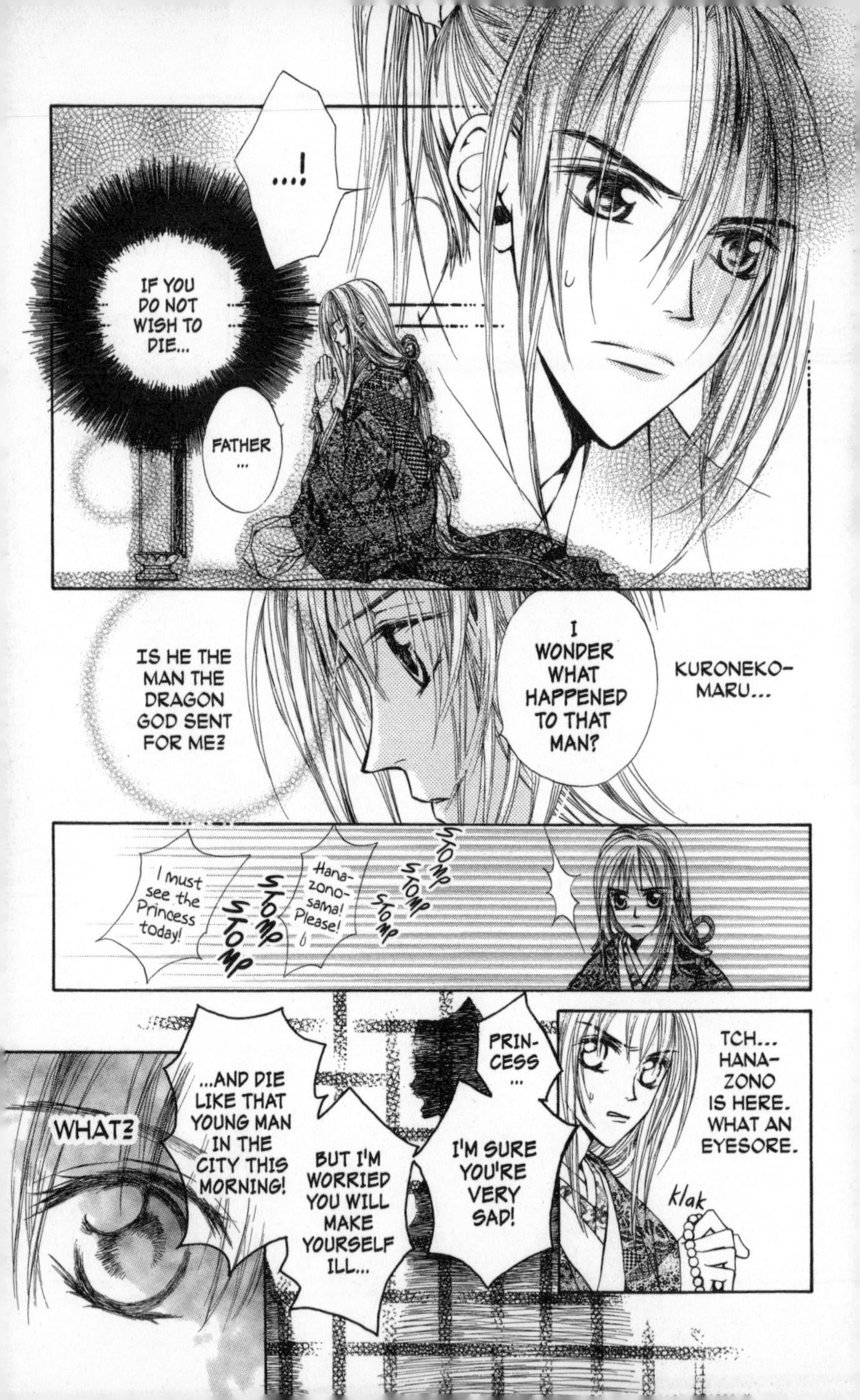

...!
IF YOU DO NOT WISH TO DIE...
FATHER ...
KURONEKO-MARU...
I WONDER WHAT HAPPENED TO THAT MAN?
IS HE THE MAN THE DRAGON GOD SENT FOR ME?
STOMP STOMP STOMP
Hana-zono-sama! Please!
STOMP STOMP
I must see the Princess today!
TCH... HANA-ZONO IS HERE. WHAT AN EYESORE.
klak
PRIN-CESS ...
I'M SURE YOU'RE VERY SAD!
BUT I'M WORRIED YOU WILL MAKE YOURSELF ILL...
...AND DIE LIKE THAT YOUNG MAN IN THE CITY THIS MORNING!
WHAT?

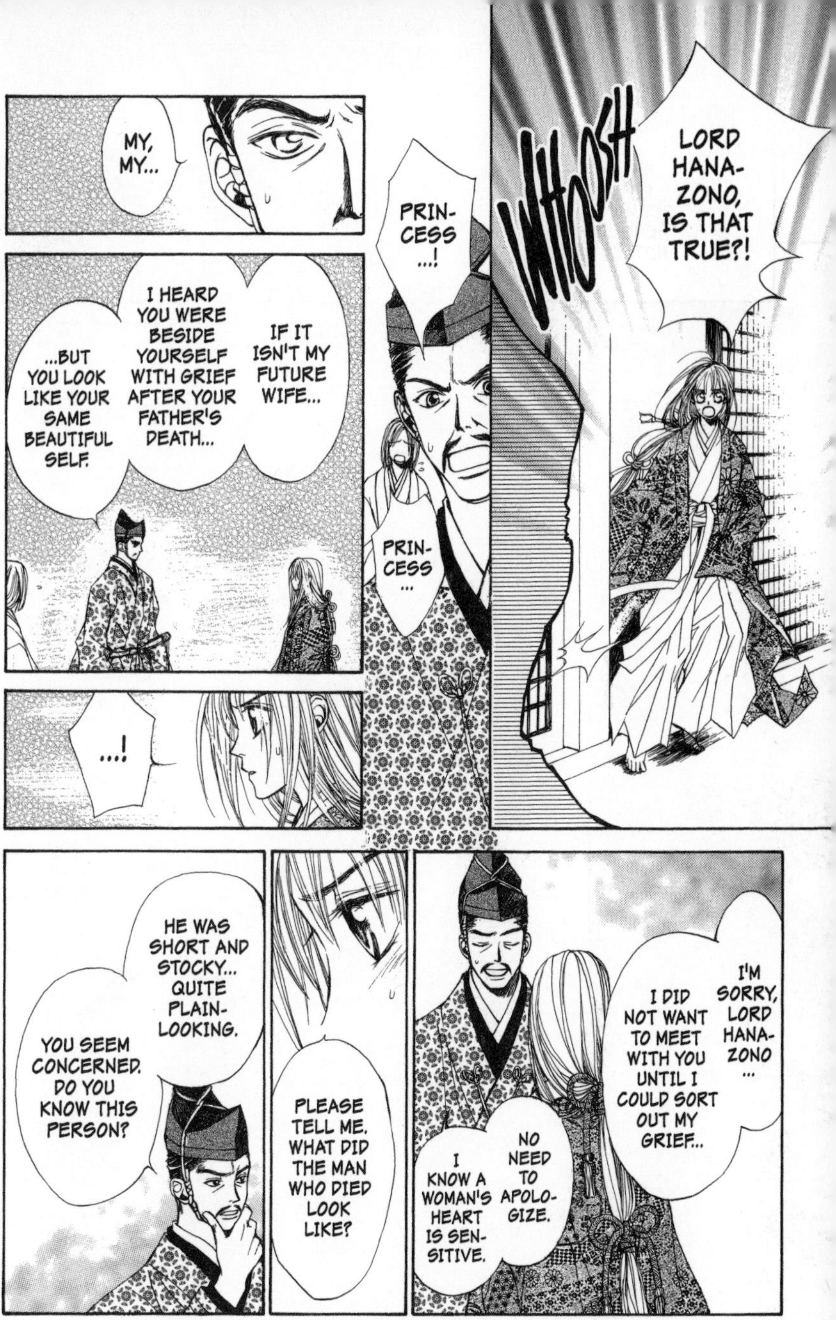
WHOOSH
LORD HANAZONO, IS THAT TRUE?!
PRINCESS...!
PRINCESS...
MY, MY...
IF IT ISN'T MY FUTURE WIFE...
I HEARD YOU WERE BESIDE YOURSELF WITH GRIEF AFTER YOUR FATHER'S DEATH...
...BUT YOU LOOK LIKE YOUR SAME BEAUTIFUL SELF.
...!
I'M SORRY, LORD HANAZONO...
I DID NOT WANT TO MEET WITH YOU UNTIL I COULD SORT OUT MY GRIEF...
NO NEED TO APOLOGIZE.
I KNOW A WOMAN'S HEART IS SENSITIVE.
PLEASE TELL ME. WHAT DID THE MAN WHO DIED LOOK LIKE?
HE WAS SHORT AND STOCKY... QUITE PLAIN-LOOKING.
YOU SEEM CONCERNED. DO YOU KNOW THIS PERSON?

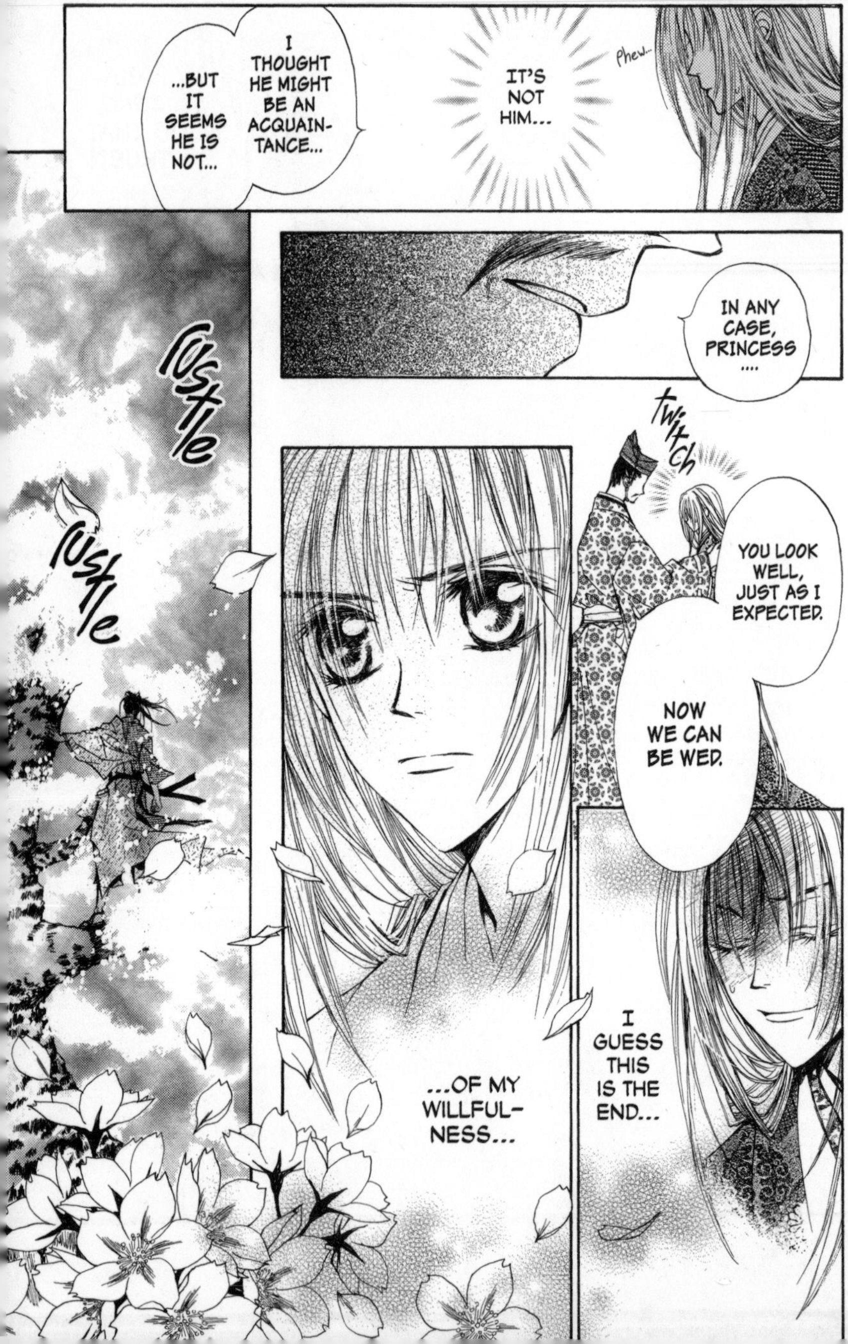

Phew...
IT'S NOT HIM...
I THOUGHT HE MIGHT BE AN ACQUAINTANCE...
...BUT IT SEEMS HE IS NOT...
IN ANY CASE, PRINCESS....
twitch
YOU LOOK WELL, JUST AS I EXPECTED.
NOW WE CAN BE WED.
I GUESS THIS IS THE END...
...OF MY WILLFULNESS...
rustle
rustle

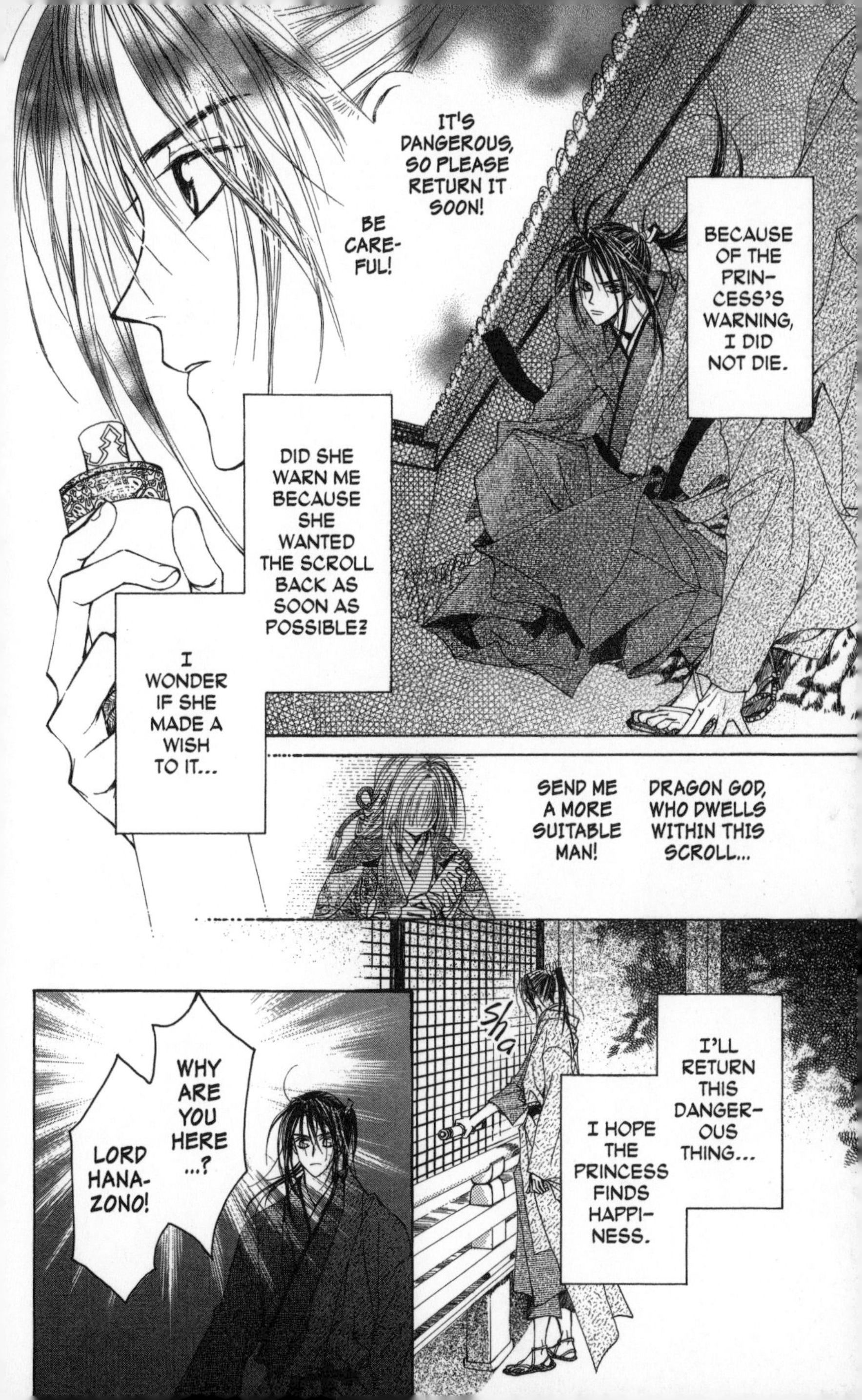
BECAUSE OF THE PRINCESS'S WARNING, I DID NOT DIE.
IT'S DANGEROUS, SO PLEASE RETURN IT SOON!
BE CAREFUL!
DID SHE WARN ME BECAUSE SHE WANTED THE SCROLL BACK AS SOON AS POSSIBLE?
I WONDER IF SHE MADE A WISH TO IT...
DRAGON GOD, WHO DWELLS WITHIN THIS SCROLL...
SEND ME A MORE SUITABLE MAN!
Sha
I'LL RETURN THIS DANGEROUS THING...
I HOPE THE PRINCESS FINDS HAPPINESS.
WHY ARE YOU HERE ...?
LORD HANAZONO!

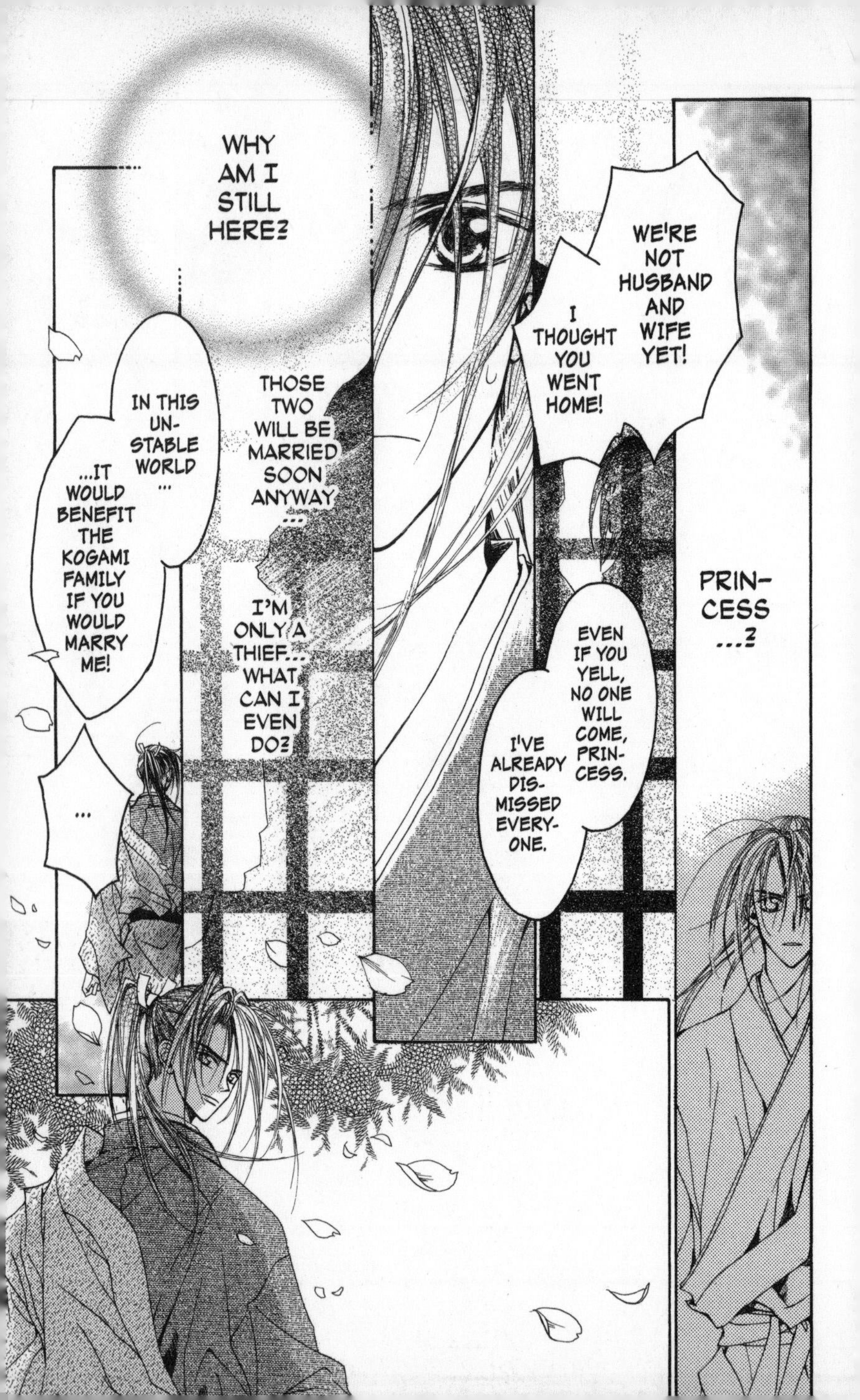
WE'RE NOT HUSBAND AND WIFE YET!
I THOUGHT YOU WENT HOME!
PRIN-CESS...?
EVEN IF YOU YELL, NO ONE WILL COME, PRIN-CESS.
I'VE ALREADY DIS-MISSED EVERY-ONE.
WHY AM I STILL HERE?
THOSE TWO WILL BE MARRIED SOON ANYWAY...
I'M ONLY A THIEF... WHAT CAN I EVEN DO?
IN THIS UN-STABLE WORLD...
...IT WOULD BENEFIT THE KOGAMI FAMILY IF YOU WOULD MARRY ME!
...

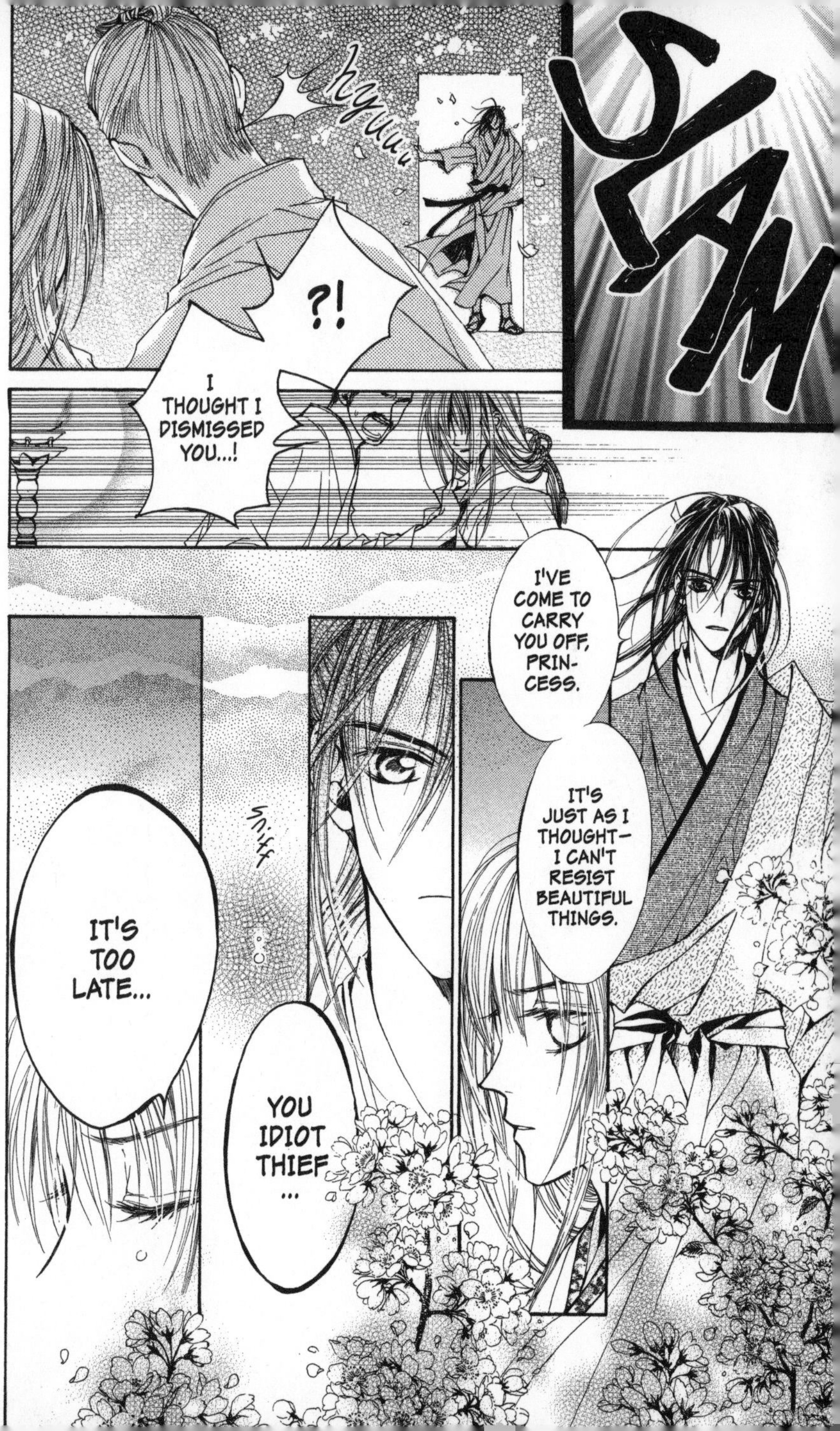
SLAM
hyuuu
?!
I THOUGHT I DISMISSED YOU...!
I'VE COME TO CARRY YOU OFF, PRIN-CESS.
IT'S JUST AS I THOUGHT— I CAN'T RESIST BEAUTIFUL THINGS.
sniff
YOU IDIOT THIEF ...
IT'S TOO LATE...

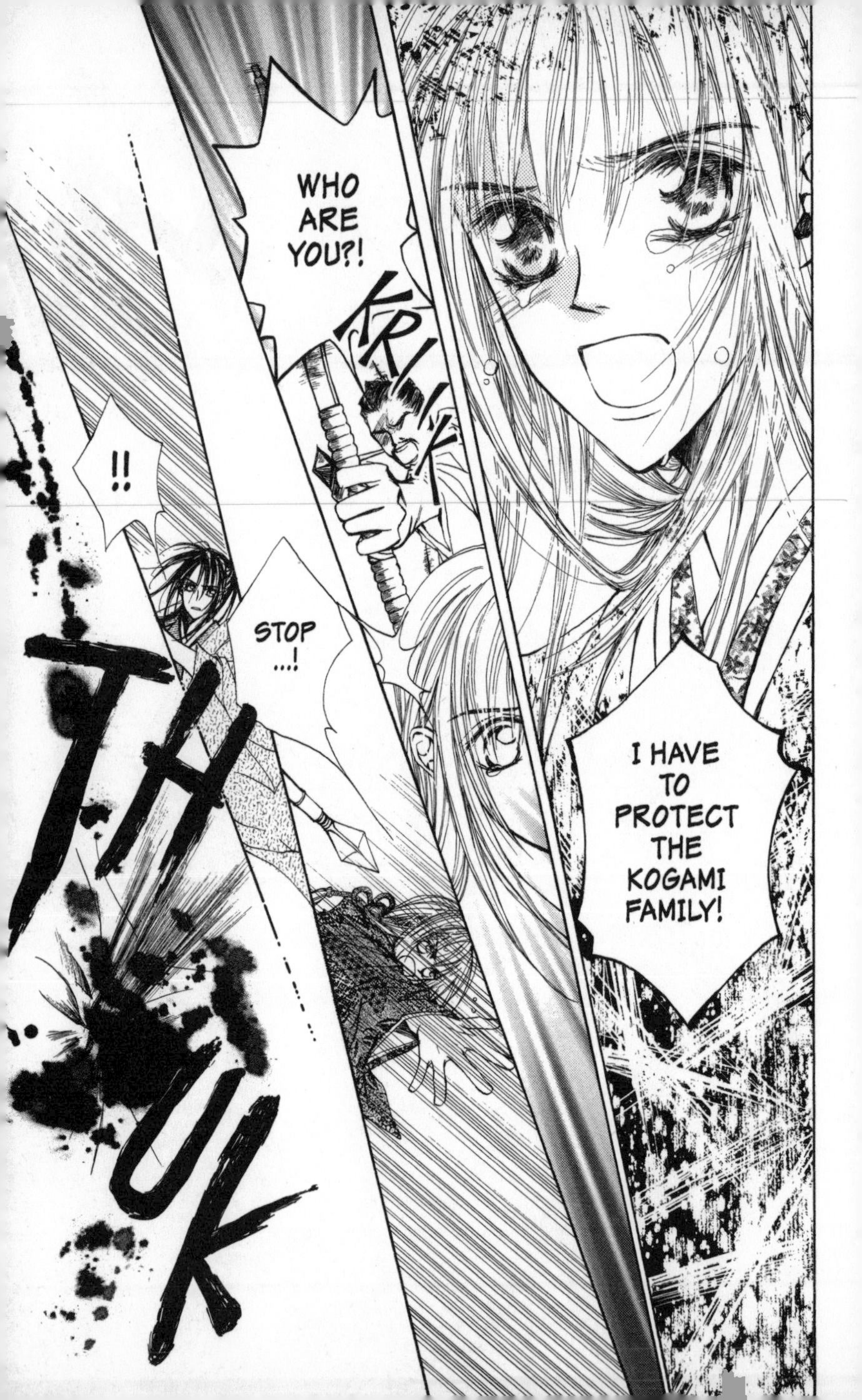
I HAVE TO PROTECT THE KOGAMI FAMILY!
WHO ARE YOU?!
KRIIK
STOP ...!
!!
THUK

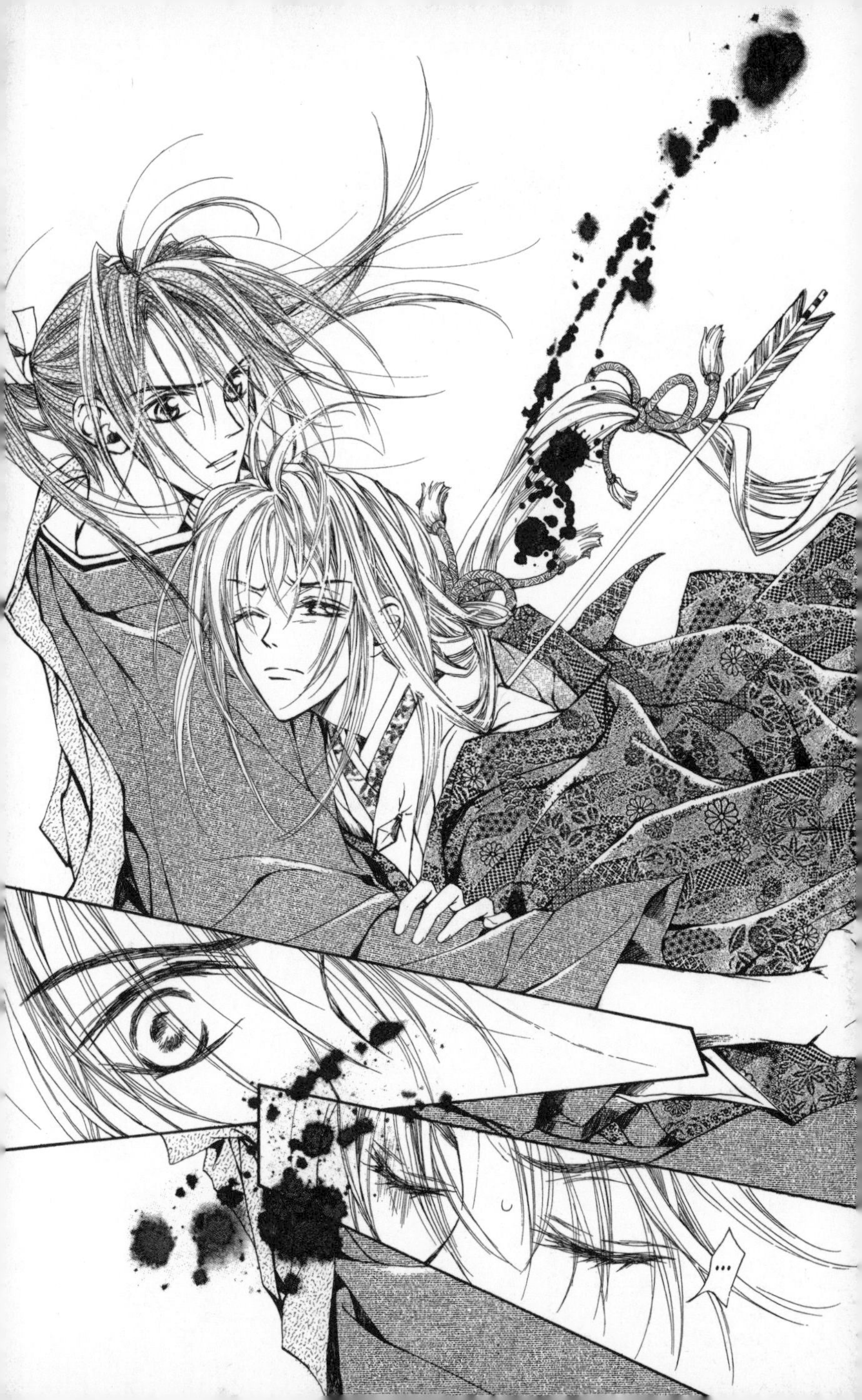
...

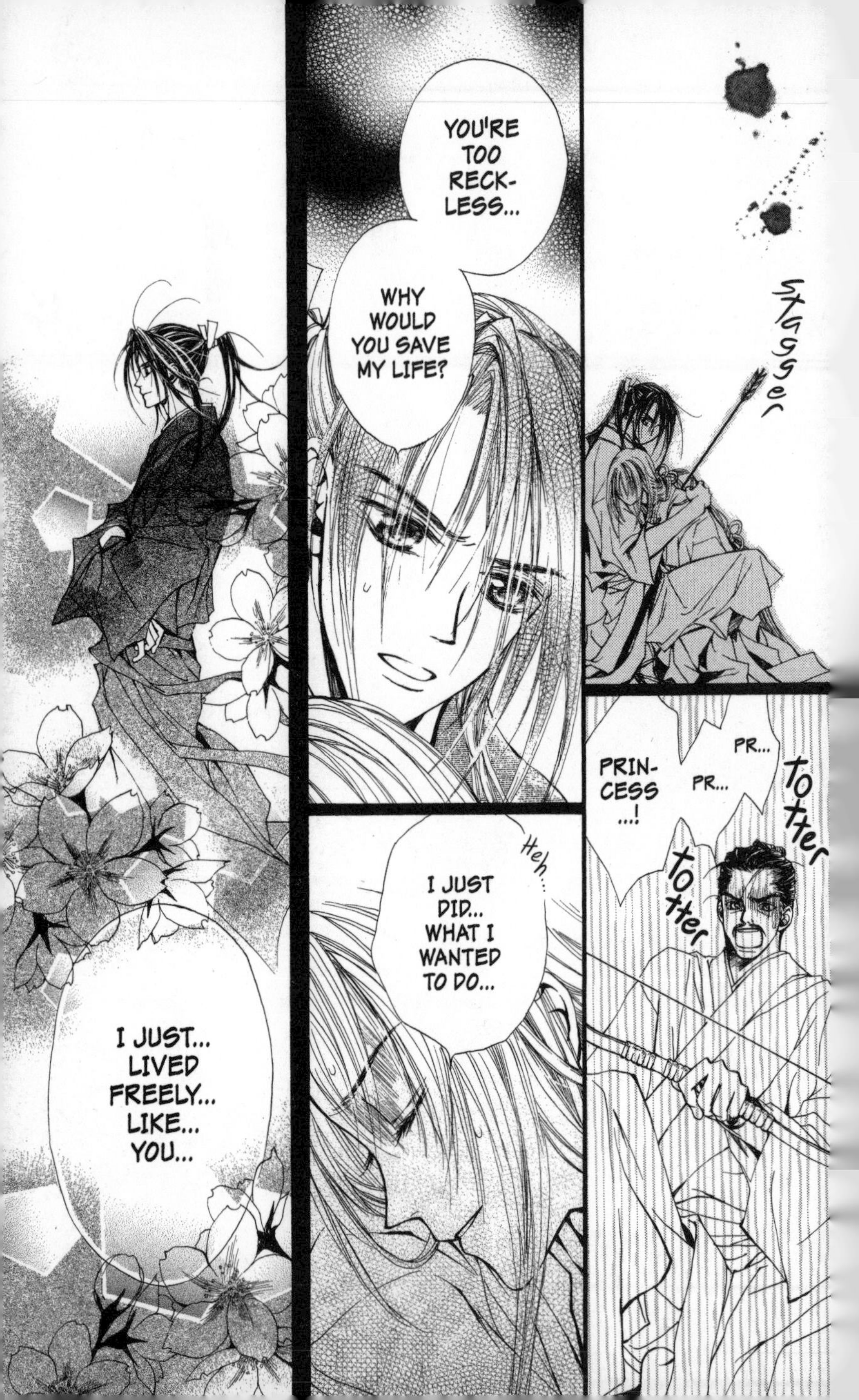
stagger
PR...
PR...
PRIN-CESS ...!
totter
totter
YOU'RE TOO RECK-LESS...
WHY WOULD YOU SAVE MY LIFE?
Heh...
I JUST DID... WHAT I WANTED TO DO...
I JUST... LIVED FREELY... LIKE... YOU...

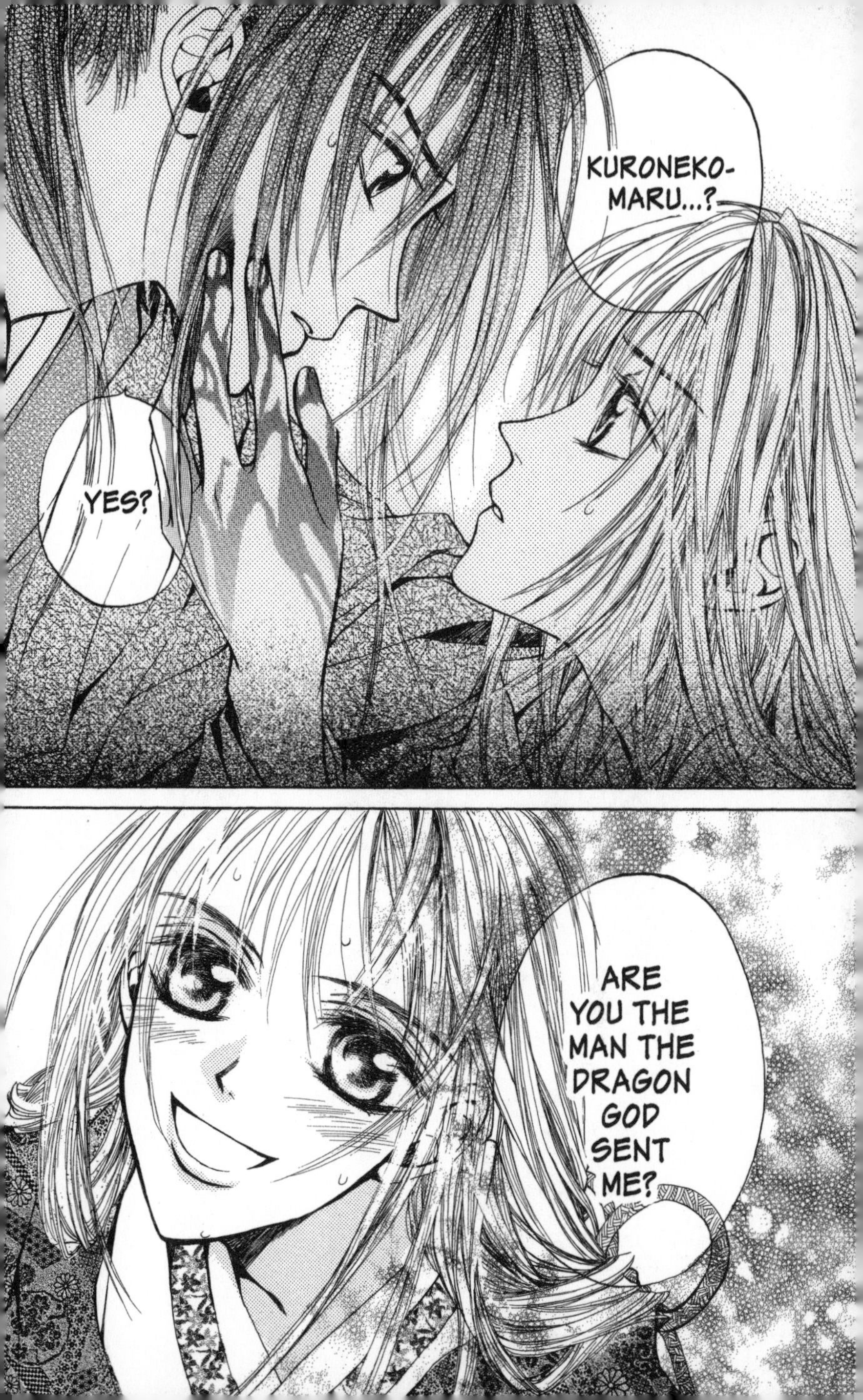
KURONEKO-MARU...?
YES?
ARE YOU THE MAN THE DRAGON GOD SENT ME?

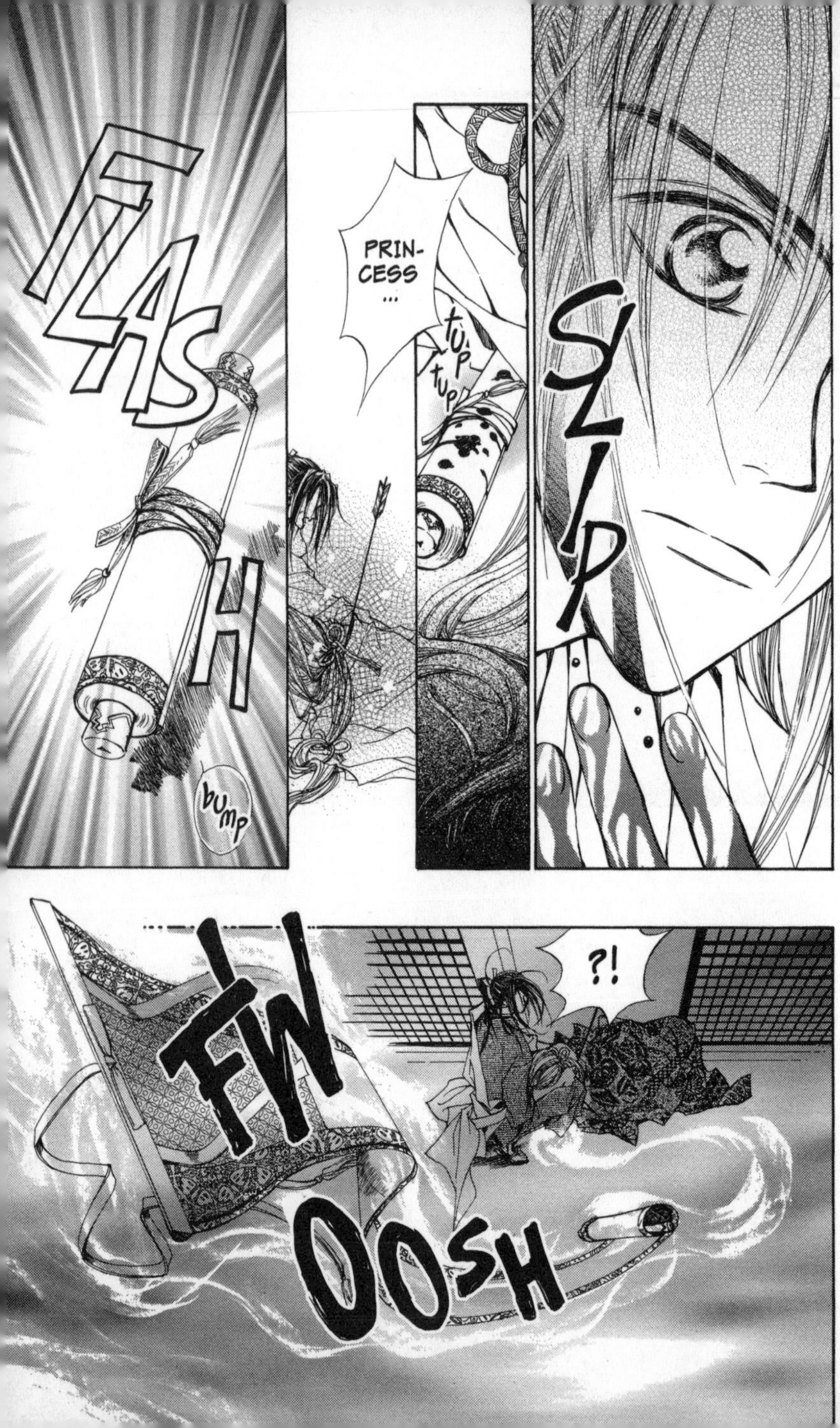
SLIP
PRINCESS...
tup tup
FLASH
bump
?!
FWOOSH

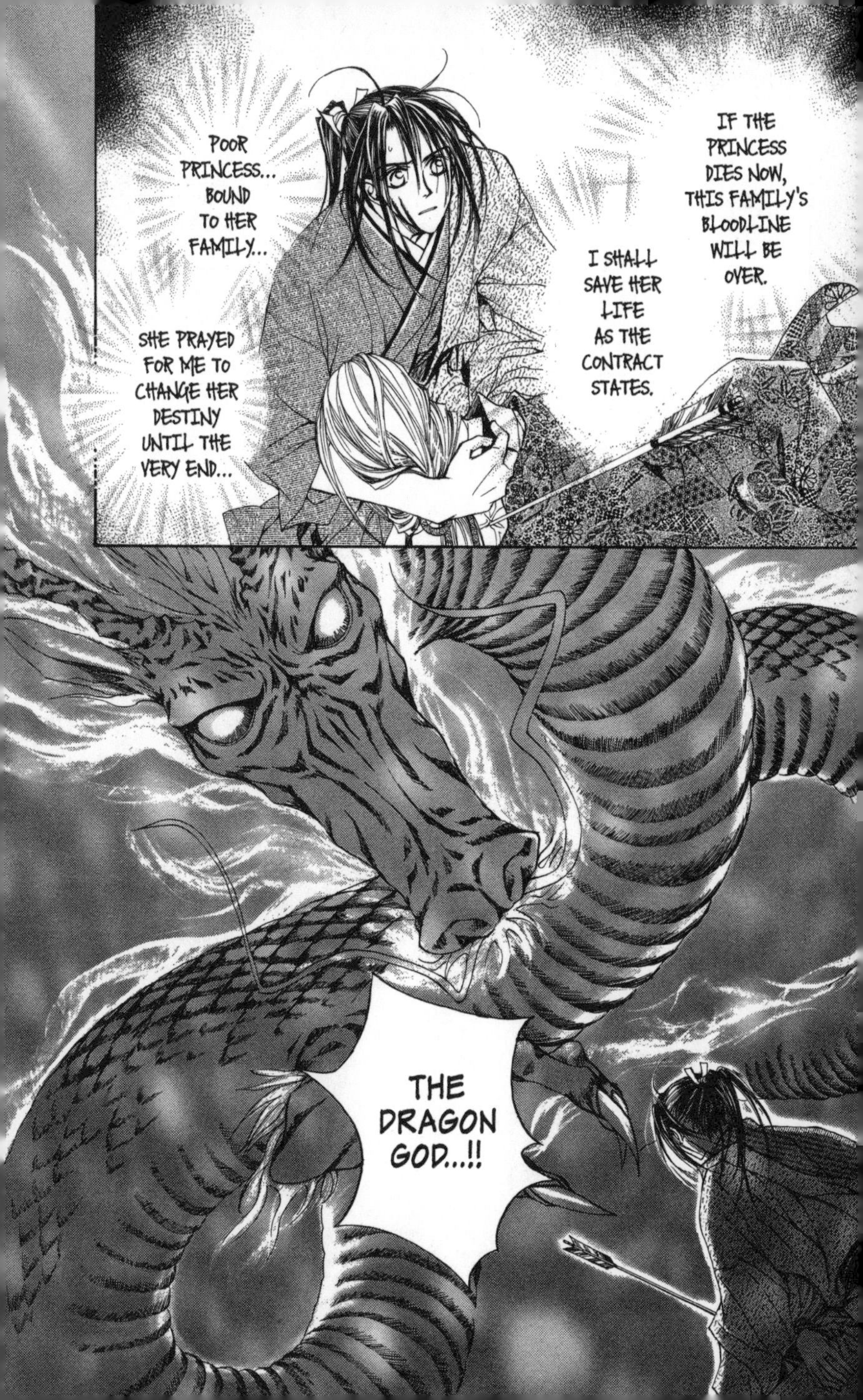
IF THE PRINCESS DIES NOW, THIS FAMILY'S BLOODLINE WILL BE OVER.
I SHALL SAVE HER LIFE AS THE CONTRACT STATES.
POOR PRINCESS... BOUND TO HER FAMILY...
SHE PRAYED FOR ME TO CHANGE HER DESTINY UNTIL THE VERY END...
THE DRAGON GOD...!!

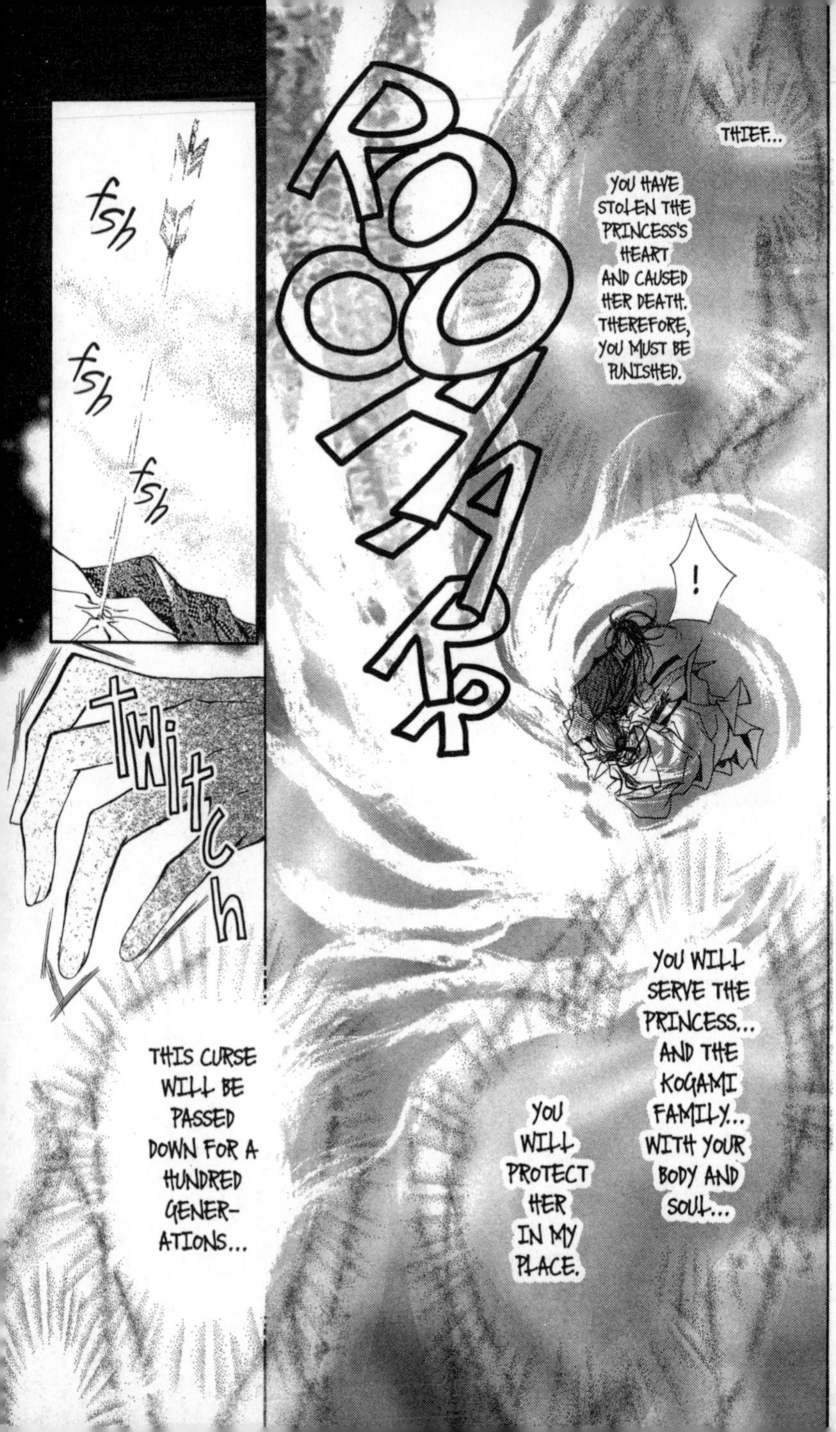
THIEF...
YOU HAVE STOLEN THE PRINCESS'S HEART AND CAUSED HER DEATH. THEREFORE, YOU MUST BE PUNISHED.
ROOOAARR
!
YOU WILL SERVE THE PRINCESS... AND THE KOGAMI FAMILY... WITH YOUR BODY AND SOUL...
YOU WILL PROTECT HER IN MY PLACE.
THIS CURSE WILL BE PASSED DOWN FOR A HUNDRED GENER-ATIONS...
fsh
fsh
fsh
twitch

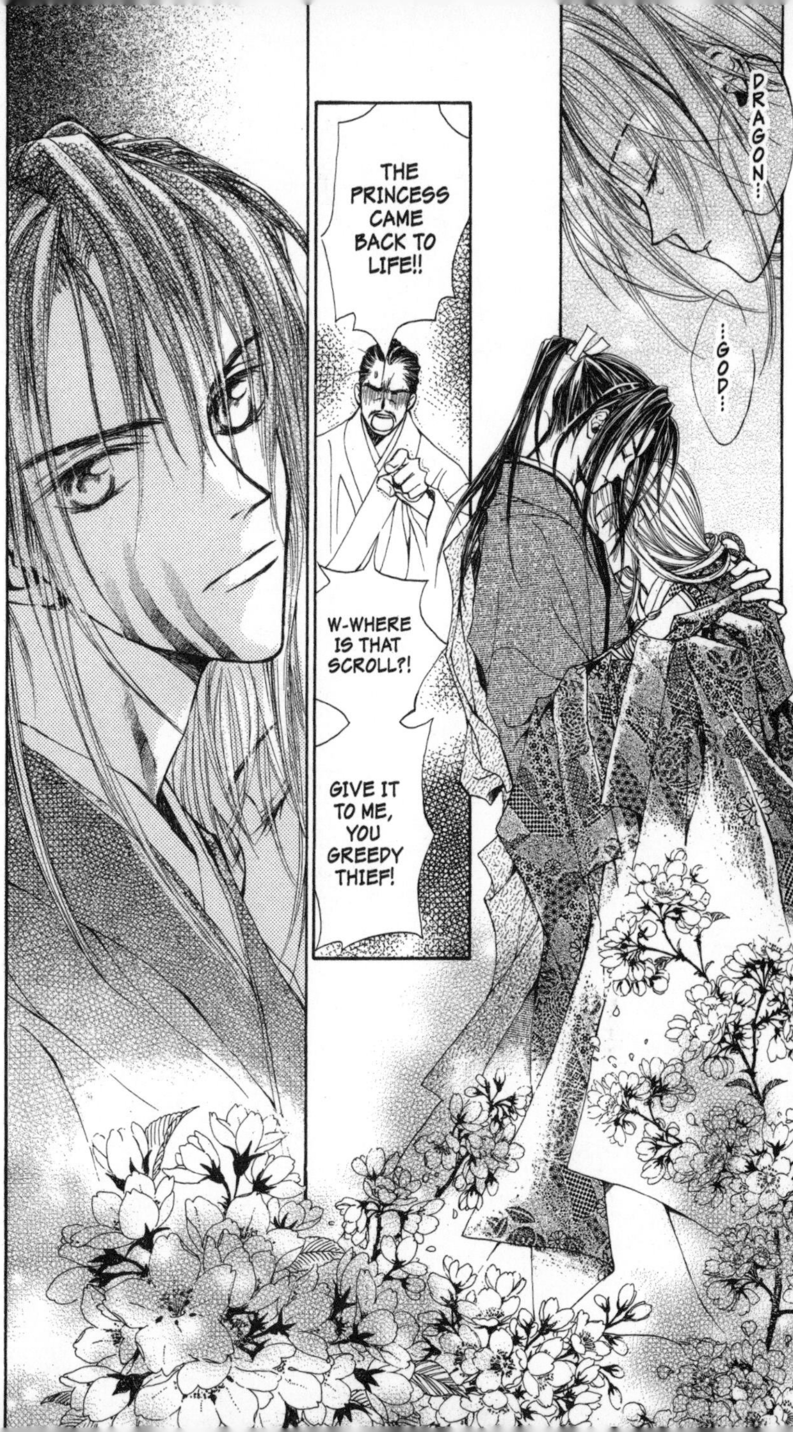
DRAGON...
...GOD...
THE PRINCESS CAME BACK TO LIFE!!
W-WHERE IS THAT SCROLL?!
GIVE IT TO ME, YOU GREEDY THIEF!

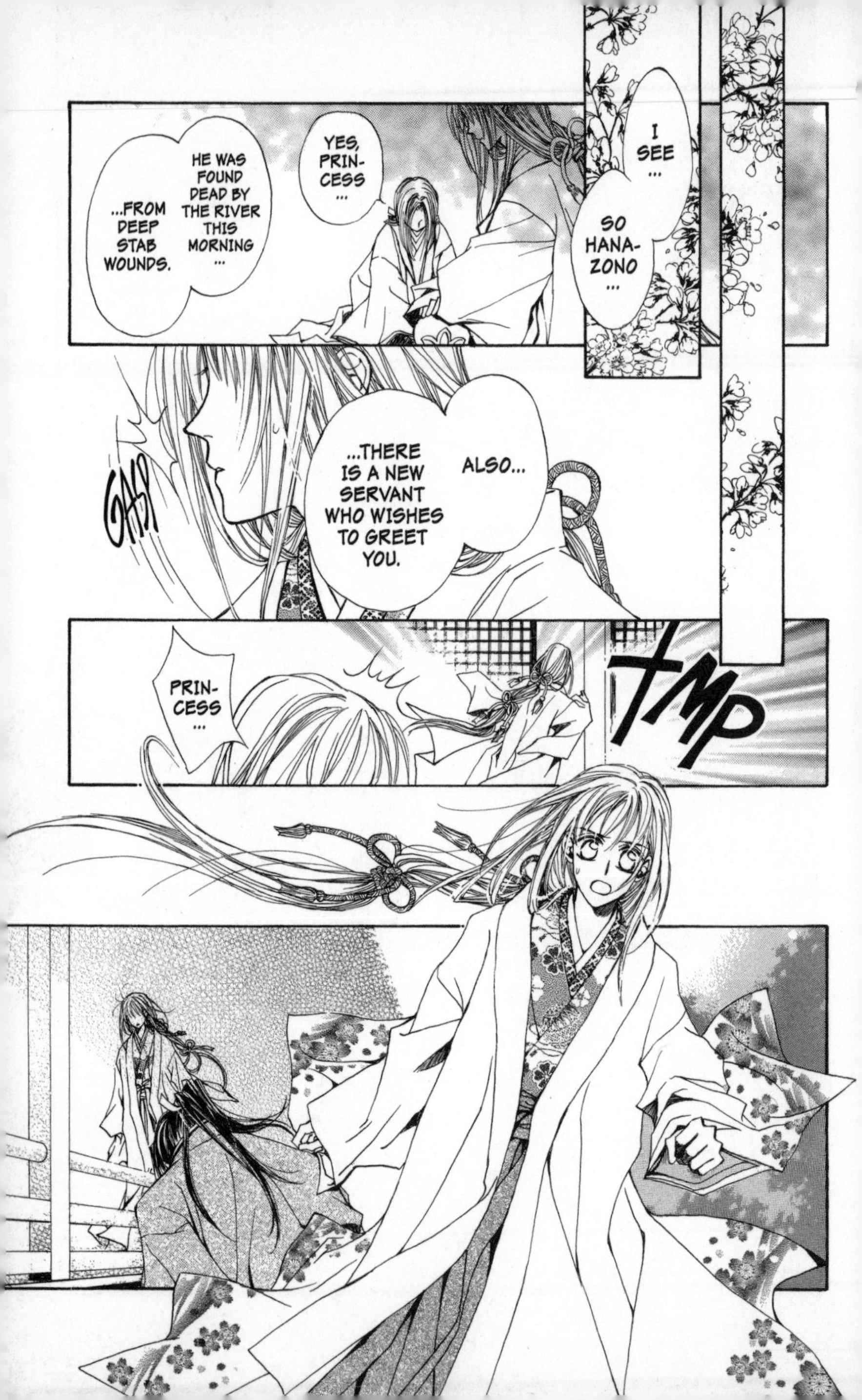
I SEE...
SO HANAZONO...
YES, PRINCESS...
HE WAS FOUND DEAD BY THE RIVER THIS MORNING...
...FROM DEEP STAB WOUNDS.
ALSO...
...THERE IS A NEW SERVANT WHO WISHES TO GREET YOU.
GASP
TMP
PRINCESS...

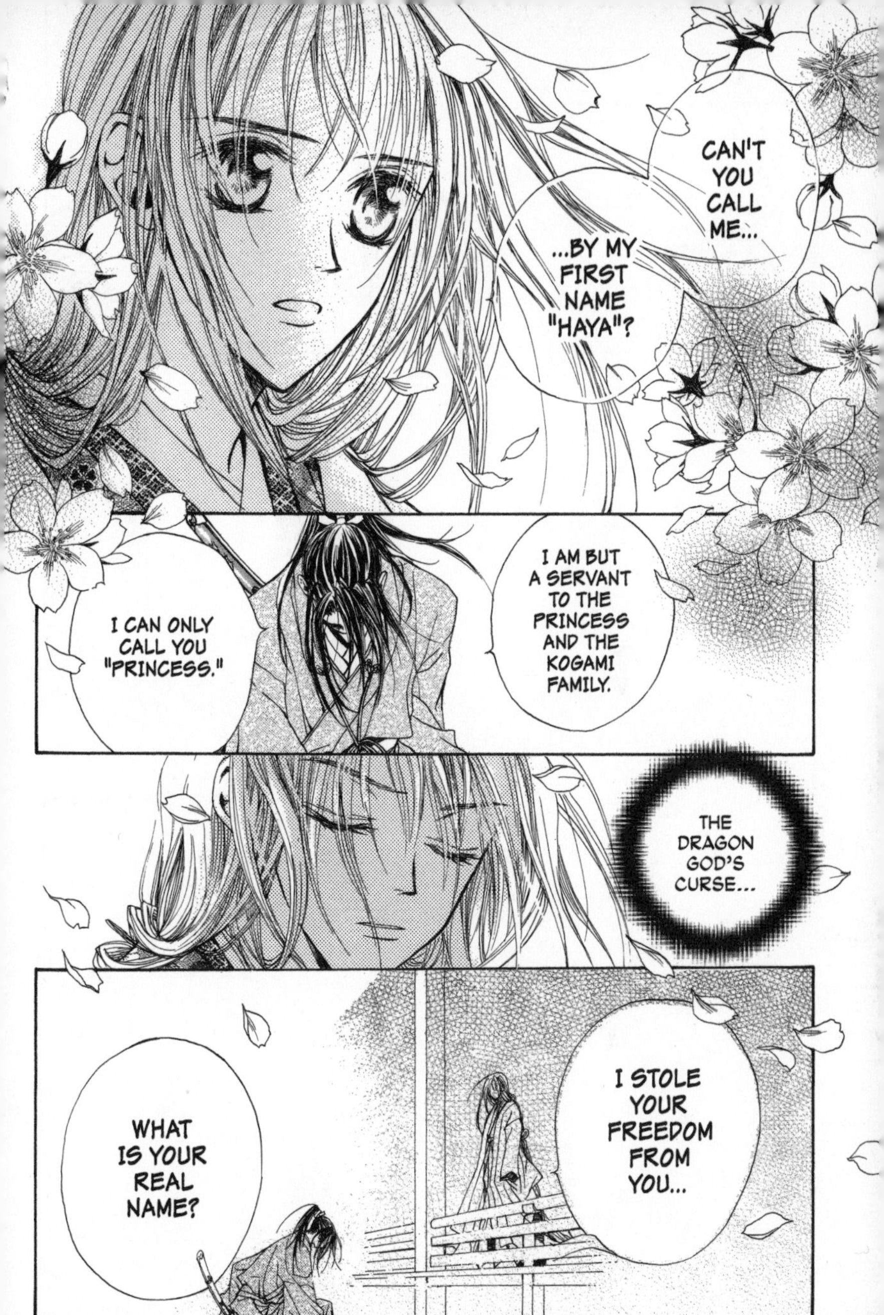
CAN'T YOU CALL ME...
...BY MY FIRST NAME "HAYA"?
I AM BUT A SERVANT TO THE PRINCESS AND THE KOGAMI FAMILY.
I CAN ONLY CALL YOU "PRINCESS."
THE DRAGON GOD'S CURSE...
I STOLE YOUR FREEDOM FROM YOU...
WHAT IS YOUR REAL NAME?

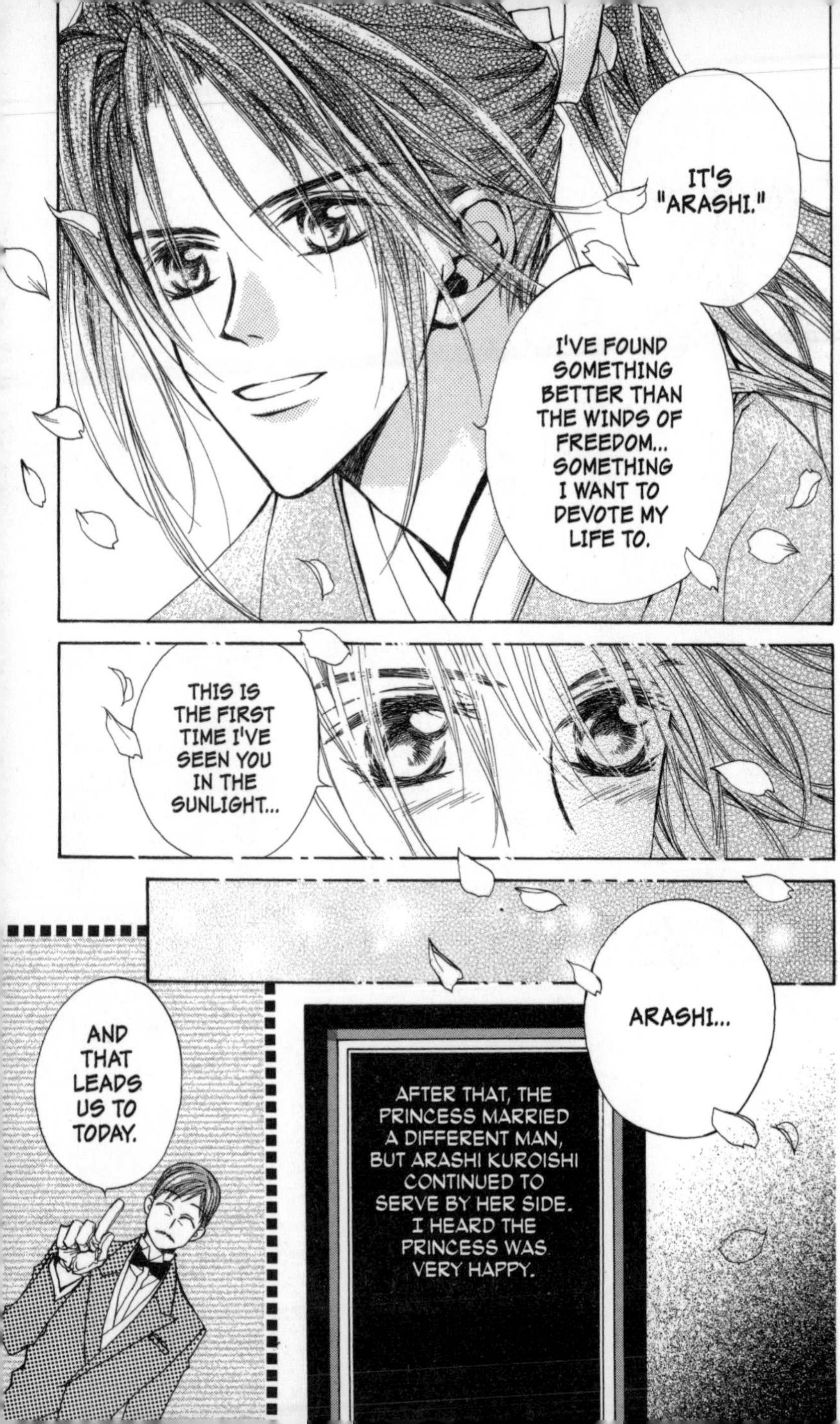
IT'S "ARASHI."
I'VE FOUND SOMETHING BETTER THAN THE WINDS OF FREEDOM... SOMETHING I WANT TO DEVOTE MY LIFE TO.
THIS IS THE FIRST TIME I'VE SEEN YOU IN THE SUNLIGHT...
ARASHI...
AFTER THAT, THE PRINCESS MARRIED A DIFFERENT MAN, BUT ARASHI KUROISHI CONTINUED TO SERVE BY HER SIDE. I HEARD THE PRINCESS WAS VERY HAPPY.
AND THAT LEADS US TO TODAY.

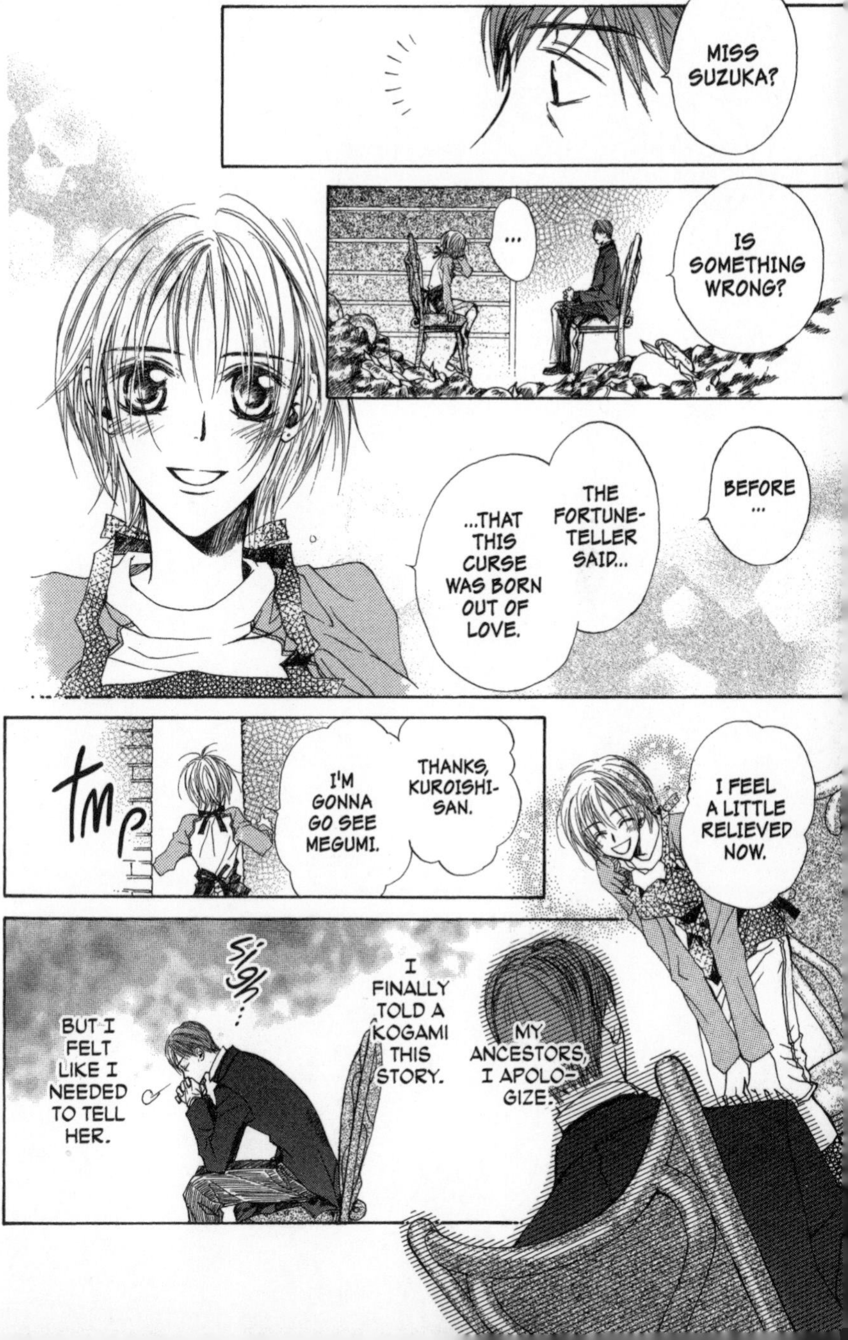
MISS SUZUKA?
IS SOMETHING WRONG?
...
BEFORE...
THE FORTUNE-TELLER SAID...
...THAT THIS CURSE WAS BORN OUT OF LOVE.
I FEEL A LITTLE RELIEVED NOW.
THANKS, KUROISHI-SAN.
I'M GONNA GO SEE MEGUMI.
tmp
MY ANCESTORS, I APOLOGIZE.
I FINALLY TOLD A KOGAMI THIS STORY.
sigh...
BUT I FELT LIKE I NEEDED TO TELL HER.

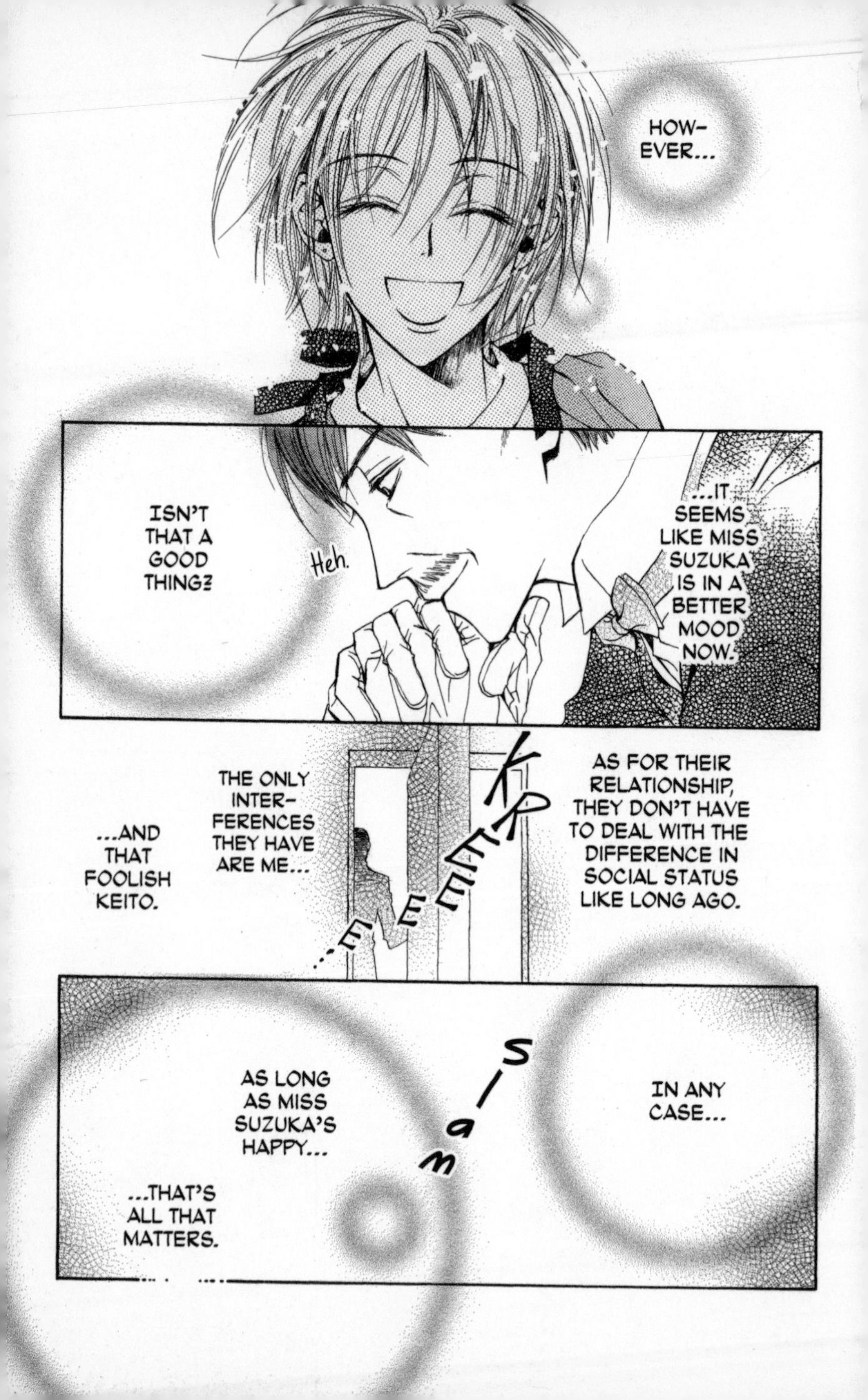
HOW-EVER...
...IT SEEMS LIKE MISS SUZUKA IS IN A BETTER MOOD NOW.
Heh.
ISN'T THAT A GOOD THING?
AS FOR THEIR RELATIONSHIP, THEY DON'T HAVE TO DEAL WITH THE DIFFERENCE IN SOCIAL STATUS LIKE LONG AGO.
KREEEEE...
THE ONLY INTER-FERENCES THEY HAVE ARE ME...
...AND THAT FOOLISH KEITO.
IN ANY CASE...
Slam
AS LONG AS MISS SUZUKA'S HAPPY...
...THAT'S ALL THAT MATTERS.

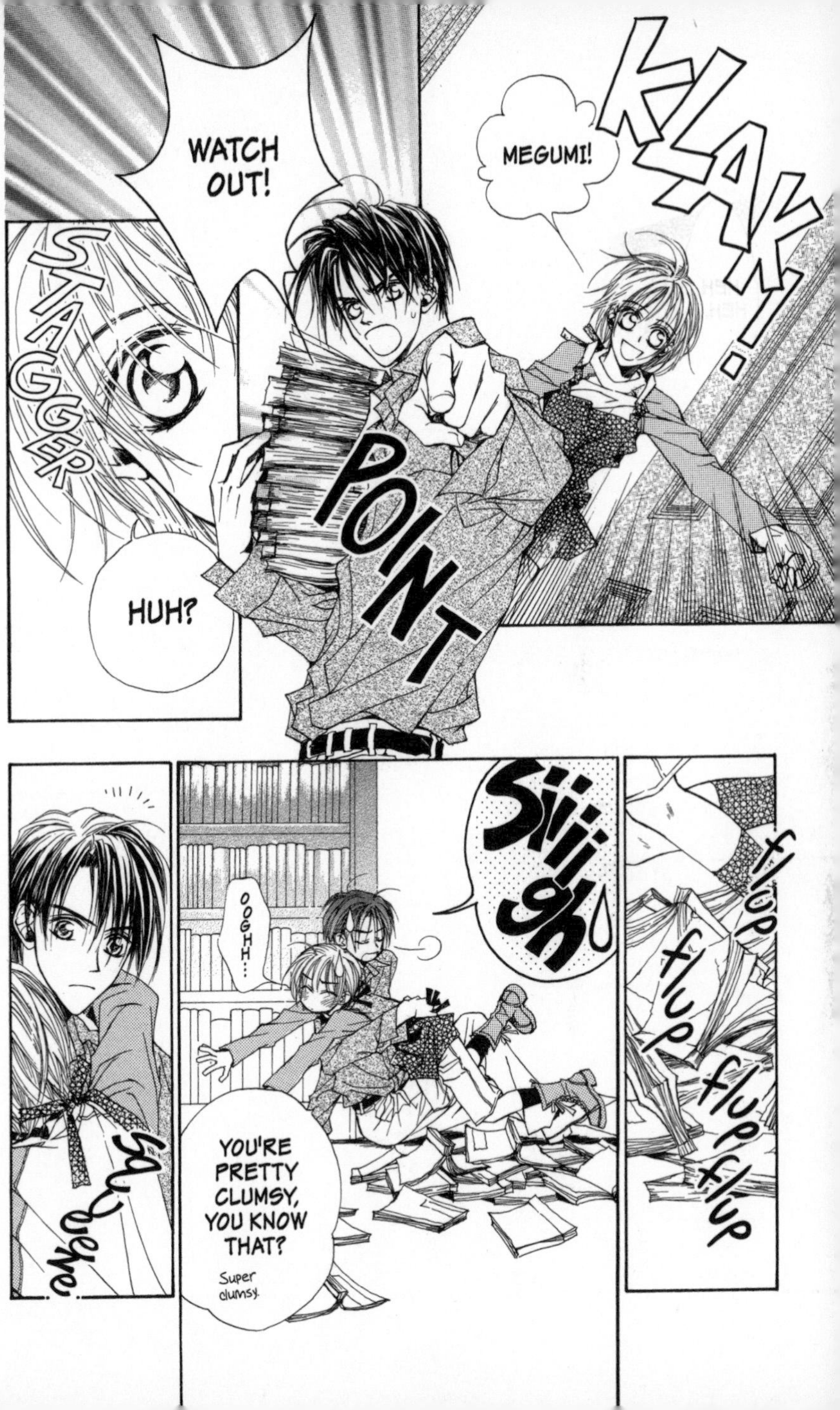

KLAK!
MEGUMI!
WATCH OUT!
POINT
STAGGER
HUH?
flup flup flup flup flup
Siiigh
OOGHH...
YOU'RE PRETTY CLUMSY, YOU KNOW THAT?
Super clumsy.
squeeze

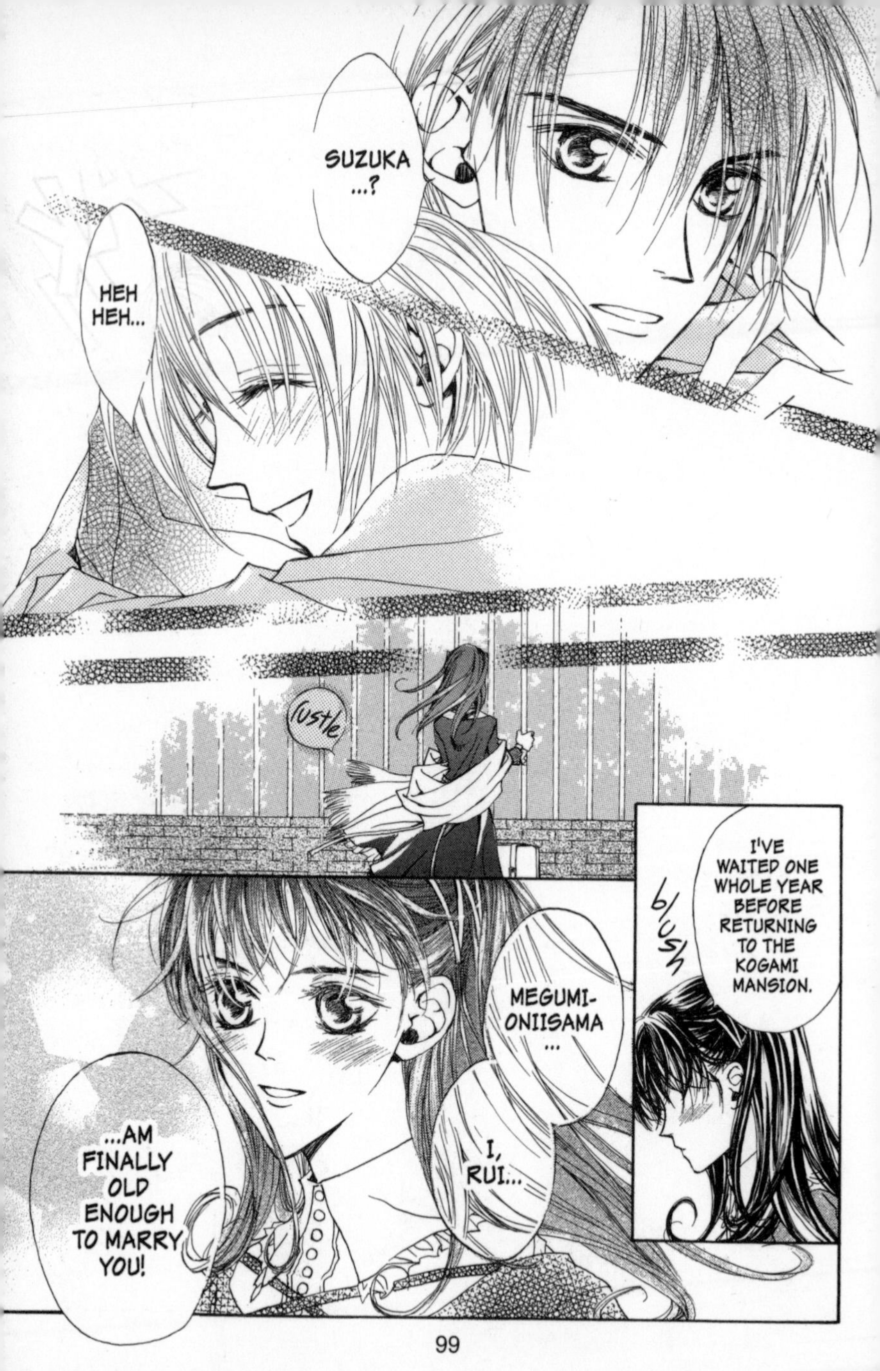
SUZUKA ...?
HEH HEH...
rustle
I'VE WAITED ONE WHOLE YEAR BEFORE RETURNING TO THE KOGAMI MANSION.
blush
MEGUMI-ONIISAMA ...
I, RUI...
...AM FINALLY OLD ENOUGH TO MARRY YOU!

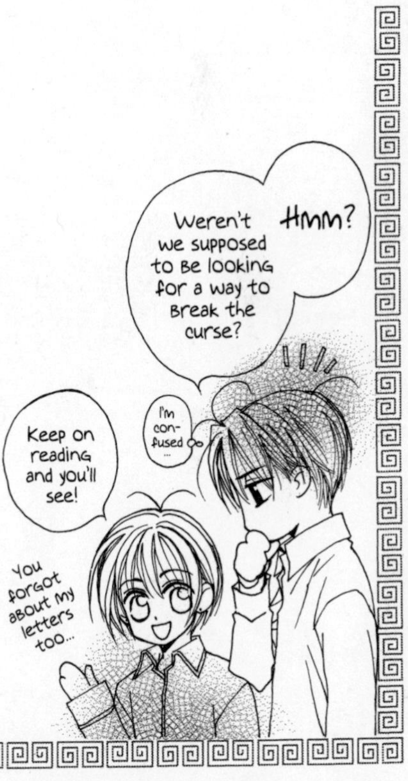
Hmm?
Weren't we supposed to be looking for a way to break the curse?
I'm con-fused ...
Keep on reading and you'll see!
You forgot about my letters too...

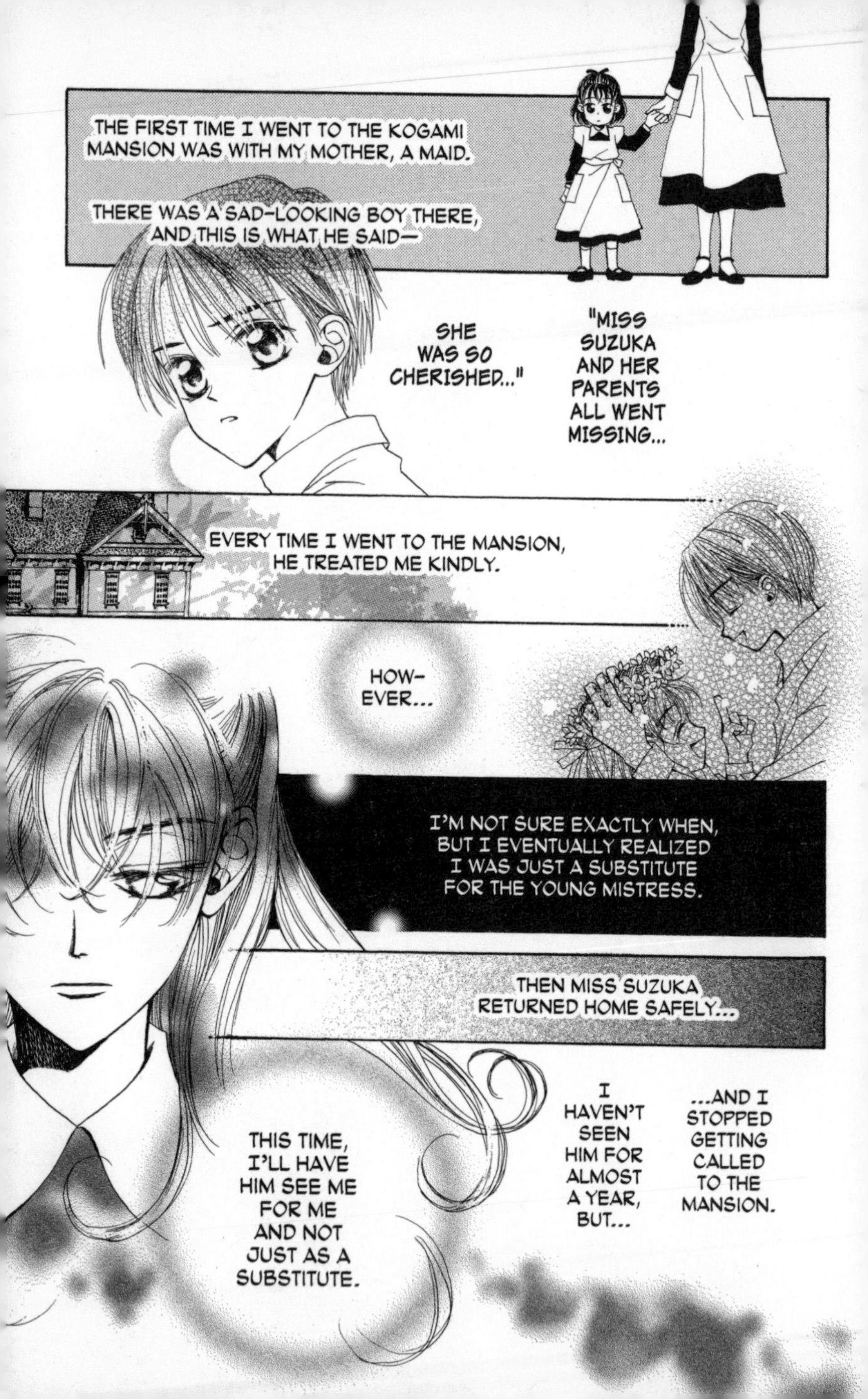
THE FIRST TIME I WENT TO THE KOGAMI MANSION WAS WITH MY MOTHER, A MAID.
THERE WAS A SAD-LOOKING BOY THERE, AND THIS IS WHAT HE SAID—
"MISS SUZUKA AND HER PARENTS ALL WENT MISSING...
SHE WAS SO CHERISHED..."
EVERY TIME I WENT TO THE MANSION, HE TREATED ME KINDLY.
HOW-EVER...
I'M NOT SURE EXACTLY WHEN, BUT I EVENTUALLY REALIZED I WAS JUST A SUBSTITUTE FOR THE YOUNG MISTRESS.
THEN MISS SUZUKA RETURNED HOME SAFELY...
...AND I STOPPED GETTING CALLED TO THE MANSION.
I HAVEN'T SEEN HIM FOR ALMOST A YEAR, BUT...
THIS TIME, I'LL HAVE HIM SEE ME FOR ME AND NOT JUST AS A SUBSTITUTE.

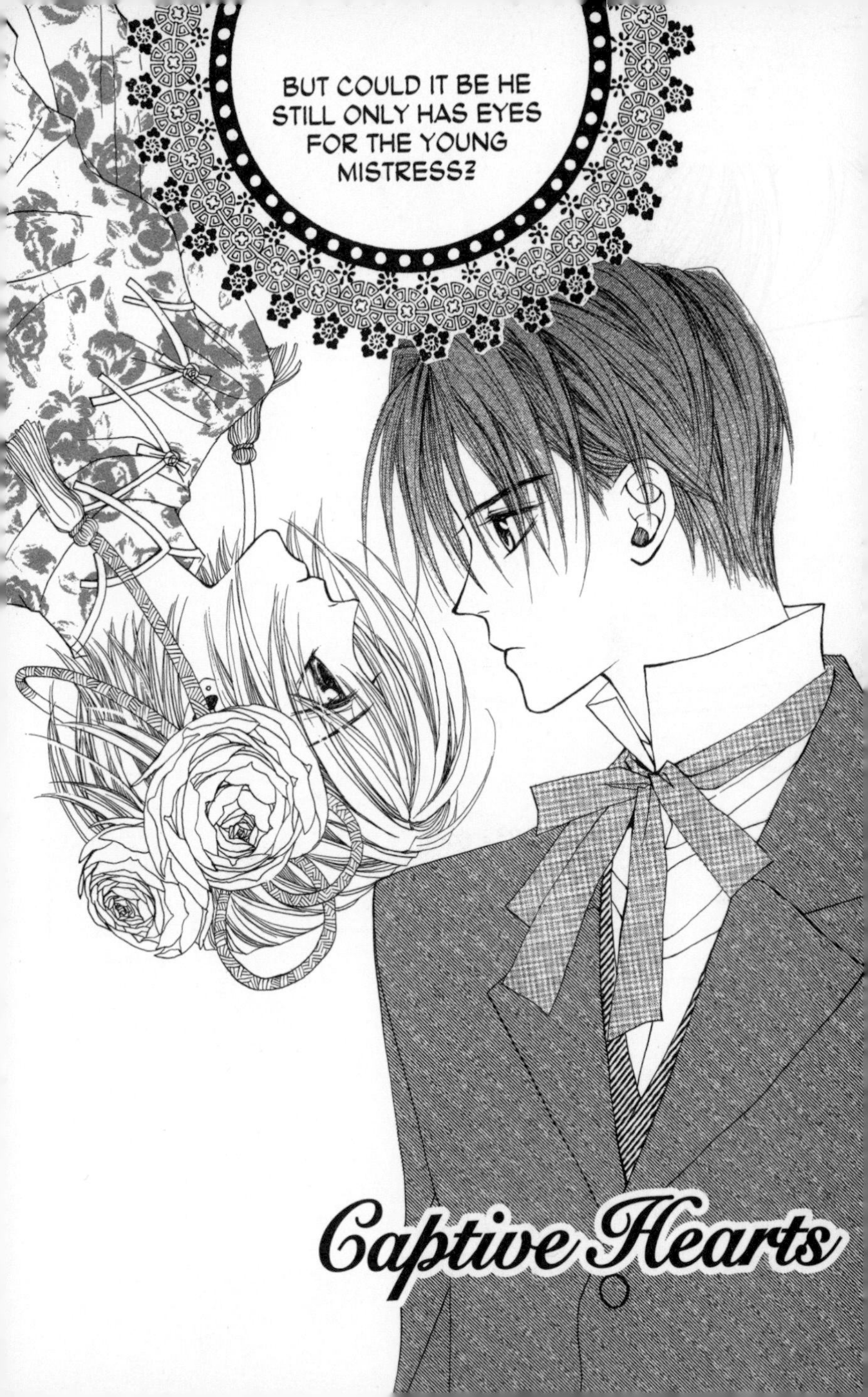
BUT COULD IT BE HE STILL ONLY HAS EYES FOR THE YOUNG MISTRESS?
Captive Hearts

WOMEN ...
BUT PRINCESS HAYA AND ARASHI-SAN...
... CHERISHED EACH OTHER FOR THE REST OF THEIR LIVES!
...ARE VERY STRONG CREA-TURES ...
CREATURES WHO FALL IN LOVE WITH SUCH STORIES...
HEY, MEGUMI. WERE YOU LISTENING TO ALL THE DETAILS ABOUT YOUR ANCESTORS?
Has been talking for 3 hours straight.
exhausted
YES. EVERY ONE.
Has been listening for 3 hours straight.
Reference to volume 1.
DAD SURE LEFT OUT A LOT WHEN HE TOLD THIS STORY TO ME EARLIER...

Backstory ④

I'm quite fond of Rui-chan. She's easy to draw and easy to understand. Suzuka is actually difficult to draw. I always have to think very hard, like, "What is she thinking about right now?" when I draw her. There are a lot of things I don't know about her yet, so I always treat her very carefully.

Megumi is...cursed, so I have to consider many things with him too! (Laugh)

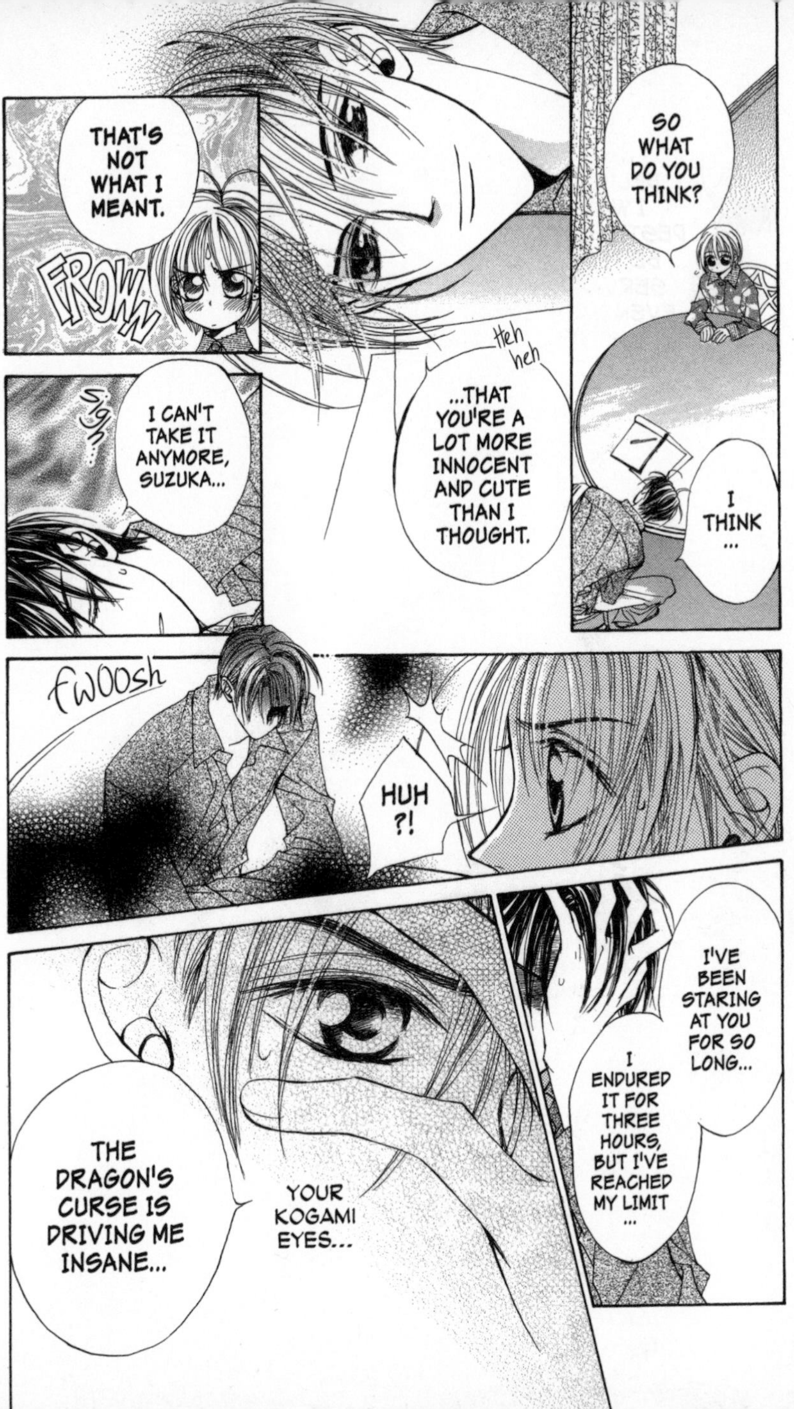
SO WHAT DO YOU THINK?
I THINK...
heh heh
...THAT YOU'RE A LOT MORE INNOCENT AND CUTE THAN I THOUGHT.
THAT'S NOT WHAT I MEANT.
FROWN
I CAN'T TAKE IT ANYMORE, SUZUKA...
sigh...
HUH?!
fwoosh
I'VE BEEN STARING AT YOU FOR SO LONG...
I ENDURED IT FOR THREE HOURS, BUT I'VE REACHED MY LIMIT...
YOUR KOGAMI EYES...
THE DRAGON'S CURSE IS DRIVING ME INSANE...

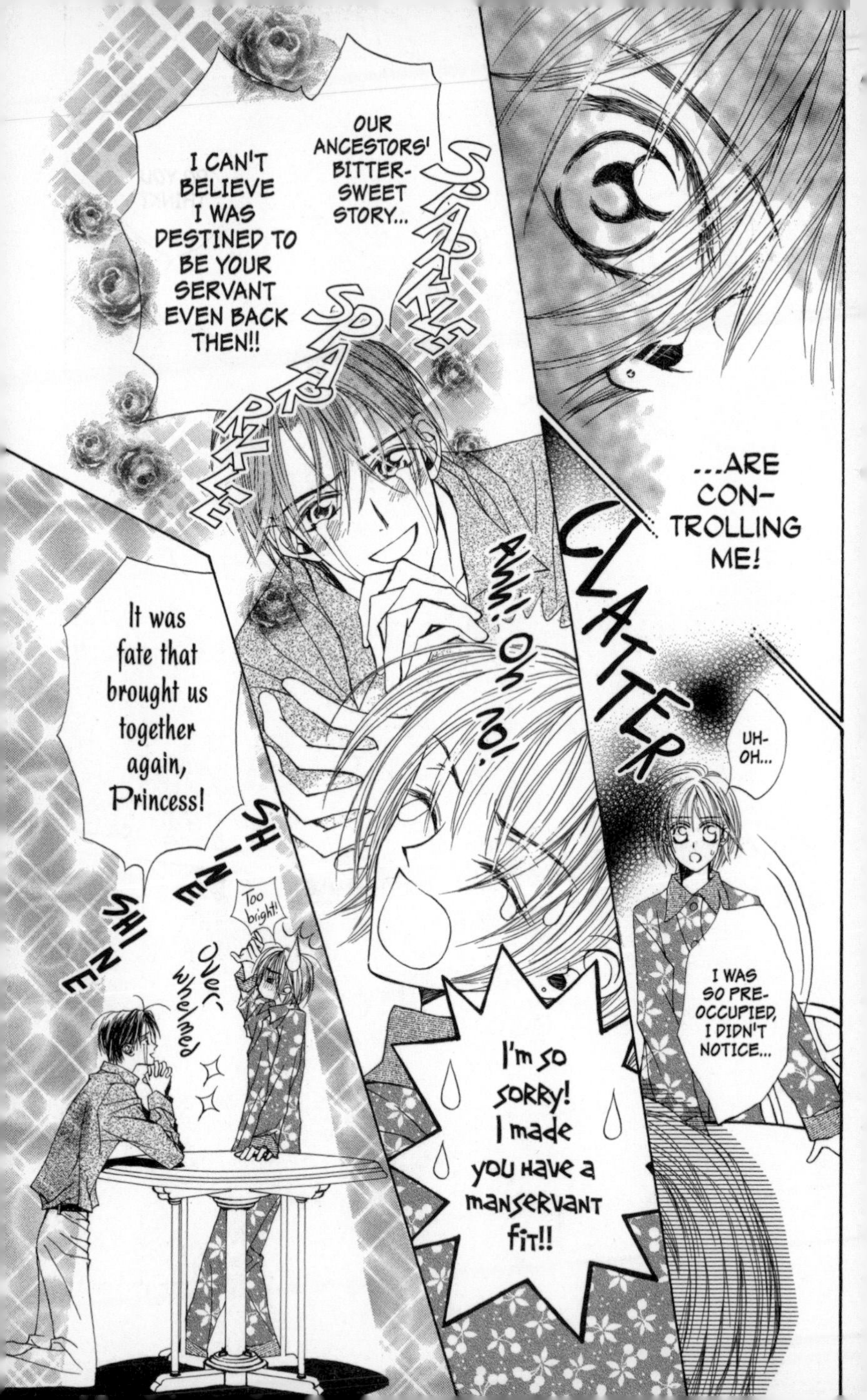
...ARE CON-TROLLING ME!
OUR ANCESTORS' BITTER-SWEET STORY...
I CAN'T BELIEVE I WAS DESTINED TO BE YOUR SERVANT EVEN BACK THEN!!
SPARKLE
SPARKLE
CLATTER
UH-OH...
I WAS SO PRE-OCCUPIED, I DIDN'T NOTICE...
AHH! OH NO!
I'm so SORRY! I made you have a manservant fit!!
It was fate that brought us together again, Princess!
SHINE
SHINE
Too bright!
Over-whelmed

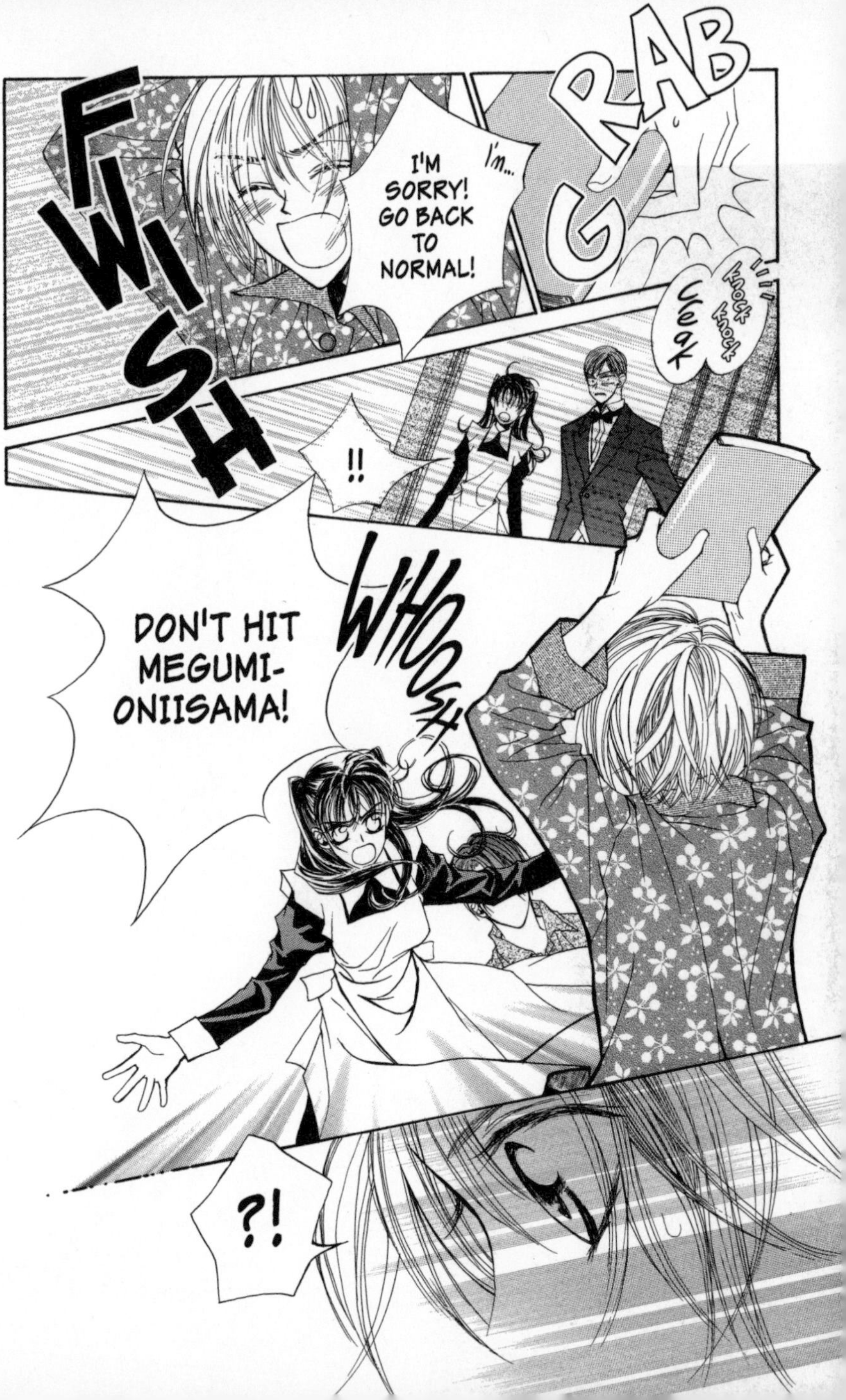
GRAB
knock knock
creak
I'm...
I'M SORRY! GO BACK TO NORMAL!
FWISH
!!
WHOOSH
DON'T HIT MEGUMI-ONIISAMA!
?!

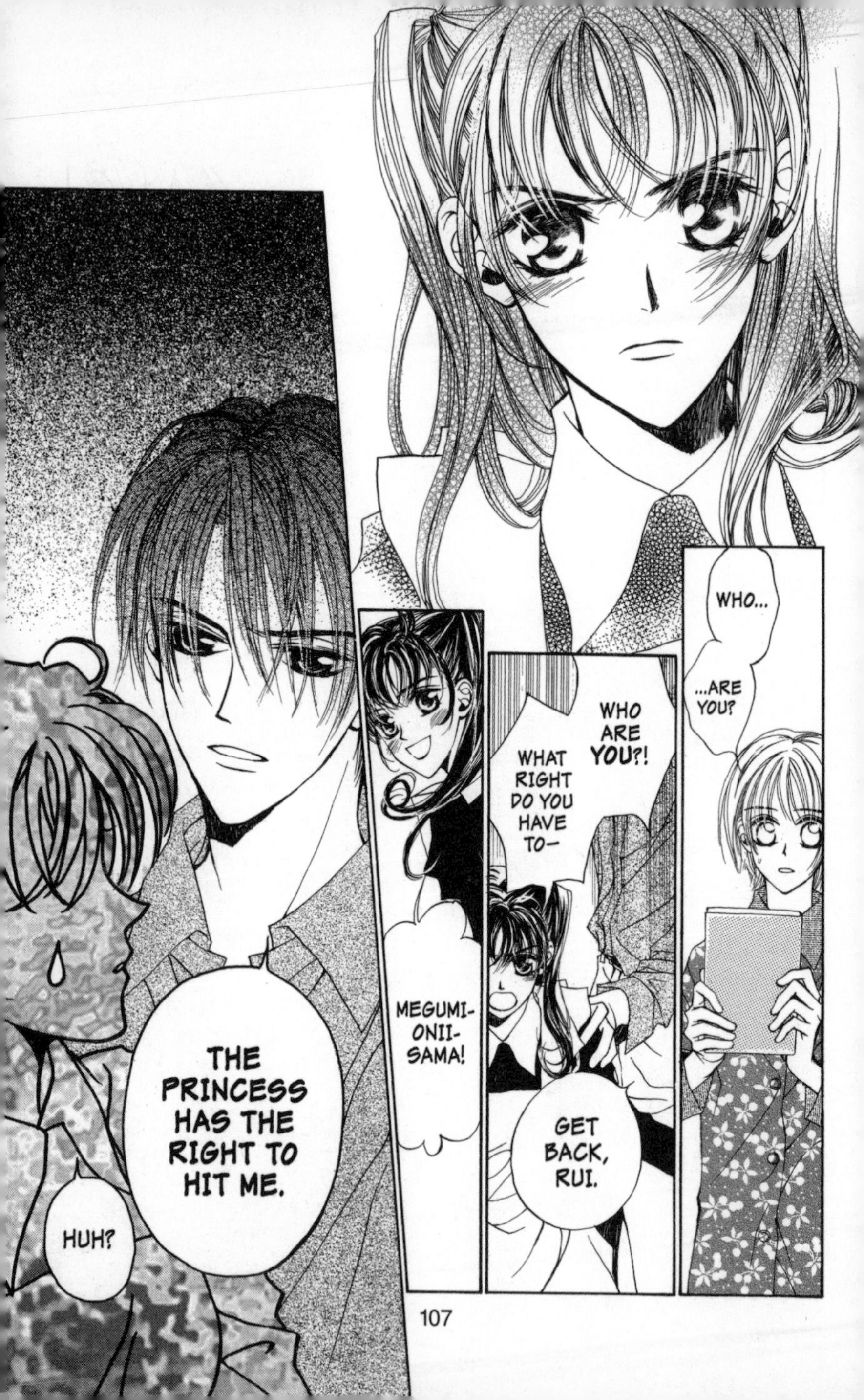
WHO...
...ARE YOU?
WHO ARE **YOU**?!
WHAT RIGHT DO YOU HAVE TO—
GET BACK, RUI.
MEGUMI-ONII-SAMA!
THE PRINCESS HAS THE RIGHT TO HIT ME.
HUH?

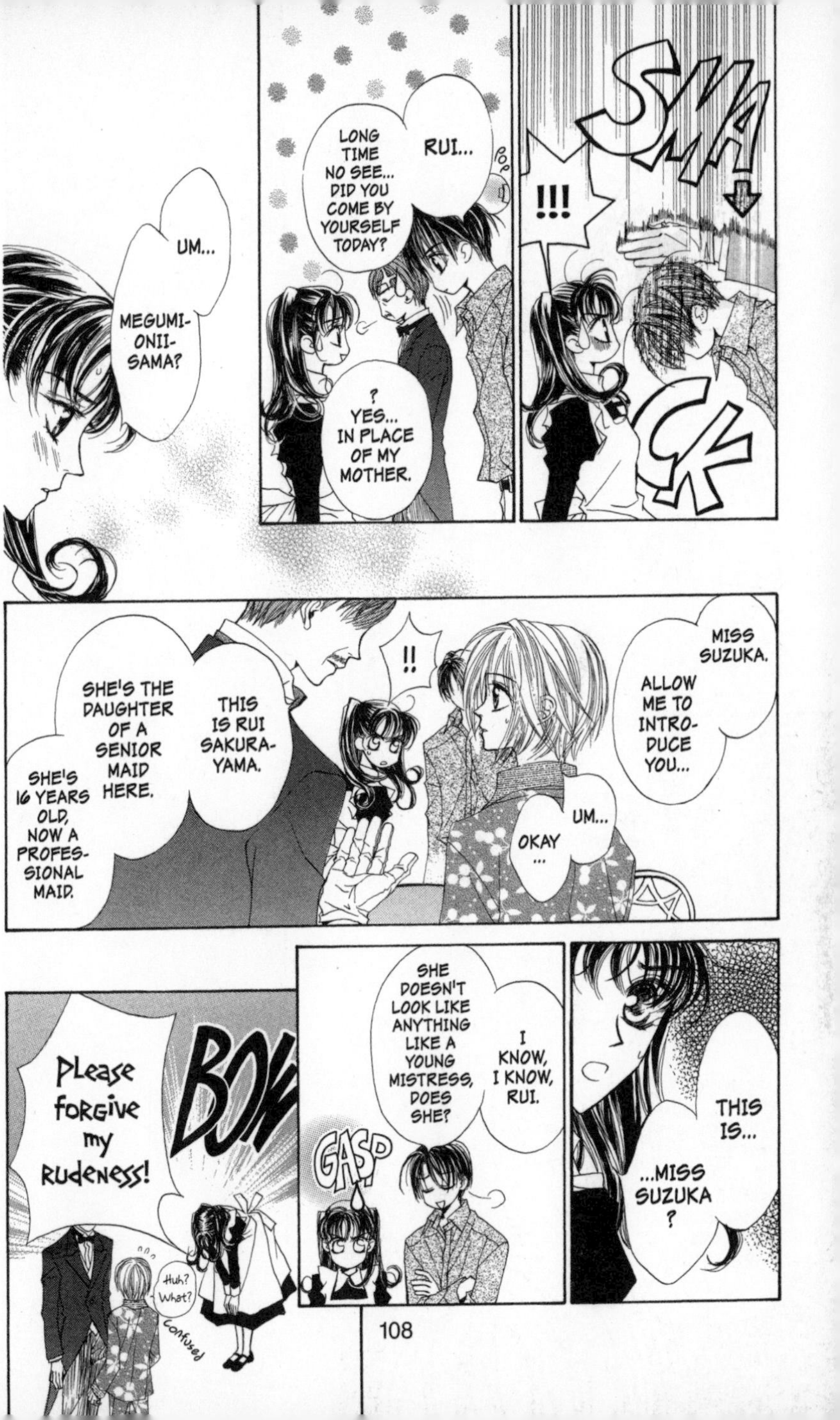
SMACK
!!!
RUI...
POP
LONG TIME NO SEE... DID YOU COME BY YOURSELF TODAY?
? YES... IN PLACE OF MY MOTHER.
UM...
MEGUMI-ONII-SAMA?
MISS SUZUKA.
ALLOW ME TO INTRO-DUCE YOU...
UM...
OKAY ...
!!
THIS IS RUI SAKURA-YAMA.
SHE'S THE DAUGHTER OF A SENIOR MAID HERE.
SHE'S 16 YEARS OLD, NOW A PROFES-SIONAL MAID.
THIS IS...
...MISS SUZUKA ?
I KNOW, I KNOW, RUI.
SHE DOESN'T LOOK LIKE ANYTHING LIKE A YOUNG MISTRESS, DOES SHE?
GASP
BOW
Please forgive my rudeness!
Huh? What?
Confused

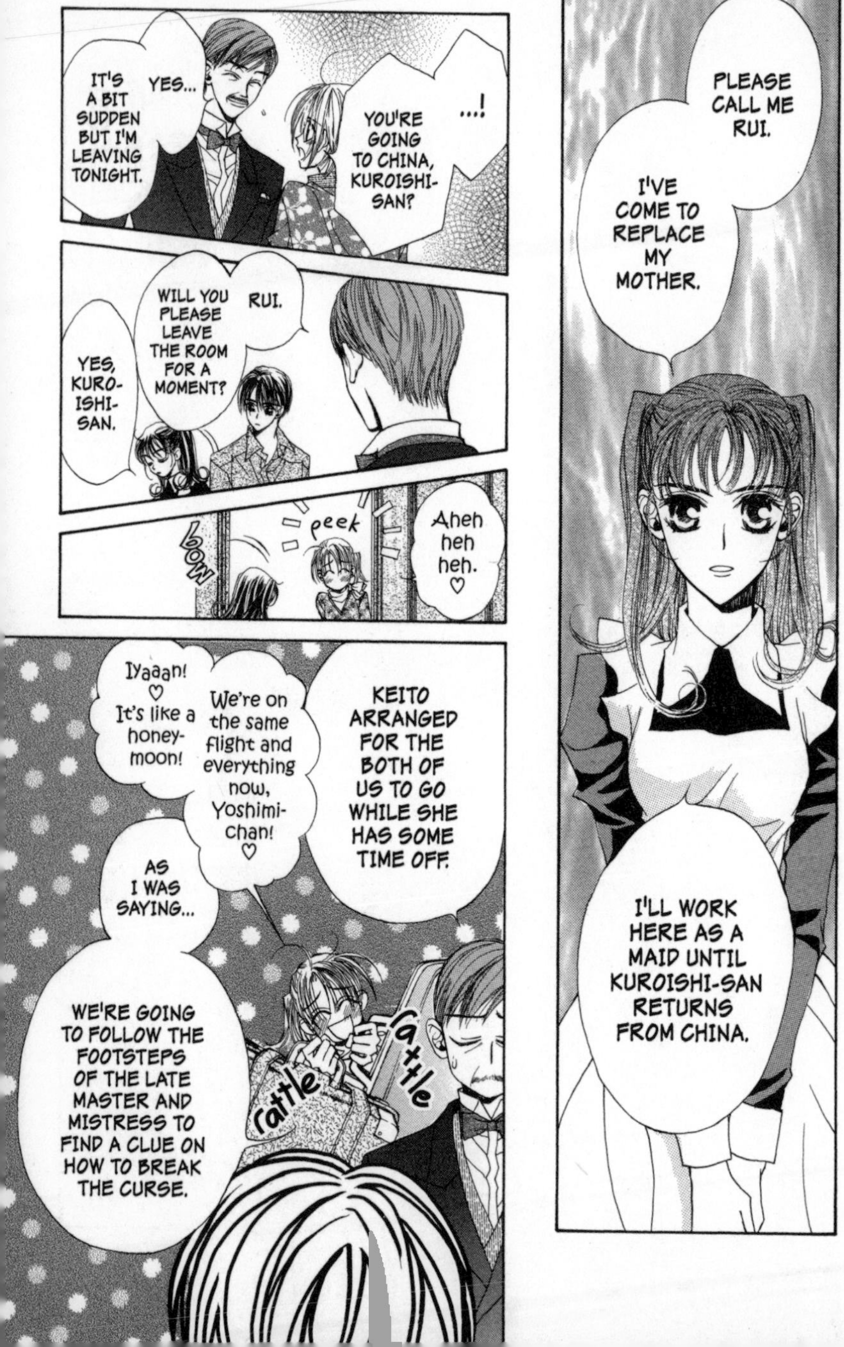
PLEASE CALL ME RUI.
I'VE COME TO REPLACE MY MOTHER.
I'LL WORK HERE AS A MAID UNTIL KUROISHI-SAN RETURNS FROM CHINA.
...!
YOU'RE GOING TO CHINA, KUROISHI-SAN?
YES...
IT'S A BIT SUDDEN BUT I'M LEAVING TONIGHT.
RUI.
WILL YOU PLEASE LEAVE THE ROOM FOR A MOMENT?
YES, KURO-ISHI-SAN.
Aheh heh heh. ♡
peek
bow
KEITO ARRANGED FOR THE BOTH OF US TO GO WHILE SHE HAS SOME TIME OFF.
We're on the same flight and everything now, Yoshimi-chan! ♡
Iyaaan! ♡ It's like a honey-moon!
AS I WAS SAYING...
WE'RE GOING TO FOLLOW THE FOOTSTEPS OF THE LATE MASTER AND MISTRESS TO FIND A CLUE ON HOW TO BREAK THE CURSE.
rattle
rattle

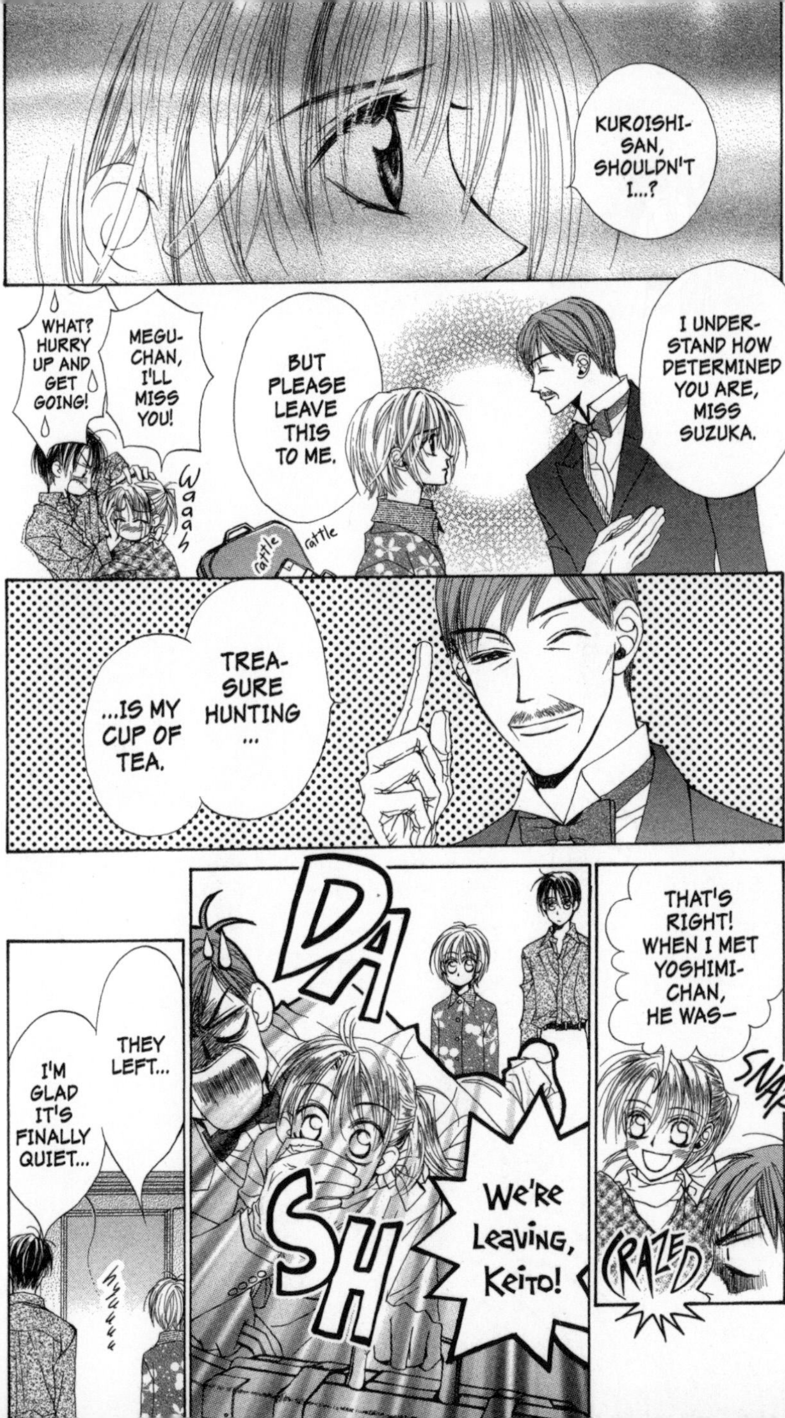
KUROISHI-SAN, SHOULDN'T I...?
I UNDER-STAND HOW DETERMINED YOU ARE, MISS SUZUKA.
BUT PLEASE LEAVE THIS TO ME.
rattle
rattle
MEGU-CHAN, I'LL MISS YOU!
Waaah
WHAT? HURRY UP AND GET GOING!
TREA-SURE HUNTING ...
...IS MY CUP OF TEA.
THAT'S RIGHT! WHEN I MET YOSHIMI-CHAN, HE WAS—
SNAP
CRAZED
DASH
We're Leaving, Keito!
THEY LEFT...
I'M GLAD IT'S FINALLY QUIET...

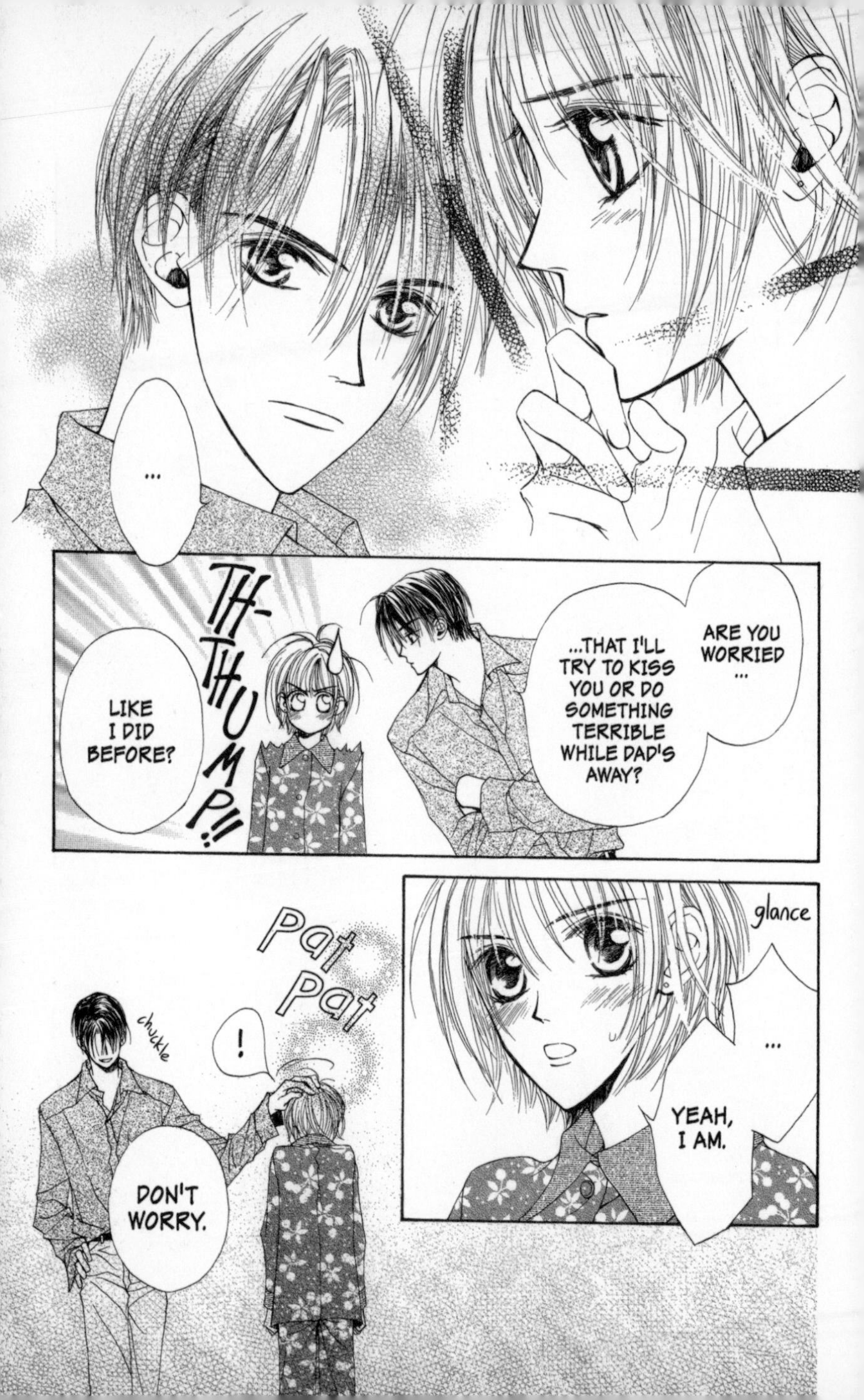
...
ARE YOU WORRIED ...
...THAT I'LL TRY TO KISS YOU OR DO SOMETHING TERRIBLE WHILE DAD'S AWAY?
TH-THUMP!!
LIKE I DID BEFORE?
glance
... YEAH, I AM.
Pat Pat
chuckle
!
DON'T WORRY.

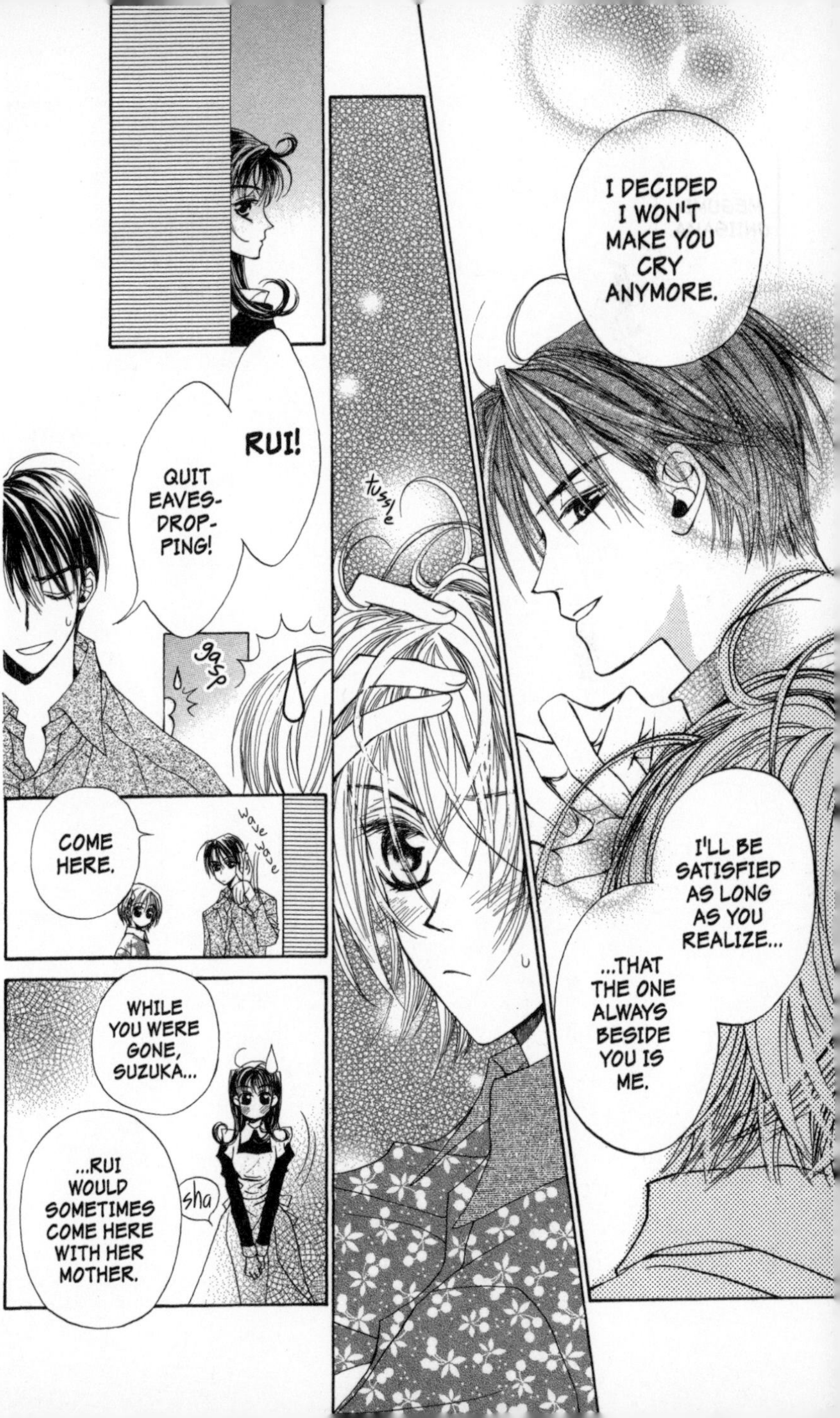
I DECIDED I WON'T MAKE YOU CRY ANYMORE.
I'LL BE SATISFIED AS LONG AS YOU REALIZE...
...THAT THE ONE ALWAYS BESIDE YOU IS ME.
tussle
RUI! QUIT EAVES-DROP-PING!
gasp
COME HERE.
wave wave
WHILE YOU WERE GONE, SUZUKA...
sha
...RUI WOULD SOMETIMES COME HERE WITH HER MOTHER.

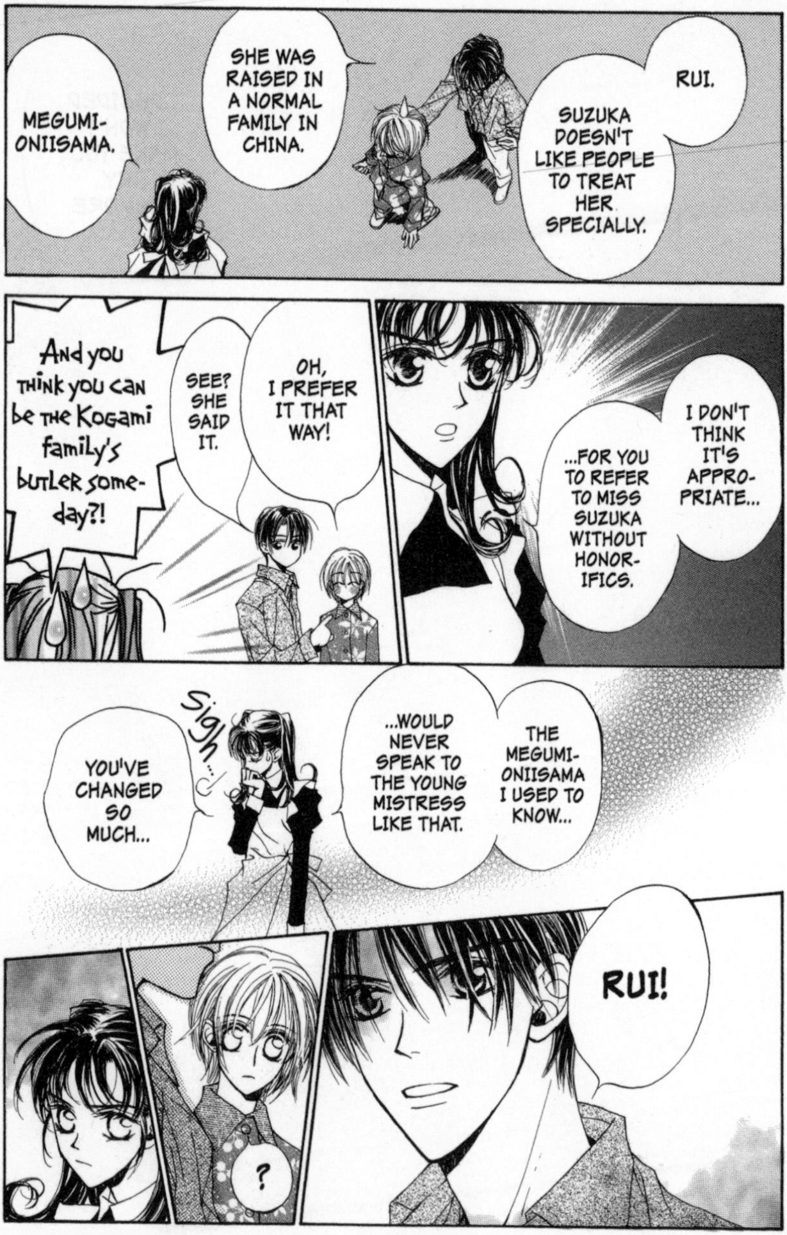
RUI.
SUZUKA DOESN'T LIKE PEOPLE TO TREAT HER SPECIALLY.
SHE WAS RAISED IN A NORMAL FAMILY IN CHINA.
MEGUMI-ONIISAMA.
I DON'T THINK IT'S APPROPRIATE...
...FOR YOU TO REFER TO MISS SUZUKA WITHOUT HONORIFICS.
OH, I PREFER IT THAT WAY!
SEE? SHE SAID IT.
And you think you can be the Kogami family's butler someday?!
THE MEGUMI-ONIISAMA I USED TO KNOW...
...WOULD NEVER SPEAK TO THE YOUNG MISTRESS LIKE THAT.
Sigh...
YOU'VE CHANGED SO MUCH...
RUI!
?

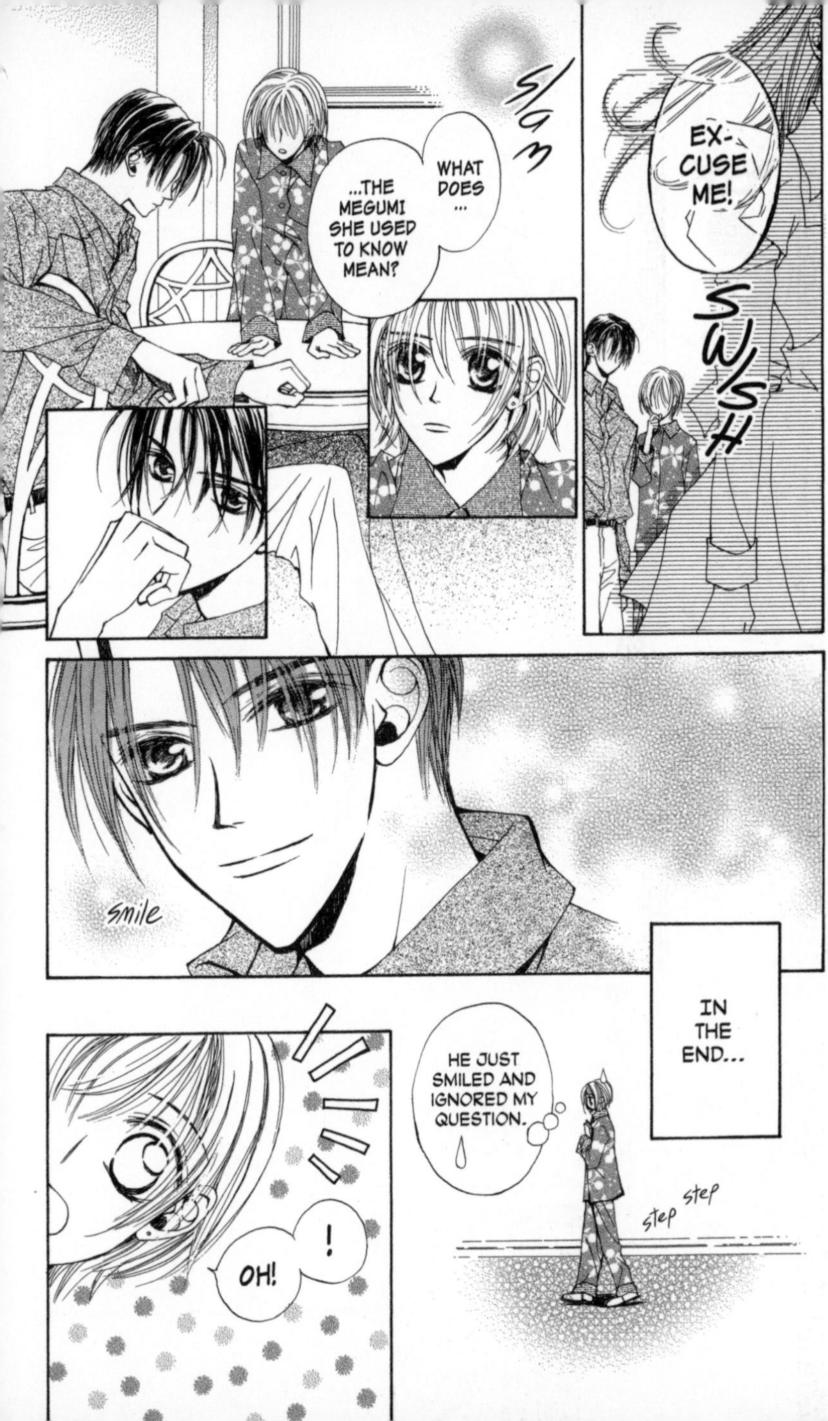
EX-CUSE ME!
SWISH
SLAM
WHAT DOES... ...THE MEGUMI SHE USED TO KNOW MEAN?
smile
IN THE END...
HE JUST SMILED AND IGNORED MY QUESTION.
step step
!
OH!

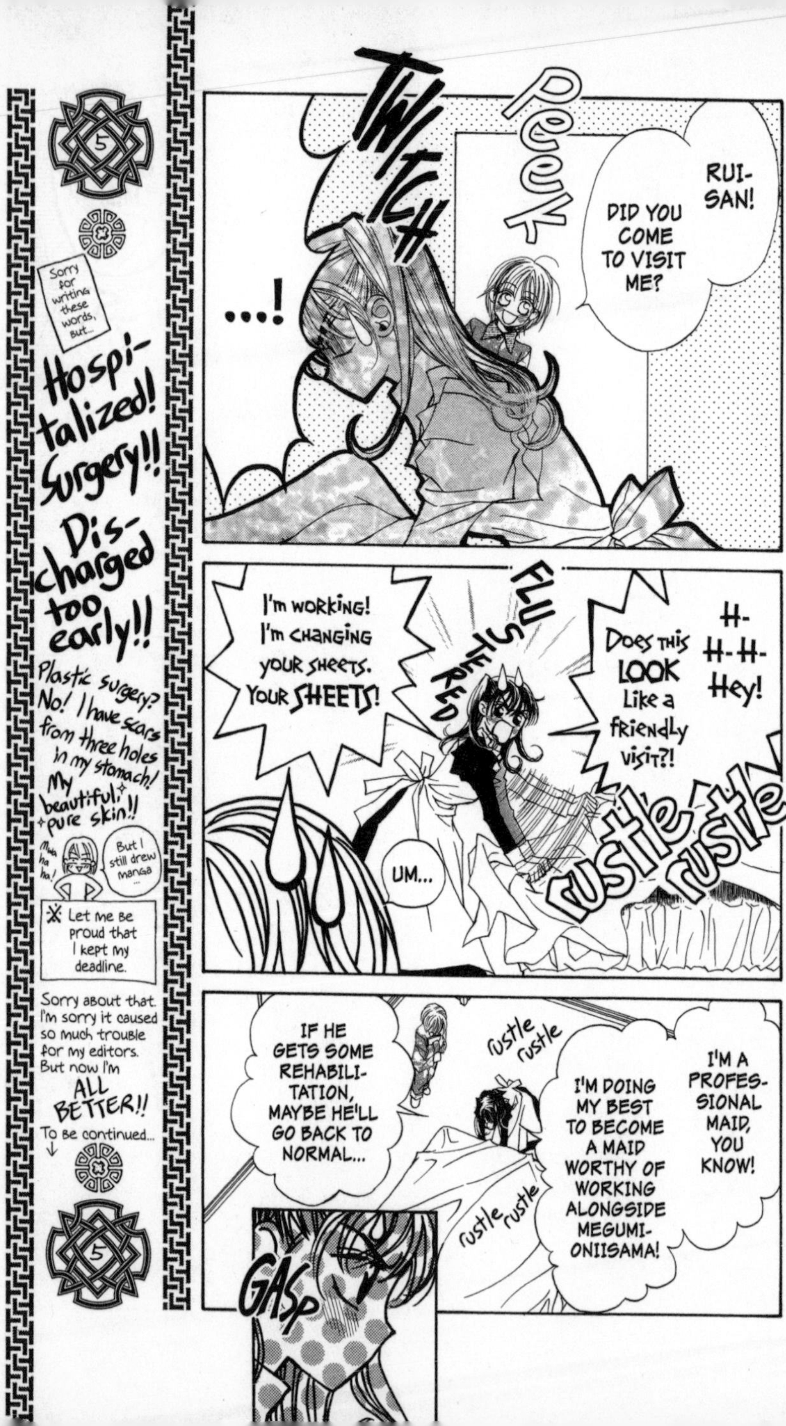
RUI-SAN!
DID YOU COME TO VISIT ME?
PEEK
TWITCH
...!
H-H-H-Hey!
Does this LOOK like a friendly visit?!
FLUSTERED
I'm working! I'm changing your sheets. Your SHEETS!
rustle rustle
UM...
I'M A PROFESSIONAL MAID, YOU KNOW!
I'M DOING MY BEST TO BECOME A MAID WORTHY OF WORKING ALONGSIDE MEGUMI-ONIISAMA!
rustle rustle
IF HE GETS SOME REHABILITATION, MAYBE HE'LL GO BACK TO NORMAL...
rustle rustle
GASP

5

Sorry for writing these words, but...

Hospitalized! Surgery!! Discharged too early!!

Plastic surgery? No! I have scars from three holes in my stomach! My beautiful, pure skin!!

Mwa ha ha!

But I still drew manga...

※ Let me be proud that I kept my deadline.

Sorry about that. I'm sorry it caused so much trouble for my editors. But now I'm ALL BETTER!!

To be continued...

5

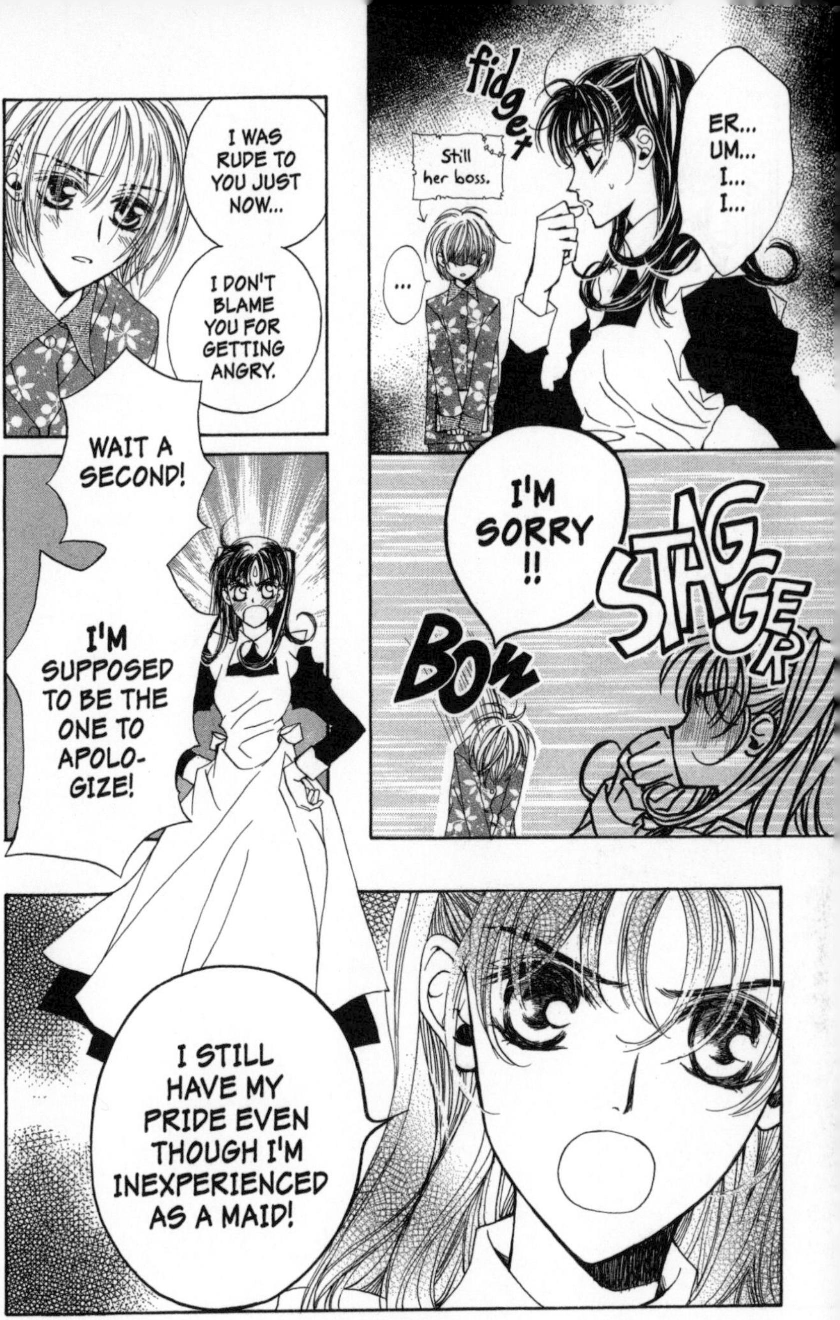

fidget
ER... UM... I... I...
Still her boss.
...
I WAS RUDE TO YOU JUST NOW...
I DON'T BLAME YOU FOR GETTING ANGRY.
I'M SORRY !!
STAGGER
BOW
WAIT A SECOND!
I'M SUPPOSED TO BE THE ONE TO APOLO-GIZE!
I STILL HAVE MY PRIDE EVEN THOUGH I'M INEXPERIENCED AS A MAID!

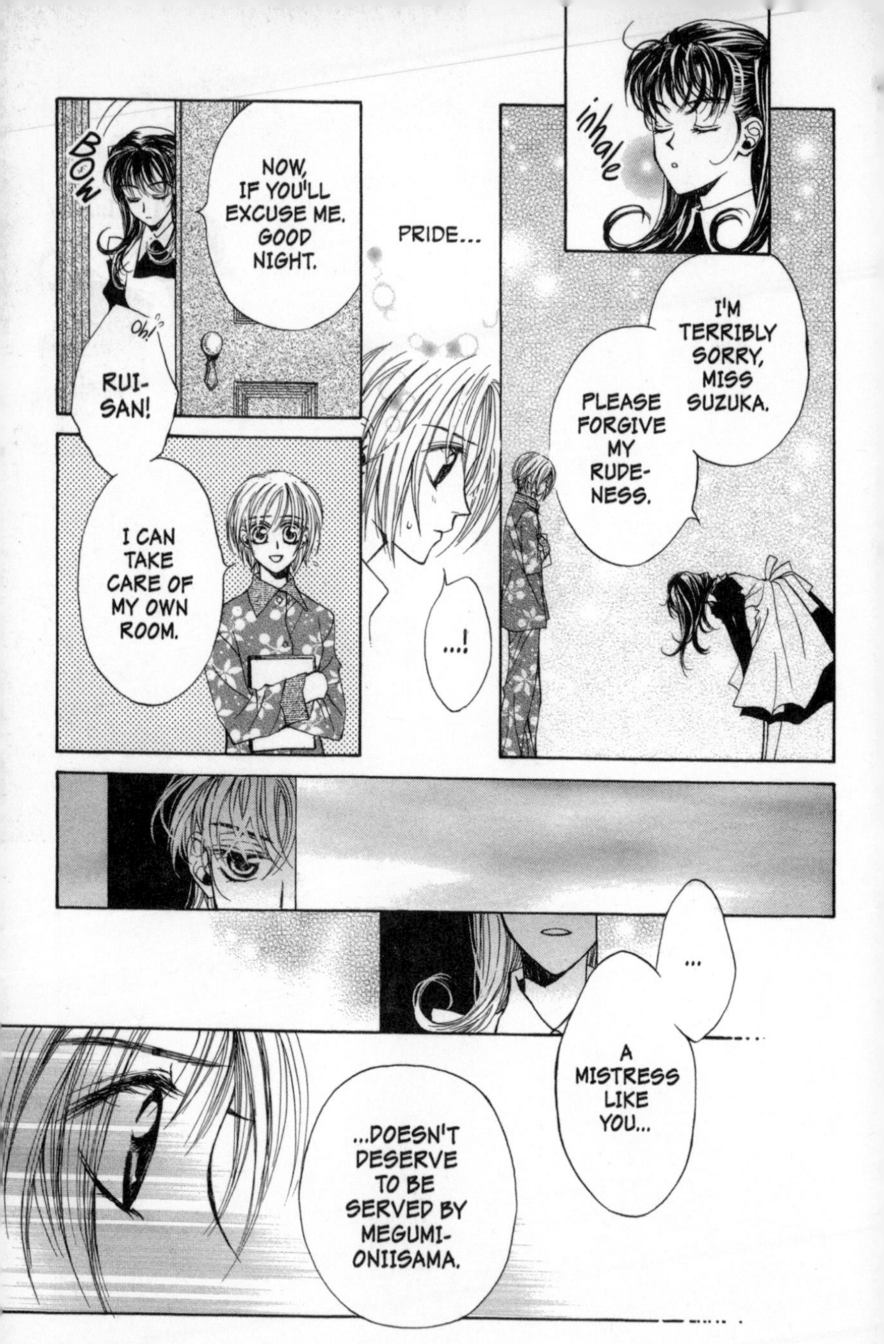
inhale
I'M TERRIBLY SORRY, MISS SUZUKA.
PLEASE FORGIVE MY RUDE-NESS.
PRIDE...
...!
BOW
NOW, IF YOU'LL EXCUSE ME. GOOD NIGHT.
Oh!
RUI-SAN!
I CAN TAKE CARE OF MY OWN ROOM.
...
A MISTRESS LIKE YOU...
...DOESN'T DESERVE TO BE SERVED BY MEGUMI-ONIISAMA.

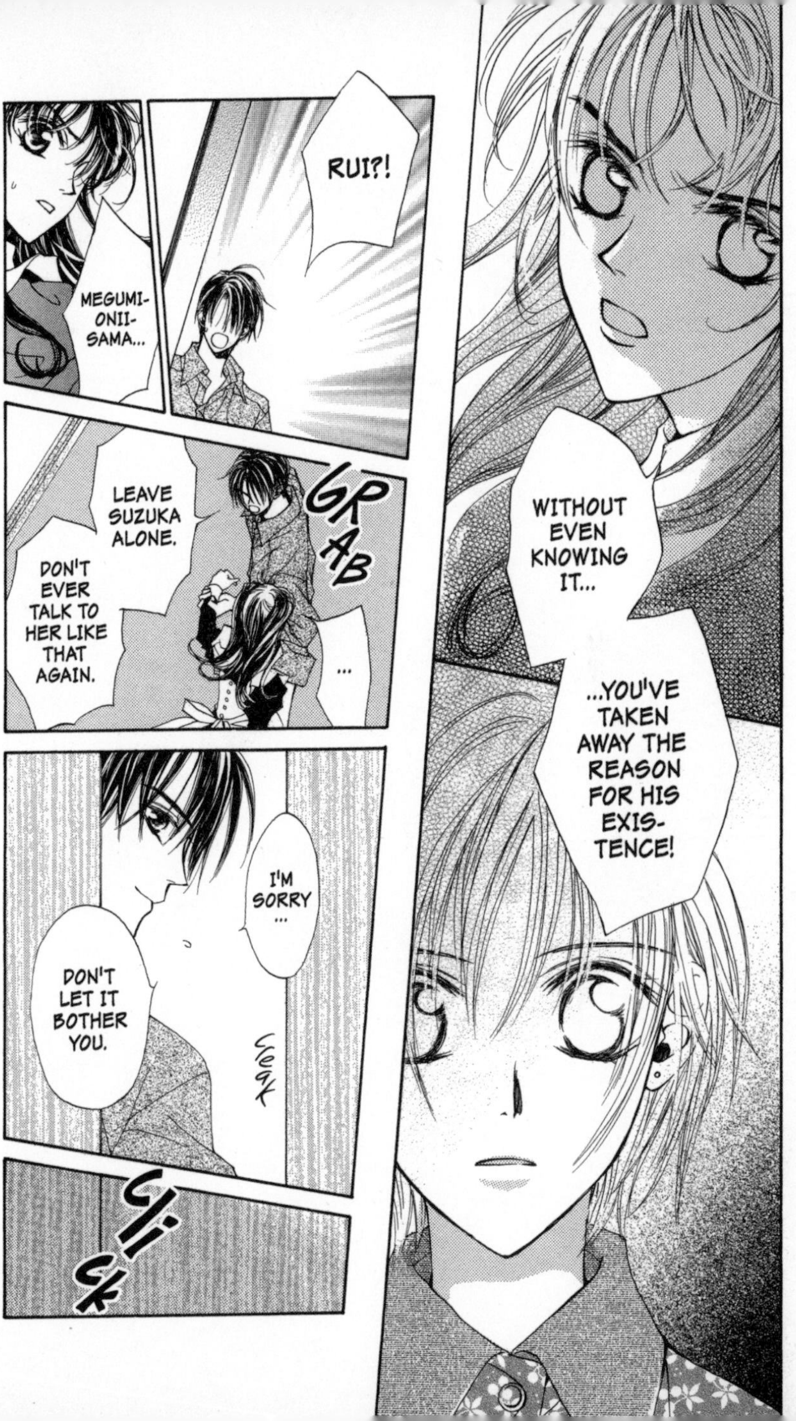
WITHOUT EVEN KNOWING IT...
...YOU'VE TAKEN AWAY THE REASON FOR HIS EXISTENCE!
RUI?!
MEGUMI-ONII-SAMA...
GRAB
LEAVE SUZUKA ALONE.
DON'T EVER TALK TO HER LIKE THAT AGAIN.
...
I'M SORRY ...
DON'T LET IT BOTHER YOU.
creak
CLICK

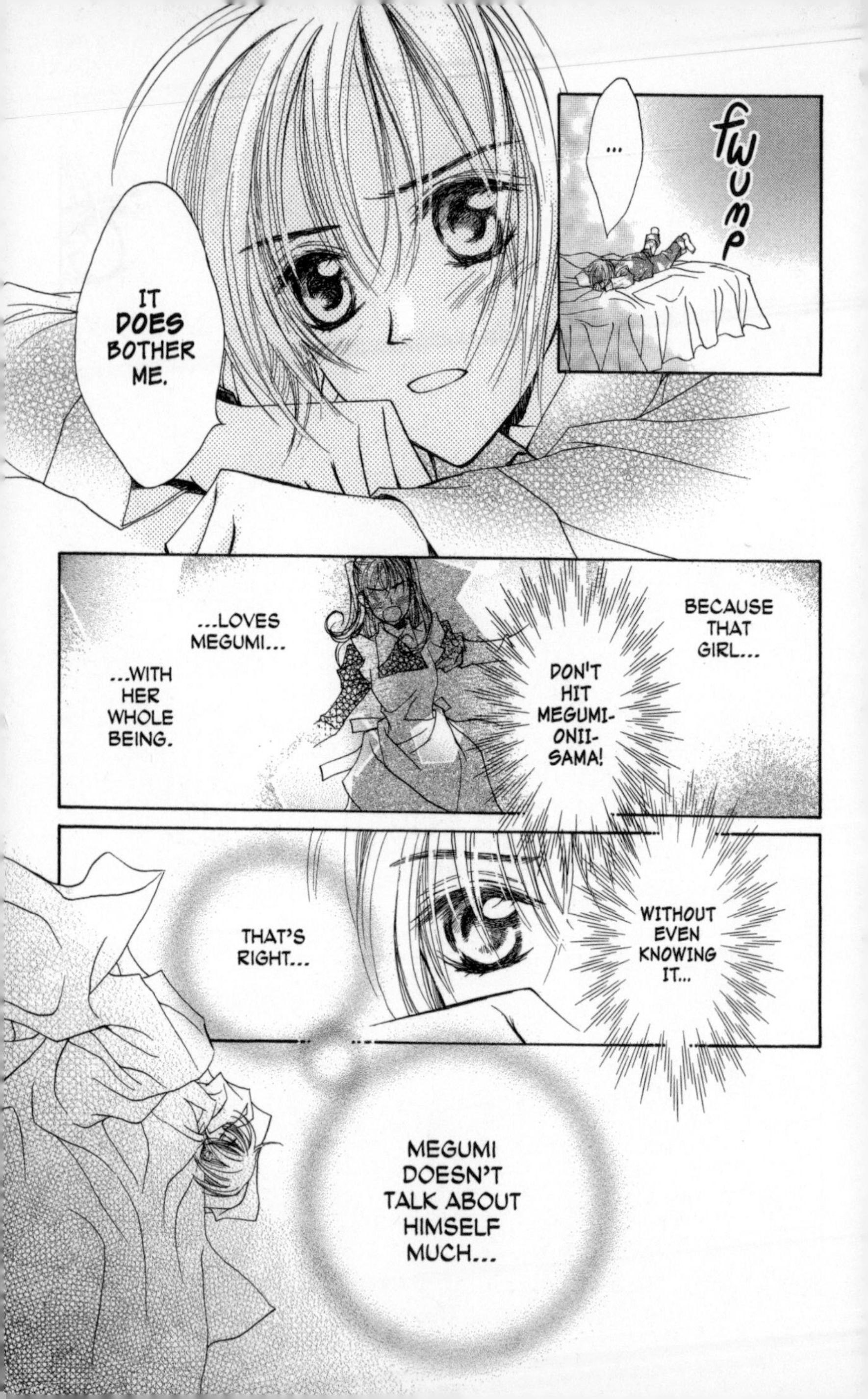
...
FWUMP
IT DOES BOTHER ME.
BECAUSE THAT GIRL...
DON'T HIT MEGUMI-ONII-SAMA!
...LOVES MEGUMI...
...WITH HER WHOLE BEING.
WITHOUT EVEN KNOWING IT...
THAT'S RIGHT...
MEGUMI DOESN'T TALK ABOUT HIMSELF MUCH...

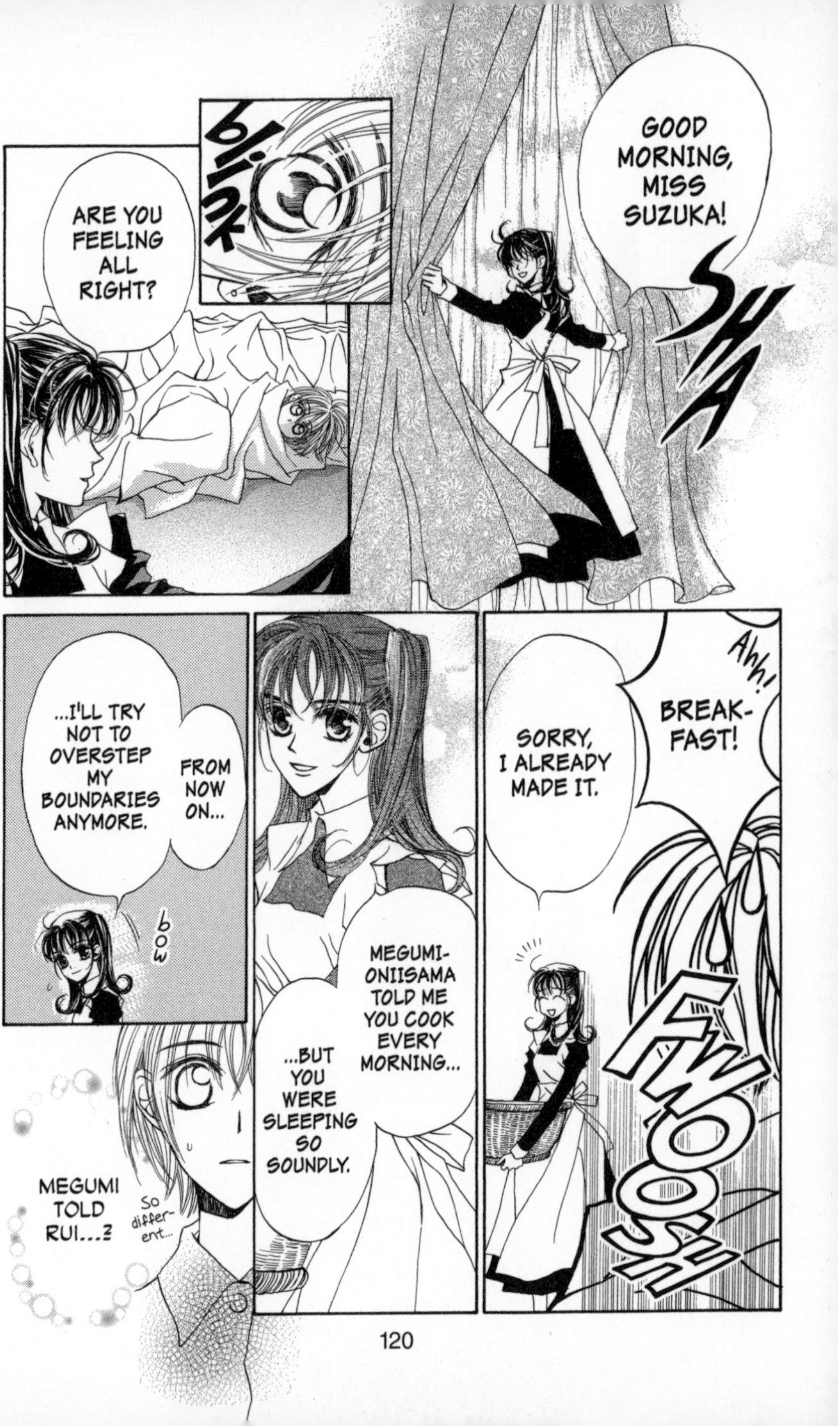
GOOD MORNING, MISS SUZUKA!
SHA
ARE YOU FEELING ALL RIGHT?
Ahh!
BREAK-FAST!
SORRY, I ALREADY MADE IT.
FWOOSH
MEGUMI-ONIISAMA TOLD ME YOU COOK EVERY MORNING...
...BUT YOU WERE SLEEPING SO SOUNDLY.
FROM NOW ON...
...I'LL TRY NOT TO OVERSTEP MY BOUNDARIES ANYMORE.
bow
MEGUMI TOLD RUI...?
So differ-ent...

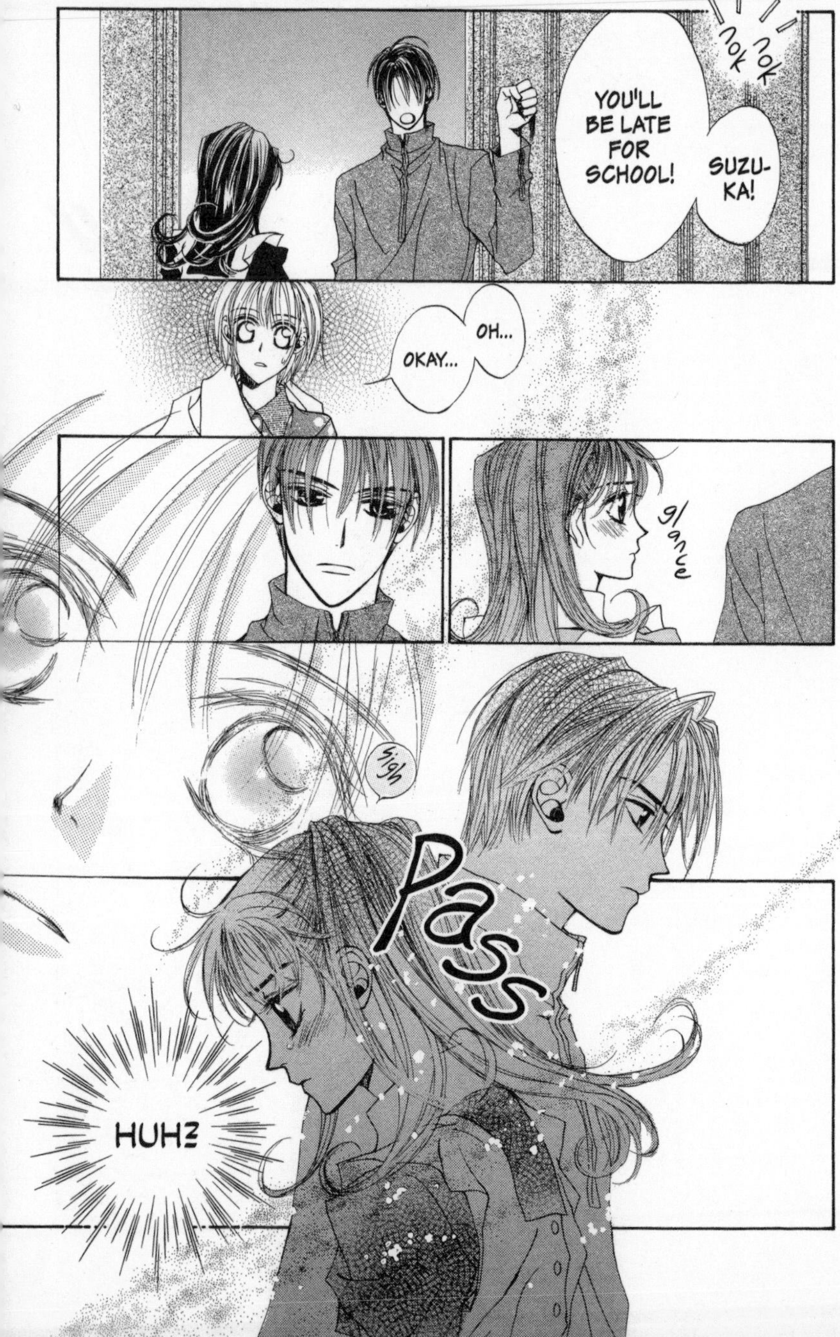
nok nok
SUZU-KA!
YOU'LL BE LATE FOR SCHOOL!
OH... OKAY...
glance
sigh
Pass
HUH?

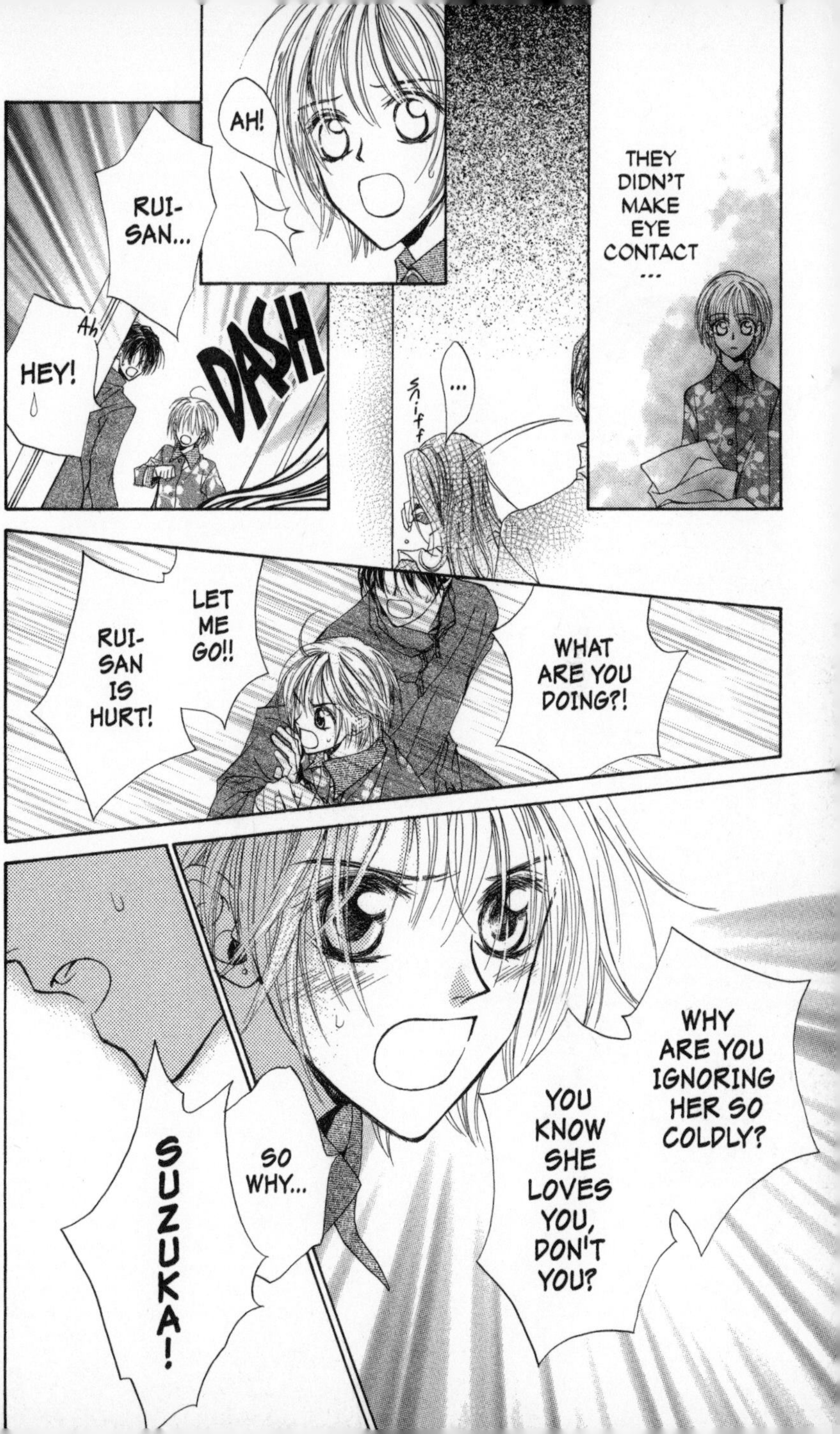
THEY DIDN'T MAKE EYE CONTACT ...
...
sniff
AH!
RUI-SAN...
DASH
Ah
HEY!
WHAT ARE YOU DOING?!
LET ME GO!!
RUI-SAN IS HURT!
WHY ARE YOU IGNORING HER SO COLDLY?
YOU KNOW SHE LOVES YOU, DON'T YOU?
SO WHY...
SUZUKA!

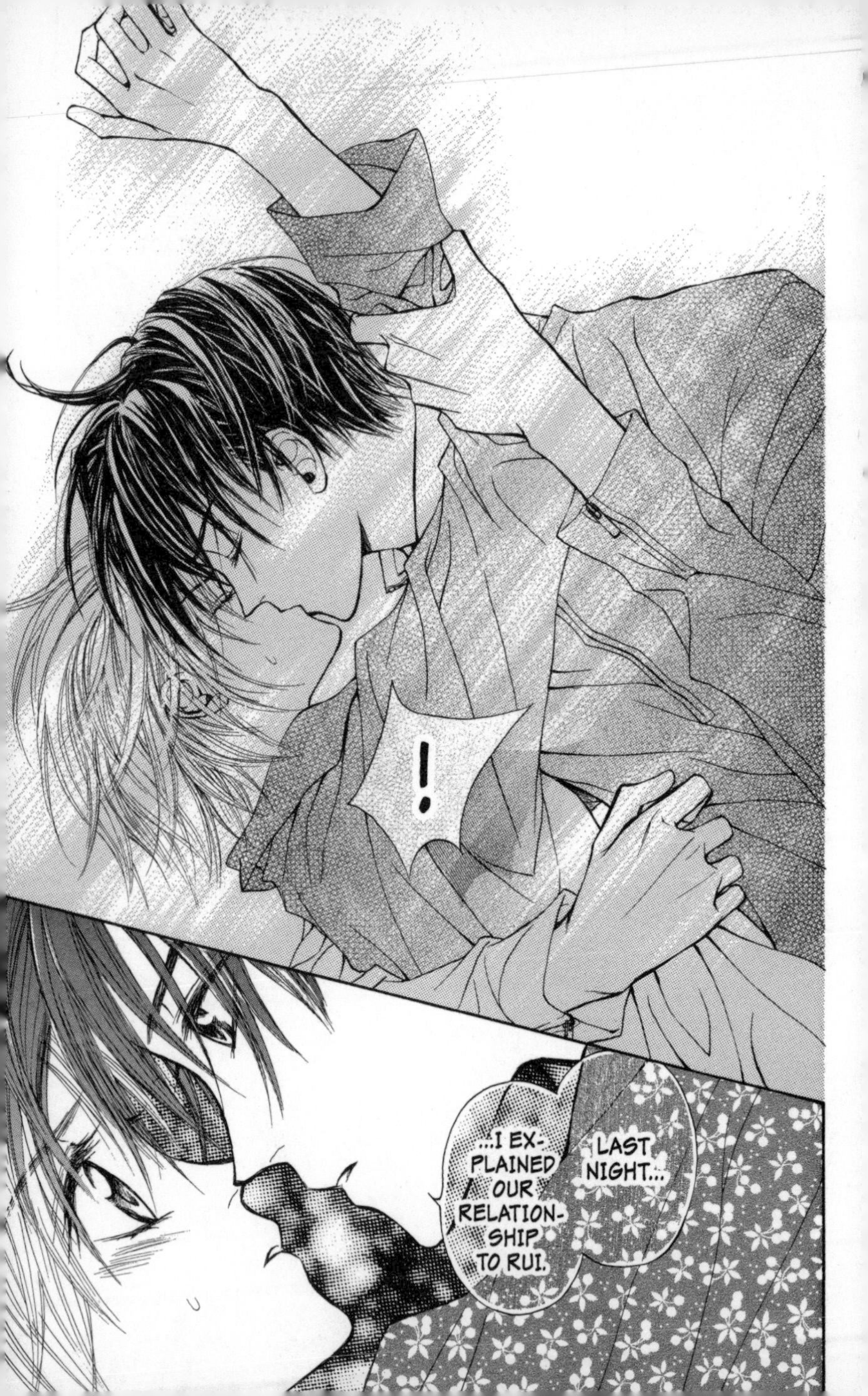
!
LAST NIGHT...
...I EX-PLAINED OUR RELATION-SHIP TO RUI.

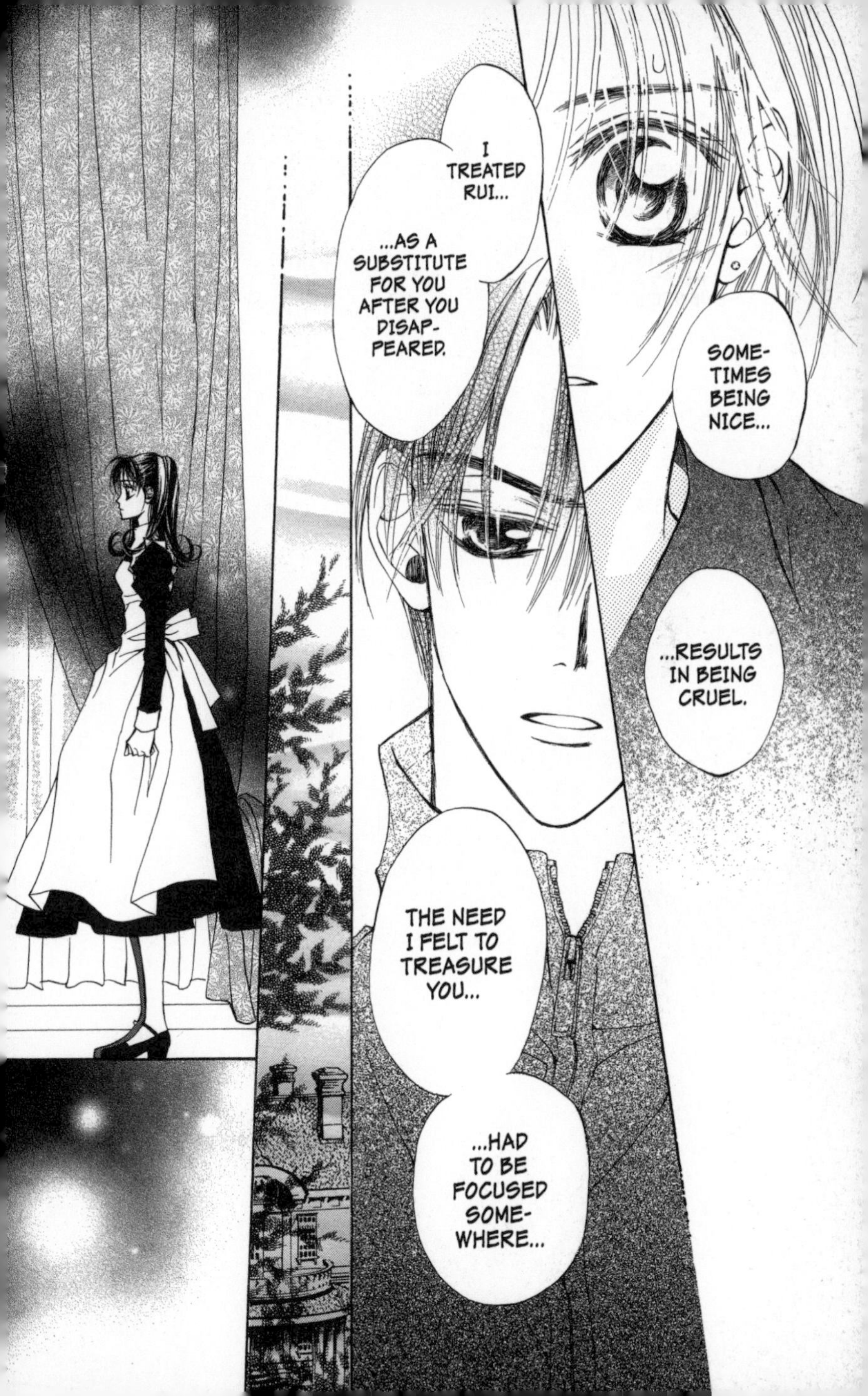
I TREATED RUI...
...AS A SUBSTITUTE FOR YOU AFTER YOU DISAP-PEARED.
SOME-TIMES BEING NICE...
...RESULTS IN BEING CRUEL.
THE NEED I FELT TO TREASURE YOU...
...HAD TO BE FOCUSED SOME-WHERE...

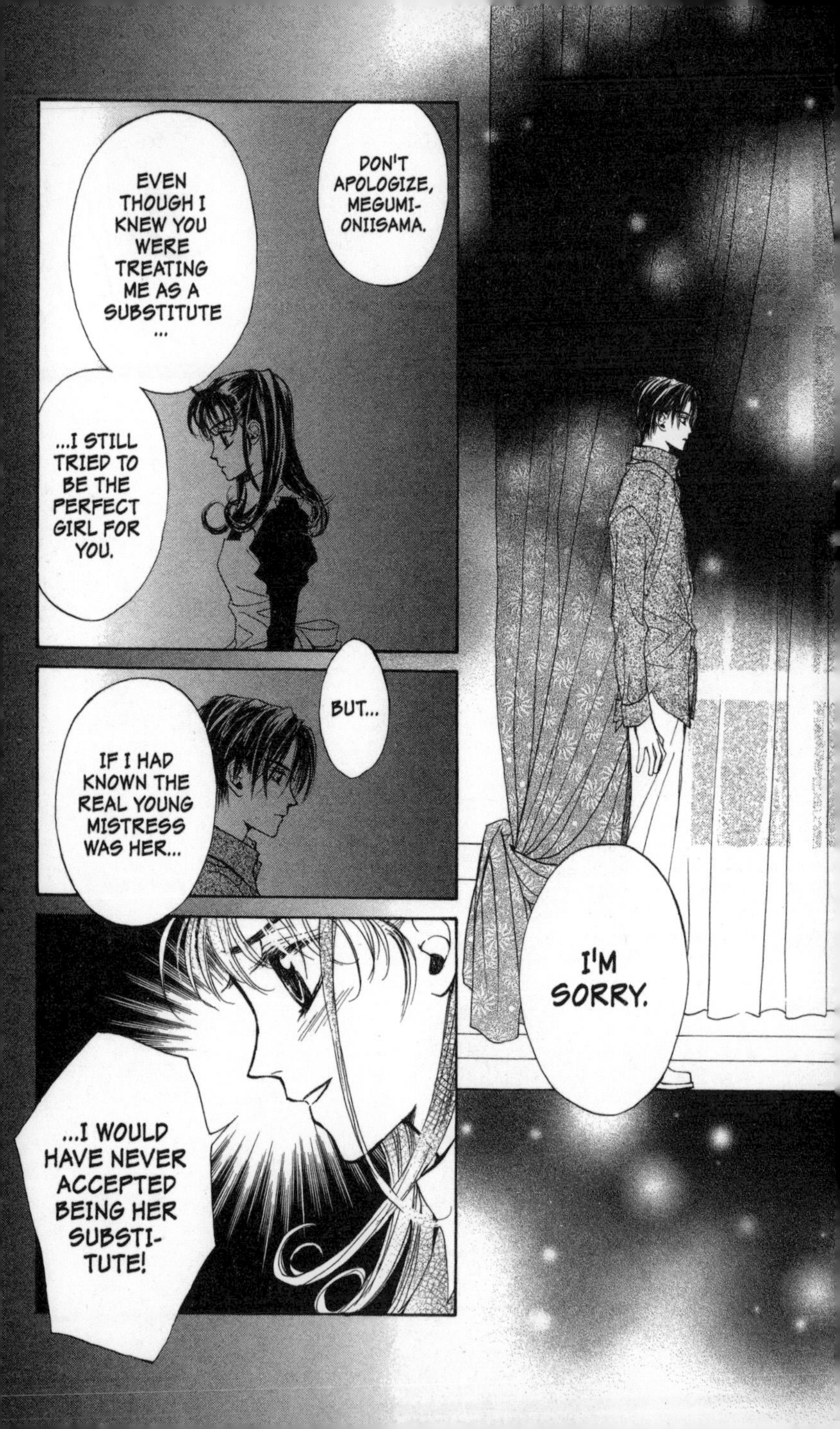
I'M SORRY.
DON'T APOLOGIZE, MEGUMI-ONIISAMA.
EVEN THOUGH I KNEW YOU WERE TREATING ME AS A SUBSTITUTE...
...I STILL TRIED TO BE THE PERFECT GIRL FOR YOU.
BUT...
IF I HAD KNOWN THE REAL YOUNG MISTRESS WAS HER...
...I WOULD HAVE NEVER ACCEPTED BEING HER SUBSTI-TUTE!

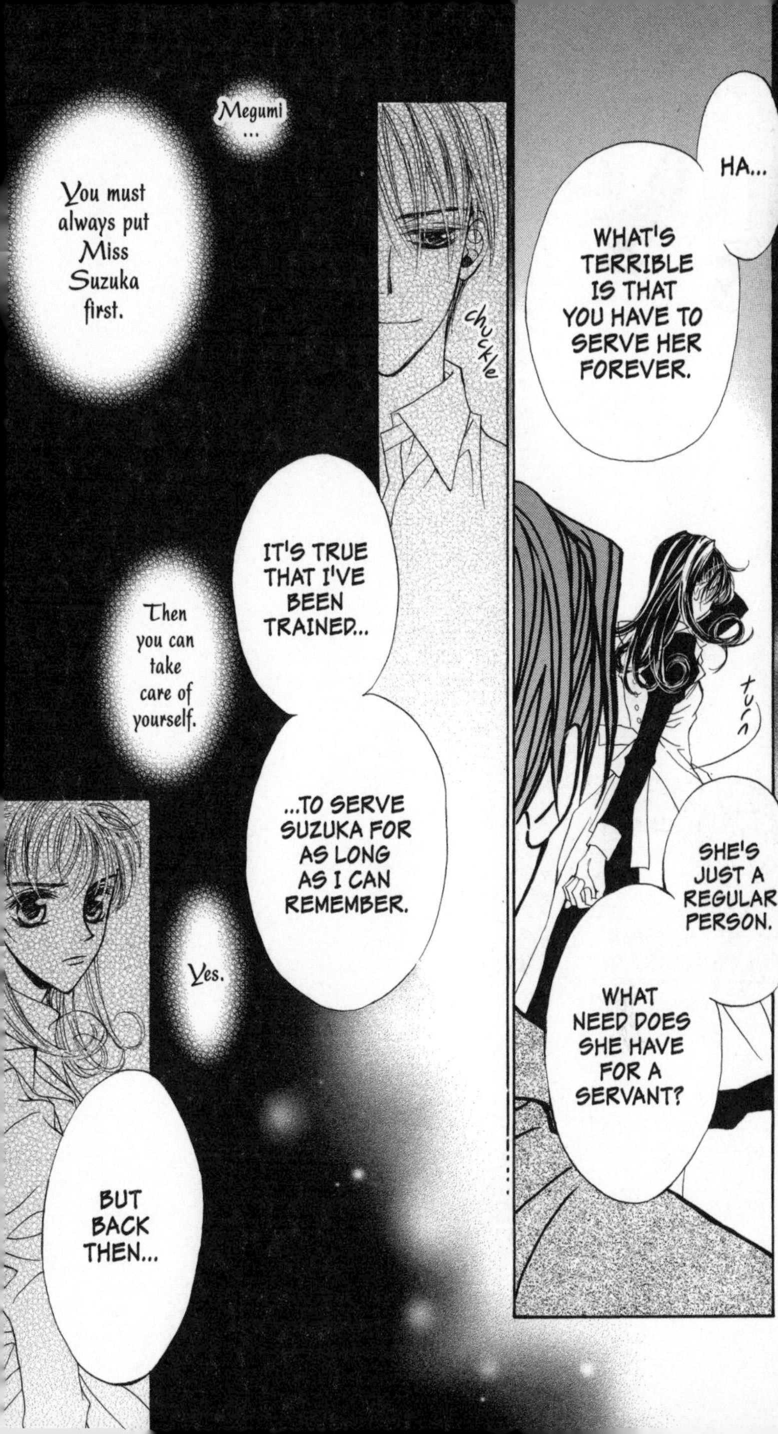
HA...
WHAT'S TERRIBLE IS THAT YOU HAVE TO SERVE HER FOREVER.
turn
SHE'S JUST A REGULAR PERSON.
WHAT NEED DOES SHE HAVE FOR A SERVANT?
chuckle
IT'S TRUE THAT I'VE BEEN TRAINED...
...TO SERVE SUZUKA FOR AS LONG AS I CAN REMEMBER.
Megumi ...
You must always put Miss Suzuka first.
Then you can take care of yourself.
Yes.
BUT BACK THEN...

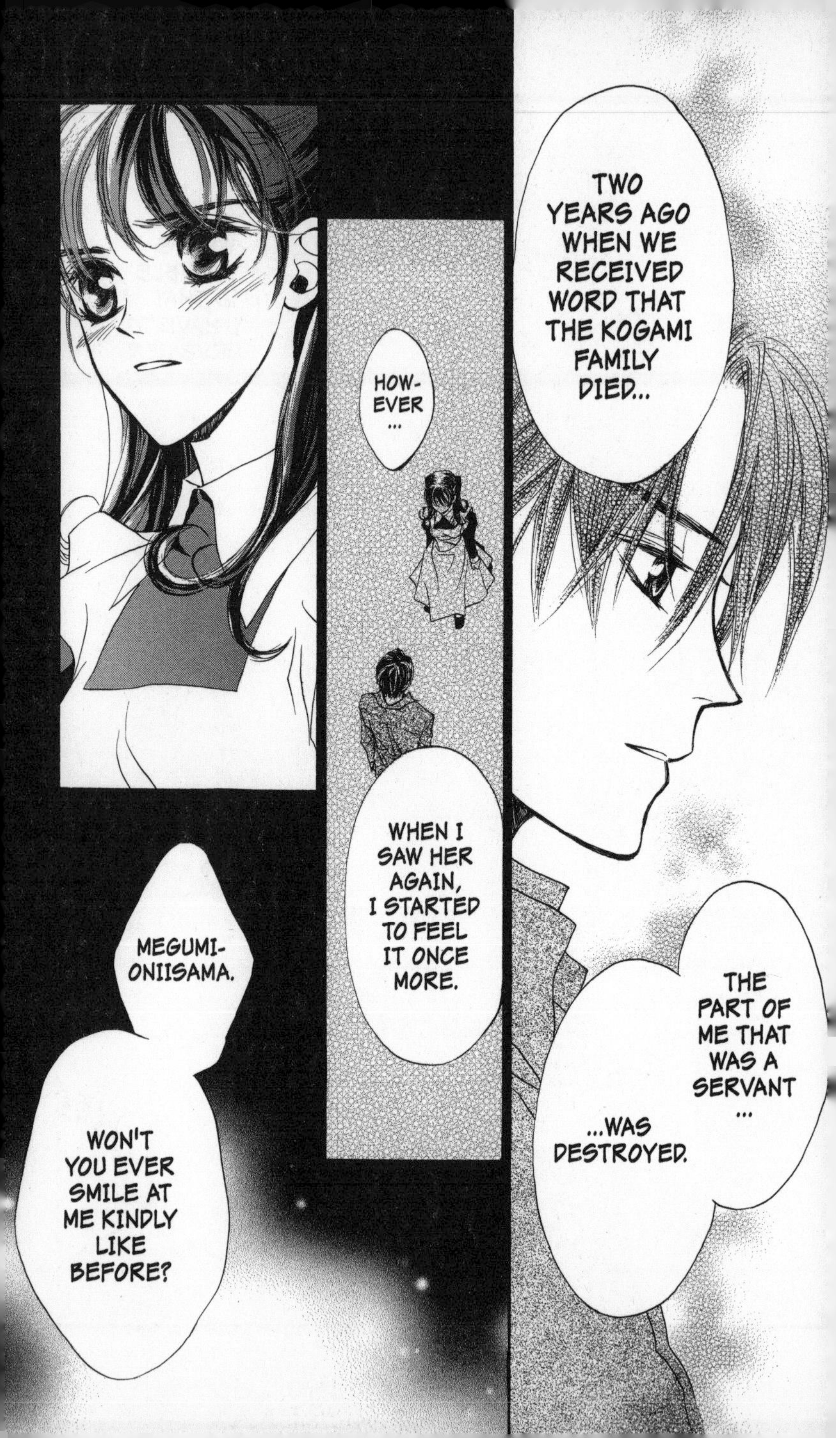
TWO YEARS AGO WHEN WE RECEIVED WORD THAT THE KOGAMI FAMILY DIED...
THE PART OF ME THAT WAS A SERVANT...
...WAS DESTROYED.
HOW-EVER...
WHEN I SAW HER AGAIN, I STARTED TO FEEL IT ONCE MORE.
MEGUMI-ONIISAMA.
WON'T YOU EVER SMILE AT ME KINDLY LIKE BEFORE?

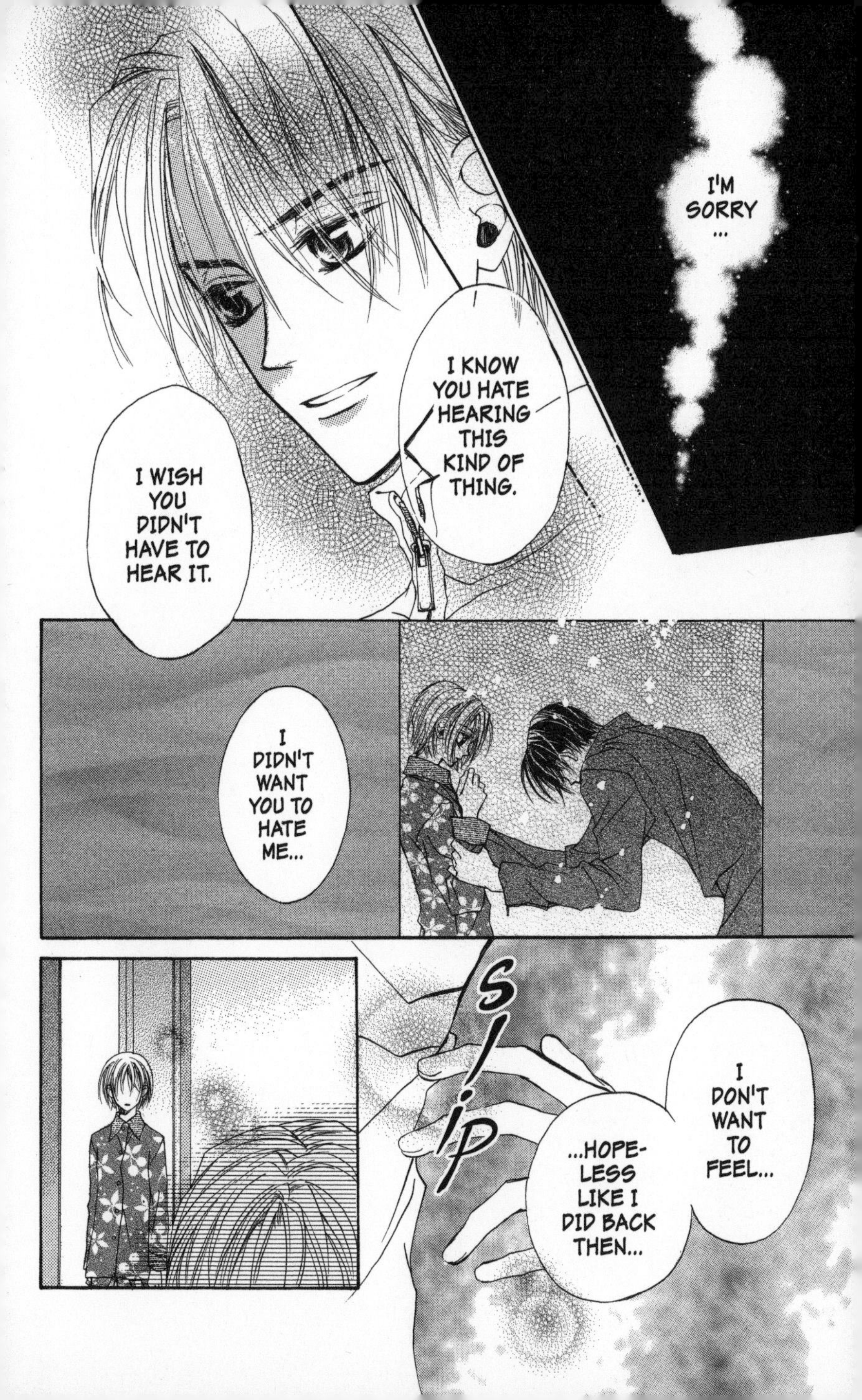
I'M SORRY...
I KNOW YOU HATE HEARING THIS KIND OF THING.
I WISH YOU DIDN'T HAVE TO HEAR IT.
I DIDN'T WANT YOU TO HATE ME...
SLIP
I DON'T WANT TO FEEL...
...HOPE-LESS LIKE I DID BACK THEN...

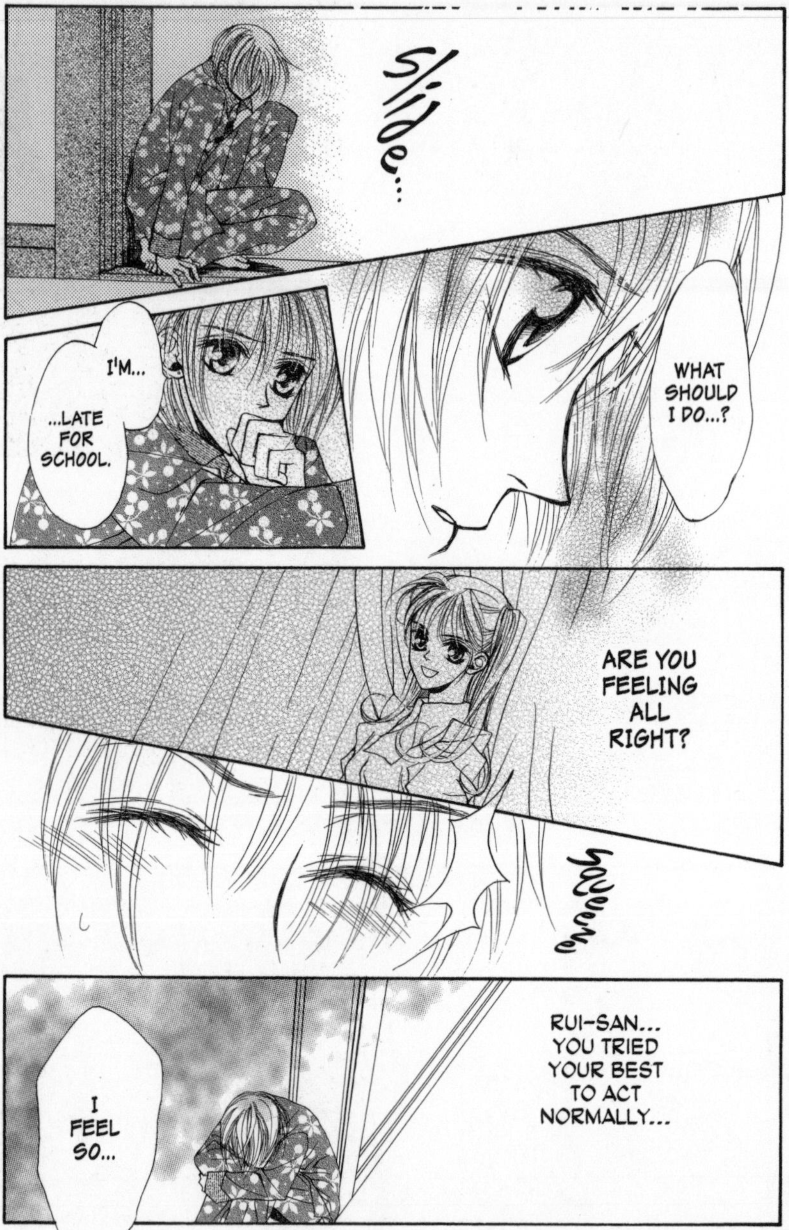
slide...
WHAT SHOULD I DO...?
I'M...
...LATE FOR SCHOOL.
ARE YOU FEELING ALL RIGHT?
squeeze
RUI-SAN... YOU TRIED YOUR BEST TO ACT NORMALLY...
I FEEL SO...

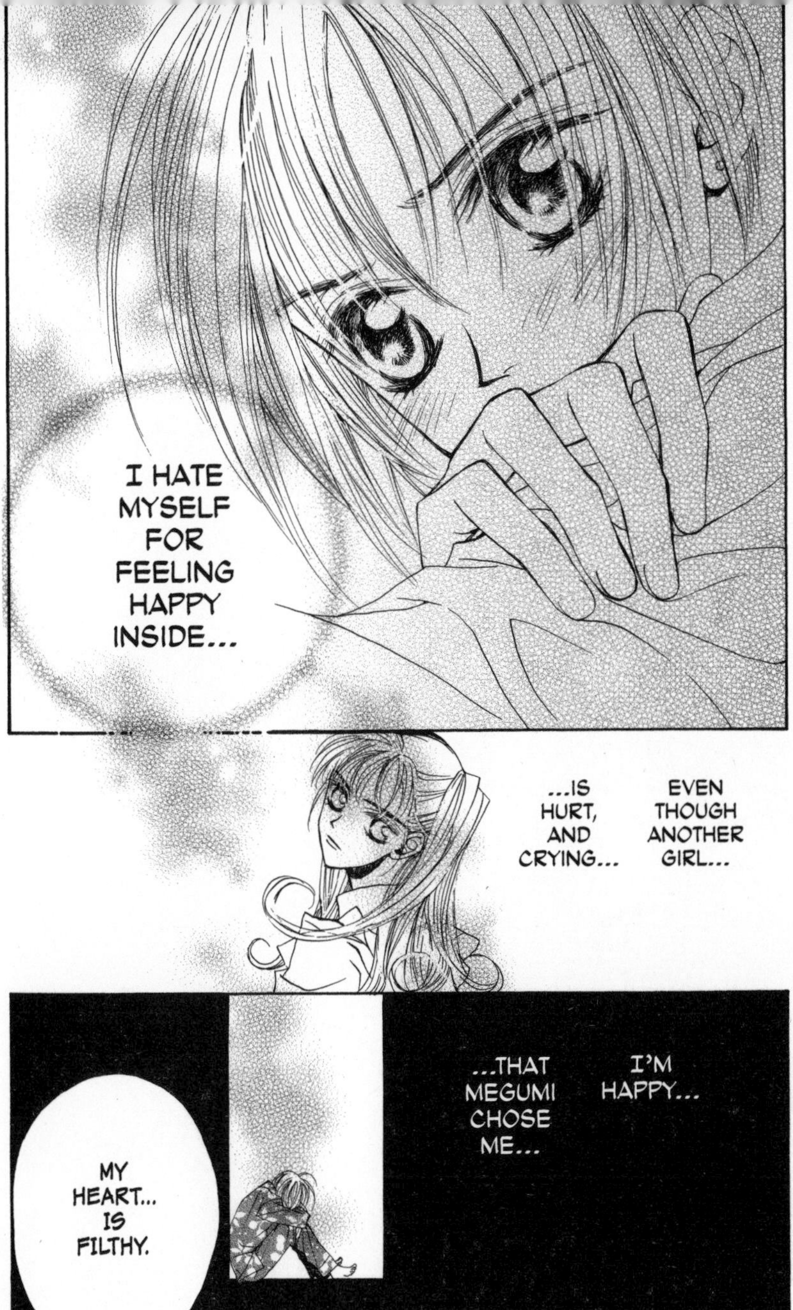
I HATE MYSELF FOR FEELING HAPPY INSIDE...
EVEN THOUGH ANOTHER GIRL...
...IS HURT, AND CRYING...
I'M HAPPY...
...THAT MEGUMI CHOSE ME...
MY HEART... IS FILTHY.

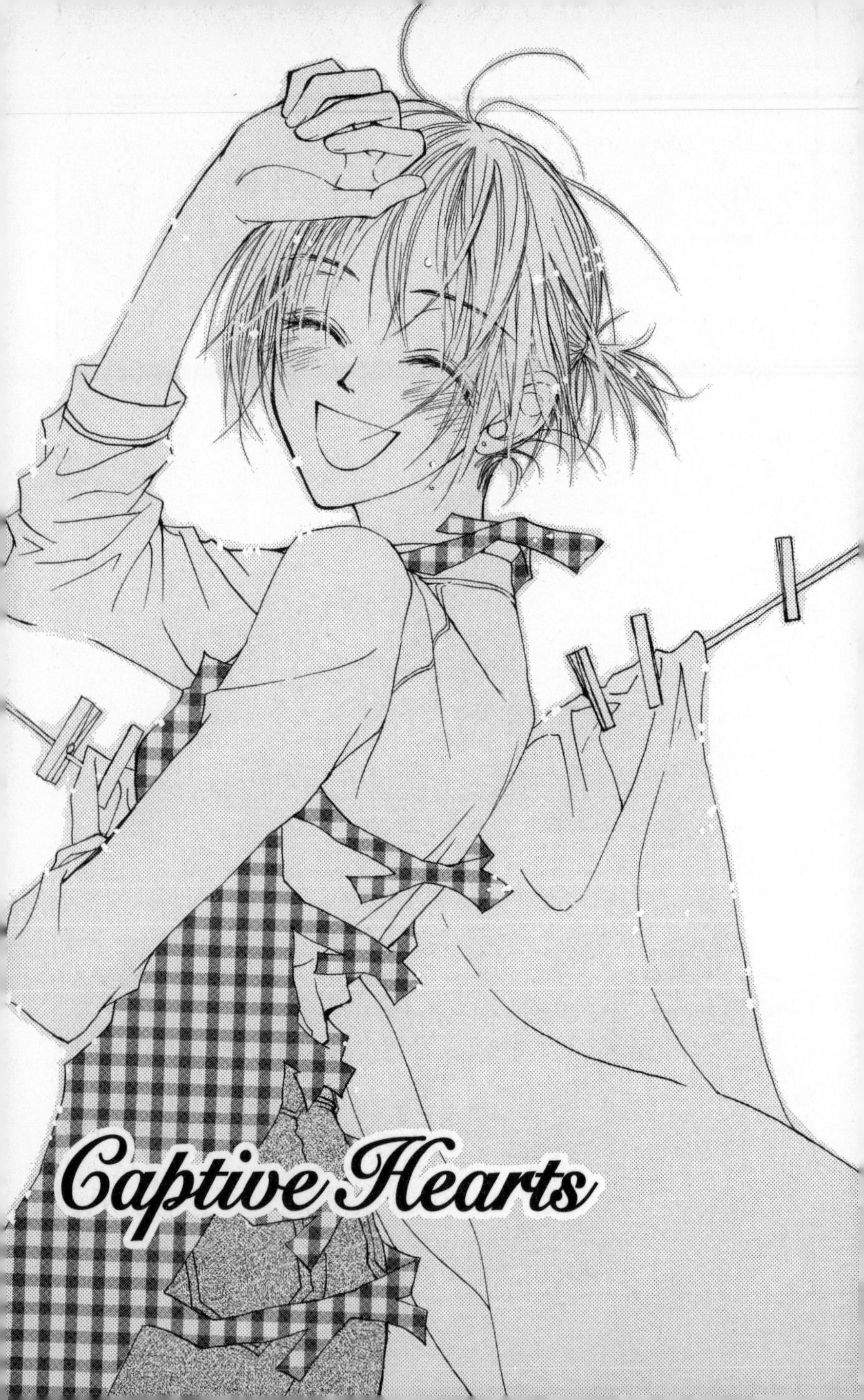
Captive Hearts

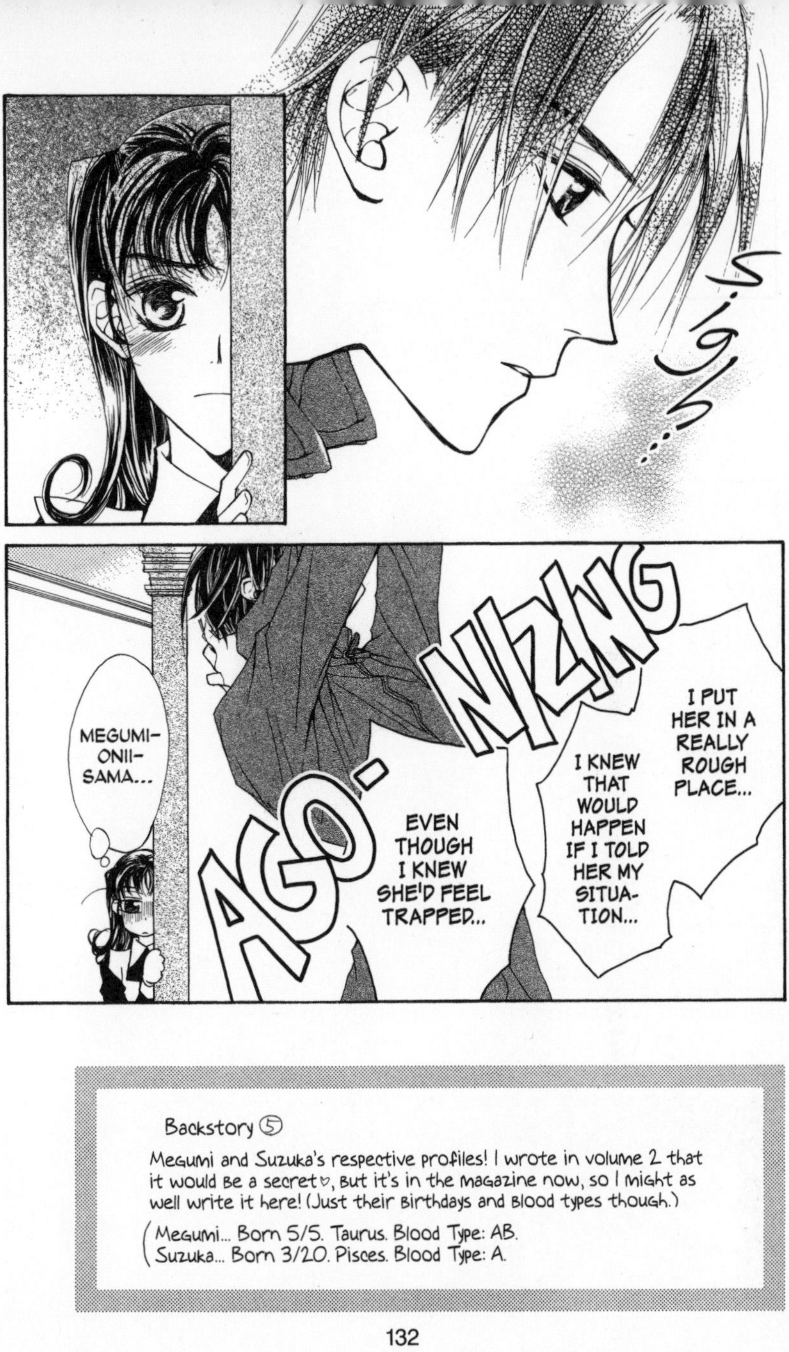
Sigh...
I PUT HER IN A REALLY ROUGH PLACE...
I KNEW THAT WOULD HAPPEN IF I TOLD HER MY SITUATION...
EVEN THOUGH I KNEW SHE'D FEEL TRAPPED...
AGO-NIZING
MEGUMI-ONII-SAMA...

Backstory ⑤

Megumi and Suzuka's respective profiles! I wrote in volume 2 that it would be a secret♡, but it's in the magazine now, so I might as well write it here! (Just their birthdays and blood types though.)

Megumi... Born 5/5. Taurus. Blood Type: AB.
Suzuka... Born 3/20. Pisces. Blood Type: A.

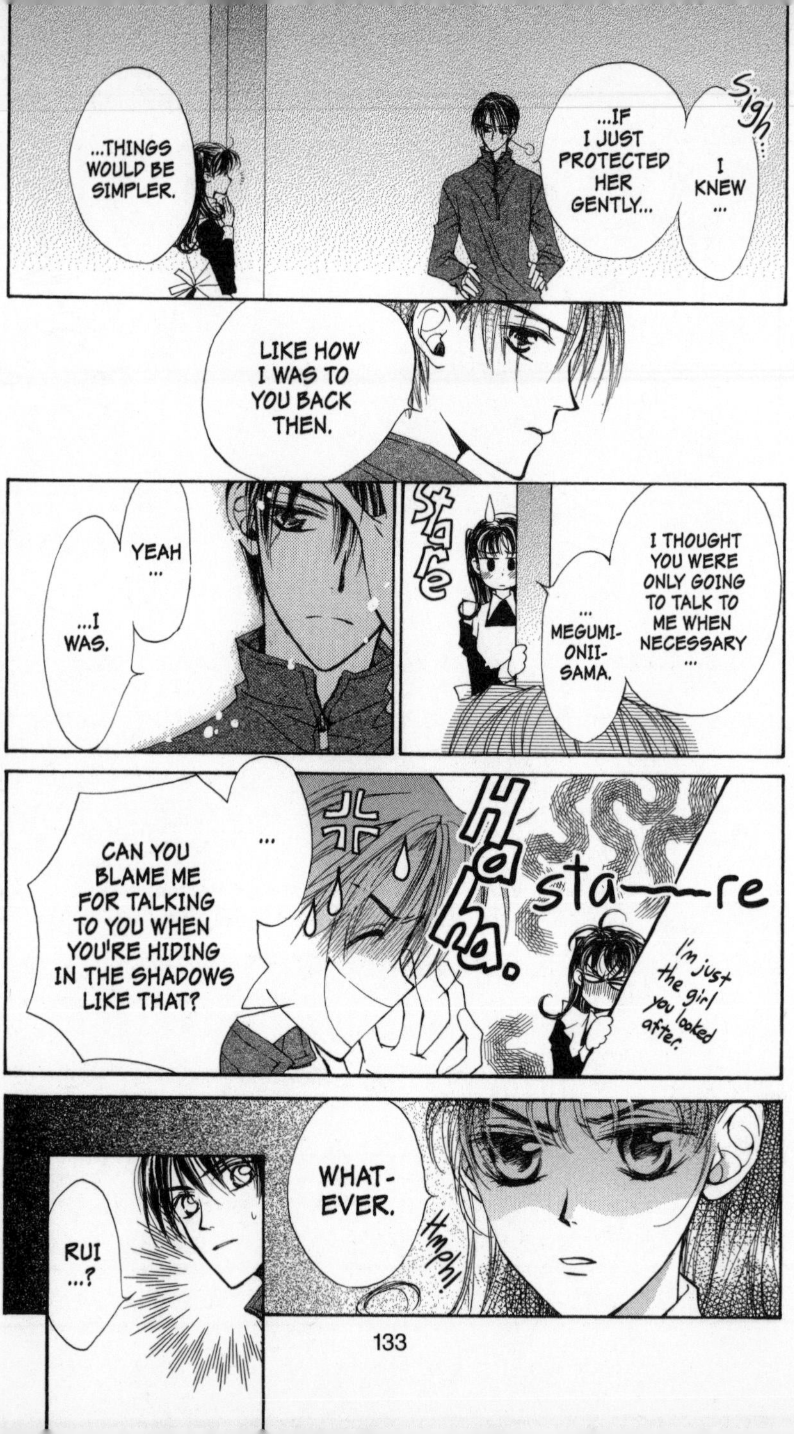
Sigh...
I KNEW ...
...IF I JUST PROTECTED HER GENTLY...
...THINGS WOULD BE SIMPLER.
LIKE HOW I WAS TO YOU BACK THEN.
I THOUGHT YOU WERE ONLY GOING TO TALK TO ME WHEN NECESSARY ...
... MEGUMI-ONII-SAMA.
stare
YEAH ...
...I WAS.
sta——re
I'm just the girl you looked after.
Ha ha.
...
CAN YOU BLAME ME FOR TALKING TO YOU WHEN YOU'RE HIDING IN THE SHADOWS LIKE THAT?
WHAT-EVER.
Hmph!
RUI ...?

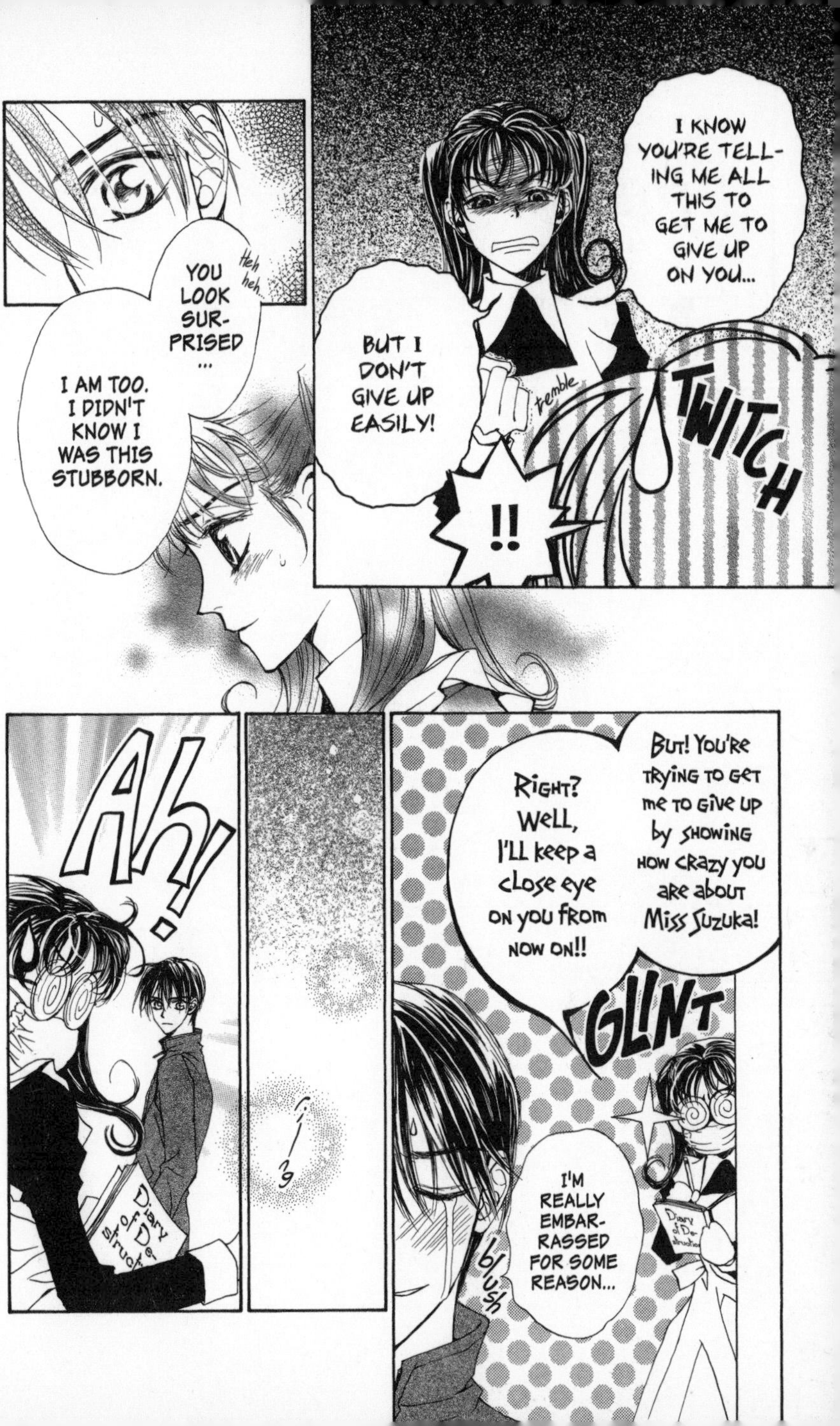
I KNOW YOU'RE TELL-ING ME ALL THIS TO GET ME TO GIVE UP ON YOU...
BUT I DON'T GIVE UP EASILY!
tremble
TWITCH
!!
YOU LOOK SUR-PRISED...
Heh heh
I AM TOO. I DIDN'T KNOW I WAS THIS STUBBORN.
But! You're trying to get me to give up by showing how crazy you are about Miss Suzuka!
Right? Well, I'll keep a close eye on you from now on!!
GLINT
Diary of De-struction
I'M REALLY EMBAR-RASSED FOR SOME REASON...
blush
Ah!

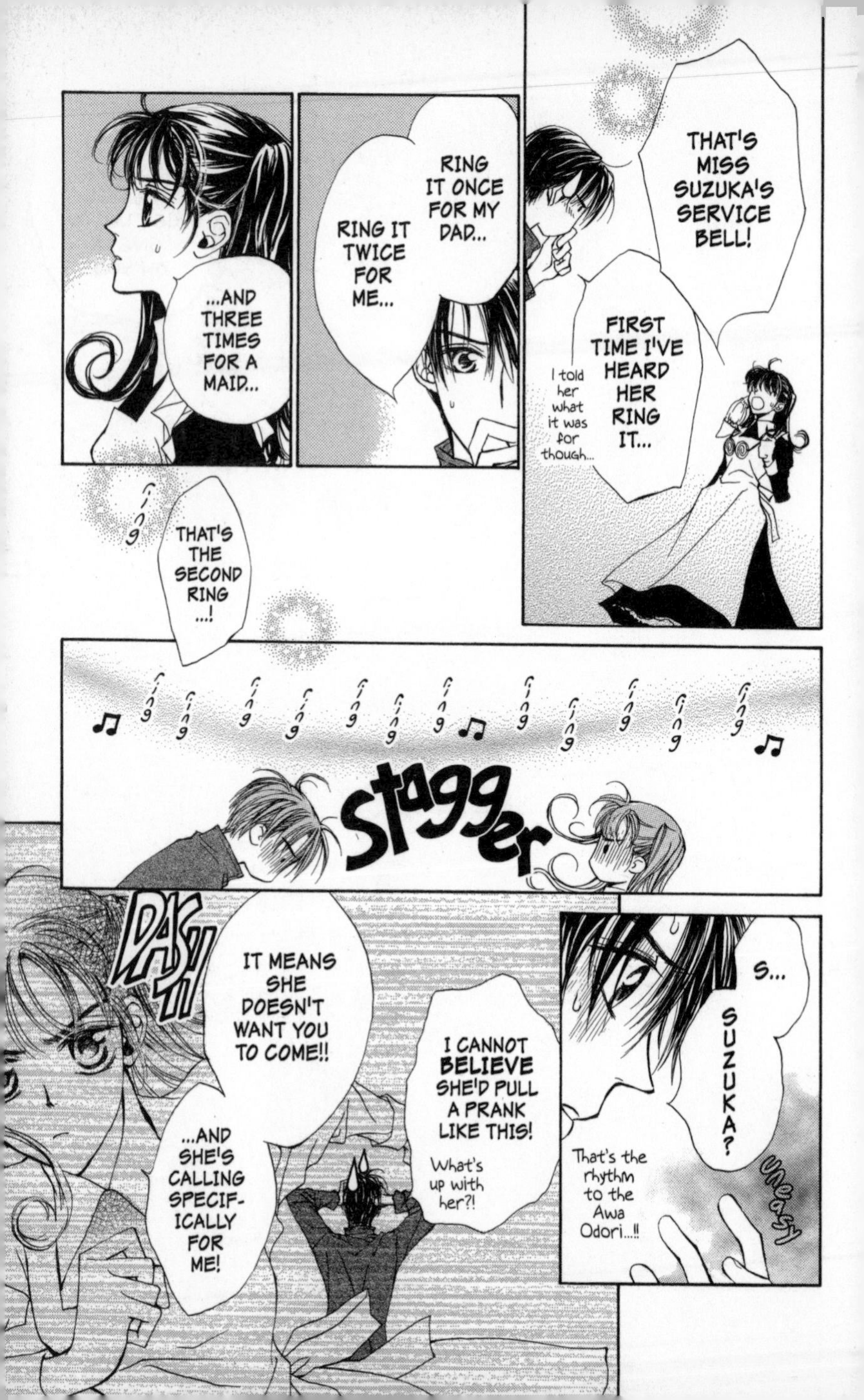
THAT'S MISS SUZUKA'S SERVICE BELL!
FIRST TIME I'VE HEARD HER RING IT...
I told her what it was for though...
RING IT ONCE FOR MY DAD...
RING IT TWICE FOR ME...
...AND THREE TIMES FOR A MAID...
ring
THAT'S THE SECOND RING...!
ring ring ring ring ring ring ring ring ring ring ring ring
stagger
S...
SUZUKA?
uneasy
That's the rhythm to the Awa Odori...!!
DASH
IT MEANS SHE DOESN'T WANT YOU TO COME!!
I CANNOT **BELIEVE** SHE'D PULL A PRANK LIKE THIS!
What's up with her?!
...AND SHE'S CALLING SPECIFICALLY FOR ME!

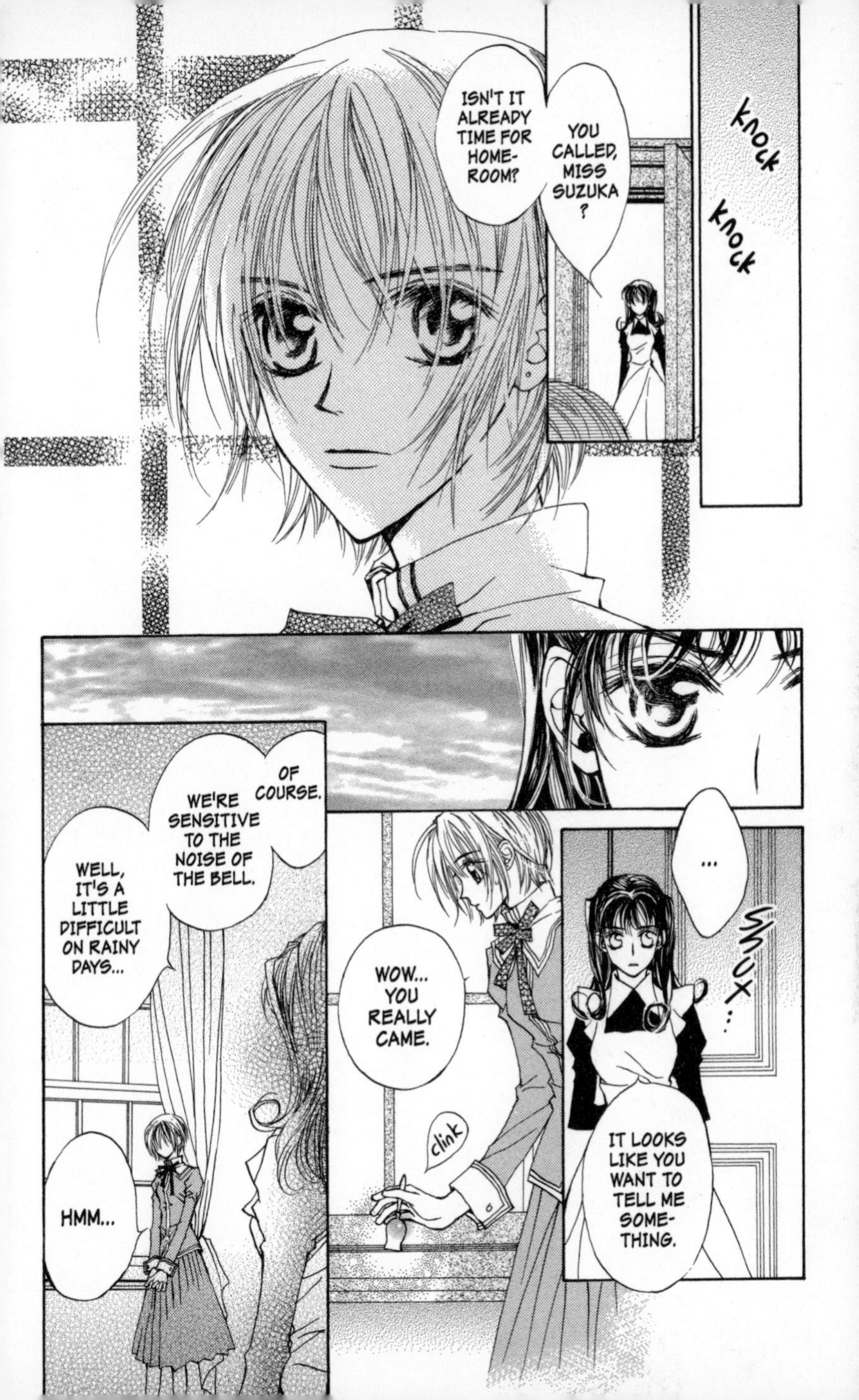
knock
knock
YOU CALLED, MISS SUZUKA?
ISN'T IT ALREADY TIME FOR HOME-ROOM?
...
SHUT...
IT LOOKS LIKE YOU WANT TO TELL ME SOME-THING.
WOW... YOU REALLY CAME.
clink
OF COURSE.
WE'RE SENSITIVE TO THE NOISE OF THE BELL.
WELL, IT'S A LITTLE DIFFICULT ON RAINY DAYS...
HMM...

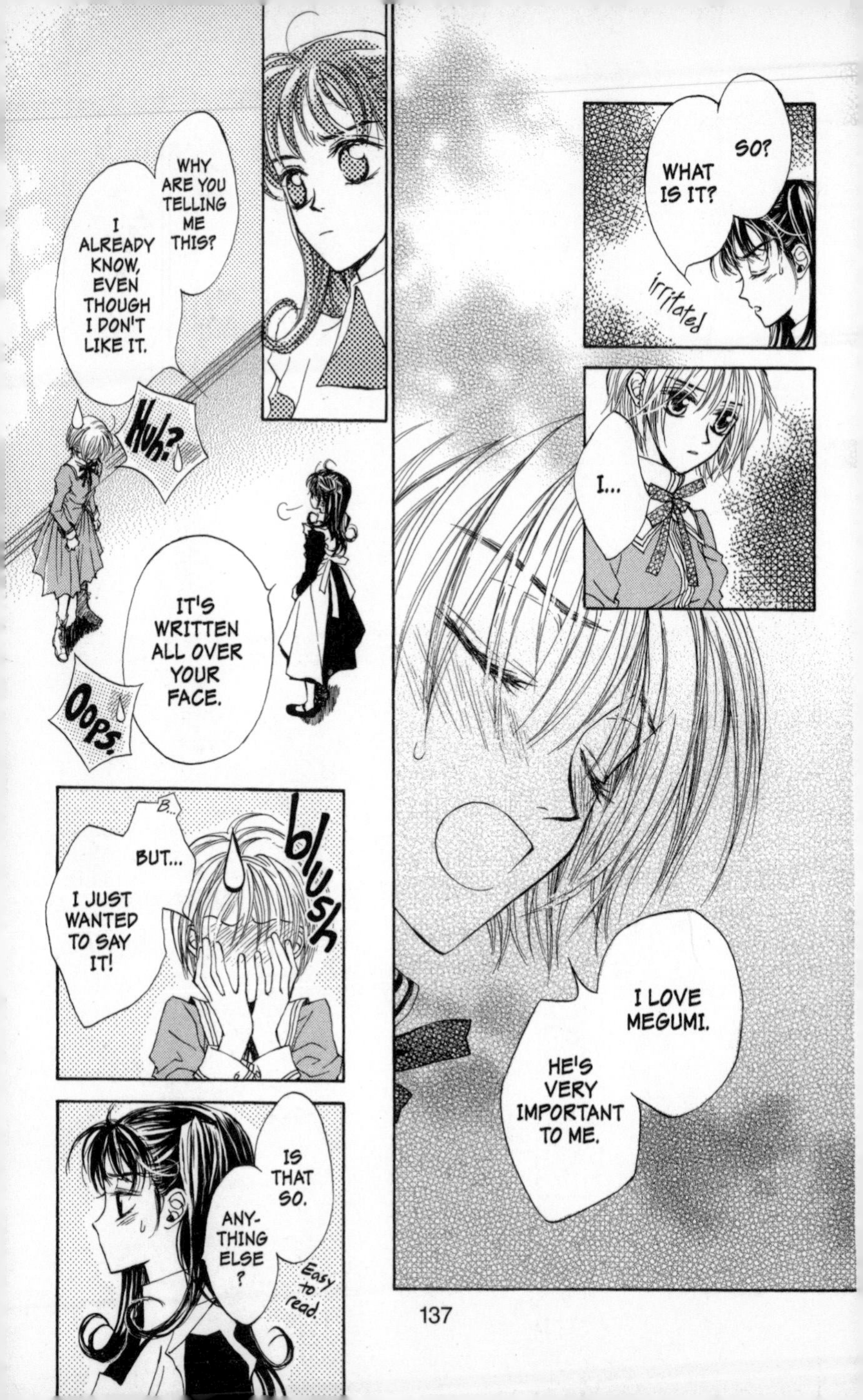

SO?
WHAT IS IT?
irritated
I...
I LOVE MEGUMI.
HE'S VERY IMPORTANT TO ME.
WHY ARE YOU TELLING ME THIS?
I ALREADY KNOW, EVEN THOUGH I DON'T LIKE IT.
Huh?
IT'S WRITTEN ALL OVER YOUR FACE.
Oops.
B...
blush
BUT...
I JUST WANTED TO SAY IT!
IS THAT SO.
ANYTHING ELSE?
Easy to read.

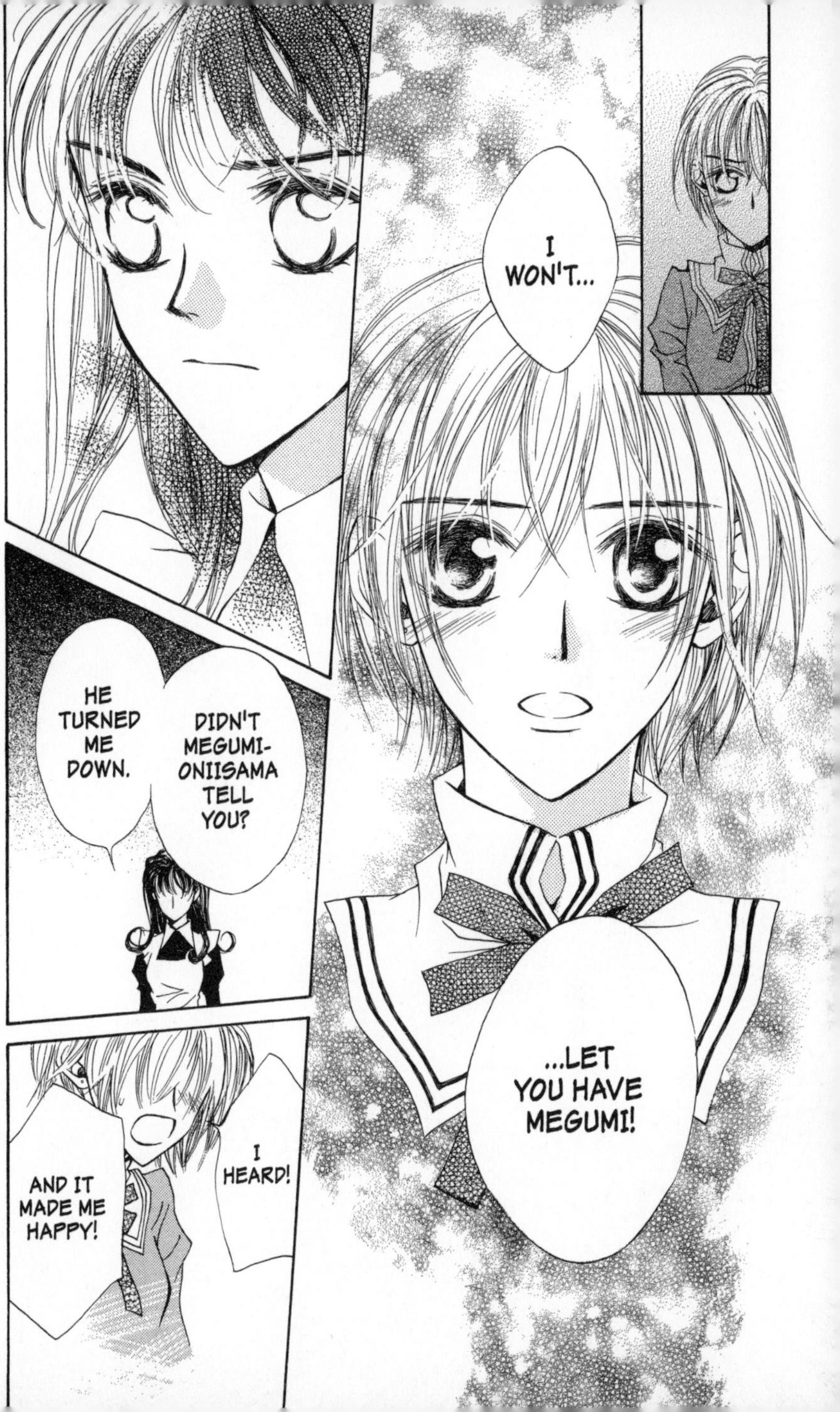
I WON'T...
...LET YOU HAVE MEGUMI!
DIDN'T MEGUMI-ONIISAMA TELL YOU?
HE TURNED ME DOWN.
I HEARD!
AND IT MADE ME HAPPY!

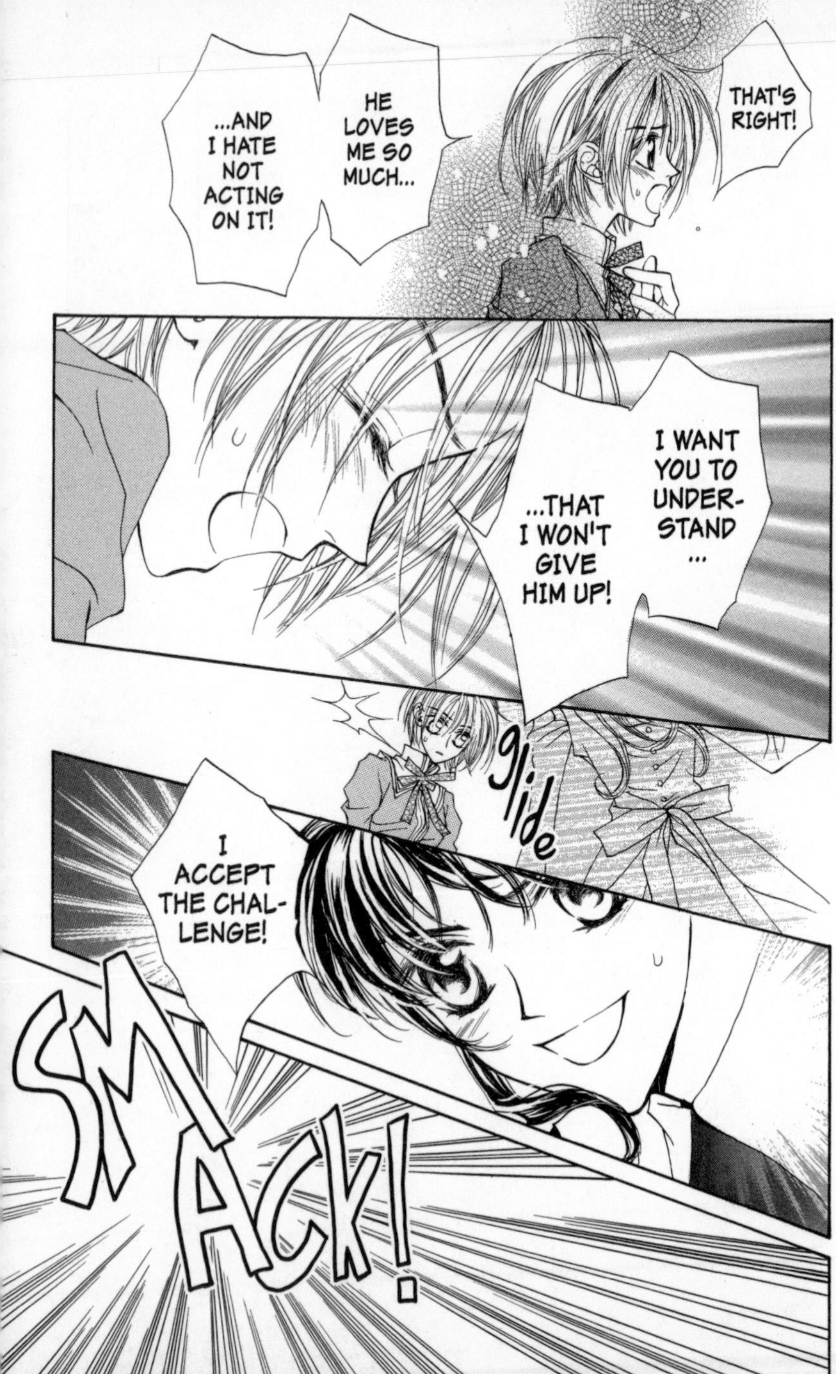
THAT'S RIGHT!
HE LOVES ME SO MUCH...
...AND I HATE NOT ACTING ON IT!
I WANT YOU TO UNDER-STAND ...
...THAT I WON'T GIVE HIM UP!
glide
I ACCEPT THE CHAL-LENGE!
SMACK!

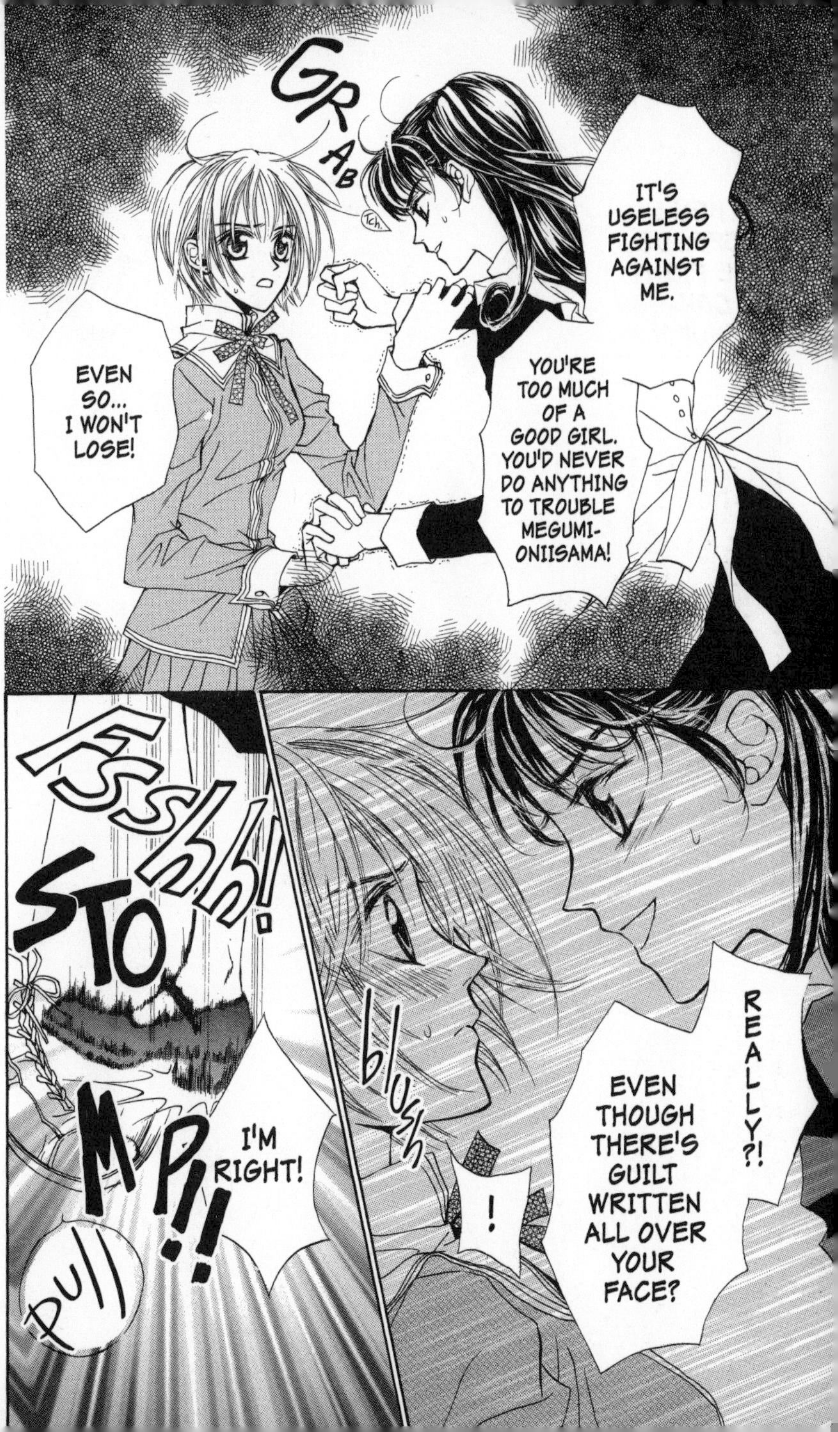
GRAB
Tch.
IT'S USELESS FIGHTING AGAINST ME.
YOU'RE TOO MUCH OF A GOOD GIRL. YOU'D NEVER DO ANYTHING TO TROUBLE MEGUMI-ONIISAMA!
EVEN SO... I WON'T LOSE!
REALLY?!
EVEN THOUGH THERE'S GUILT WRITTEN ALL OVER YOUR FACE?
!
blush
I'M RIGHT!
FSShh!!
STOMP!!
pull

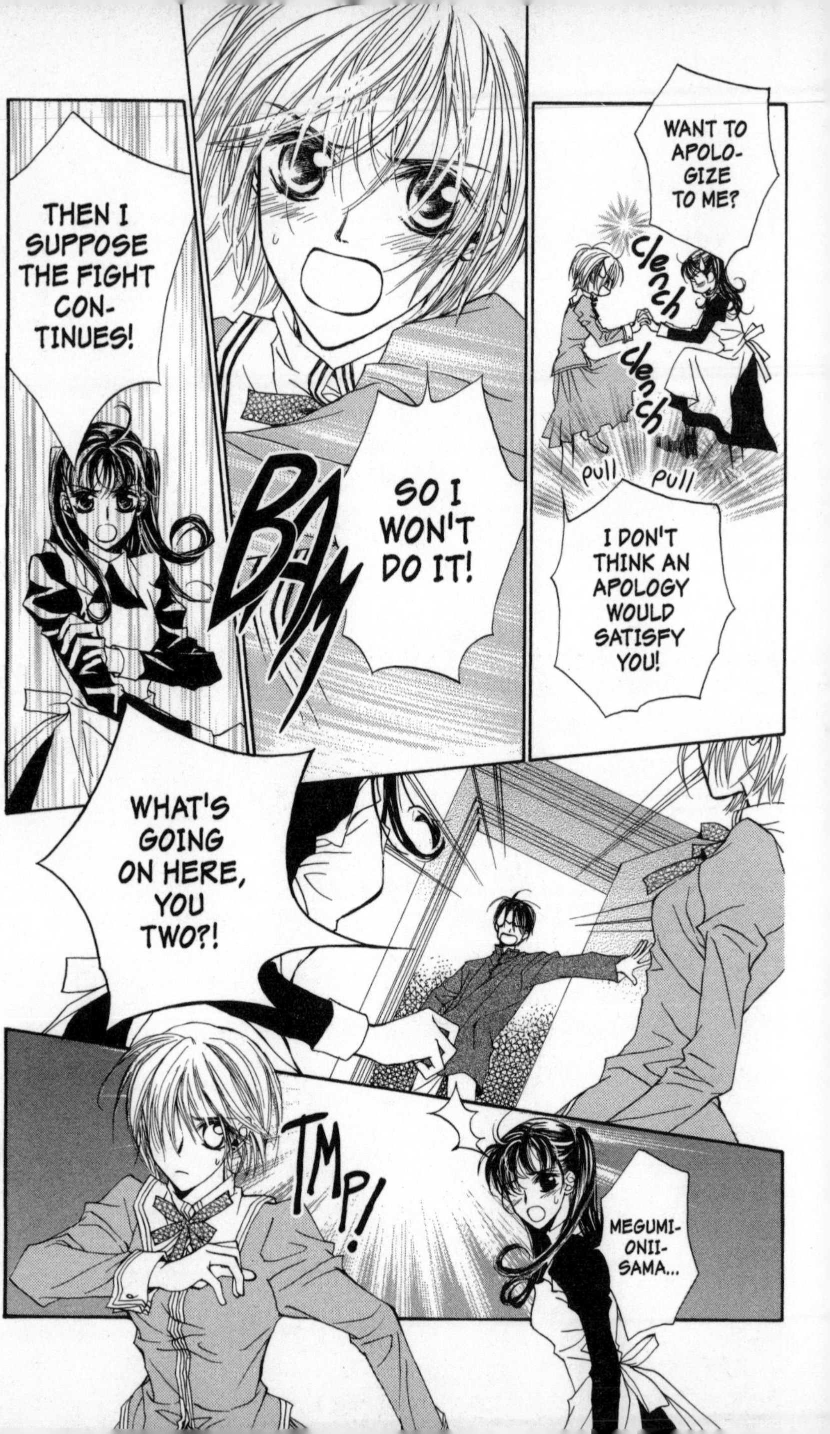
WANT TO APOLOGIZE TO ME?
clench clench
pull pull
I DON'T THINK AN APOLOGY WOULD SATISFY YOU!
BAM
SO I WON'T DO IT!
THEN I SUPPOSE THE FIGHT CONTINUES!
WHAT'S GOING ON HERE, YOU TWO?!
TMP!
MEGUMI-ONII-SAMA...

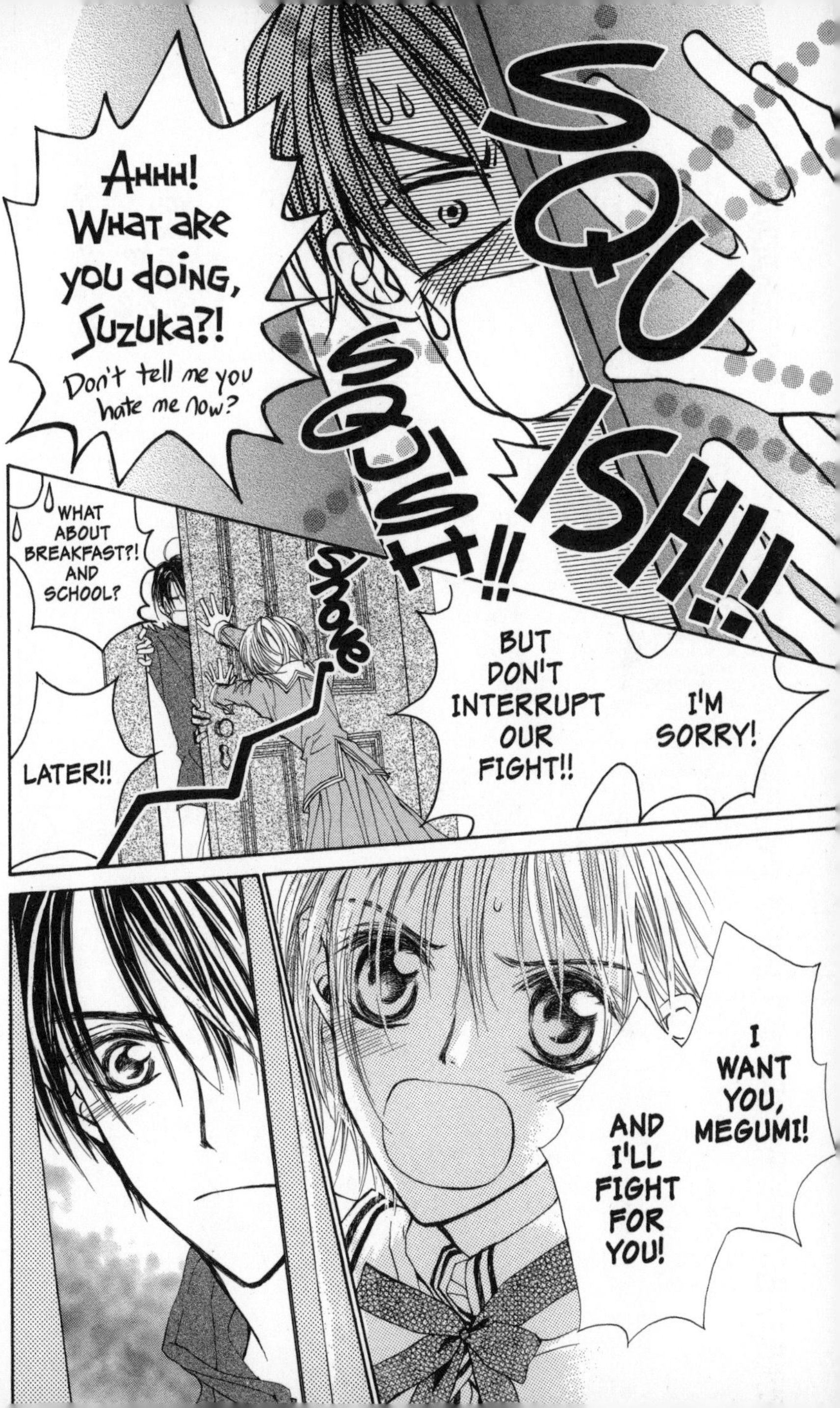
SQUISH!!
SQUISH!!
Ahhh! What are you doing, Suzuka?!
Don't tell me you hate me now?
I'M SORRY!
BUT DON'T INTERRUPT OUR FIGHT!!
shove
WHAT ABOUT BREAKFAST?! AND SCHOOL?
LATER!!
I WANT YOU, MEGUMI!
AND I'LL FIGHT FOR YOU!

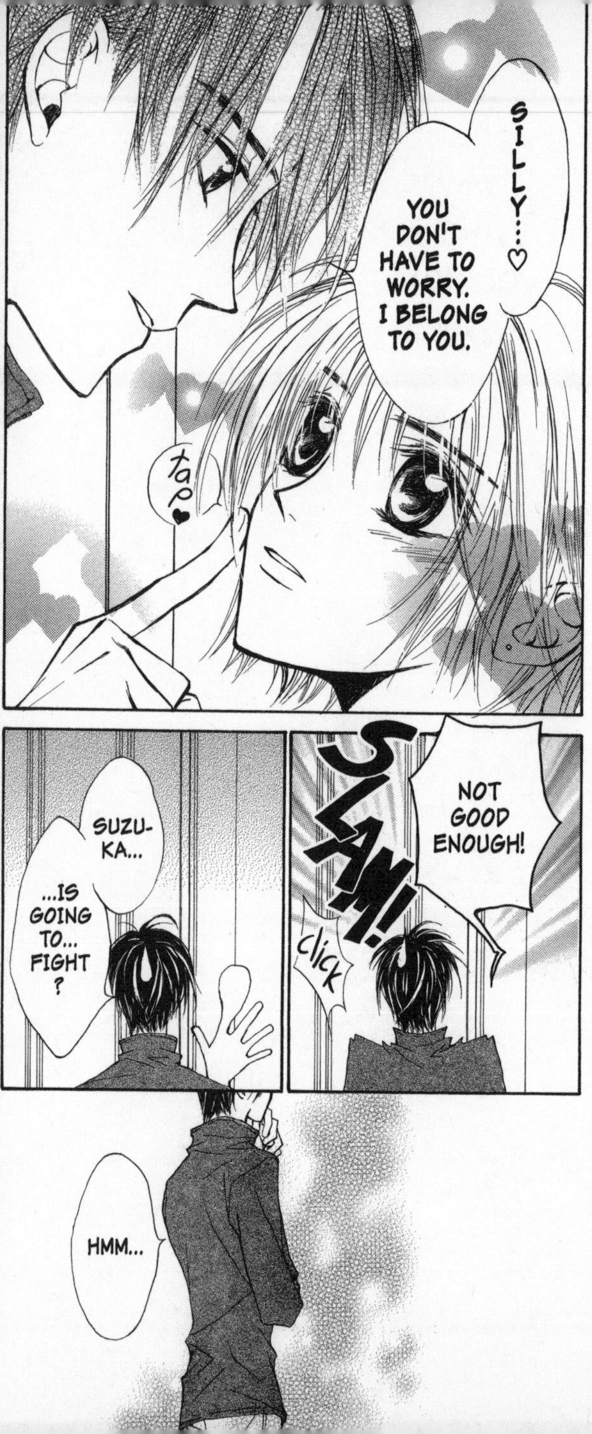
SILLY...♡
YOU DON'T HAVE TO WORRY. I BELONG TO YOU.
tap♥
SLAM!
NOT GOOD ENOUGH!
click
SUZU-KA...
...IS GOING TO... FIGHT?
HMM...

Even though I just bragged about something silly, it's a big deal (to me). That's why I wanted to write it down in this column to commemorate (?ô) it. Just ignore it, please.

Now...

It seems like I can continue drawing *Captive Hearts*. I'm so thankful! ♡ I'm so happy and for some reason... embarrassed... I thought the storyline was getting so ridiculous I might have to quit! The story gets a little more fantasy-like after this point, so I should work more on the romance...I'll do my best!

Please continue reading the series! ♡ Then you can see how high-strung I get! Yes, as my editor says, "Hino-san, you're always so high-strung..."

To be continued...
↓

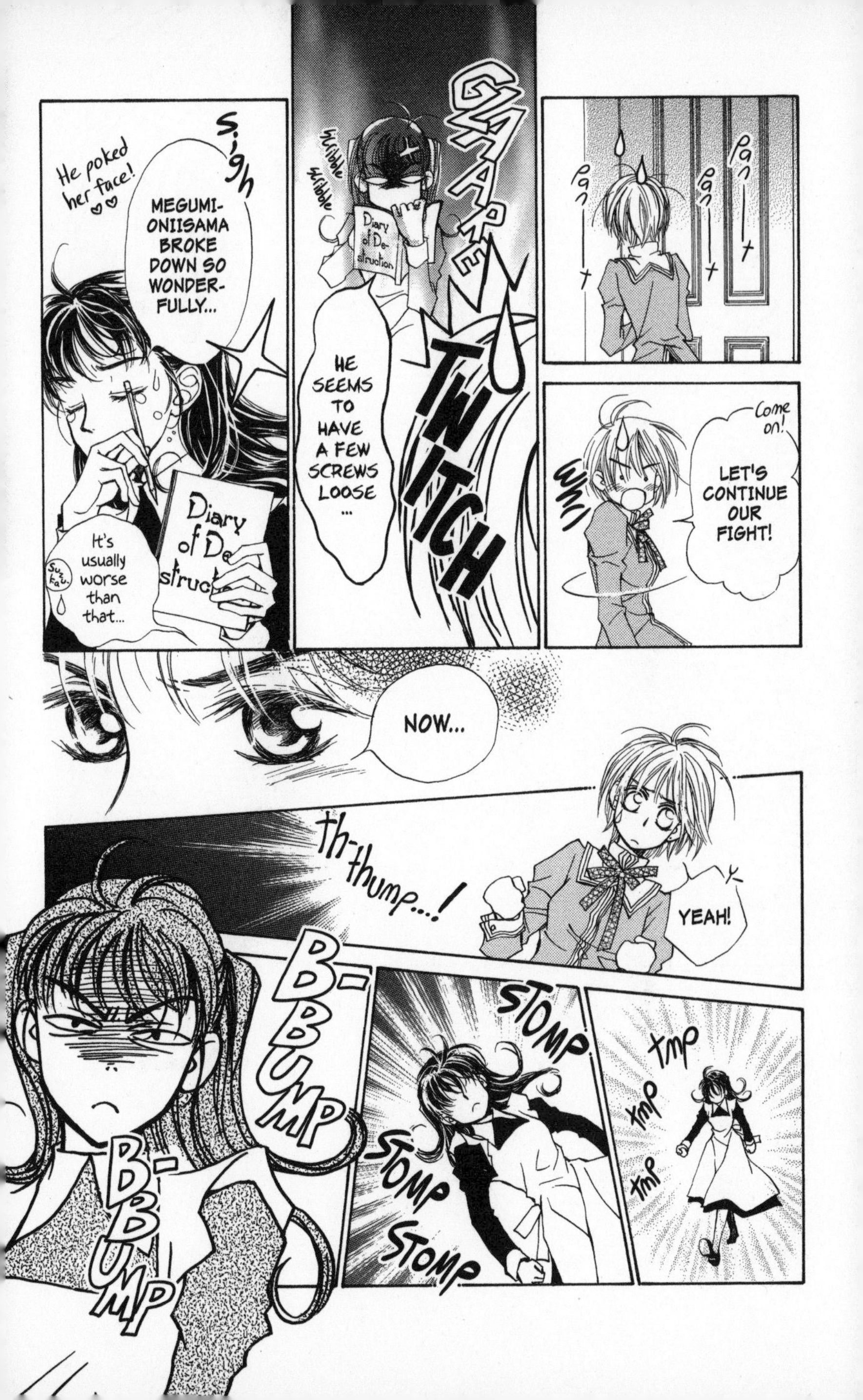
Pan—t
Pan—t
Pan—t
Pan—t
Whirl
Come on!
LET'S CONTINUE OUR FIGHT!
GLARE
scribble scribble
Diary of Destruction
HE SEEMS TO HAVE A FEW SCREWS LOOSE ...
TWITCH
Sigh
MEGUMI-ONIISAMA BROKE DOWN SO WONDERFULLY...
He poked her face!
Diary of Destruct
It's usually worse than that...
NOW...
YEAH!
th-thump...!
B-BUMP
B-BUMP
tmp tmp tmp
STOMP STOMP STOMP

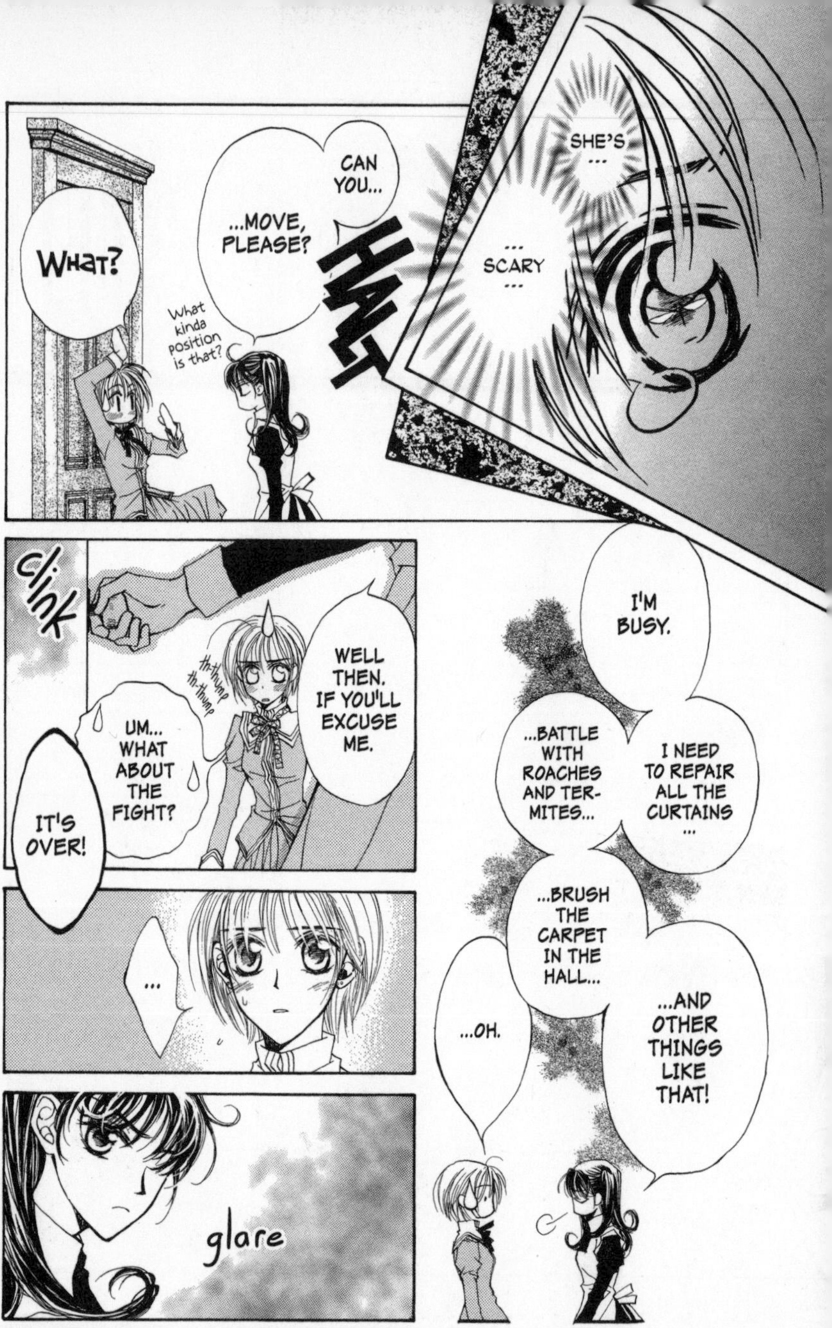
SHE'S ...
... SCARY ...
HALT
CAN YOU...
...MOVE, PLEASE?
What kinda position is that?
WHAT?
I'M BUSY.
I NEED TO REPAIR ALL THE CURTAINS ...
...BATTLE WITH ROACHES AND TER-MITES...
...BRUSH THE CARPET IN THE HALL...
...AND OTHER THINGS LIKE THAT!
...OH.
clink
WELL THEN. IF YOU'LL EXCUSE ME.
th-thump th-thump
UM... WHAT ABOUT THE FIGHT?
IT'S OVER!
...
glare

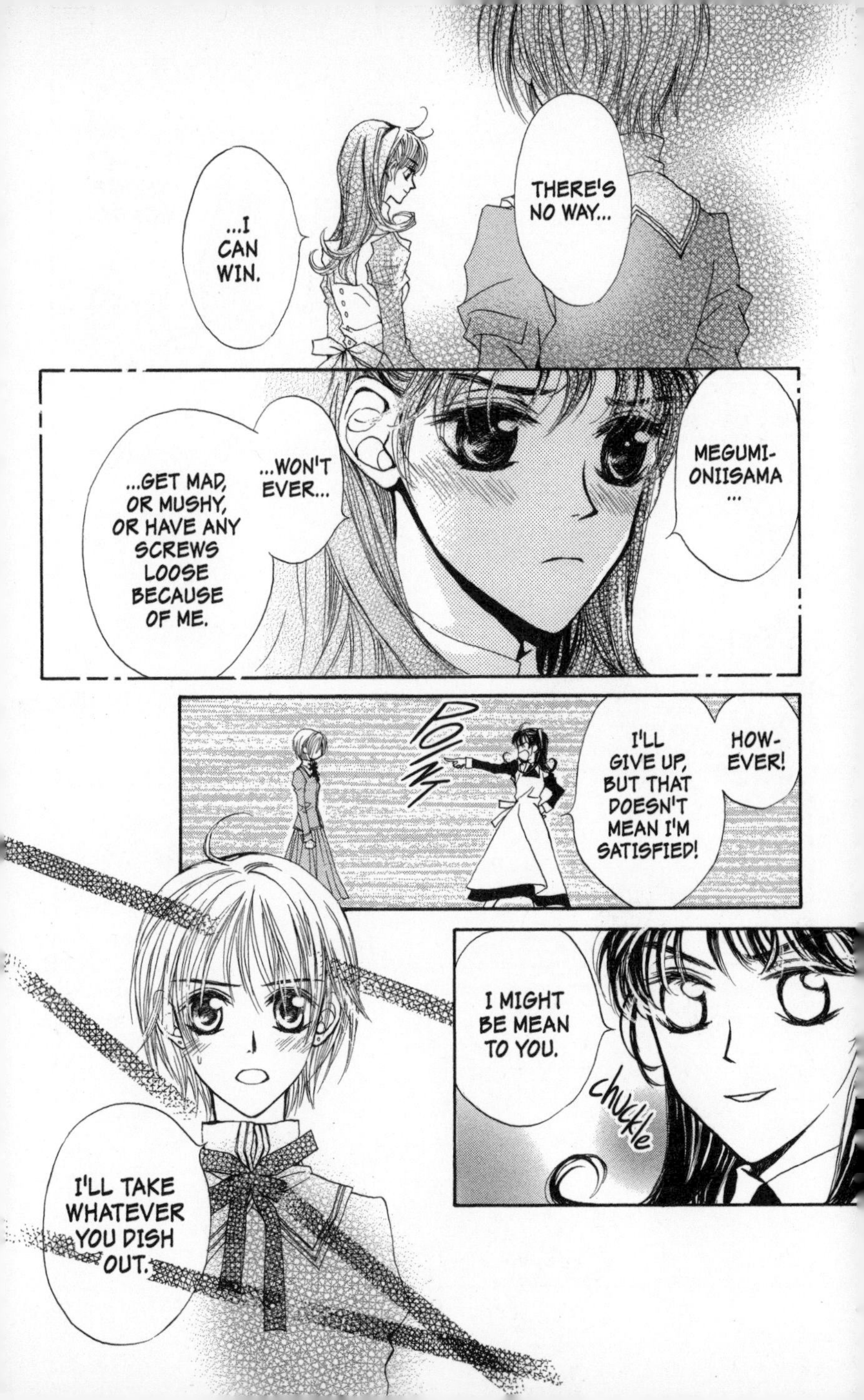
THERE'S NO WAY...
...I CAN WIN.
MEGUMI-ONIISAMA ...
...WON'T EVER...
...GET MAD, OR MUSHY, OR HAVE ANY SCREWS LOOSE BECAUSE OF ME.
HOW-EVER!
I'LL GIVE UP, BUT THAT DOESN'T MEAN I'M SATISFIED!
BOING
I MIGHT BE MEAN TO YOU.
chuckle
I'LL TAKE WHATEVER YOU DISH OUT.

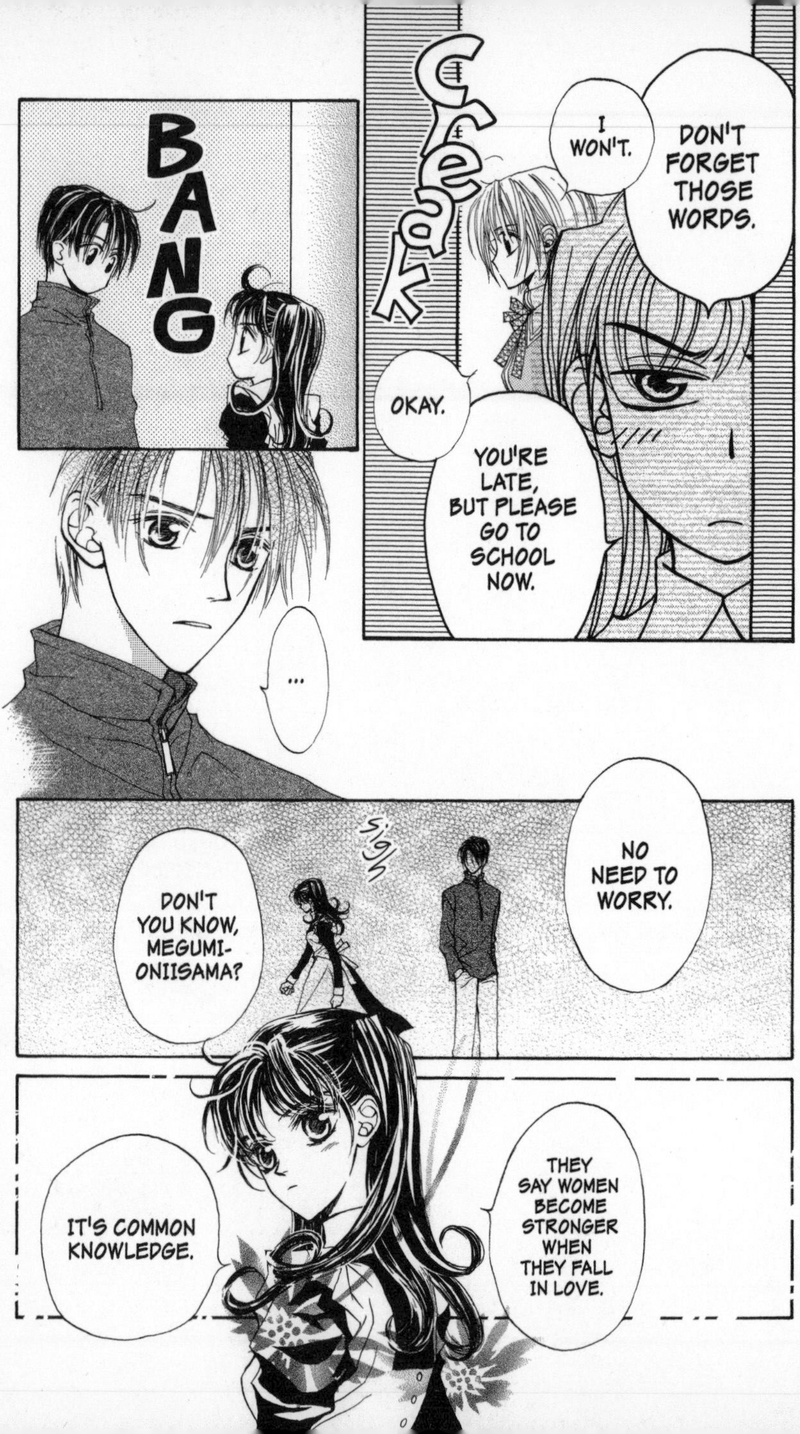
DON'T FORGET THOSE WORDS.
I WON'T.
Creak
YOU'RE LATE, BUT PLEASE GO TO SCHOOL NOW.
OKAY.
BANG
...
NO NEED TO WORRY.
sigh
DON'T YOU KNOW, MEGUMI-ONIISAMA?
THEY SAY WOMEN BECOME STRONGER WHEN THEY FALL IN LOVE.
IT'S COMMON KNOWLEDGE.

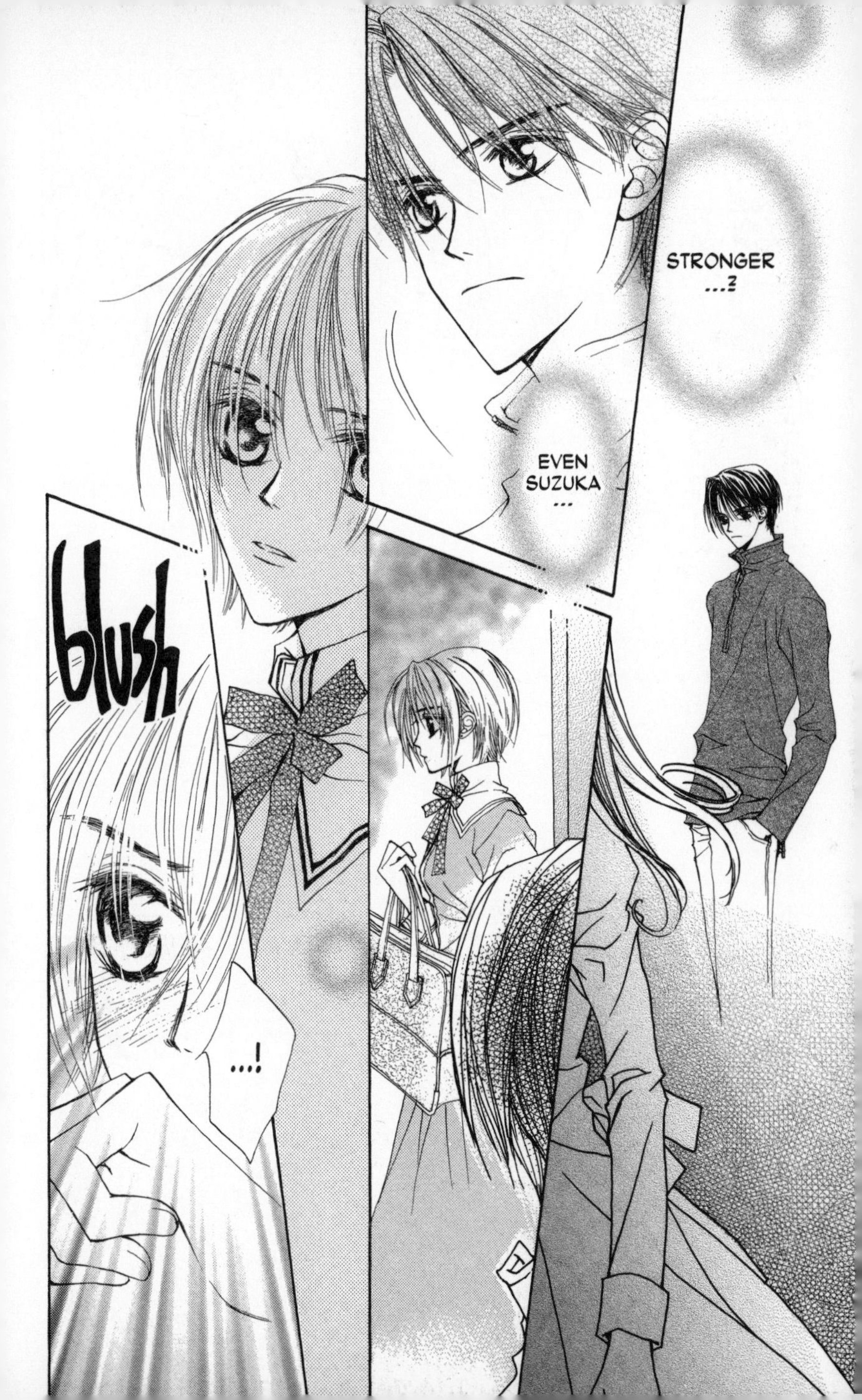
STRONGER ...?
EVEN SUZUKA ...
blush
...!

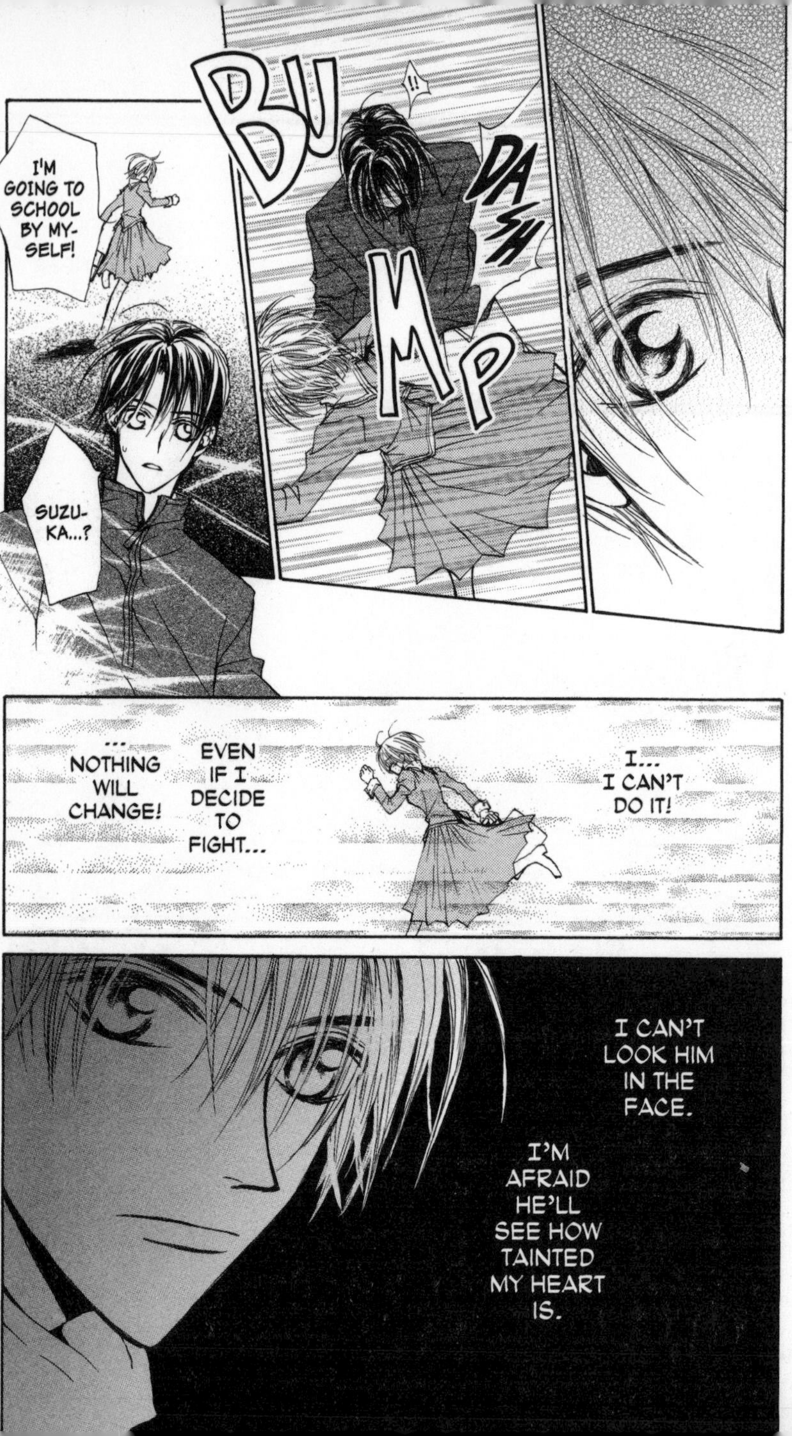
BUMP
!!
DASH
I'M GOING TO SCHOOL BY MY-SELF!
SUZU-KA...?
I... I CAN'T DO IT!
EVEN IF I DECIDE TO FIGHT...
... NOTHING WILL CHANGE!
I CAN'T LOOK HIM IN THE FACE.
I'M AFRAID HE'LL SEE HOW TAINTED MY HEART IS.

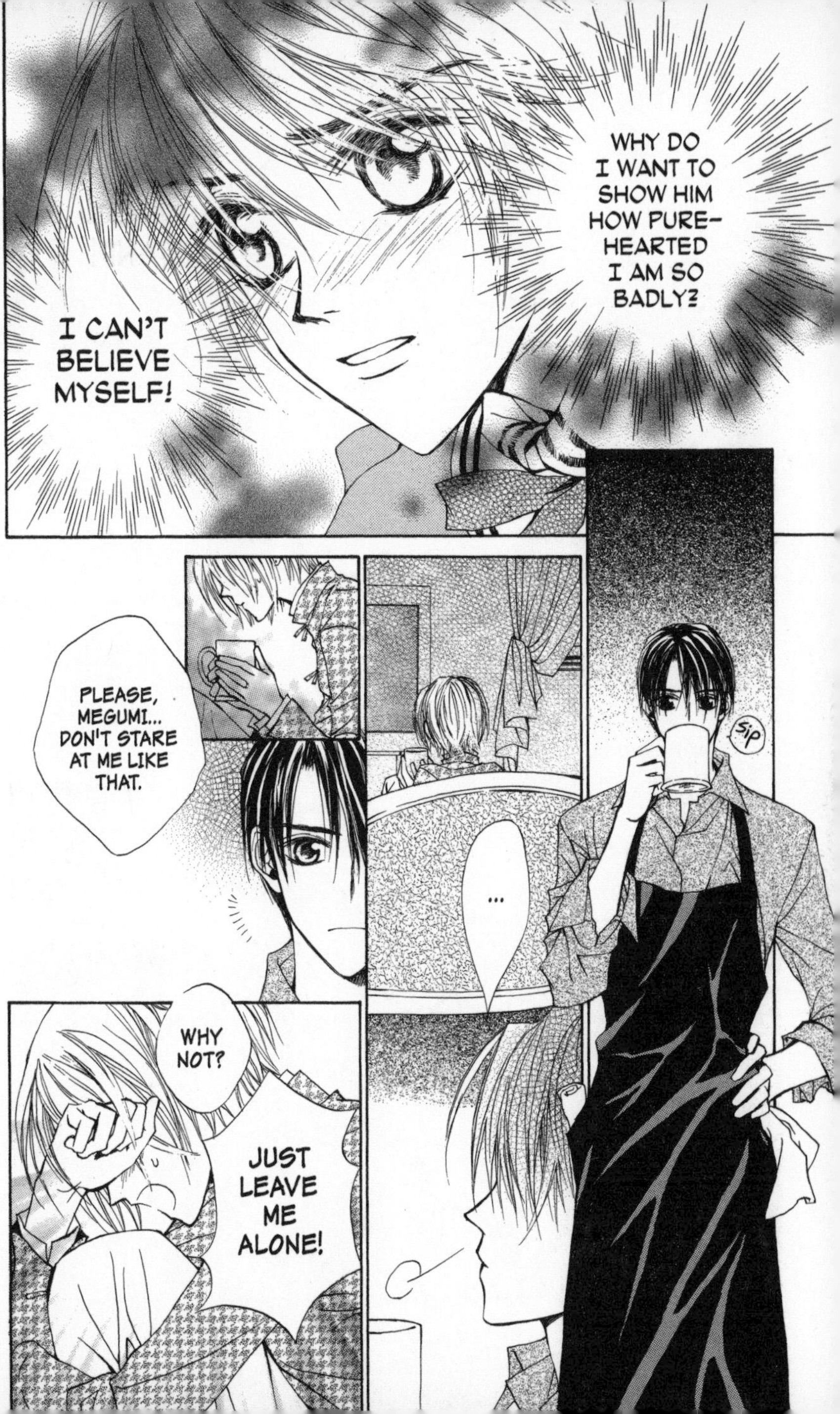
WHY DO I WANT TO SHOW HIM HOW PURE-HEARTED I AM SO BADLY?
I CAN'T BELIEVE MYSELF!
Sip
...
PLEASE, MEGUMI... DON'T STARE AT ME LIKE THAT.
WHY NOT?
JUST LEAVE ME ALONE!

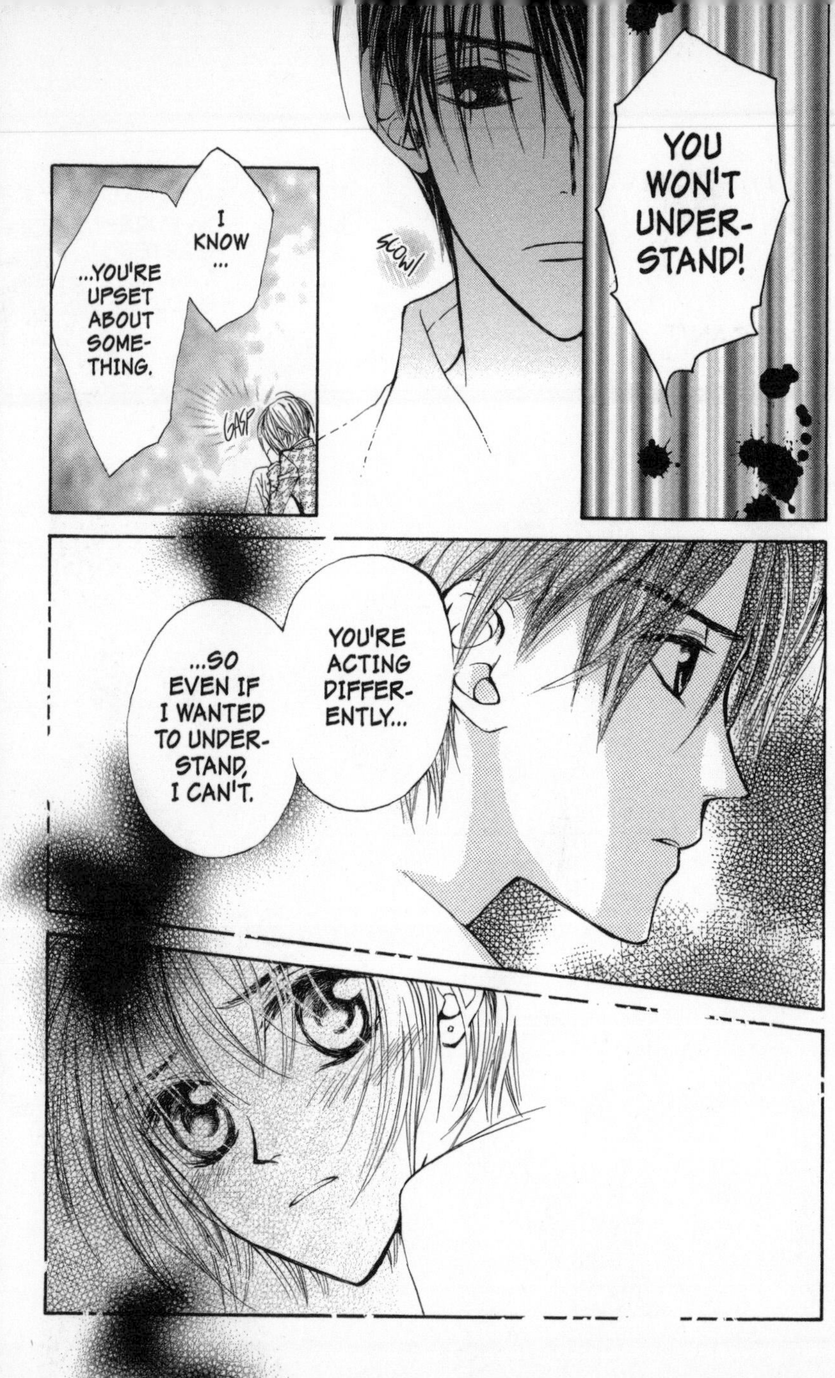
YOU WON'T UNDER-STAND!
SCOWL
I KNOW ...
...YOU'RE UPSET ABOUT SOME-THING.
GASP
YOU'RE ACTING DIFFER-ENTLY...
...SO EVEN IF I WANTED TO UNDER-STAND, I CAN'T.

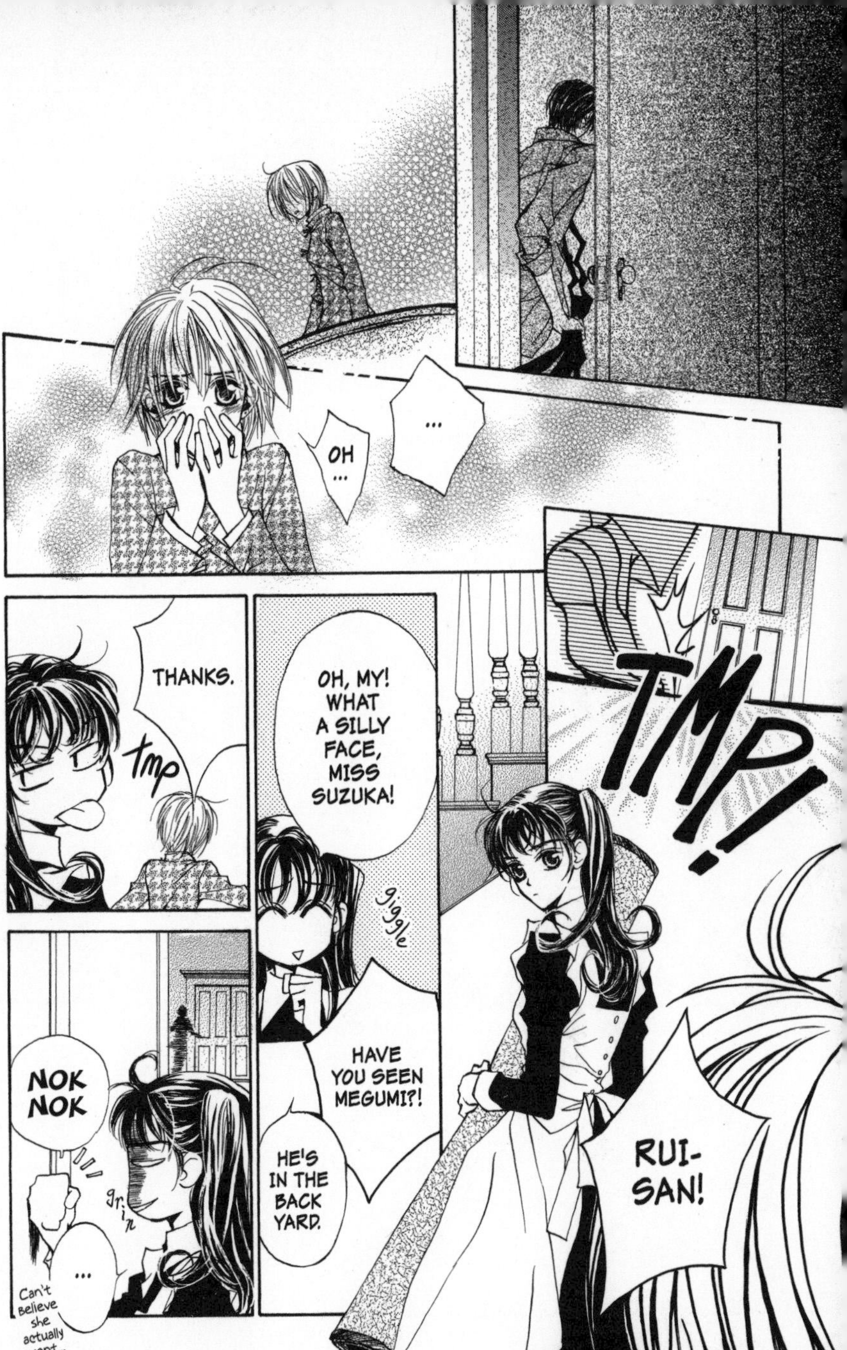
...
OH ...
TMP!!
RUI-SAN!
HAVE YOU SEEN MEGUMI?!
HE'S IN THE BACK YARD.
OH, MY! WHAT A SILLY FACE, MISS SUZUKA!
giggle
THANKS.
tmp
NOK NOK
grin
...
Can't believe she actually went...

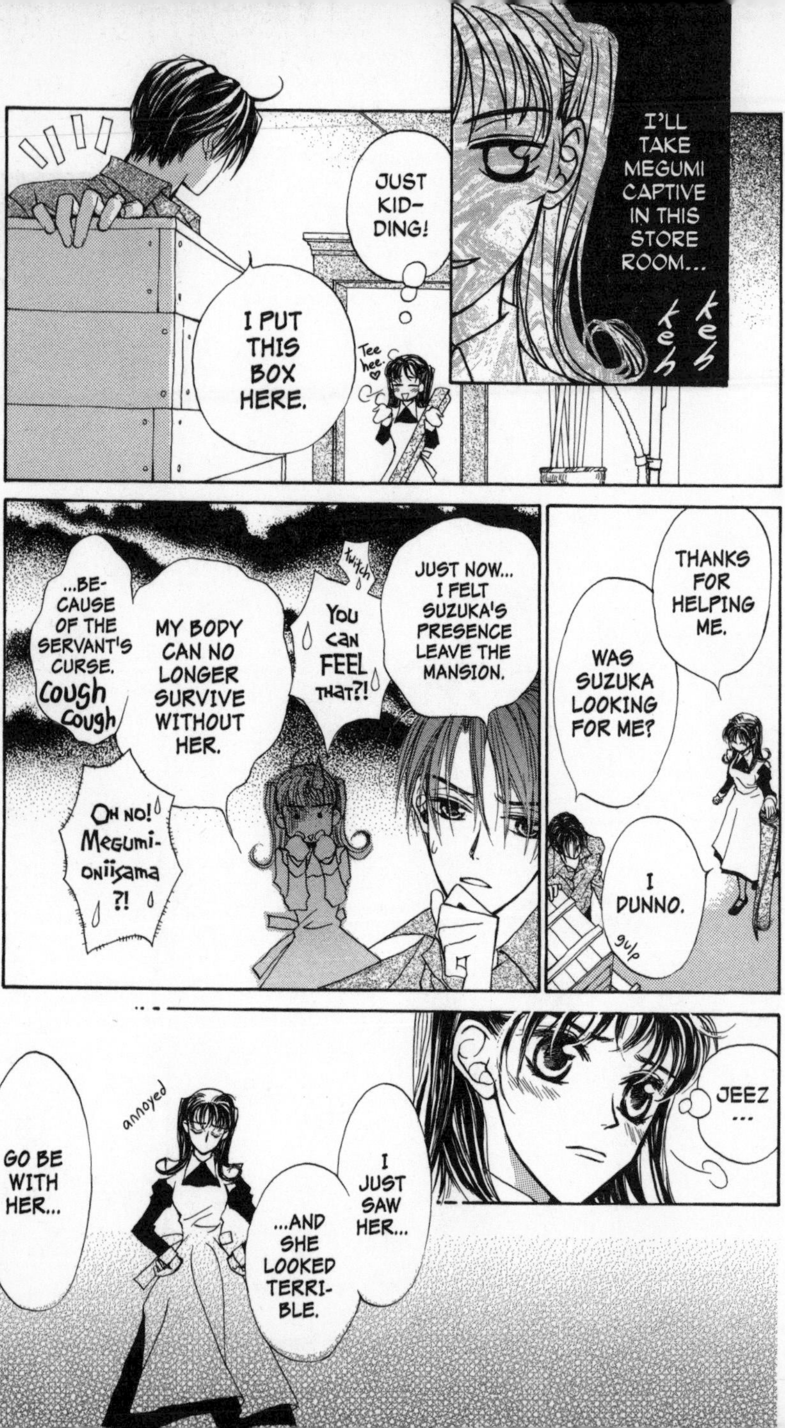
I'LL TAKE MEGUMI CAPTIVE IN THIS STORE ROOM...
keh keh
JUST KID-DING!
I PUT THIS BOX HERE.
Tee hee.
THANKS FOR HELPING ME.
WAS SUZUKA LOOKING FOR ME?
I DUNNO.
gulp
JUST NOW... I FELT SUZUKA'S PRESENCE LEAVE THE MANSION.
twitch
You can FEEL THAT?!
MY BODY CAN NO LONGER SURVIVE WITHOUT HER.
...BE-CAUSE OF THE SERVANT'S CURSE.
Cough cough
OH NO! Megumi-oniisama ?!
JEEZ...
I JUST SAW HER...
...AND SHE LOOKED TERRI-BLE.
annoyed
GO BE WITH HER...

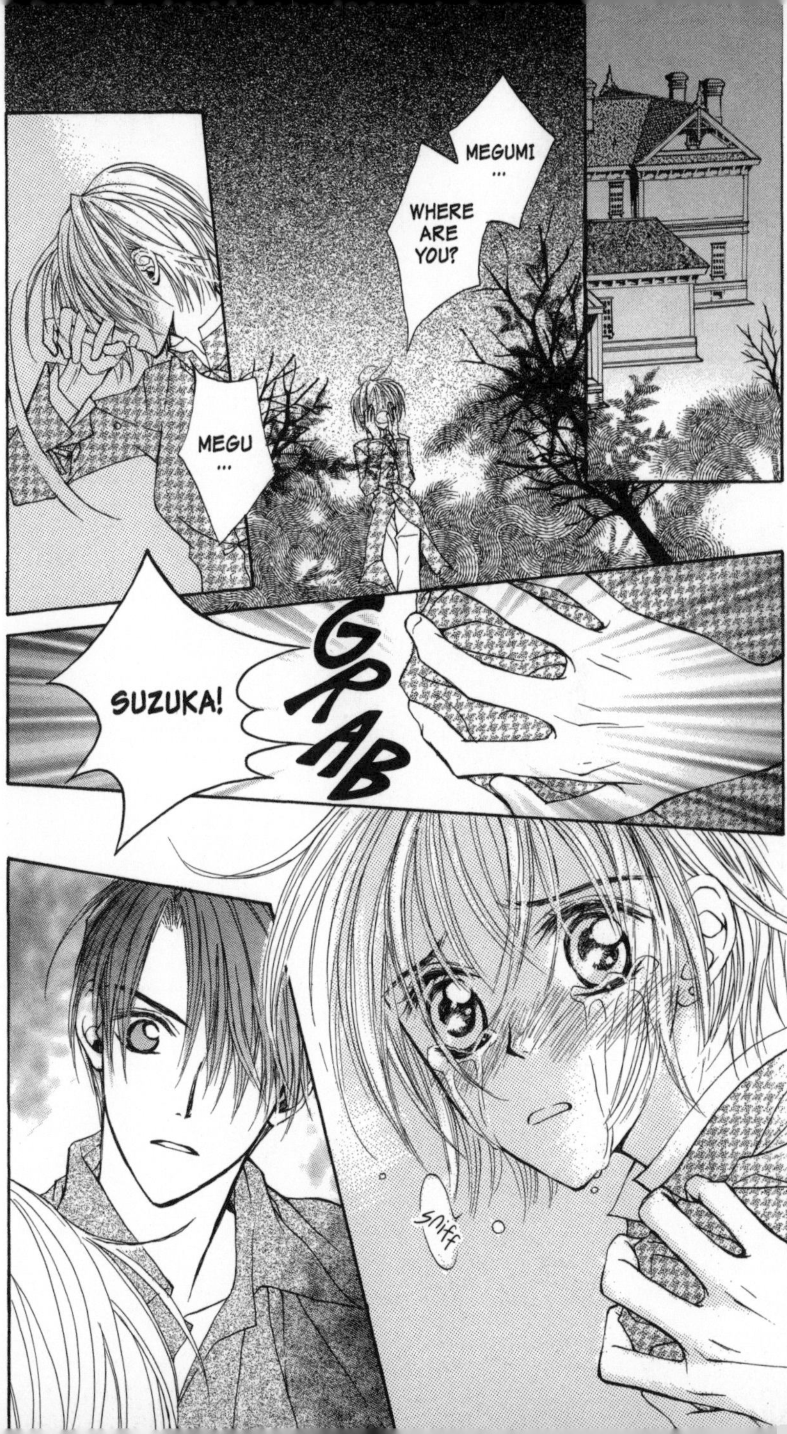
MEGUMI ...
WHERE ARE YOU?
MEGU ...
GRAB
SUZUKA!
sniff

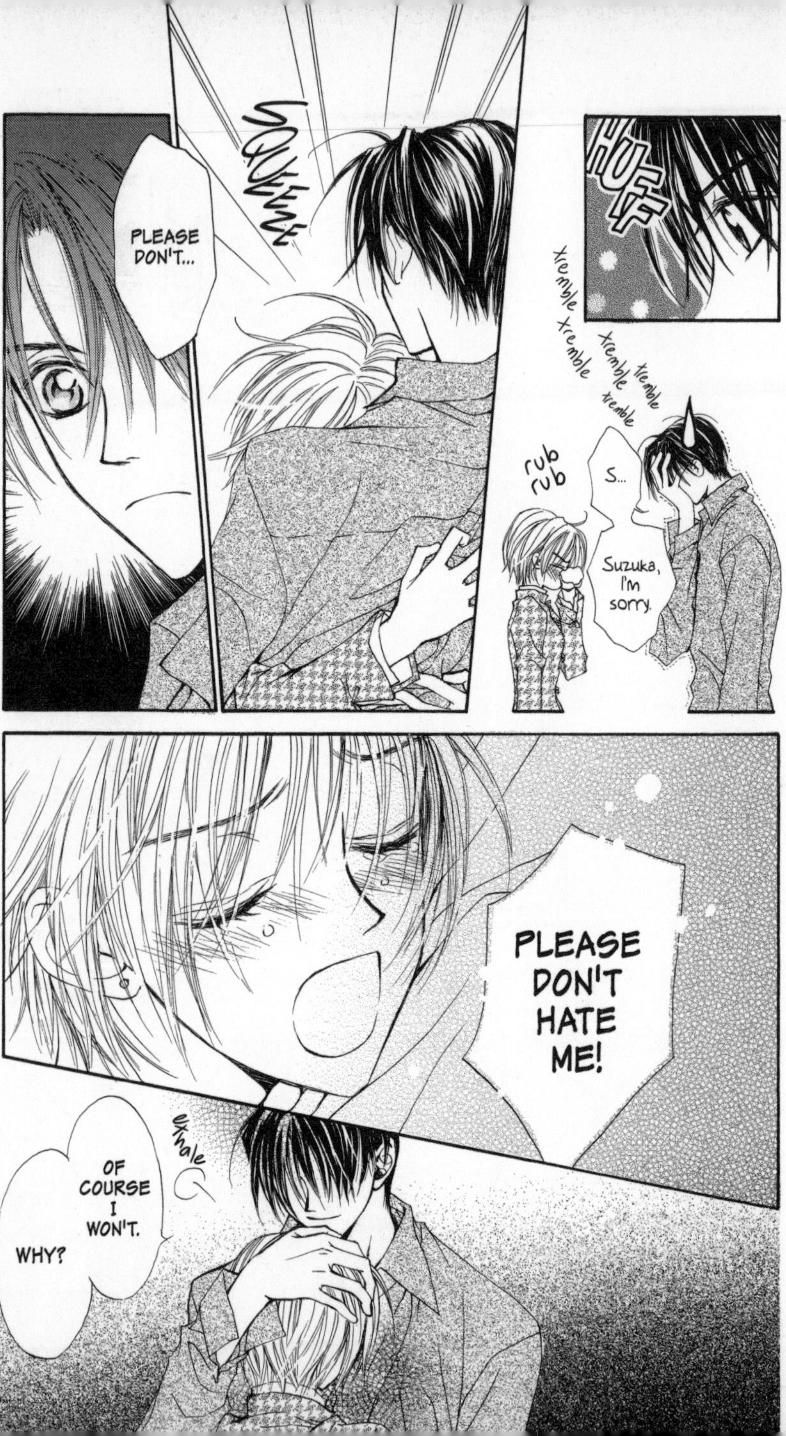
HUFF
tremble tremble tremble tremble tremble
S...
rub rub
Suzuka, I'm sorry.
SQUEEZE
PLEASE DON'T...
PLEASE DON'T HATE ME!
exhale
OF COURSE I WON'T.
WHY?

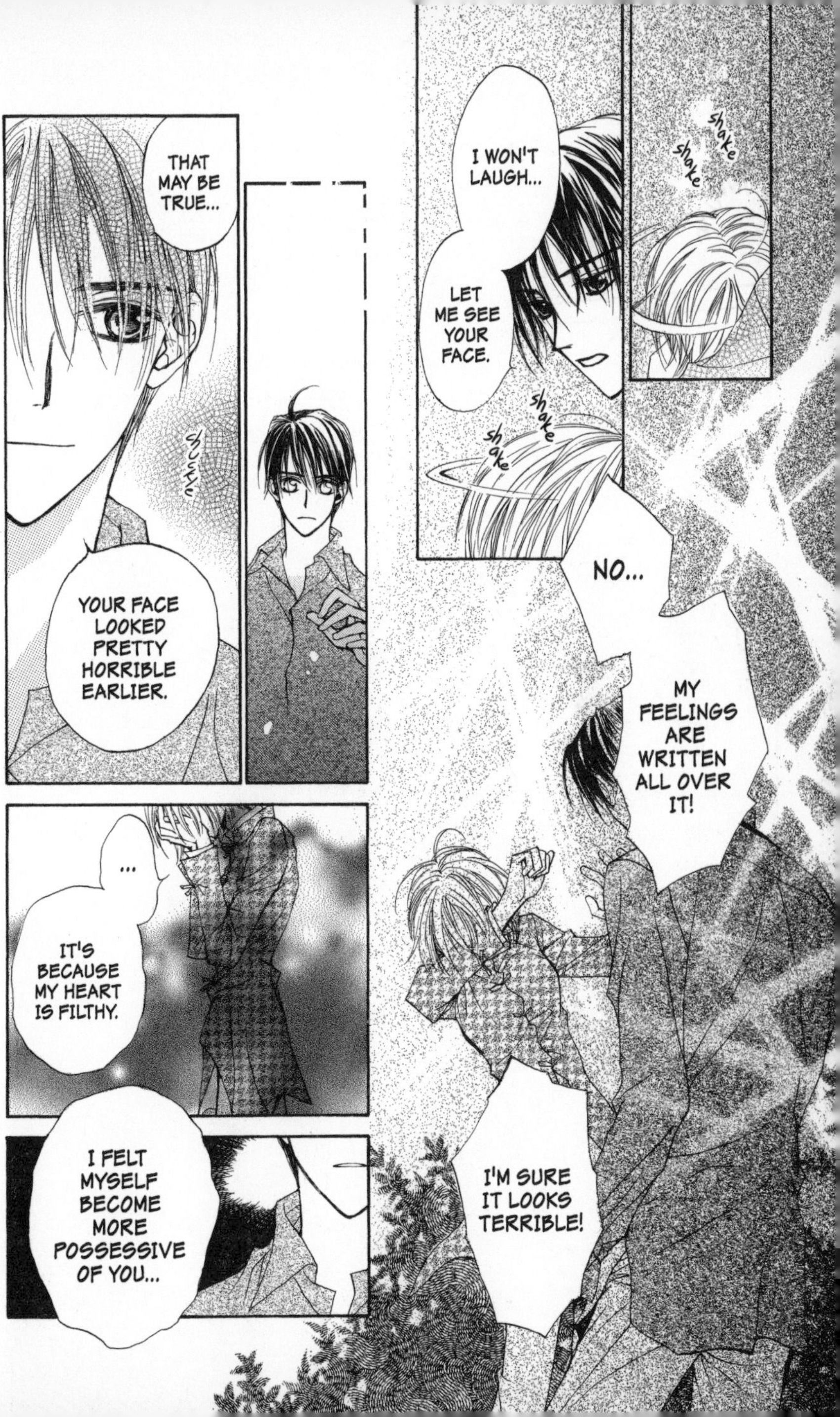
shake
shake
I WON'T LAUGH...
LET ME SEE YOUR FACE.
shake
shake
NO...
MY FEELINGS ARE WRITTEN ALL OVER IT!
I'M SURE IT LOOKS TERRIBLE!
THAT MAY BE TRUE...
chuckle
YOUR FACE LOOKED PRETTY HORRIBLE EARLIER.
...
IT'S BECAUSE MY HEART IS FILTHY.
I FELT MYSELF BECOME MORE POSSESSIVE OF YOU...

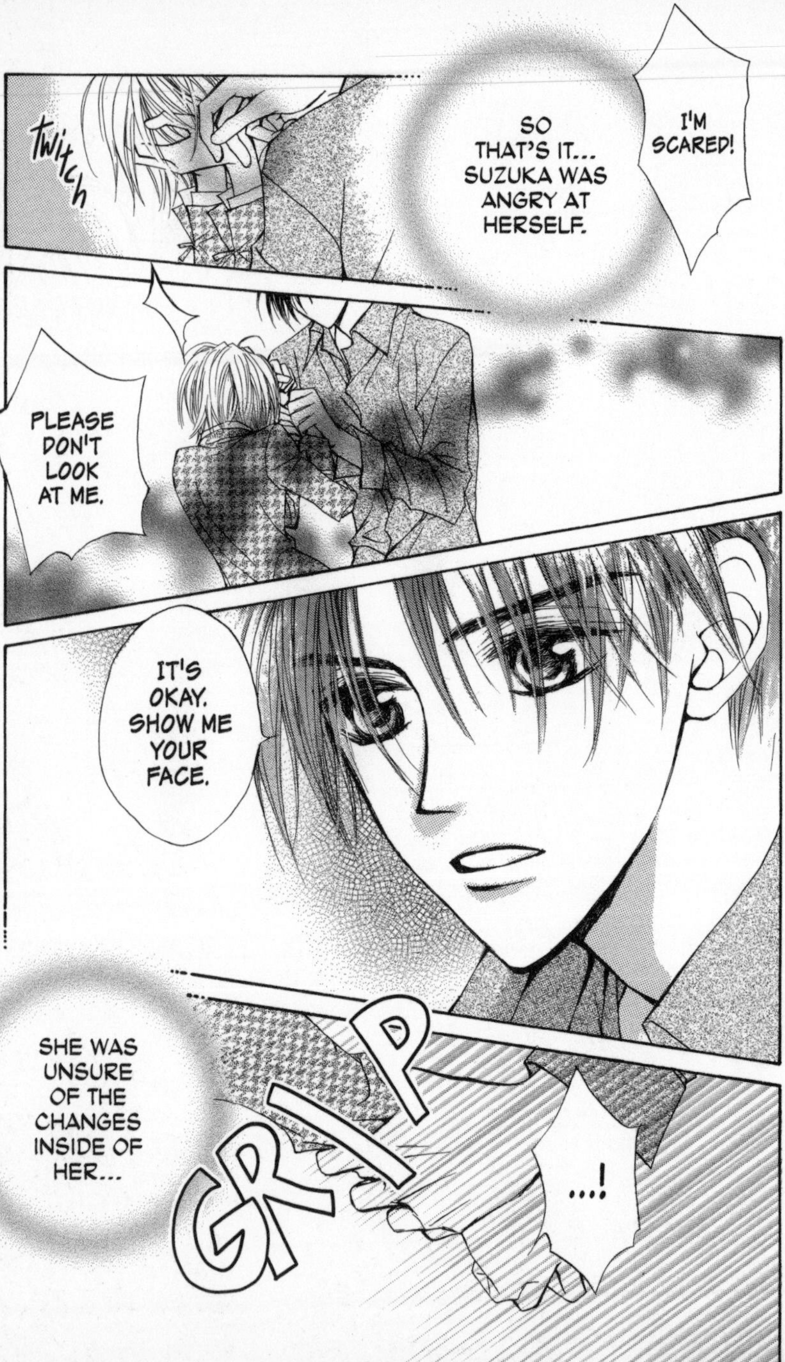
I'M SCARED!
SO THAT'S IT... SUZUKA WAS ANGRY AT HERSELF.
twitch
PLEASE DON'T LOOK AT ME.
IT'S OKAY. SHOW ME YOUR FACE.
...!
GRIP
SHE WAS UNSURE OF THE CHANGES INSIDE OF HER...

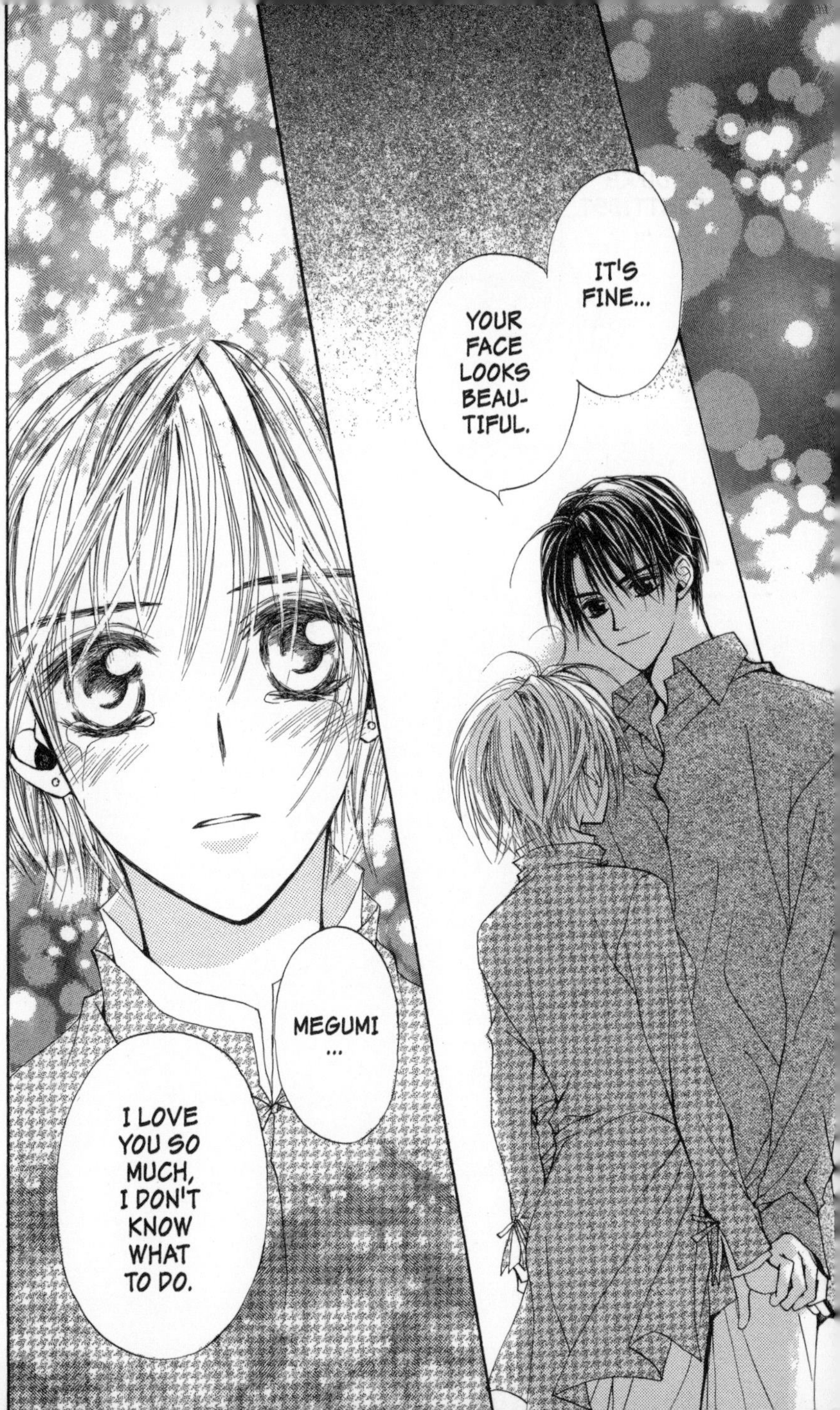
IT'S FINE...
YOUR FACE LOOKS BEAU-TIFUL.
MEGUMI ...
I LOVE YOU SO MUCH, I DON'T KNOW WHAT TO DO.

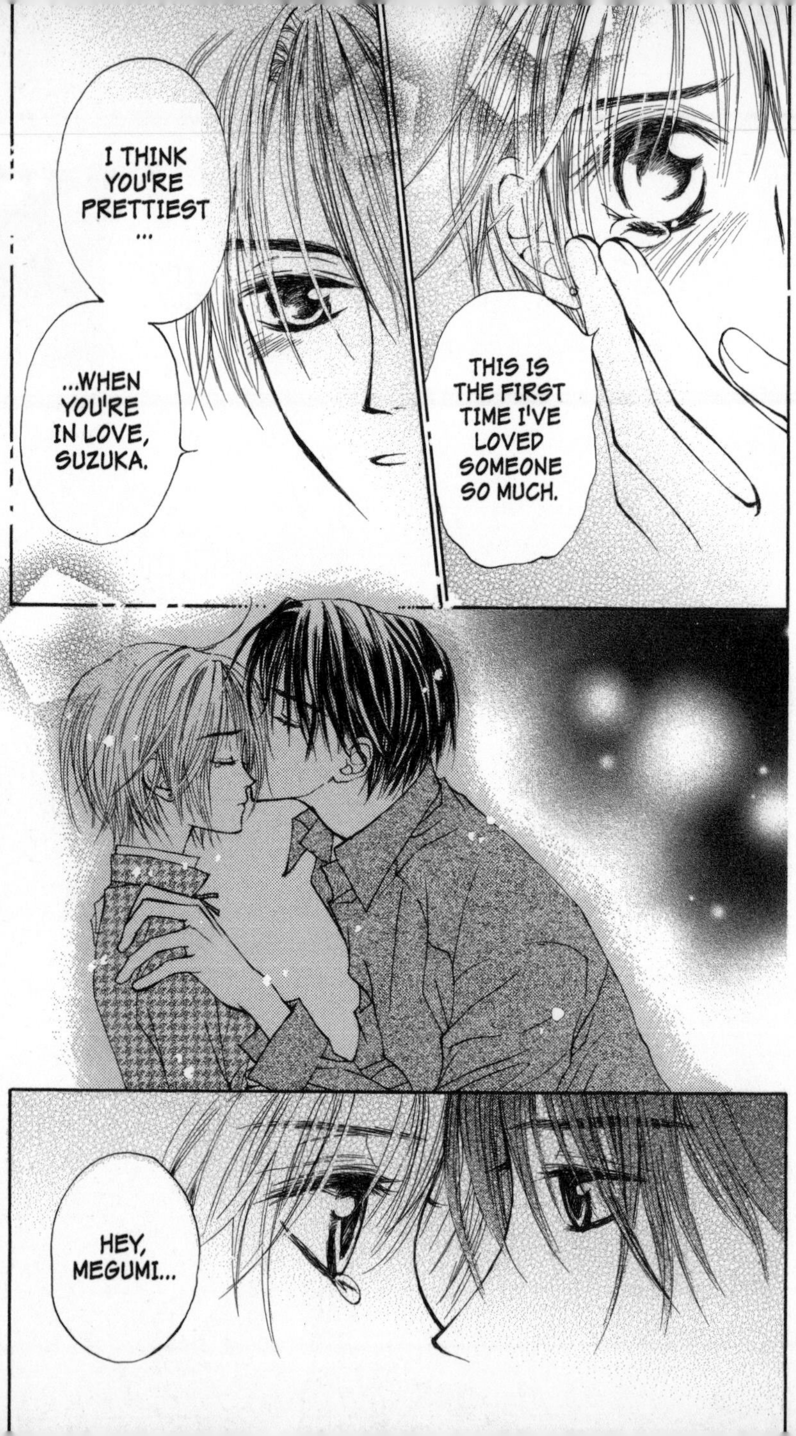
THIS IS THE FIRST TIME I'VE LOVED SOMEONE SO MUCH.
I THINK YOU'RE PRETTIEST ...
...WHEN YOU'RE IN LOVE, SUZUKA.
HEY, MEGUMI...

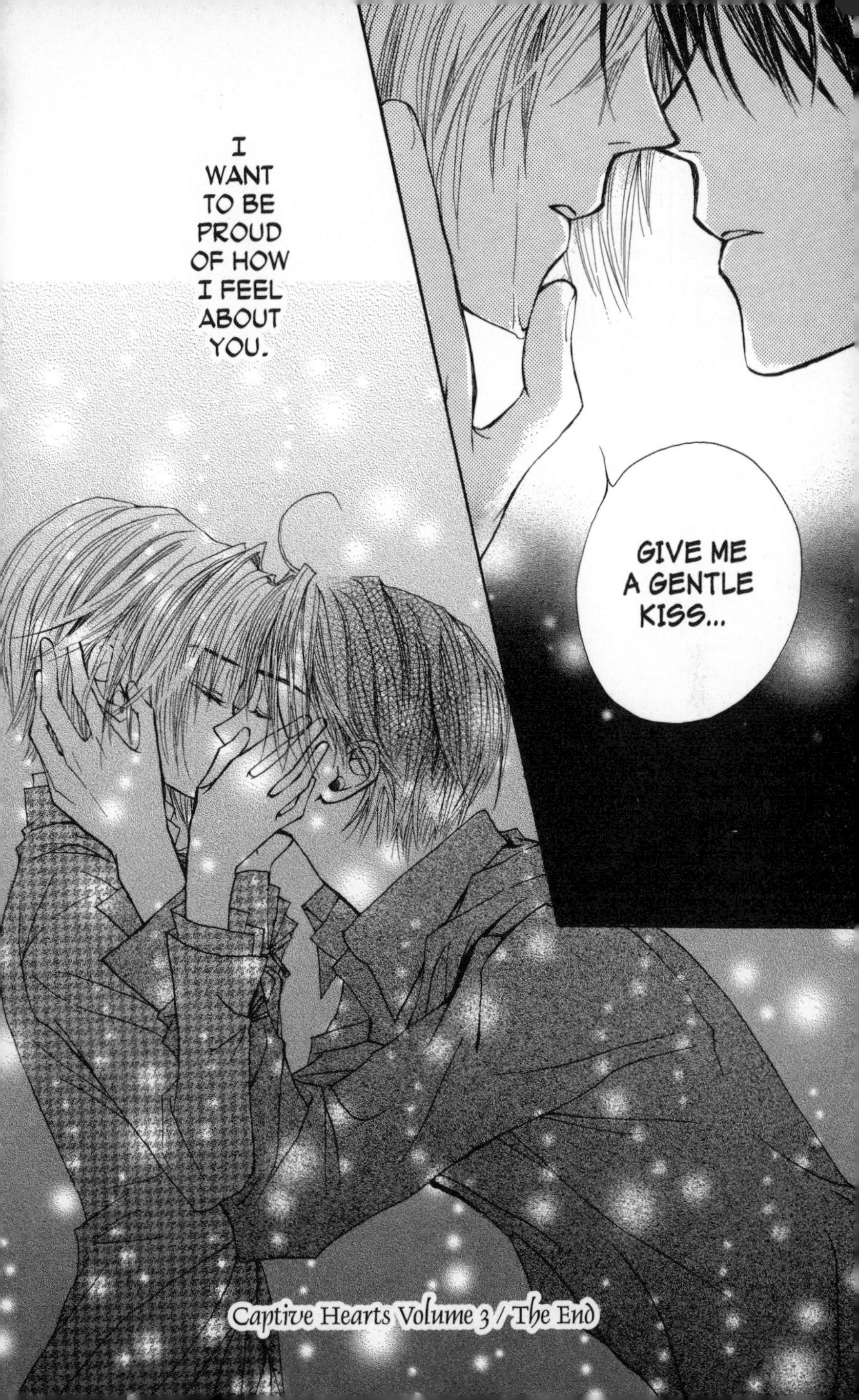
GIVE ME A GENTLE KISS...
I WANT TO BE PROUD OF HOW I FEEL ABOUT YOU.
Captive Hearts Volume 3 / The End

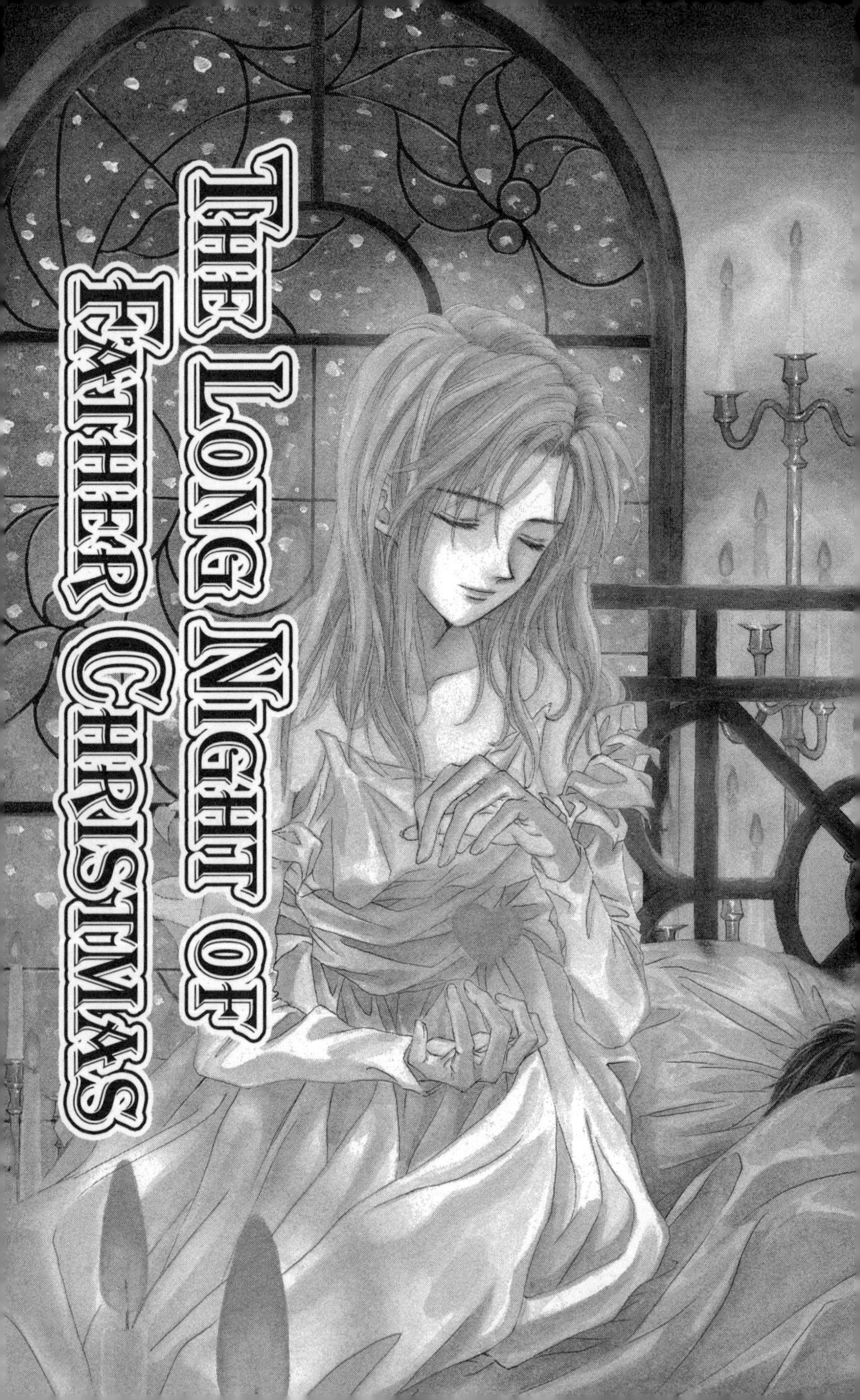
The Long Night of Father Christmas

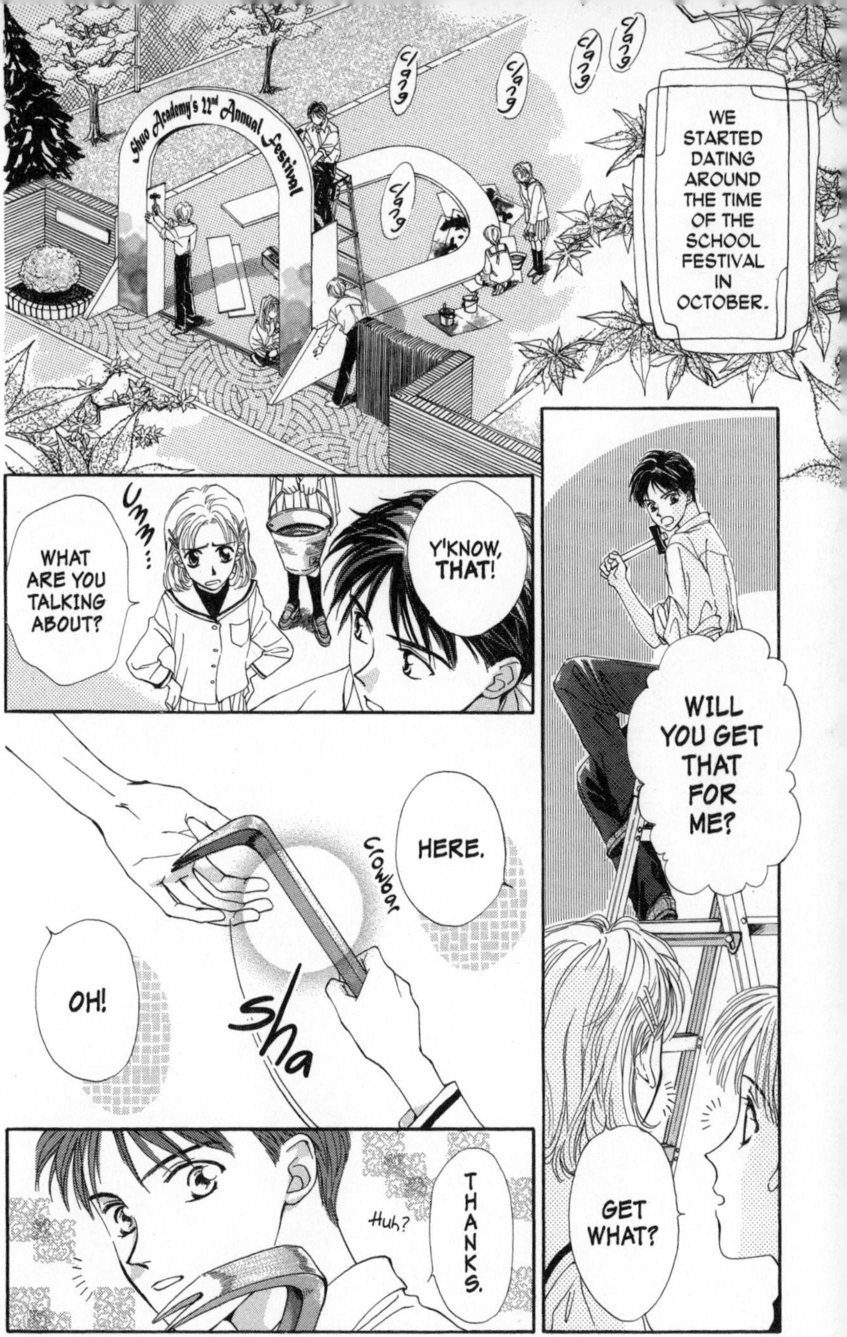
clang
clang
clang
clang
clang
Shuo Academy's 22nd Annual Festival
WE STARTED DATING AROUND THE TIME OF THE SCHOOL FESTIVAL IN OCTOBER.
WILL YOU GET THAT FOR ME?
GET WHAT?
Y'KNOW, THAT!
Umm...
WHAT ARE YOU TALKING ABOUT?
HERE.
Crowbar
OH!
sha
THANKS.
Huh?

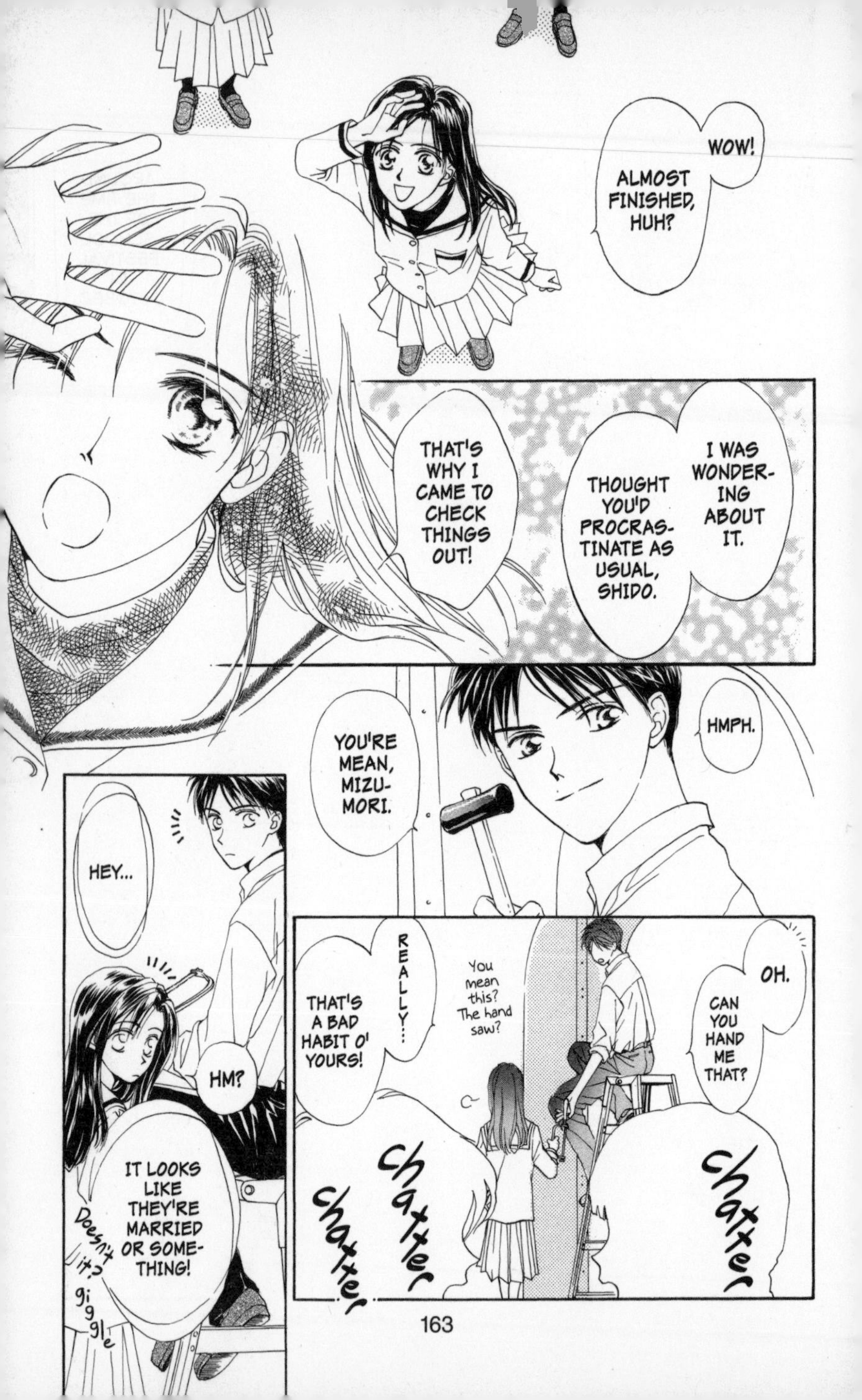
WOW!
ALMOST FINISHED, HUH?
I WAS WONDERING ABOUT IT.
THOUGHT YOU'D PROCRASTINATE AS USUAL, SHIDO.
THAT'S WHY I CAME TO CHECK THINGS OUT!
HMPH.
YOU'RE MEAN, MIZUMORI.
OH.
CAN YOU HAND ME THAT?
You mean this? The hand saw?
REALLY...
THAT'S A BAD HABIT O' YOURS!
Chatter
Chatter
chatter
HEY...
HM?
IT LOOKS LIKE THEY'RE MARRIED OR SOMETHING!
Doesn't it?
giggle

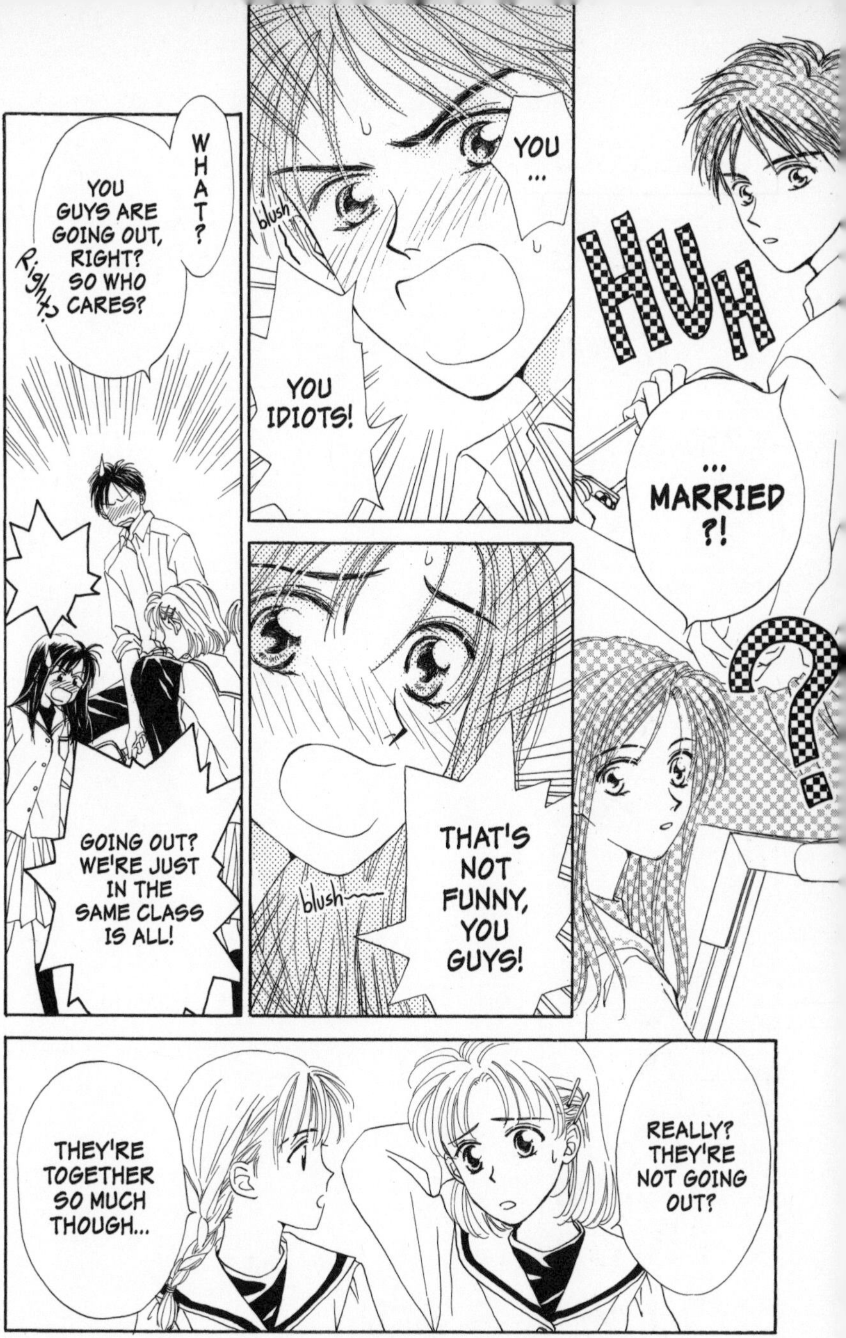
HUH
... MARRIED ?!
?
YOU ...
YOU IDIOTS!
blush
THAT'S NOT FUNNY, YOU GUYS!
blush~~
WHAT?
YOU GUYS ARE GOING OUT, RIGHT? SO WHO CARES?
Right?
GOING OUT? WE'RE JUST IN THE SAME CLASS IS ALL!
REALLY? THEY'RE NOT GOING OUT?
THEY'RE TOGETHER SO MUCH THOUGH...

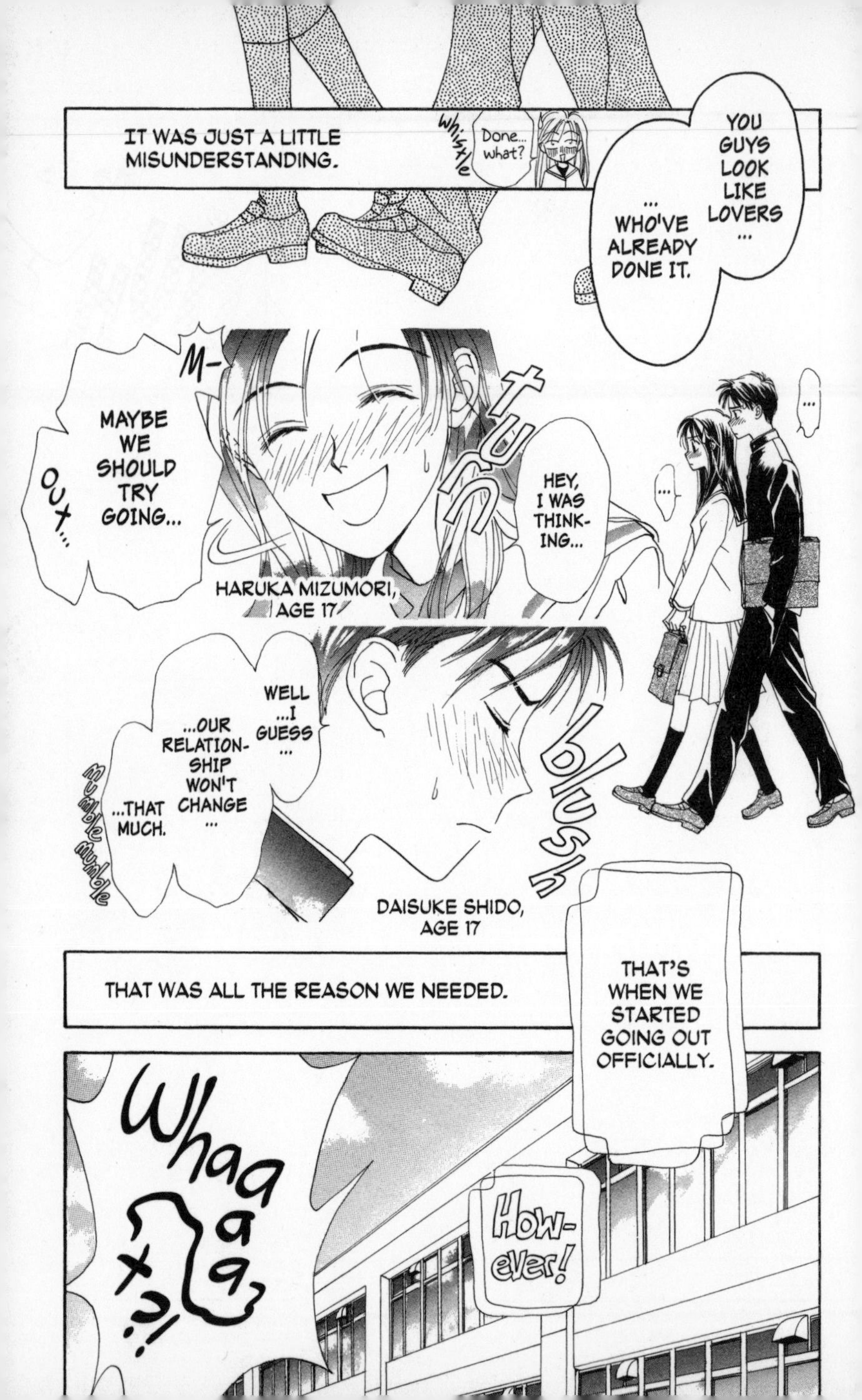
YOU GUYS LOOK LIKE LOVERS ...
... WHO'VE ALREADY DONE IT.
whistle
Done... what?
IT WAS JUST A LITTLE MISUNDERSTANDING.
...
...
tug
HEY, I WAS THINKING-ING...
M-
MAYBE WE SHOULD TRY GOING...
OUT...
HARUKA MIZUMORI, AGE 17
blush
WELL ...I GUESS ...
...OUR RELATIONSHIP WON'T CHANGE ...
...THAT MUCH.
mumble mumble
DAISUKE SHIDO, AGE 17
THAT'S WHEN WE STARTED GOING OUT OFFICIALLY.
THAT WAS ALL THE REASON WE NEEDED.
However!
Whaaaaat?!

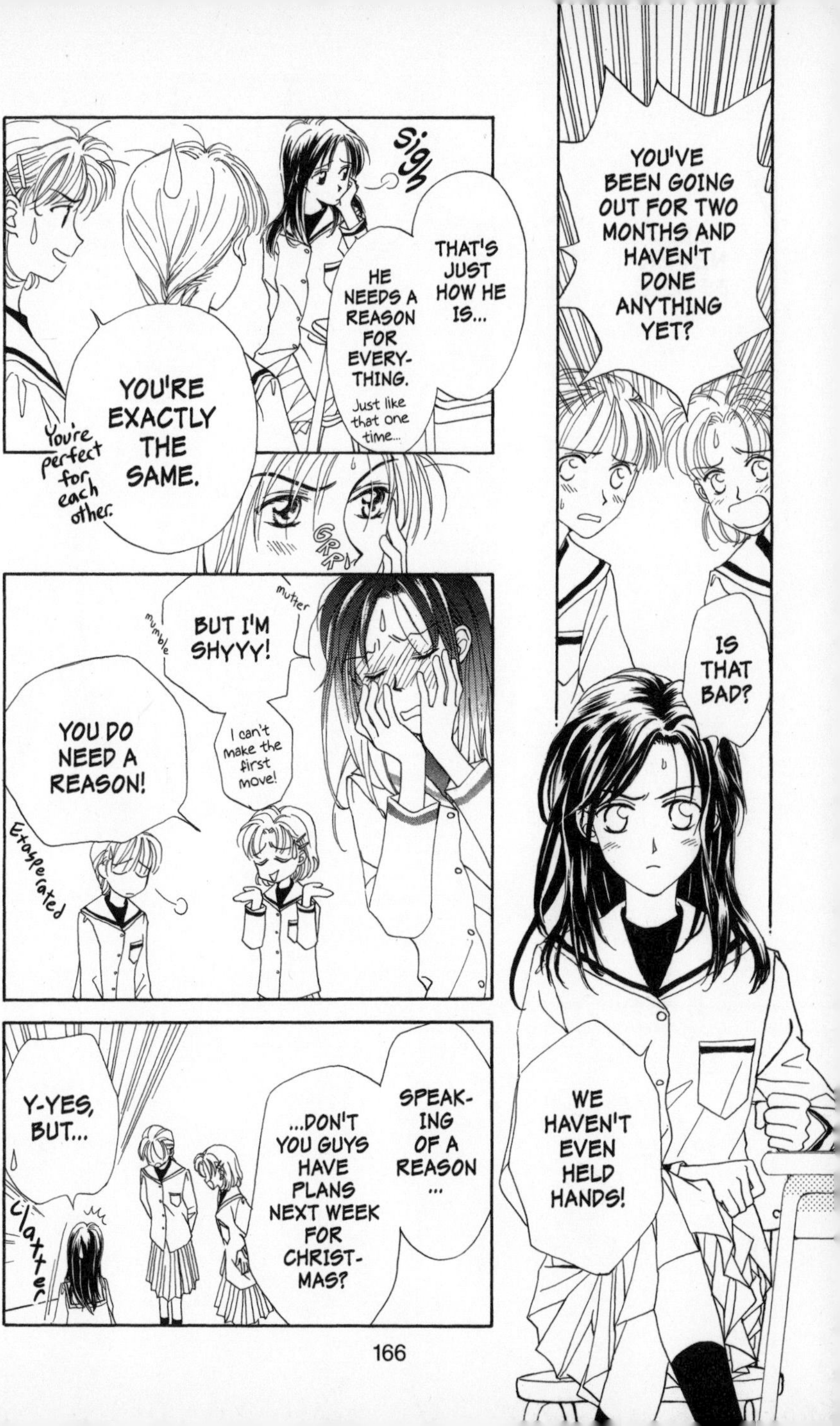
YOU'VE BEEN GOING OUT FOR TWO MONTHS AND HAVEN'T DONE ANYTHING YET?
IS THAT BAD?
WE HAVEN'T EVEN HELD HANDS!
Sigh
THAT'S JUST HOW HE IS...
HE NEEDS A REASON FOR EVERY-THING.
Just like that one time...
YOU'RE EXACTLY THE SAME.
You're perfect for each other.
GRR
mutter
BUT I'M SHYYY!
mumble
I can't make the first move!
YOU DO NEED A REASON!
Exasperated
SPEAK-ING OF A REASON ...
...DON'T YOU GUYS HAVE PLANS NEXT WEEK FOR CHRIST-MAS?
Y-YES, BUT...
Clatter

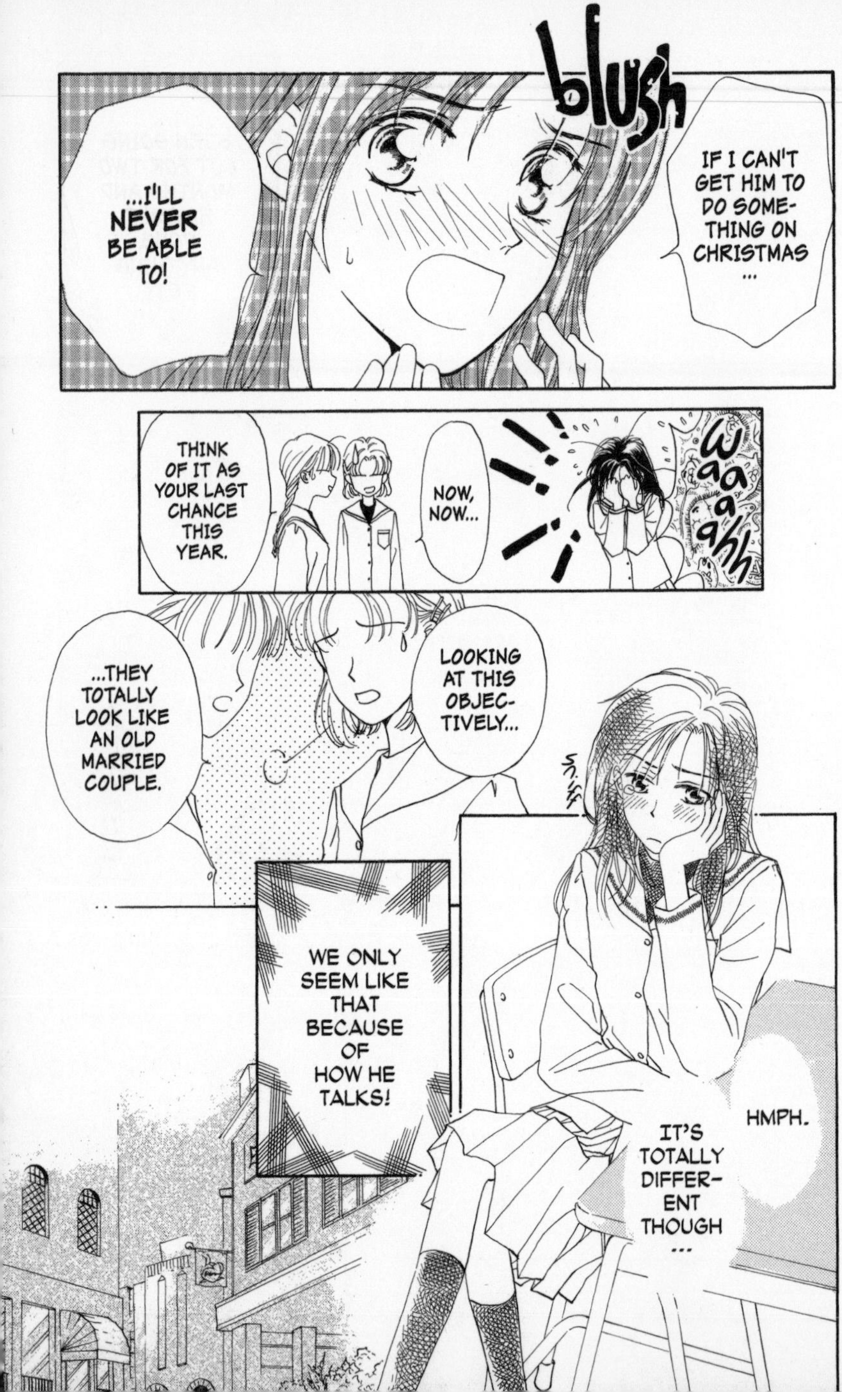
blush
IF I CAN'T GET HIM TO DO SOMETHING ON CHRISTMAS ...
...I'LL **NEVER** BE ABLE TO!
Waaaahh
NOW, NOW...
THINK OF IT AS YOUR LAST CHANCE THIS YEAR.
LOOKING AT THIS OBJECTIVELY...
...THEY TOTALLY LOOK LIKE AN OLD MARRIED COUPLE.
sniff
HMPH.
IT'S TOTALLY DIFFERENT THOUGH ...
WE ONLY SEEM LIKE THAT BECAUSE OF HOW HE TALKS!

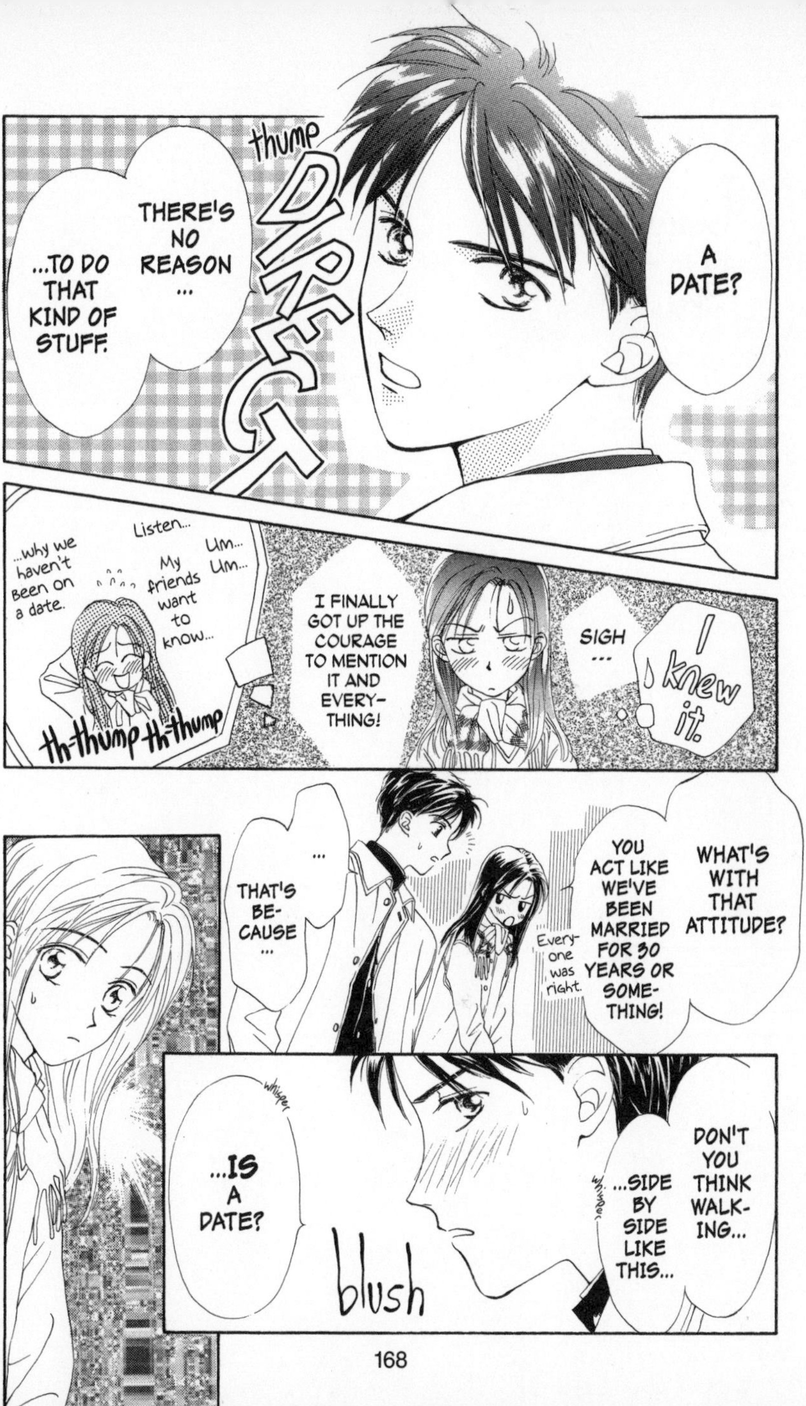
A DATE?
THERE'S NO REASON...
...TO DO THAT KIND OF STUFF.
thump
DIRECT
I knew it.
SIGH...
I FINALLY GOT UP THE COURAGE TO MENTION IT AND EVERYTHING!
Um... Um...
Listen...
My friends want to know...
...why we haven't been on a date.
th-thump th-thump
WHAT'S WITH THAT ATTITUDE?
YOU ACT LIKE WE'VE BEEN MARRIED FOR 30 YEARS OR SOMETHING!
Every-one was right.
...
THAT'S BE-CAUSE...
DON'T YOU THINK WALK-ING...
...SIDE BY SIDE LIKE THIS...
whisper
...IS A DATE?
whisper
blush

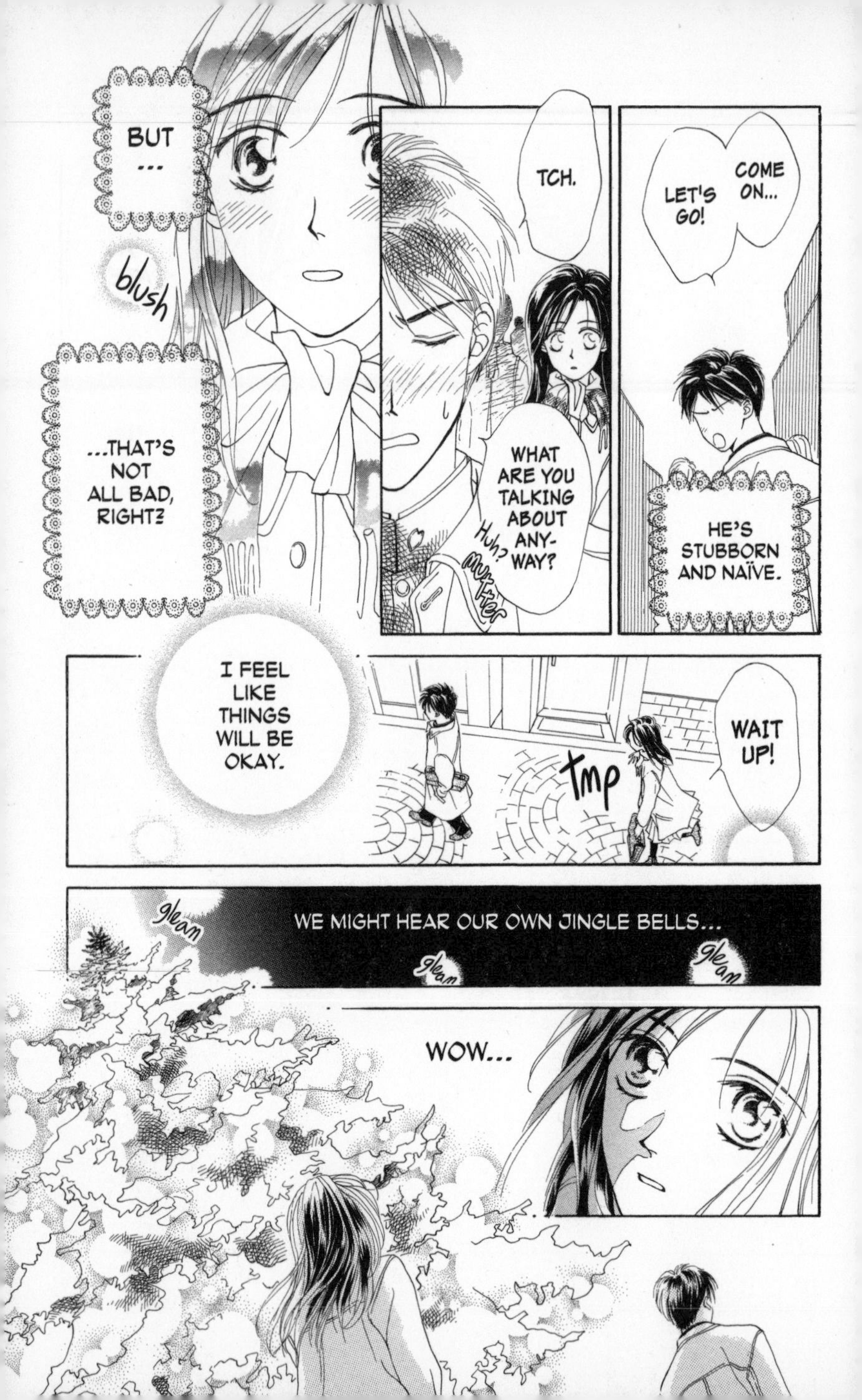
COME ON...
LET'S GO!
HE'S STUBBORN AND NAÏVE.
TCH.
WHAT ARE YOU TALKING ABOUT ANY-WAY?
Huh?
mutter
BUT ...
blush
...THAT'S NOT ALL BAD, RIGHT?
WAIT UP!
tmp
I FEEL LIKE THINGS WILL BE OKAY.
gleam
WE MIGHT HEAR OUR OWN JINGLE BELLS...
gleam
gleam
WOW...

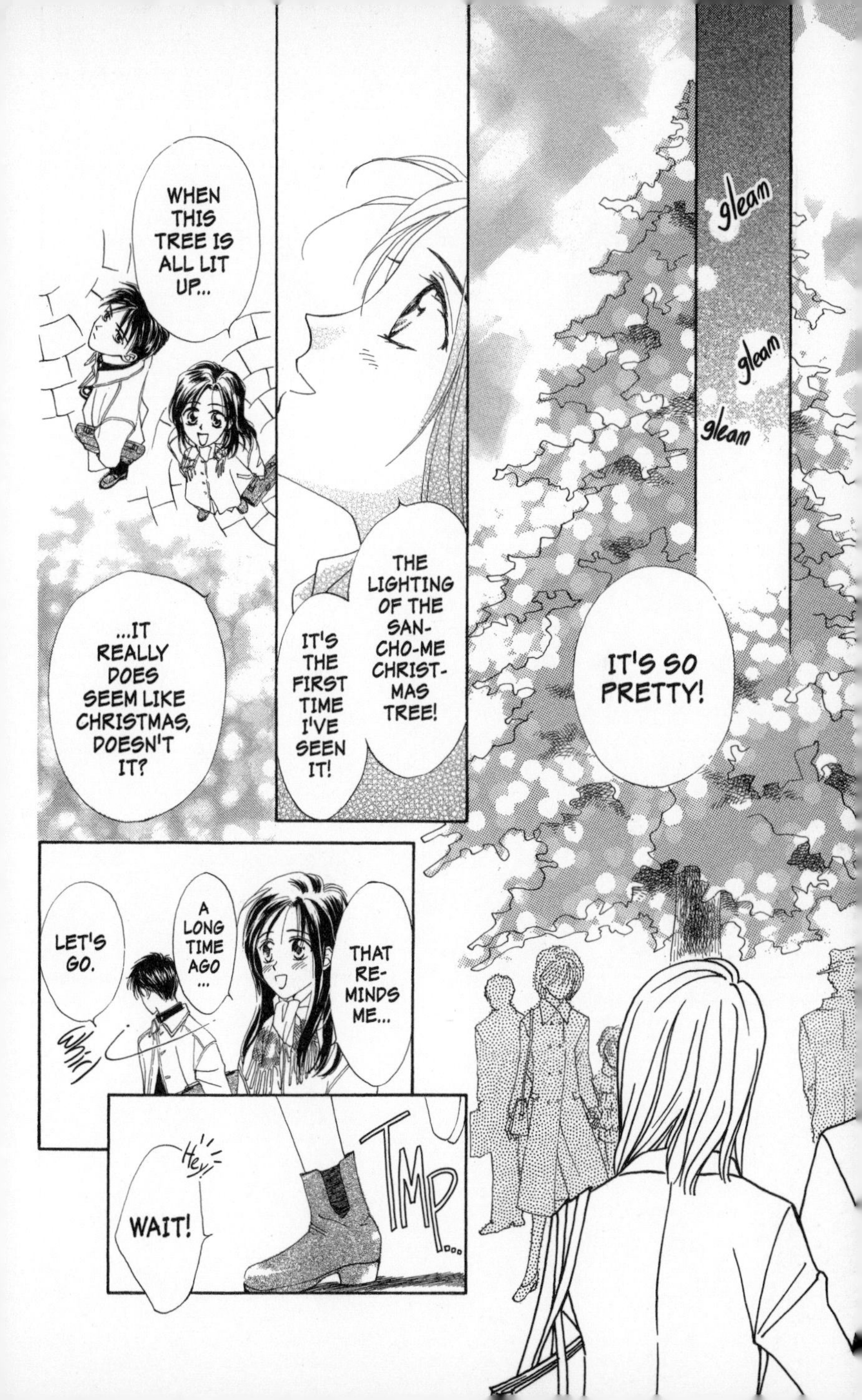
gleam
gleam
gleam
IT'S SO PRETTY!
THE LIGHTING OF THE SAN-CHO-ME CHRIST-MAS TREE!
IT'S THE FIRST TIME I'VE SEEN IT!
WHEN THIS TREE IS ALL LIT UP...
...IT REALLY DOES SEEM LIKE CHRISTMAS, DOESN'T IT?
THAT RE-MINDS ME...
A LONG TIME AGO...
LET'S GO.
whirl
TMP...
Hey!
WAIT!

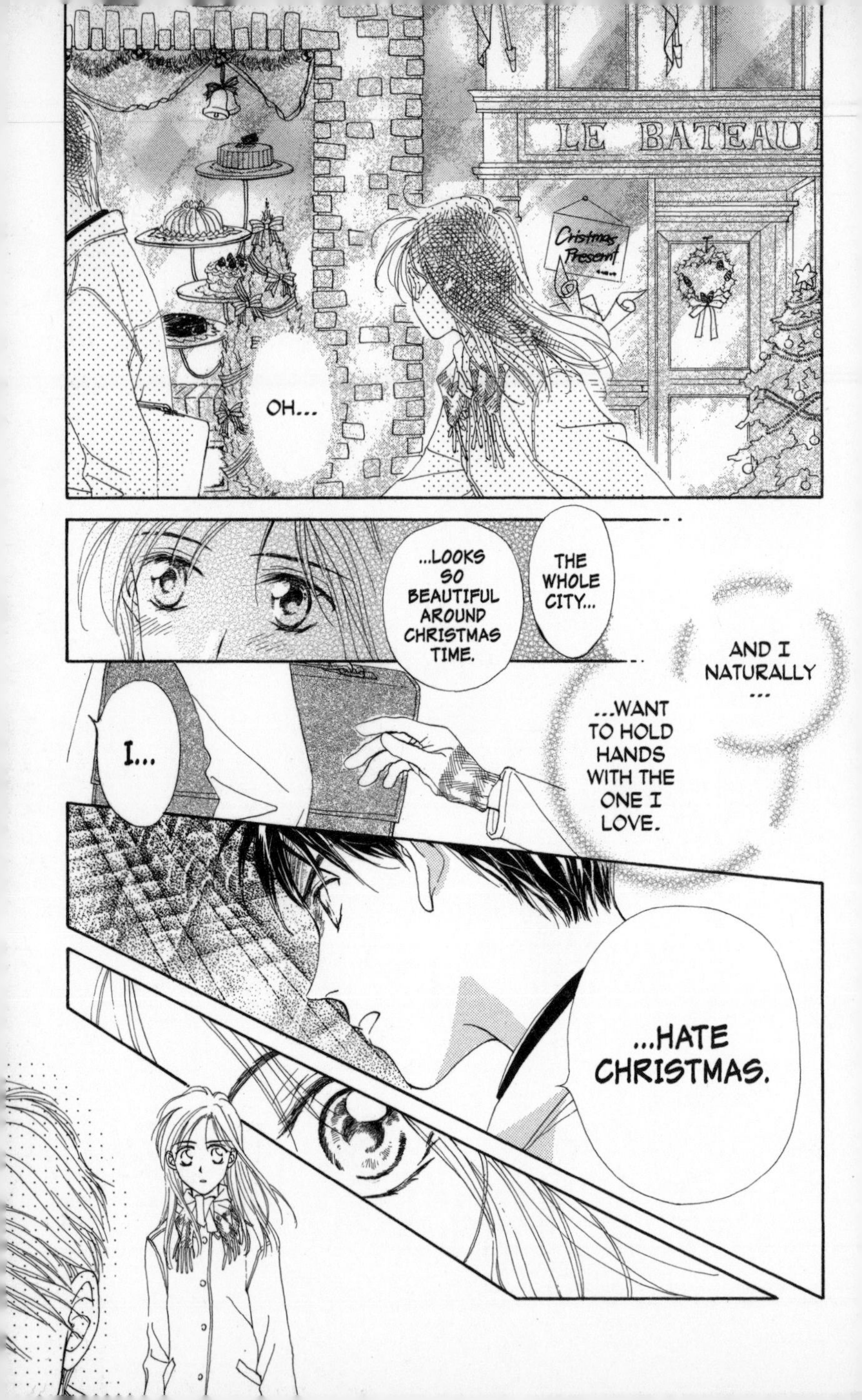
LE BATEAU
Cristmas Present
OH...
THE WHOLE CITY...
...LOOKS SO BEAUTIFUL AROUND CHRISTMAS TIME.
AND I NATURALLY ...
...WANT TO HOLD HANDS WITH THE ONE I LOVE.
I...
...HATE CHRISTMAS.

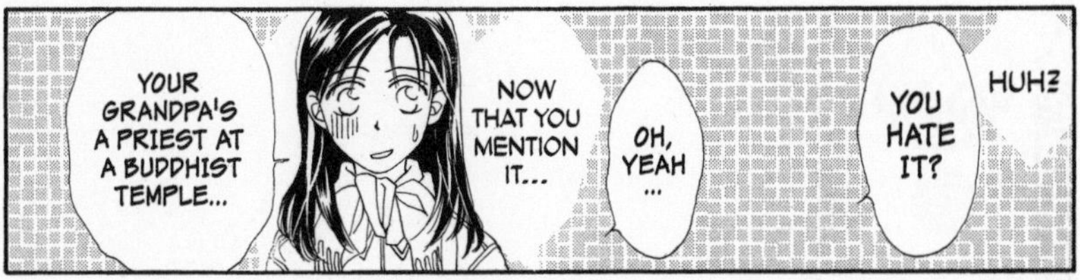
HUH?
YOU HATE IT?
OH, YEAH ...
NOW THAT YOU MENTION IT...
YOUR GRANDPA'S A PRIEST AT A BUDDHIST TEMPLE...

COULD THAT...BE THE REASON?

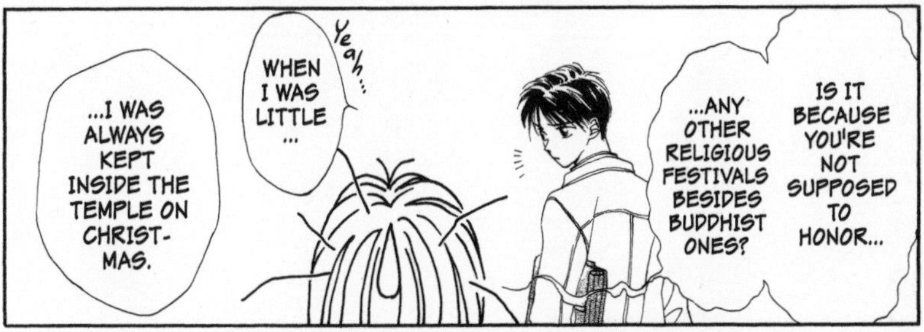
IS IT BECAUSE YOU'RE NOT SUPPOSED TO HONOR...
...ANY OTHER RELIGIOUS FESTIVALS BESIDES BUDDHIST ONES?
Yeah...
WHEN I WAS LITTLE ...
...I WAS ALWAYS KEPT INSIDE THE TEMPLE ON CHRIST-MAS.

CHRISTMAS PRESENT... CHRISTMAS DATE...

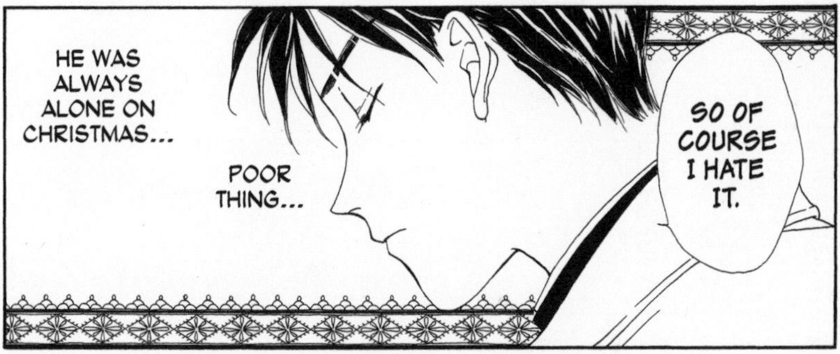
SO OF COURSE I HATE IT.
HE WAS ALWAYS ALONE ON CHRISTMAS...
POOR THING...

I HOPE HE CHANGES HIS MIND...

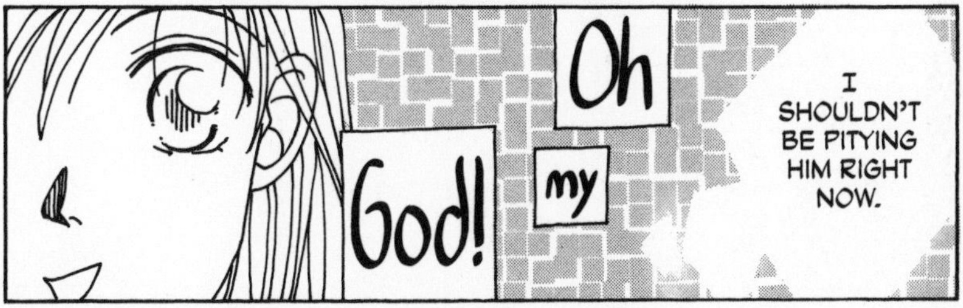
I SHOULDN'T BE PITYING HIM RIGHT NOW.
Oh my God!

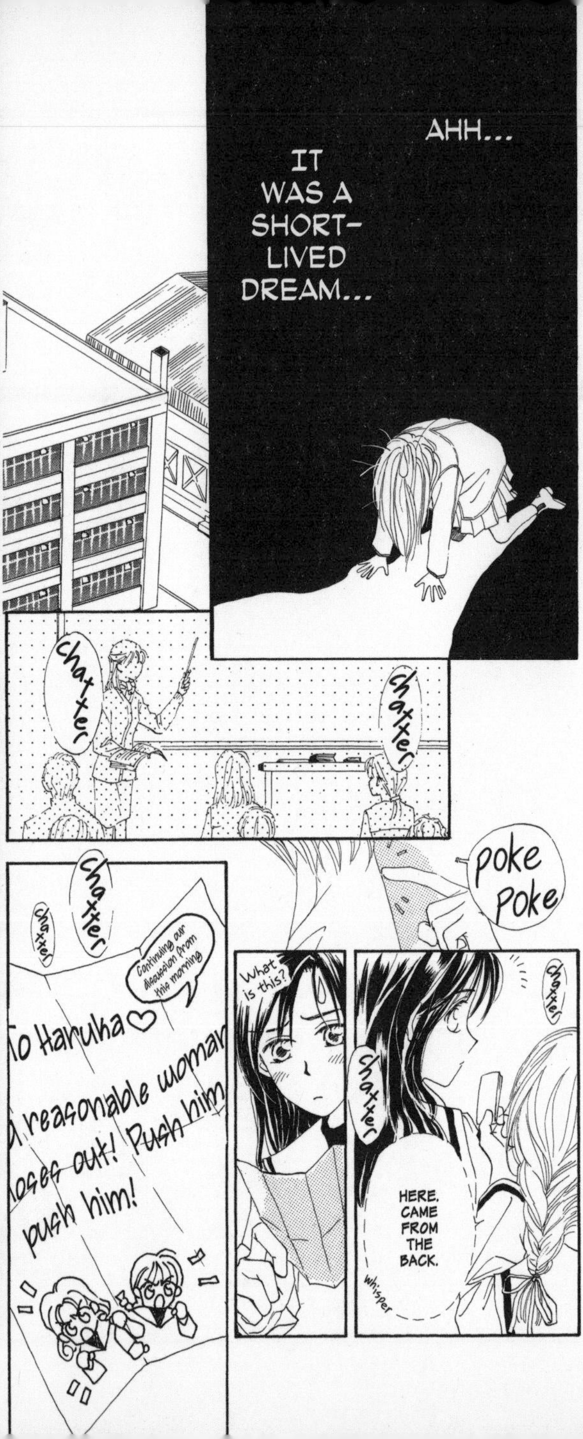
AHH...
IT WAS A SHORT-LIVED DREAM...
chatter
chatter
poke poke
chatter
HERE. CAME FROM THE BACK.
whisper
What is this?
chatter
chatter
Continuing our discussion from this morning
To Haruka ♡
reasonable woman loses out! Push him push him!

But if you're not high-strung, I don't think you can draw manga! I've decided to live as carefree as possible! (At least, that's the ideal I have...)

At some point, we transitioned from *Captive Hearts* to the manga on the right. This is a one-shot story I wrote three years ago. It's embarrassing. I wrote this one for myself. Hey, hey!

I'm usually stubborn about going to Christmas events, so this story was a message to myself—to relax about things.

But this story seems so stiff... I'm embarrassed...

Oh! I should say goodbye now. Thanks for reading!

From Masuri Hino, towards the end of 2000.

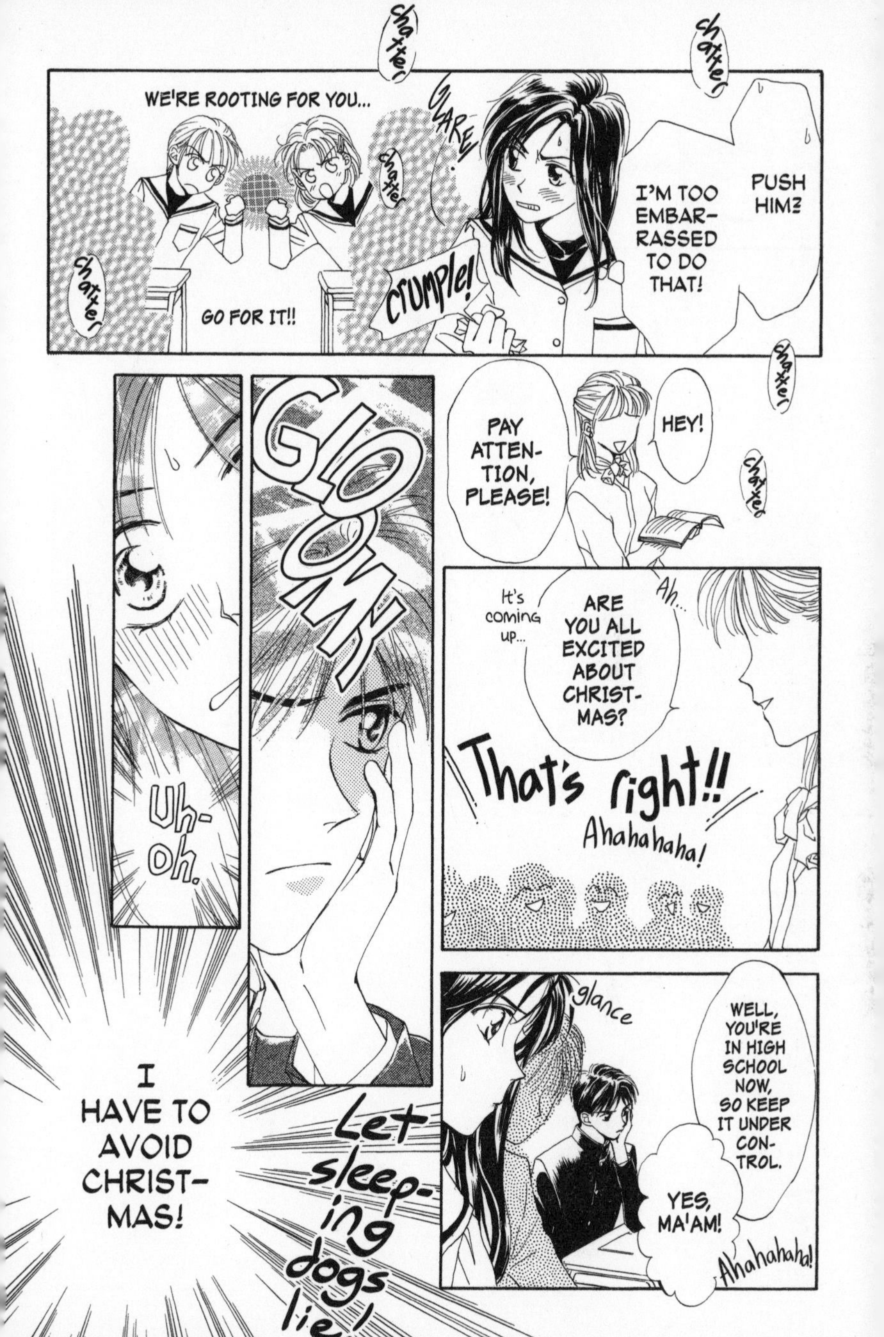
chatter
PUSH HIM?
I'M TOO EMBARRASSED TO DO THAT!
GLARE!
chatter
chatter
WE'RE ROOTING FOR YOU...
CRUMPLE!
GO FOR IT!!
chatter
chatter
HEY!
PAY ATTENTION, PLEASE!
chatter
Ah...
ARE YOU ALL EXCITED ABOUT CHRISTMAS?
It's coming up...
That's right!!
Ahahahaha!
glance
WELL, YOU'RE IN HIGH SCHOOL NOW, SO KEEP IT UNDER CONTROL.
YES, MA'AM!
Ahahahaha!
GLOOMY
Uh-oh.
I HAVE TO AVOID CHRISTMAS!
Let sleeping dogs lie!

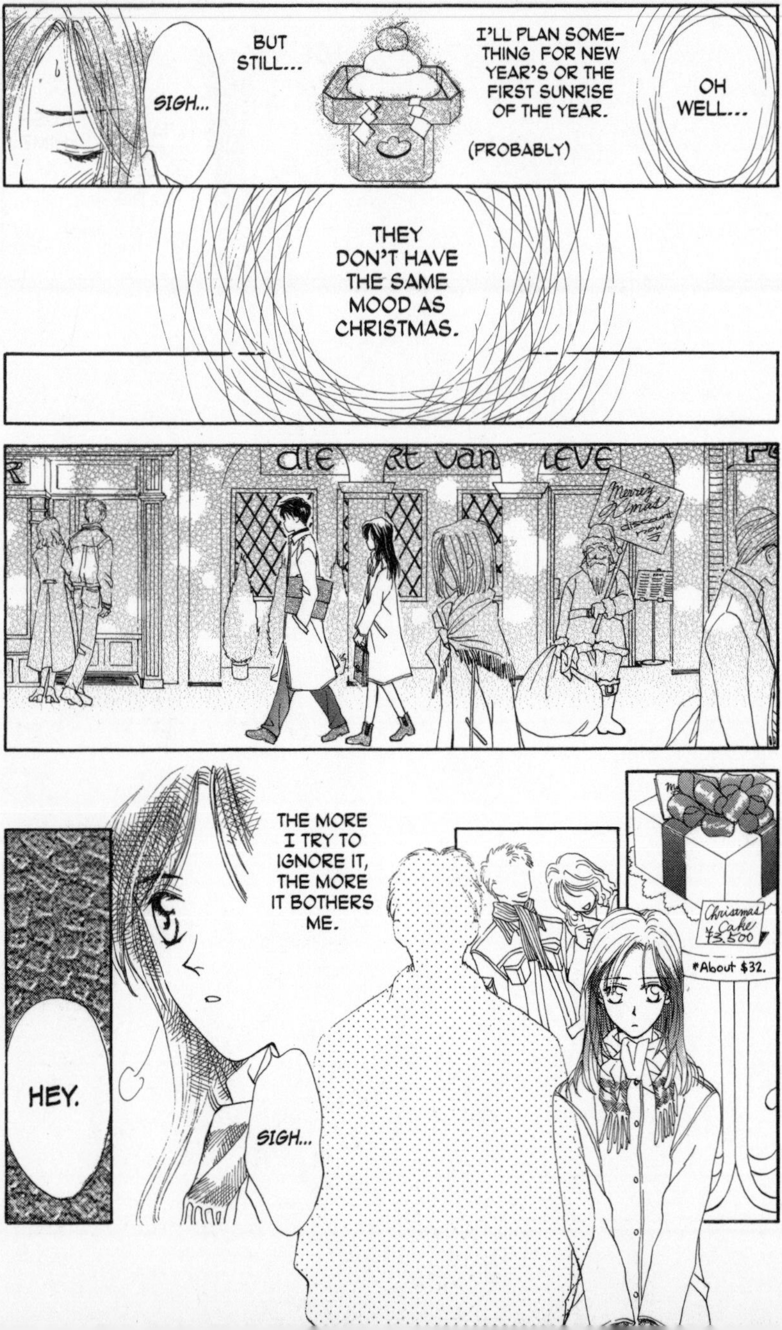
OH WELL...
I'LL PLAN SOME-THING FOR NEW YEAR'S OR THE FIRST SUNRISE OF THE YEAR.
(PROBABLY)
BUT STILL...
SIGH...
THEY DON'T HAVE THE SAME MOOD AS CHRISTMAS.
Christmas Cake ¥3,500
*About $32.
THE MORE I TRY TO IGNORE IT, THE MORE IT BOTHERS ME.
SIGH...
HEY.

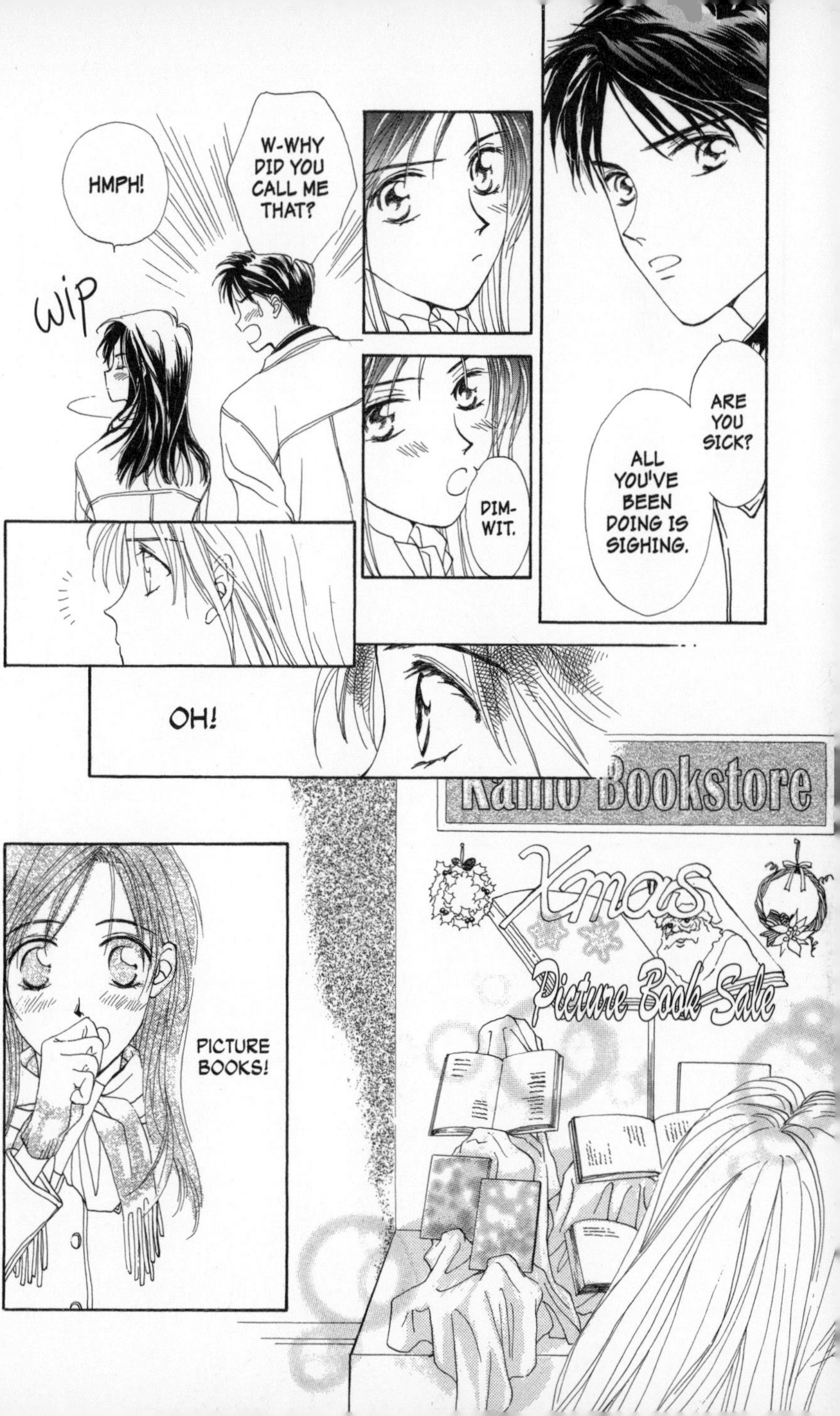

ARE YOU SICK?
ALL YOU'VE BEEN DOING IS SIGHING.
DIM-WIT.
W-WHY DID YOU CALL ME THAT?
HMPH!
wip
OH!
Bookstore
Xmas
Picture Book Sale
PICTURE BOOKS!

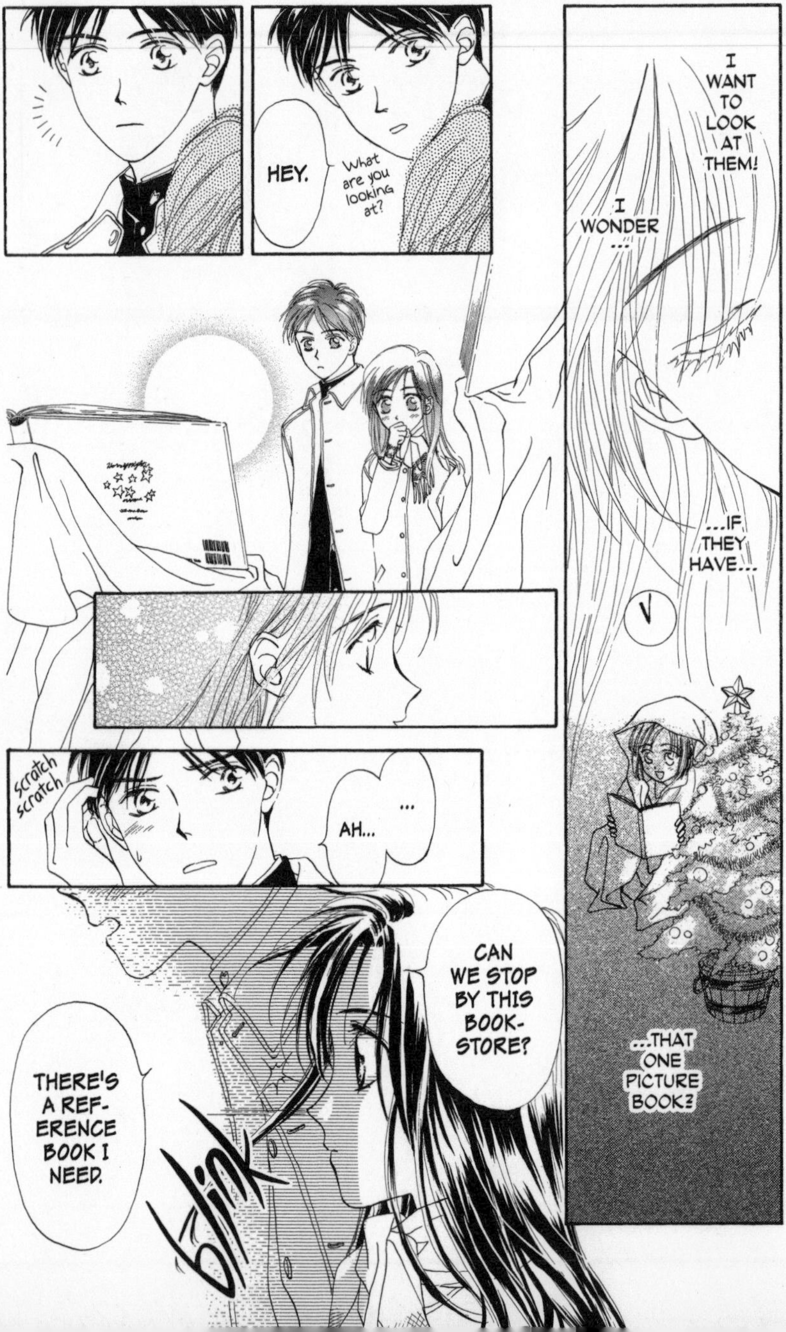
I WANT TO LOOK AT THEM!
I WONDER...
...IF THEY HAVE...
...THAT ONE PICTURE BOOK?
HEY.
What are you looking at?
...
AH...
scratch scratch
CAN WE STOP BY THIS BOOK-STORE?
THERE'S A REFERENCE BOOK I NEED.
blink

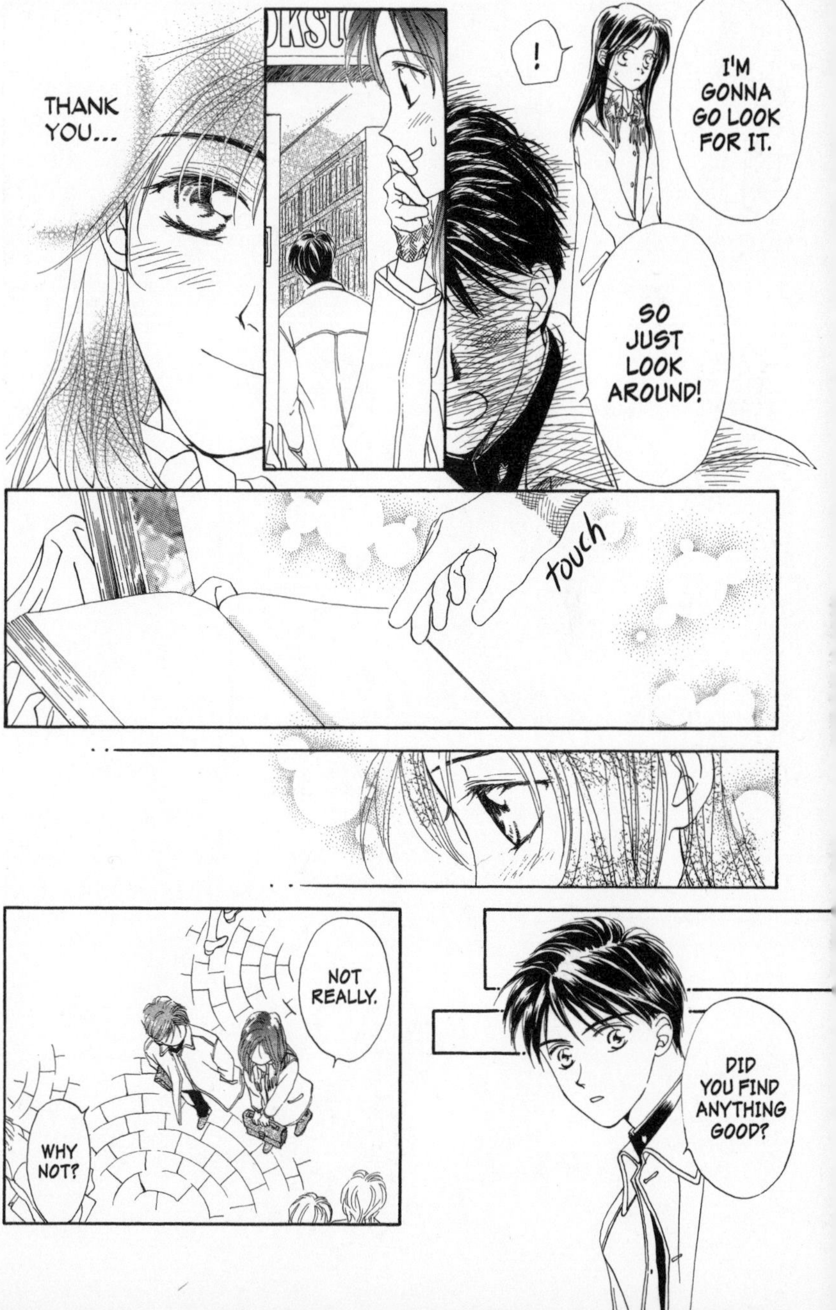
I'M GONNA GO LOOK FOR IT.
!
SO JUST LOOK AROUND!
THANK YOU...
touch
DID YOU FIND ANYTHING GOOD?
NOT REALLY.
WHY NOT?

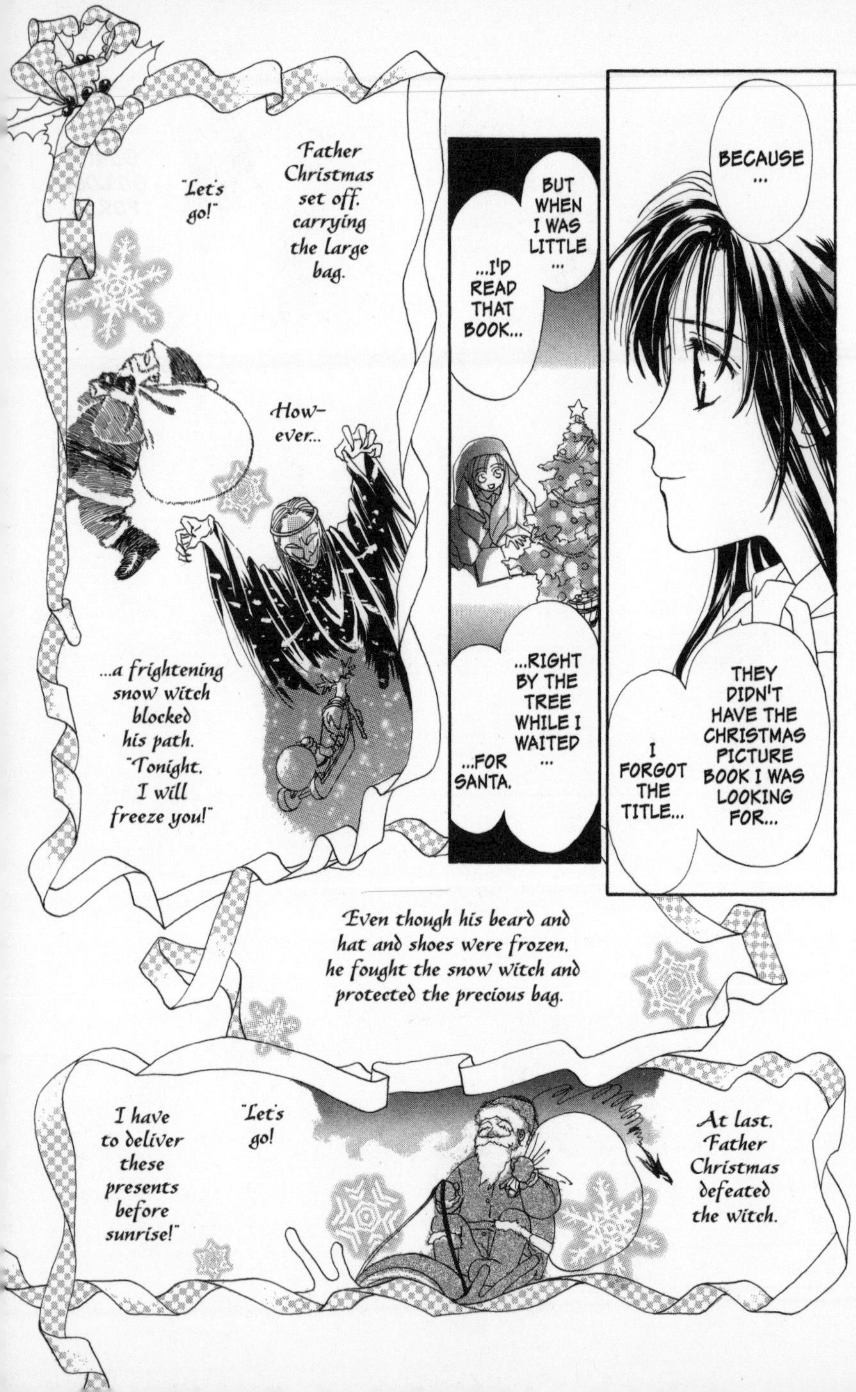
BECAUSE ...
THEY DIDN'T HAVE THE CHRISTMAS PICTURE BOOK I WAS LOOKING FOR...
I FORGOT THE TITLE...
BUT WHEN I WAS LITTLE ...
...I'D READ THAT BOOK...
...RIGHT BY THE TREE WHILE I WAITED ...
...FOR SANTA.
Father Christmas set off, carrying the large bag.
"Let's go!"
How-ever...
...a frightening snow witch blocked his path. "Tonight, I will freeze you!"
Even though his beard and hat and shoes were frozen, he fought the snow witch and protected the precious bag.
At last, Father Christmas defeated the witch.
"Let's go!
I have to deliver these presents before sunrise!"

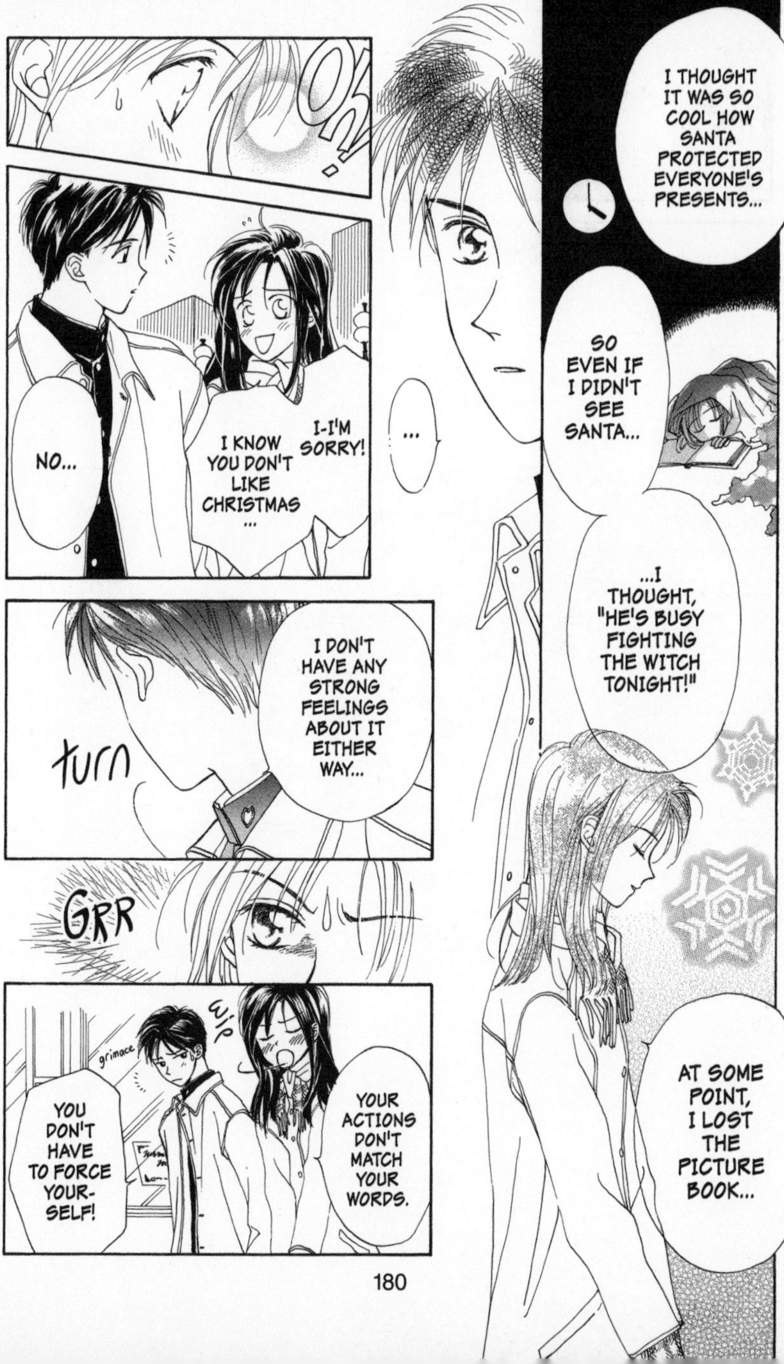
I THOUGHT IT WAS SO COOL HOW SANTA PROTECTED EVERYONE'S PRESENTS...
SO EVEN IF I DIDN'T SEE SANTA...
...I THOUGHT, "HE'S BUSY FIGHTING THE WITCH TONIGHT!"
AT SOME POINT, I LOST THE PICTURE BOOK...
...
OH!
I-I'M SORRY!
I KNOW YOU DON'T LIKE CHRISTMAS ...
NO...
I DON'T HAVE ANY STRONG FEELINGS ABOUT IT EITHER WAY...
turn
GRR
grimace
YOUR ACTIONS DON'T MATCH YOUR WORDS.
YOU DON'T HAVE TO FORCE YOURSELF!

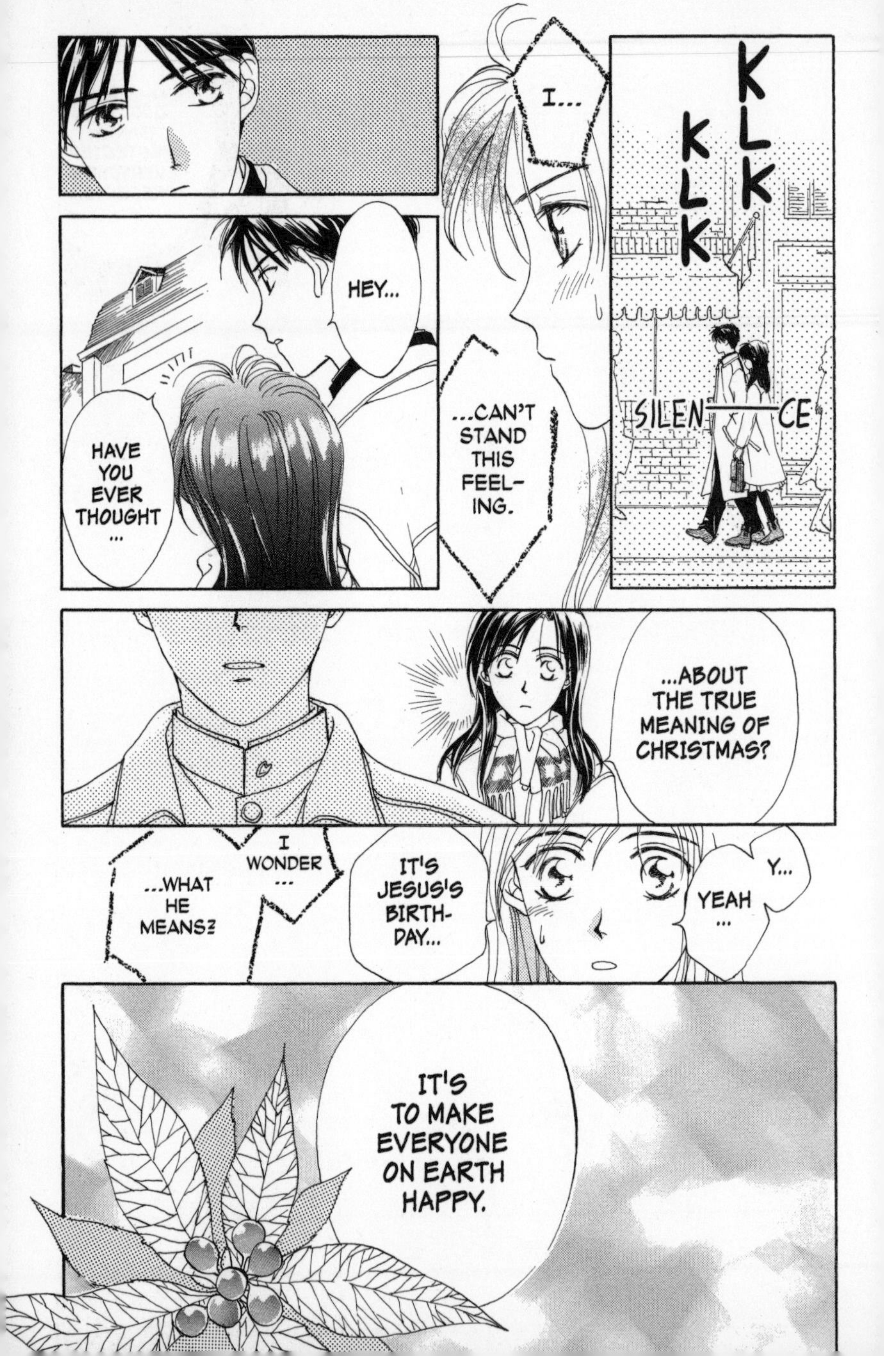
KLK KLK
SILENCE
I...
...CAN'T STAND THIS FEELING.
HEY...
HAVE YOU EVER THOUGHT...
...ABOUT THE TRUE MEANING OF CHRISTMAS?
Y... YEAH...
IT'S JESUS'S BIRTHDAY...
I WONDER...
...WHAT HE MEANS?
IT'S TO MAKE EVERYONE ON EARTH HAPPY.

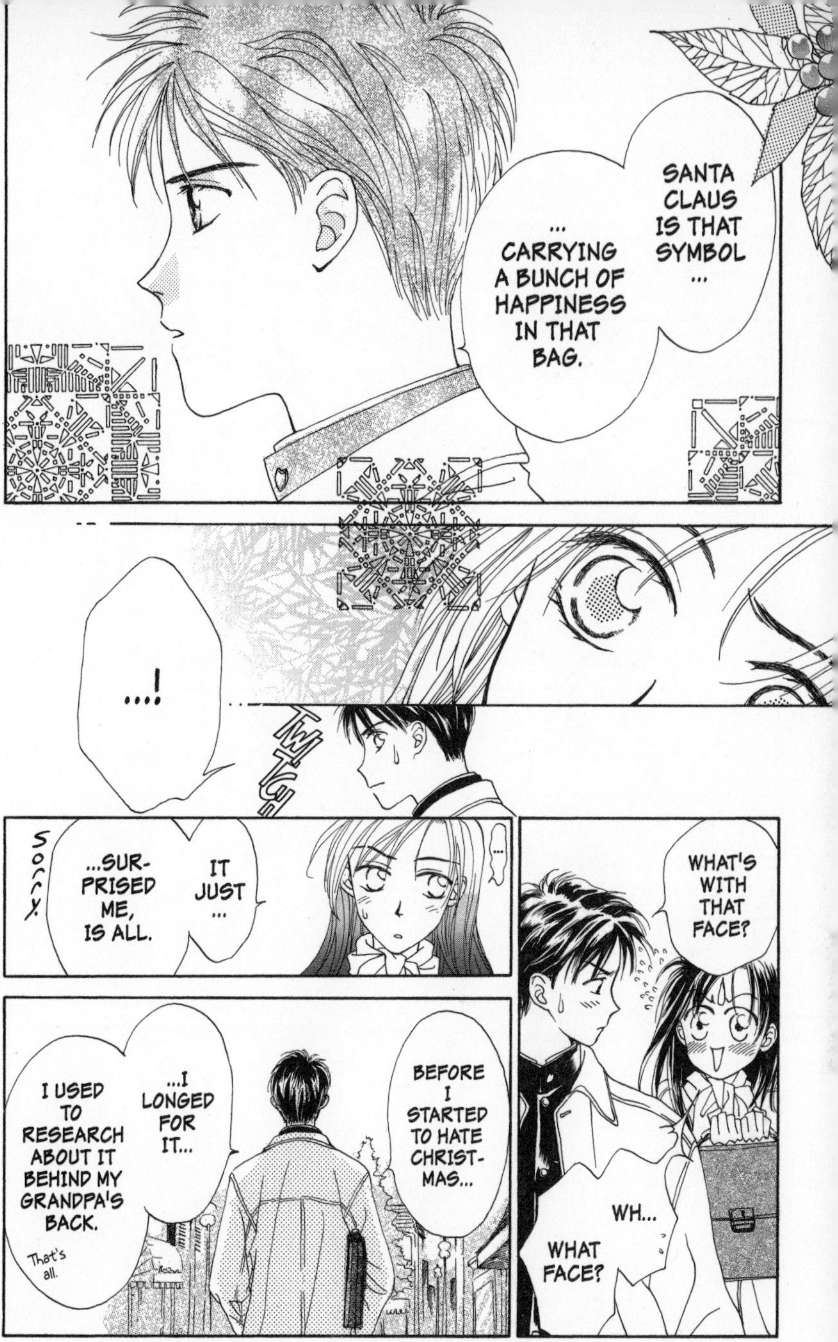
SANTA CLAUS IS THAT SYMBOL...
...CARRYING A BUNCH OF HAPPINESS IN THAT BAG.
...!
TWITCH
WHAT'S WITH THAT FACE?
WH... WHAT FACE?
...
IT JUST...
...SURPRISED ME, IS ALL.
Sorry.
BEFORE I STARTED TO HATE CHRISTMAS...
...I LONGED FOR IT...
I USED TO RESEARCH ABOUT IT BEHIND MY GRANDPA'S BACK.
That's all.

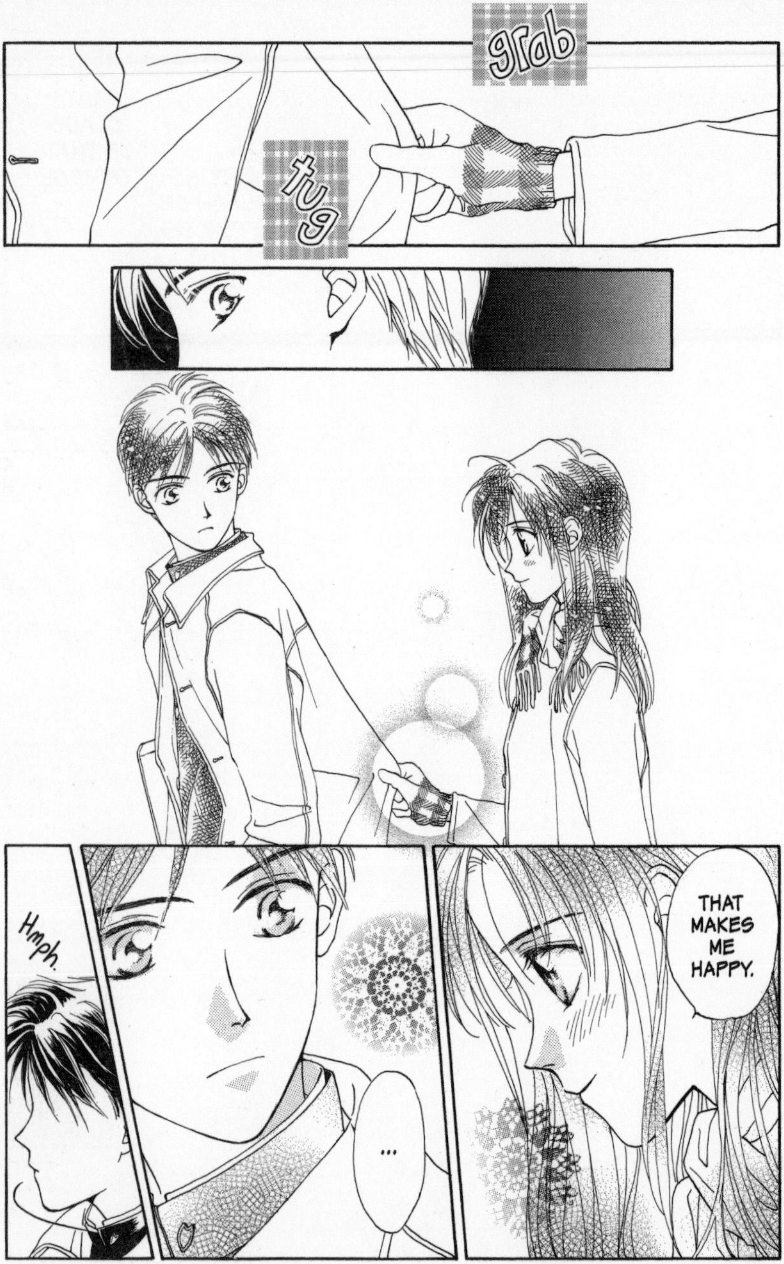
grab
tug
THAT MAKES ME HAPPY.
...
Hmph.

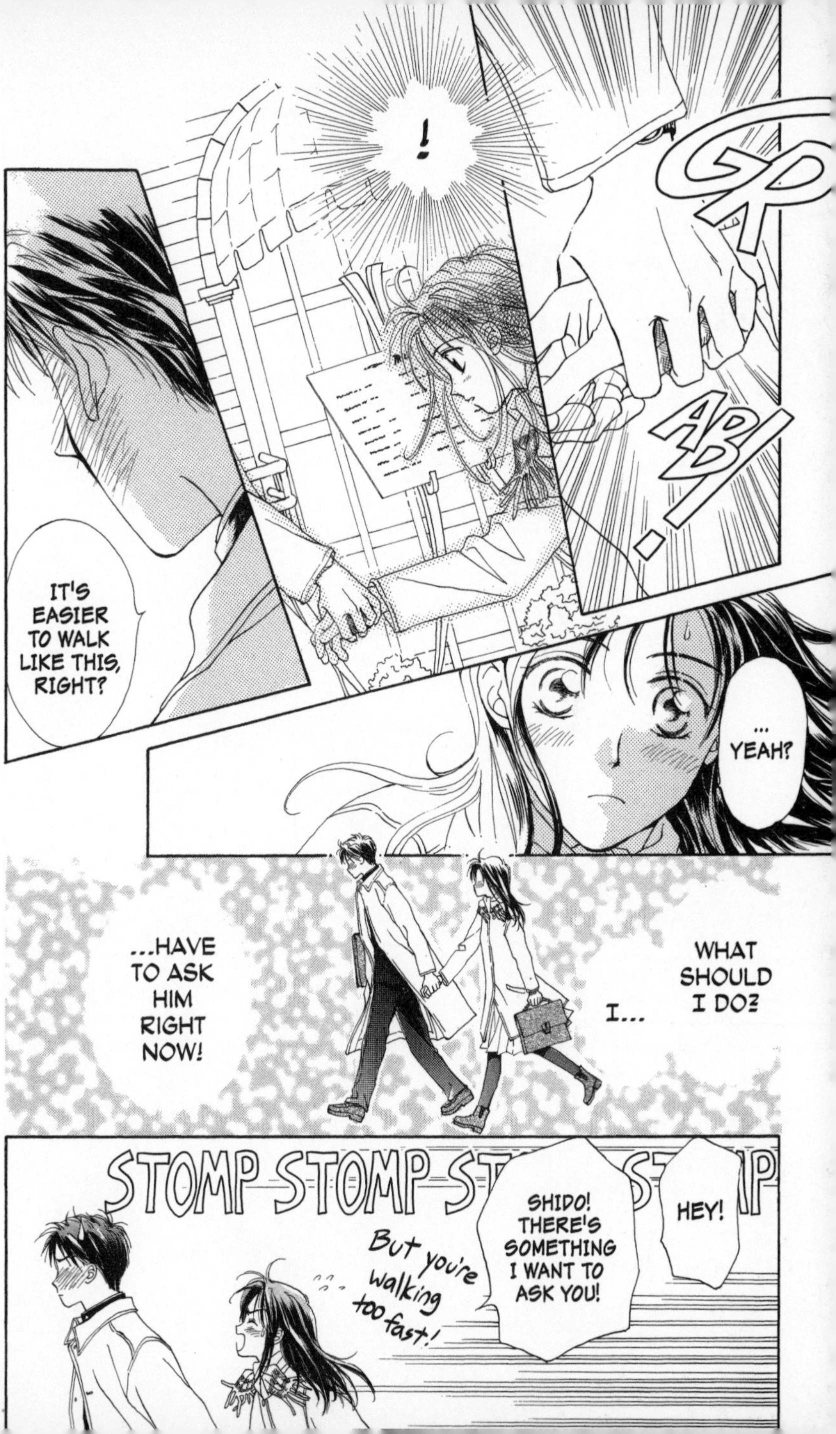
GR
AB!
!
IT'S EASIER TO WALK LIKE THIS, RIGHT?
...YEAH?
WHAT SHOULD I DO?
I...
...HAVE TO ASK HIM RIGHT NOW!
STOMP STOMP
HEY!
SHIDO! THERE'S SOMETHING I WANT TO ASK YOU!
But you're walking too fast!

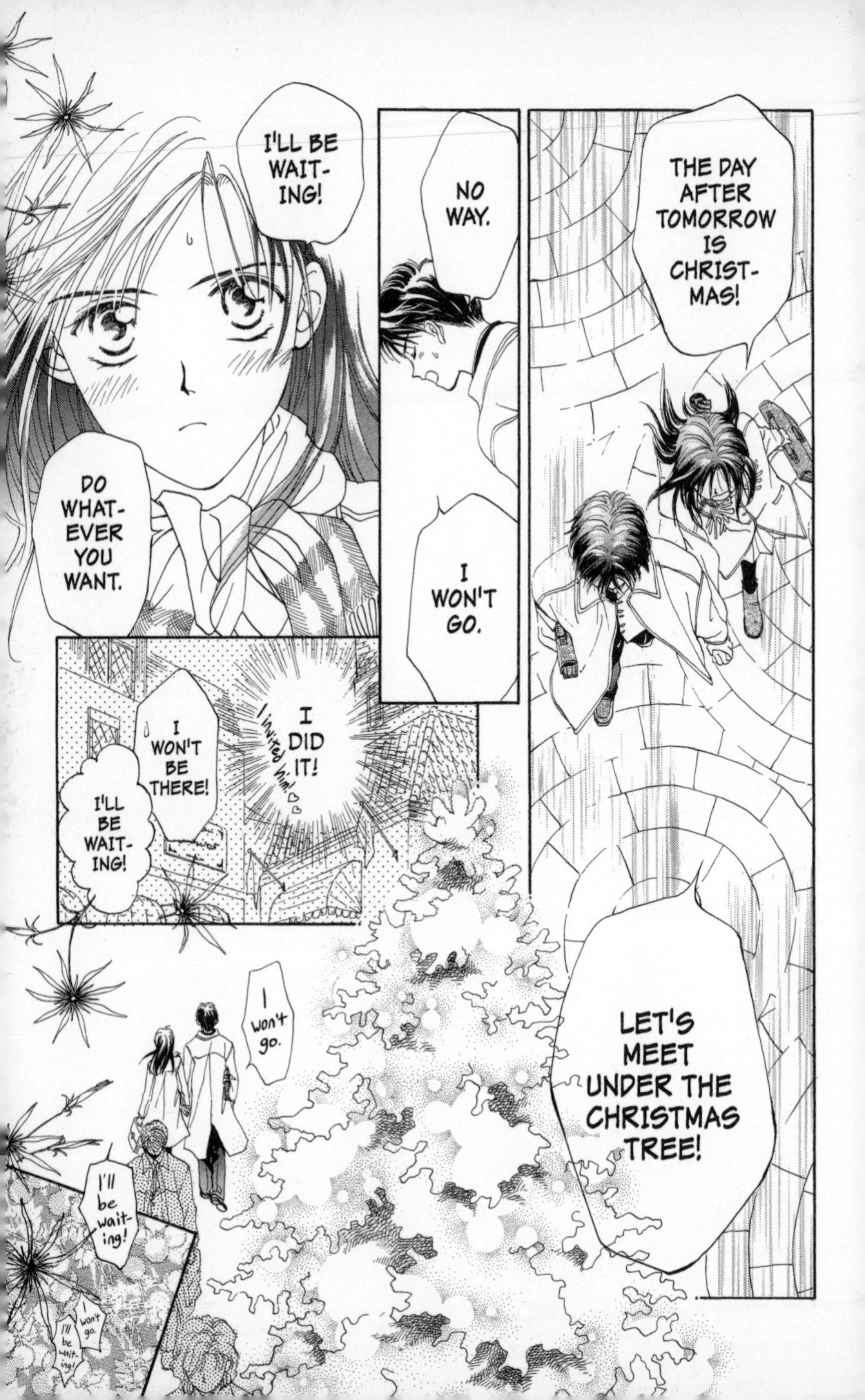
THE DAY AFTER TOMORROW IS CHRIST-MAS!
LET'S MEET UNDER THE CHRISTMAS TREE!
NO WAY.
I WON'T GO.
I'LL BE WAIT-ING!
DO WHAT-EVER YOU WANT.
I DID IT!
I invited him!
I WON'T BE THERE!
I'LL BE WAIT-ING!
I won't go.
I'll be wait-ing!
I won't go.
I'll be wait-ing!

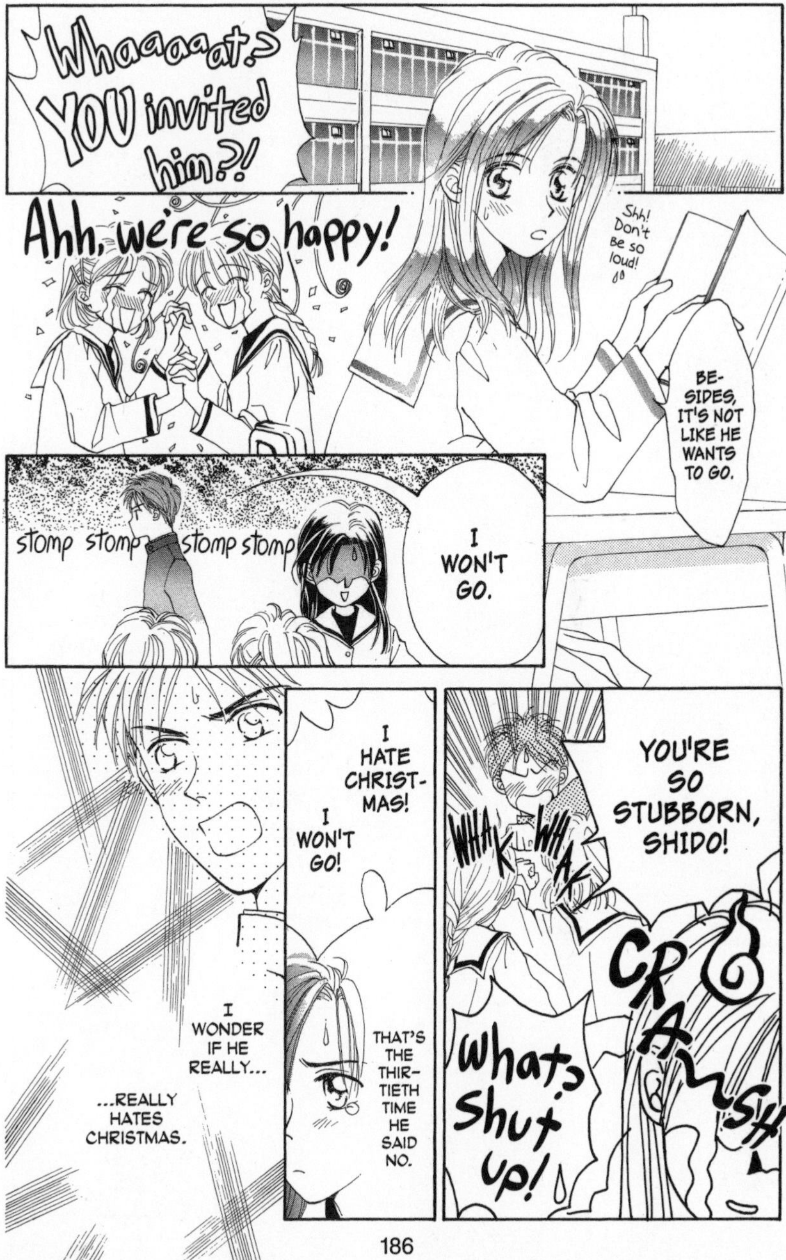
Whaaaaat? YOU invited him?!
Ahh, we're so happy!
Shh! Don't be so loud!
BE-SIDES, IT'S NOT LIKE HE WANTS TO GO.
stomp stomp stomp stomp
I WON'T GO.
YOU'RE SO STUBBORN, SHIDO!
WHAK WHAK
CRASH
What? Shut up!
I HATE CHRIST-MAS!
I WON'T GO!
THAT'S THE THIR-TIETH TIME HE SAID NO.
I WONDER IF HE REALLY...
...REALLY HATES CHRISTMAS.

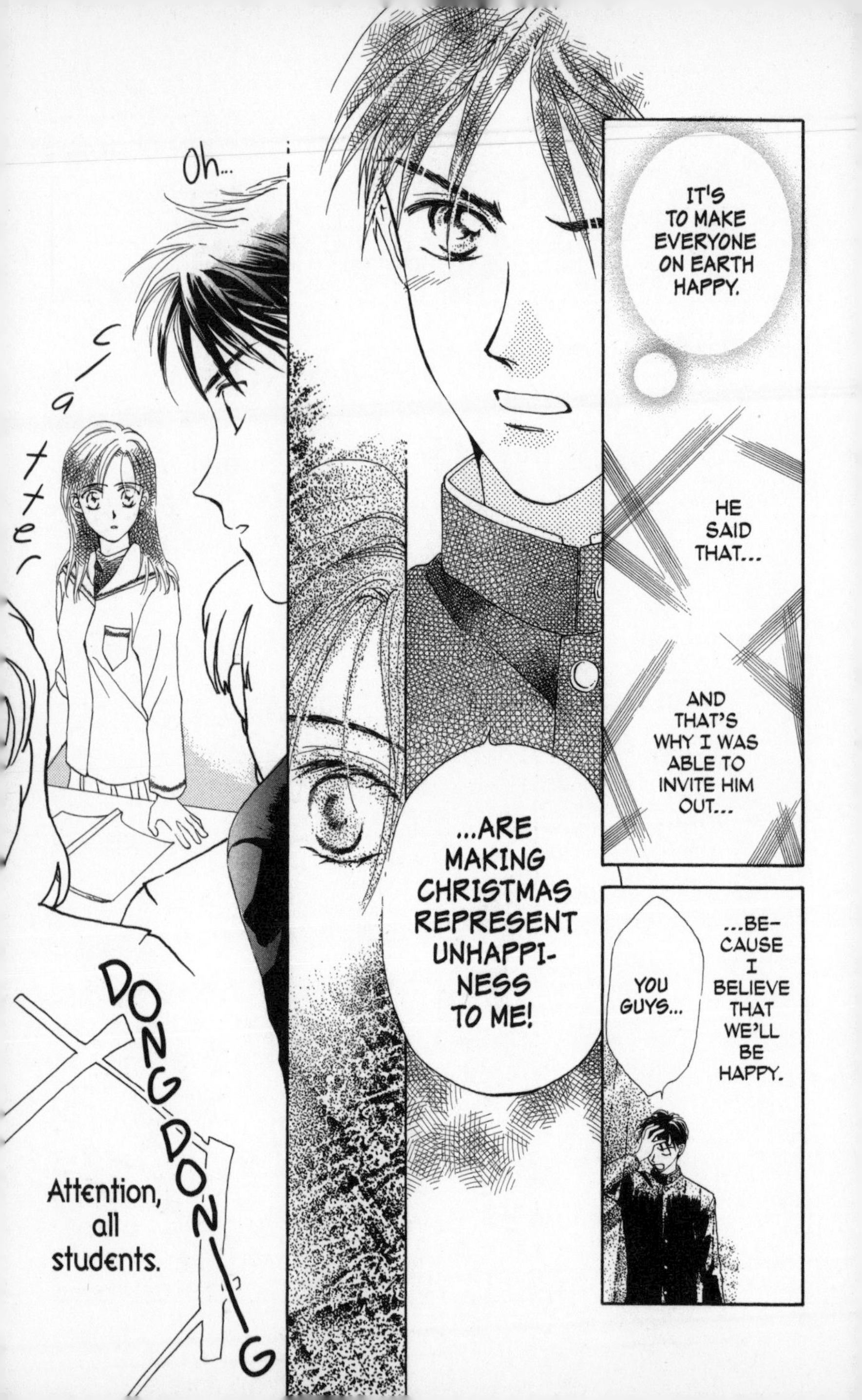
IT'S TO MAKE EVERYONE ON EARTH HAPPY.
HE SAID THAT...
AND THAT'S WHY I WAS ABLE TO INVITE HIM OUT...
...BE-CAUSE I BELIEVE THAT WE'LL BE HAPPY.
YOU GUYS...
...ARE MAKING CHRISTMAS REPRESENT UNHAPPI-NESS TO ME!
Oh...
clatter
DONG DONG
Attention, all students.

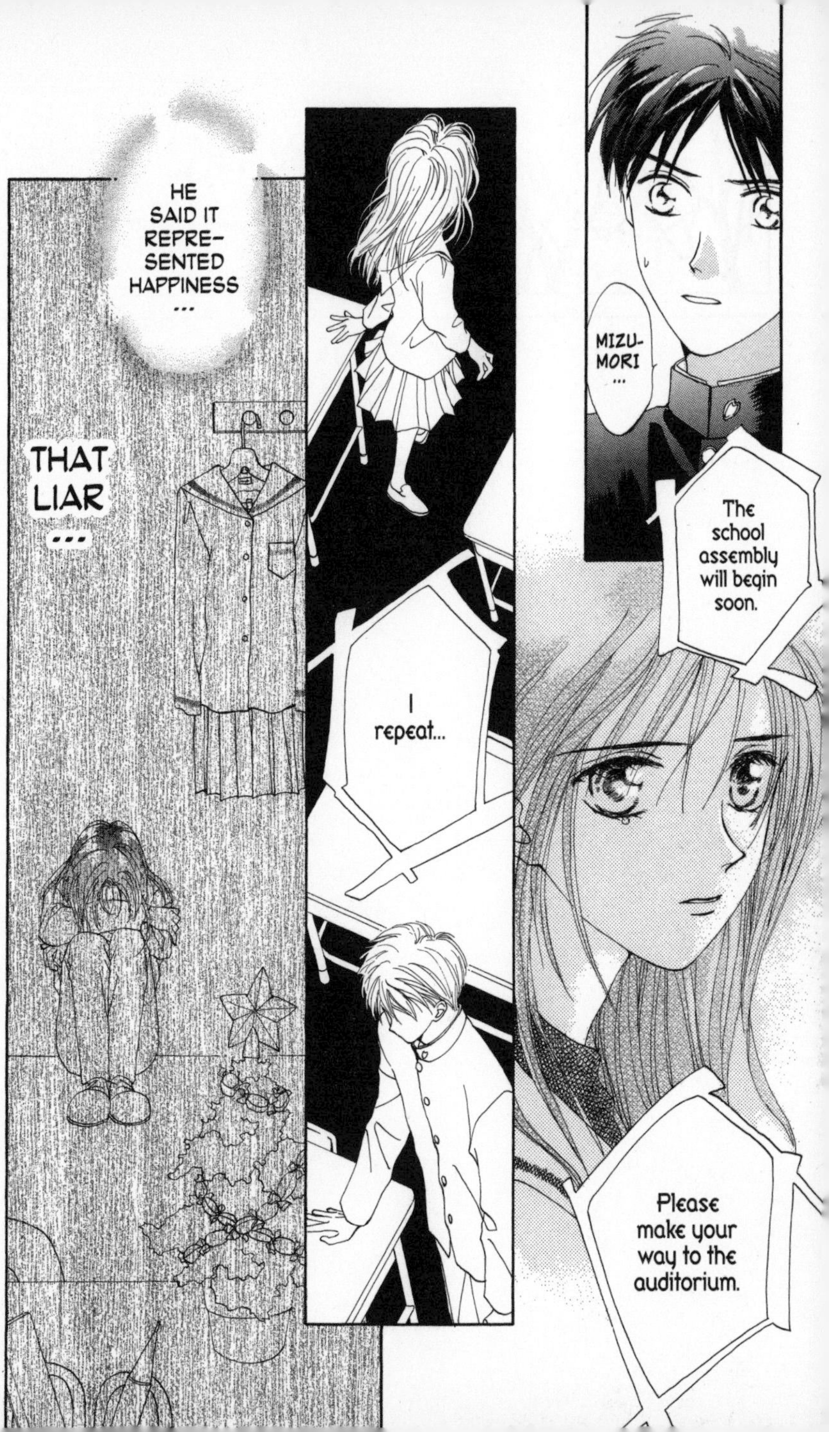
MIZU-MORI...
The school assembly will begin soon.
Please make your way to the auditorium.
I repeat...
HE SAID IT REPRE-SENTED HAPPINESS...
THAT LIAR...

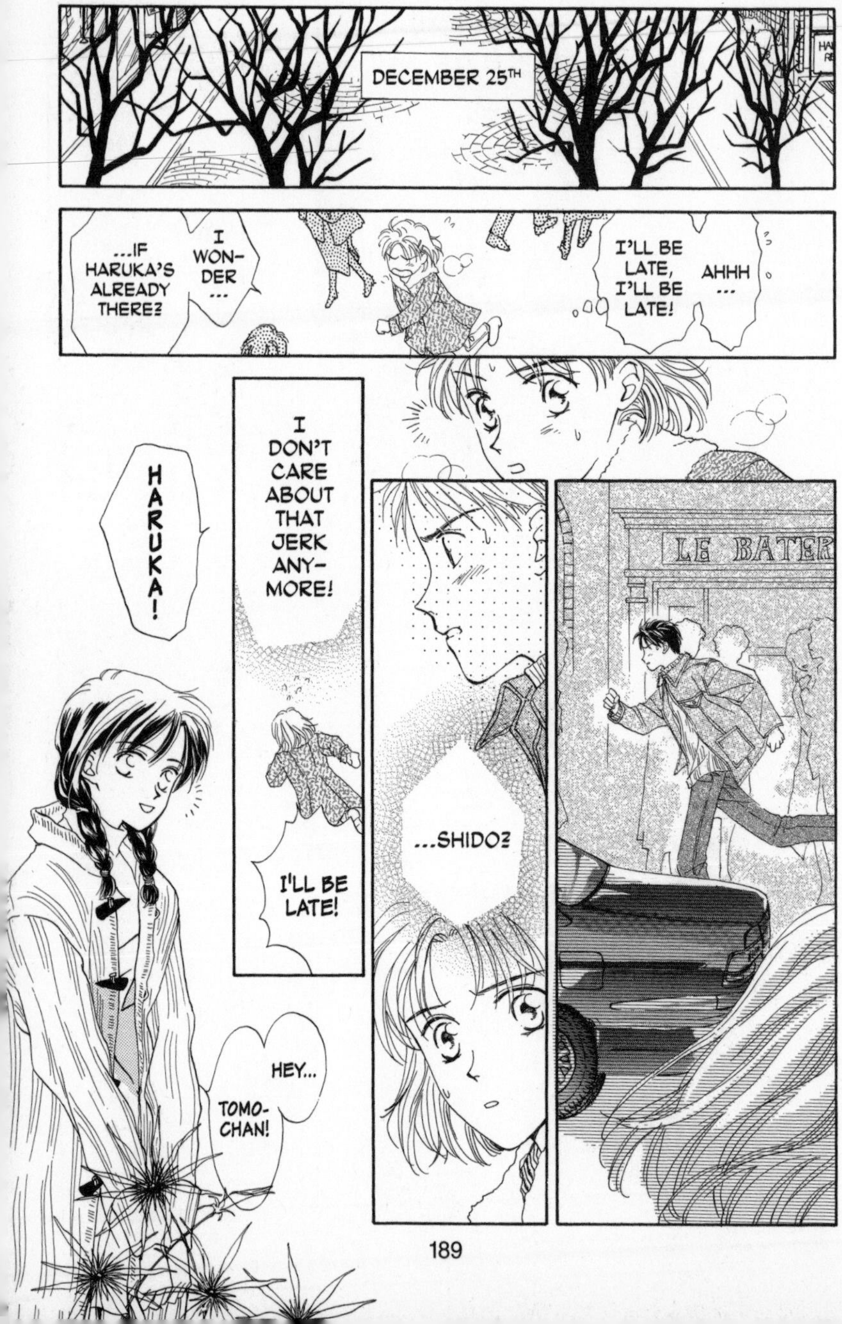
DECEMBER 25TH
AHHH...
I'LL BE LATE, I'LL BE LATE!
I WONDER...
...IF HARUKA'S ALREADY THERE?
LE BATER
...SHIDO?
I DON'T CARE ABOUT THAT JERK ANYMORE!
I'LL BE LATE!
HARUKA!
HEY... TOMO-CHAN!

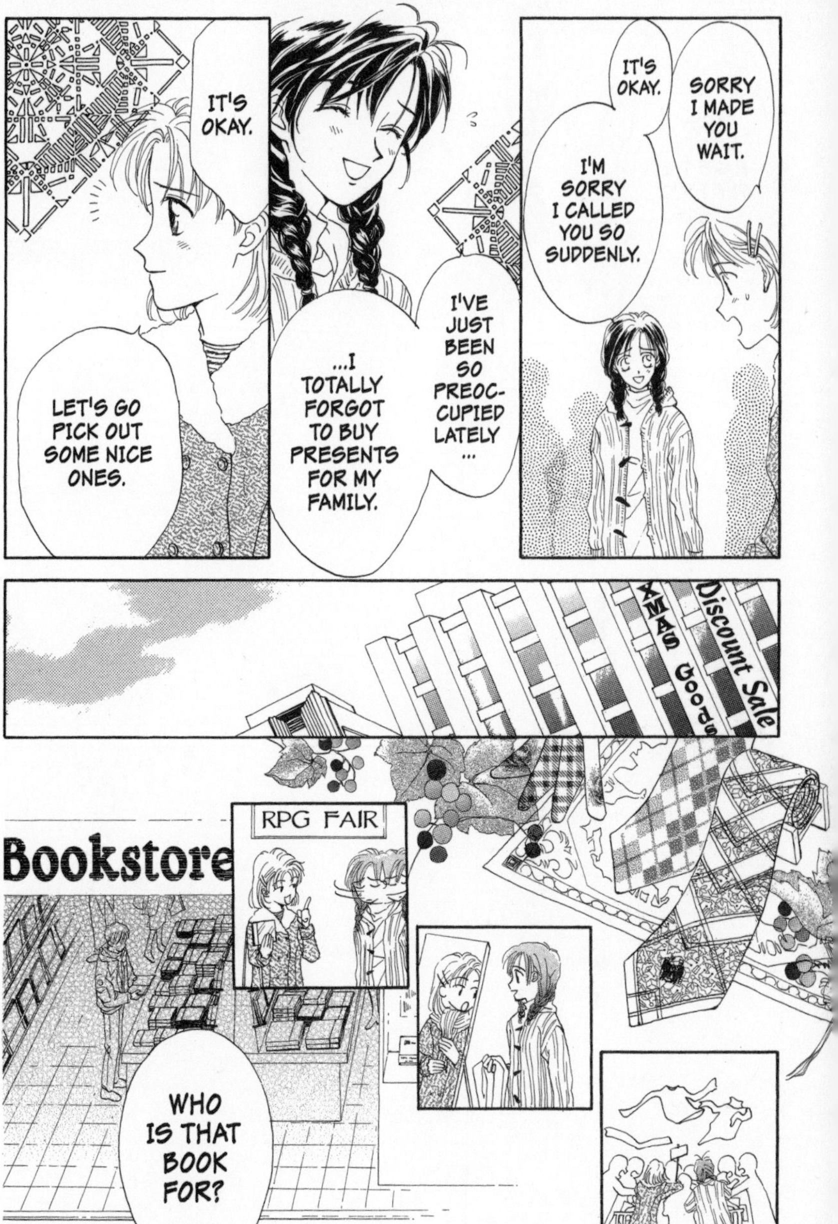
SORRY I MADE YOU WAIT.
IT'S OKAY.
I'M SORRY I CALLED YOU SO SUDDENLY.
I'VE JUST BEEN SO PREOC-CUPIED LATELY ...
...I TOTALLY FORGOT TO BUY PRESENTS FOR MY FAMILY.
IT'S OKAY.
LET'S GO PICK OUT SOME NICE ONES.
Discount Sale
XMAS Goods
RPG FAIR
Bookstore
WHO IS THAT BOOK FOR?

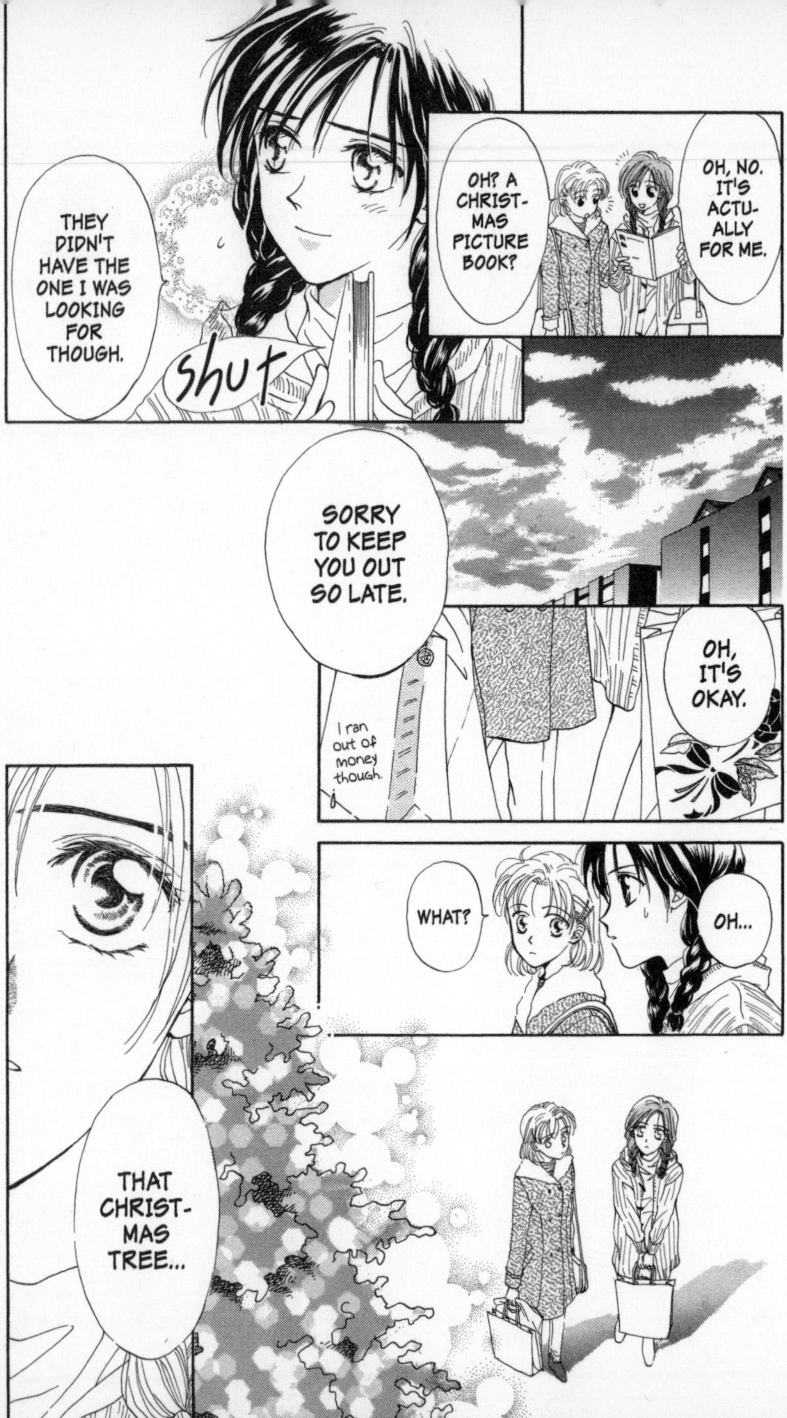
OH? A CHRIST-MAS PICTURE BOOK?
OH, NO. IT'S ACTU-ALLY FOR ME.
THEY DIDN'T HAVE THE ONE I WAS LOOKING FOR THOUGH.
shut
SORRY TO KEEP YOU OUT SO LATE.
OH, IT'S OKAY.
I ran out of money though.
OH...
WHAT?
THAT CHRIST-MAS TREE...

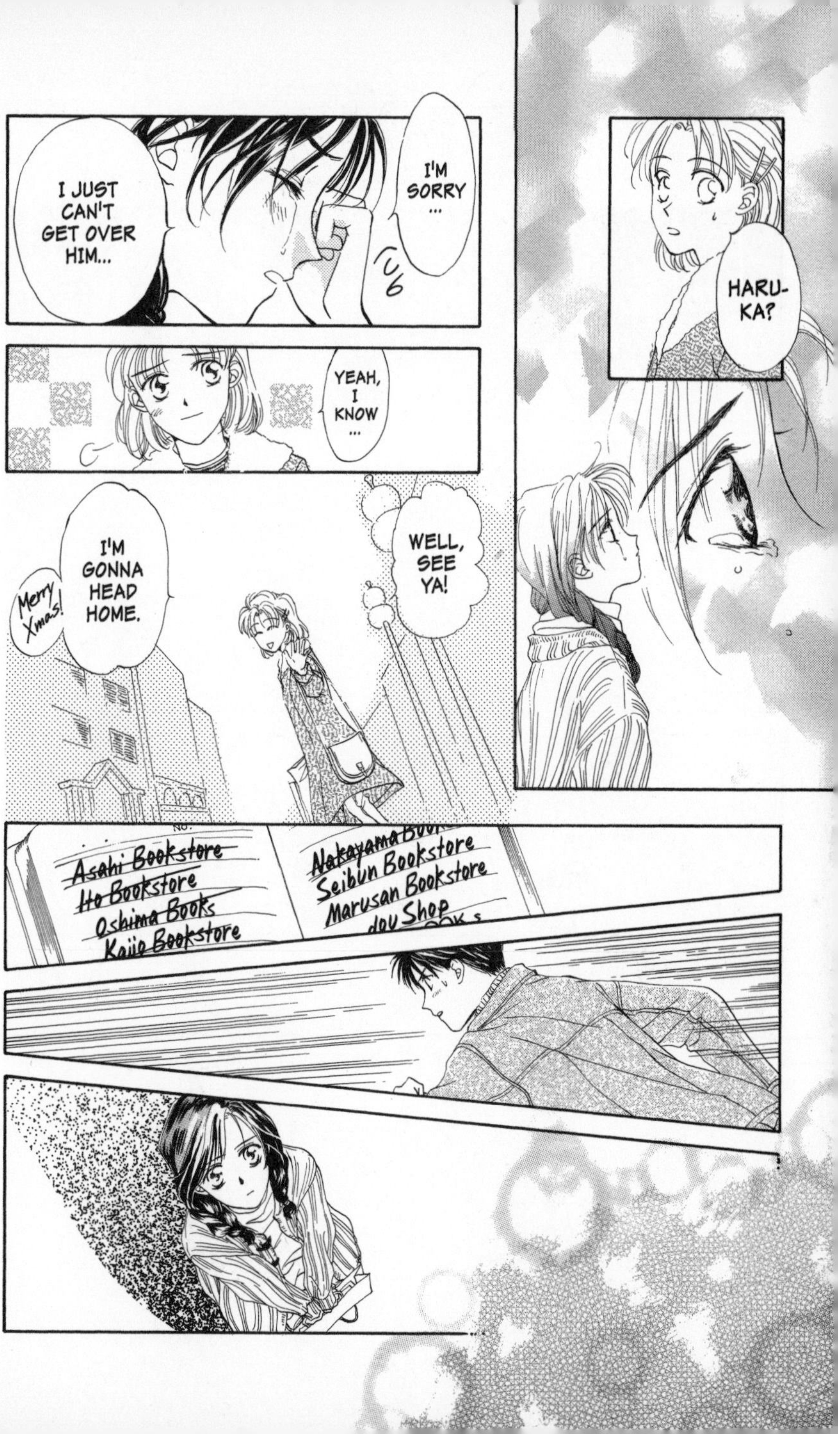
HARU-KA?
I'M SORRY...
I JUST CAN'T GET OVER HIM...
YEAH, I KNOW...
I'M GONNA HEAD HOME.
WELL, SEE YA!
Merry Xmas!
Nakayama Books
Seibun Bookstore
Marusan Bookstore
dou Shop
Asahi Bookstore
Ito Bookstore
Oshima Books
Kaijo Bookstore

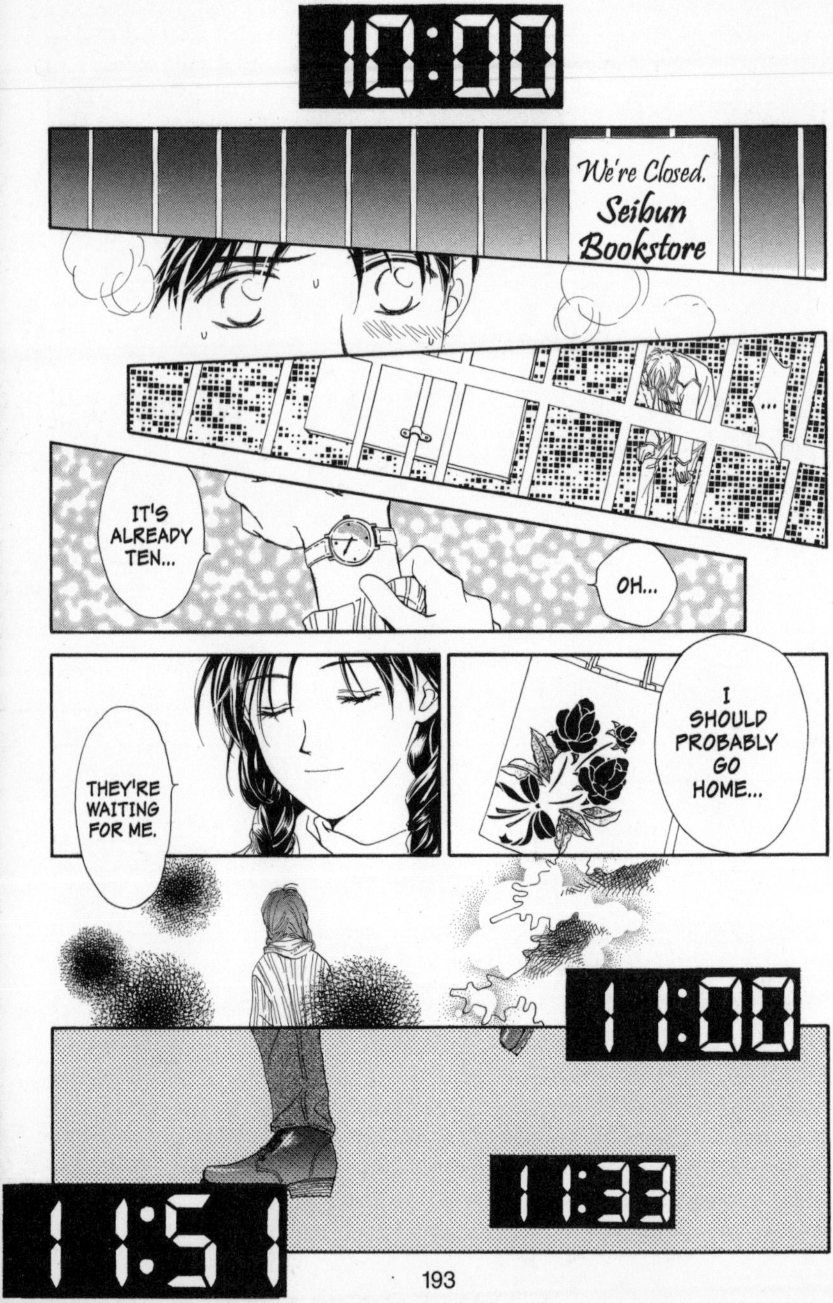
10:00
We're Closed.
Seibun Bookstore
...
OH...
IT'S ALREADY TEN...
I SHOULD PROBABLY GO HOME...
THEY'RE WAITING FOR ME.
11:00
11:33
11:51

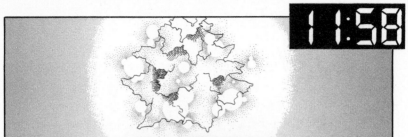

11:58

00:00

HUFF

Pant

Pant

Pant

I DOUBT SHE'LL BE HERE...

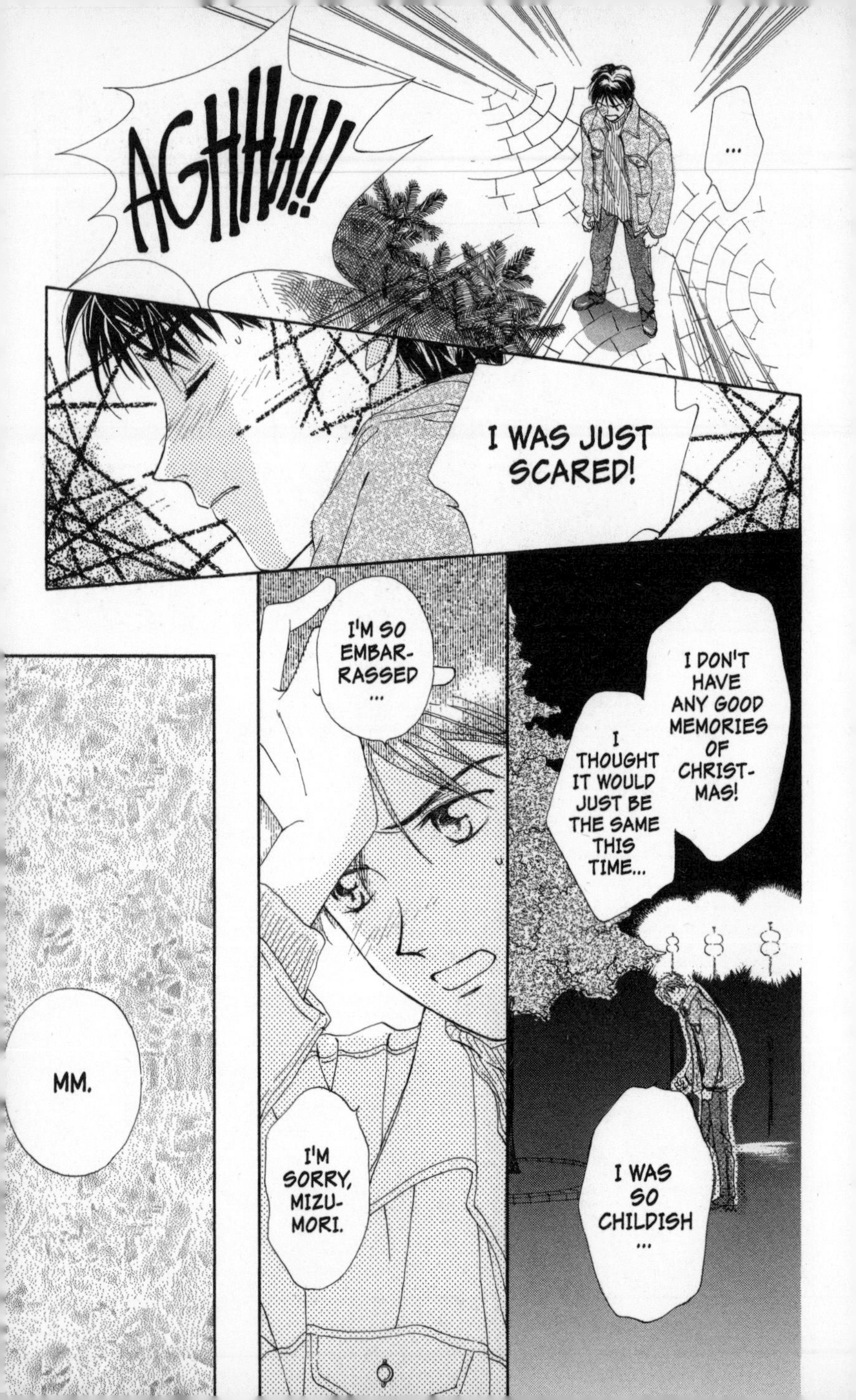
...
AGHHH!!
I WAS JUST SCARED!
I DON'T HAVE ANY GOOD MEMORIES OF CHRIST-MAS!
I THOUGHT IT WOULD JUST BE THE SAME THIS TIME...
I WAS SO CHILDISH ...
I'M SO EMBAR-RASSED ...
I'M SORRY, MIZU-MORI.
MM.

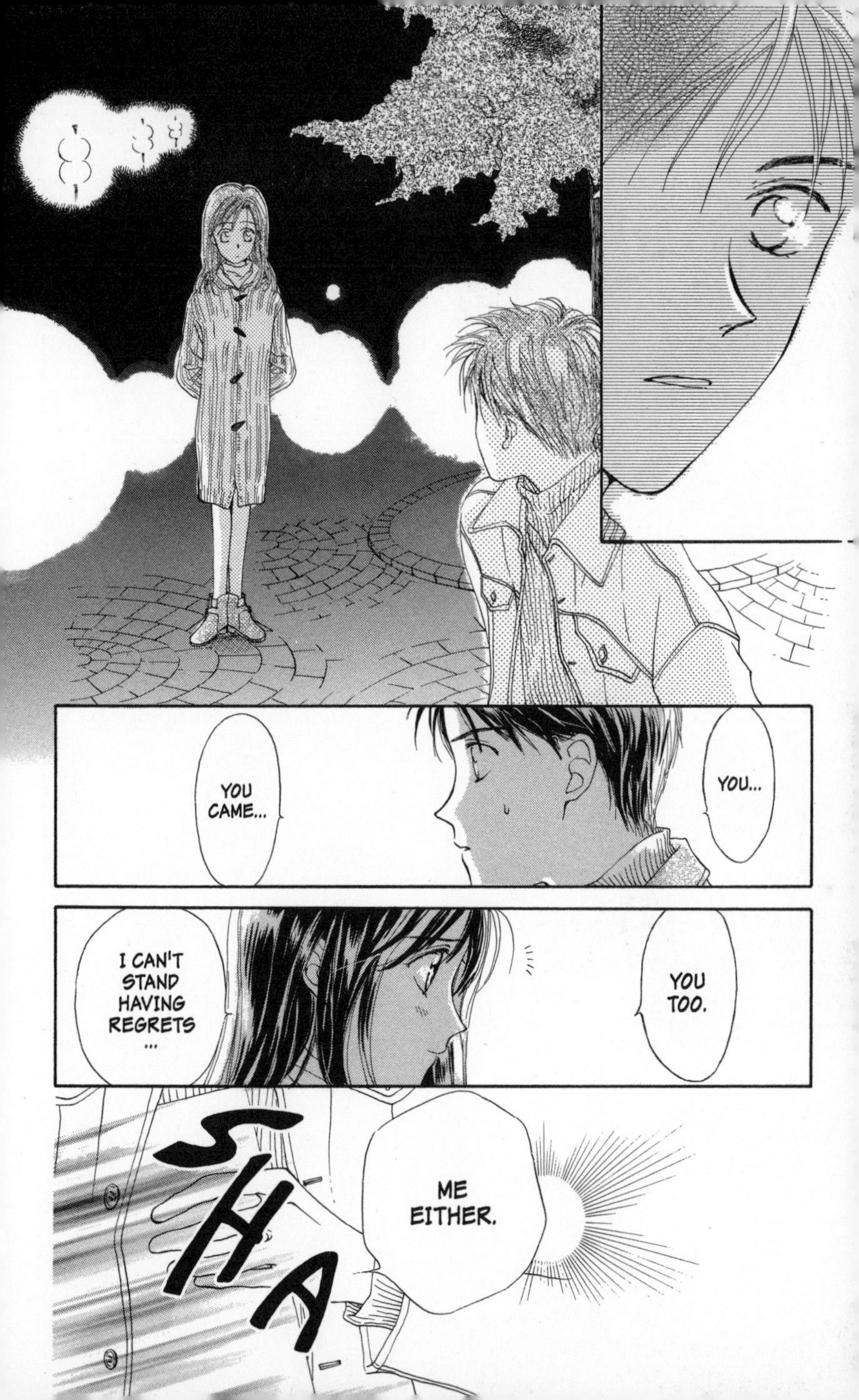
YOU...
YOU CAME...
YOU TOO.
I CAN'T STAND HAVING REGRETS ...
ME EITHER.
SHA

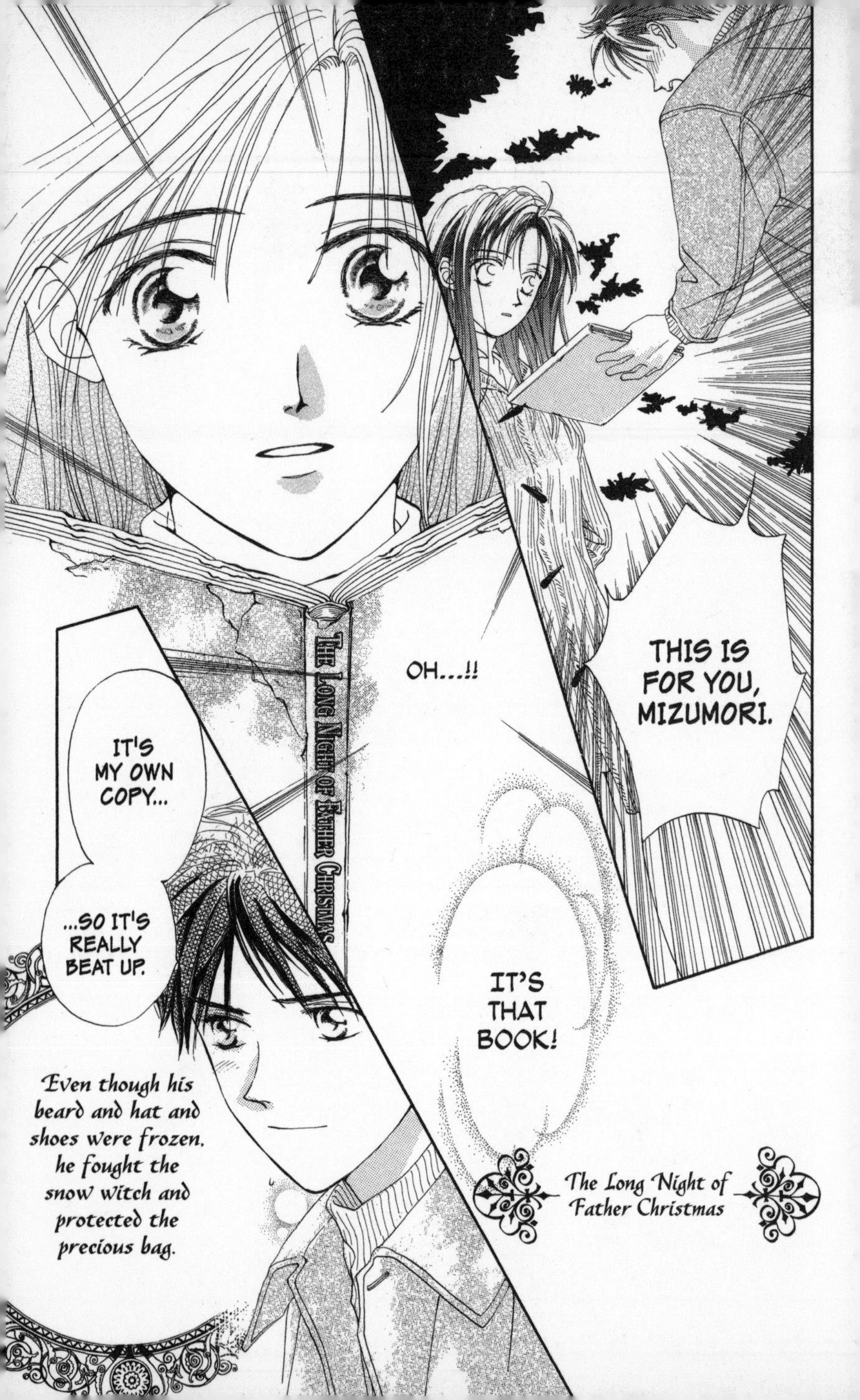
THIS IS FOR YOU, MIZUMORI.
OH...!!
IT'S THAT BOOK!
The Long Night of Father Christmas
THE LONG NIGHT OF FATHER CHRISTMAS
IT'S MY OWN COPY...
...SO IT'S REALLY BEAT UP.
Even though his beard and hat and shoes were frozen, he fought the snow witch and protected the precious bag.

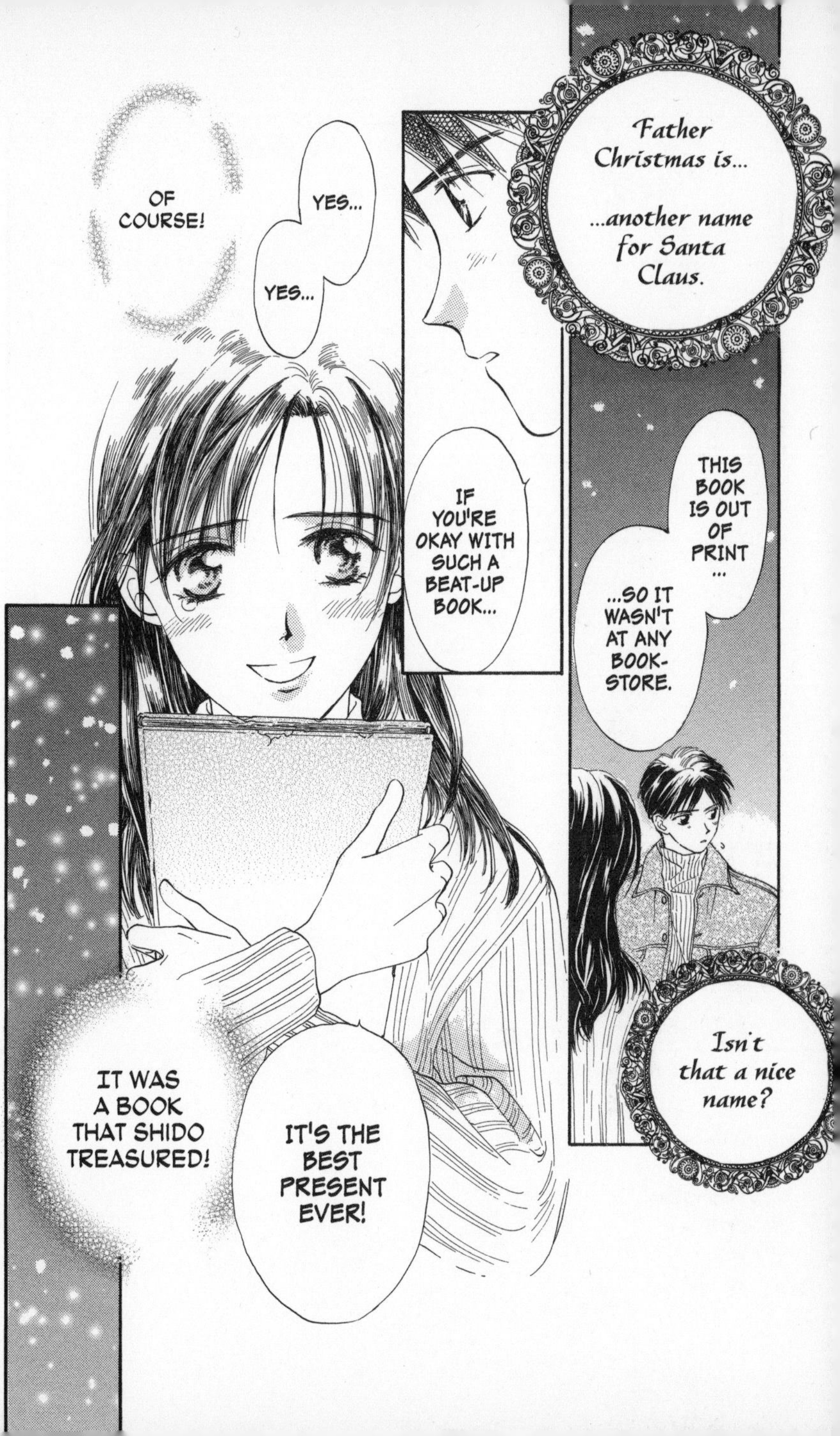
Father Christmas is...
...another name for Santa Claus.
THIS BOOK IS OUT OF PRINT ...
...SO IT WASN'T AT ANY BOOK-STORE.
Isn't that a nice name?
IF YOU'RE OKAY WITH SUCH A BEAT-UP BOOK...
YES...
YES...
OF COURSE!
IT'S THE BEST PRESENT EVER!
IT WAS A BOOK THAT SHIDO TREASURED!

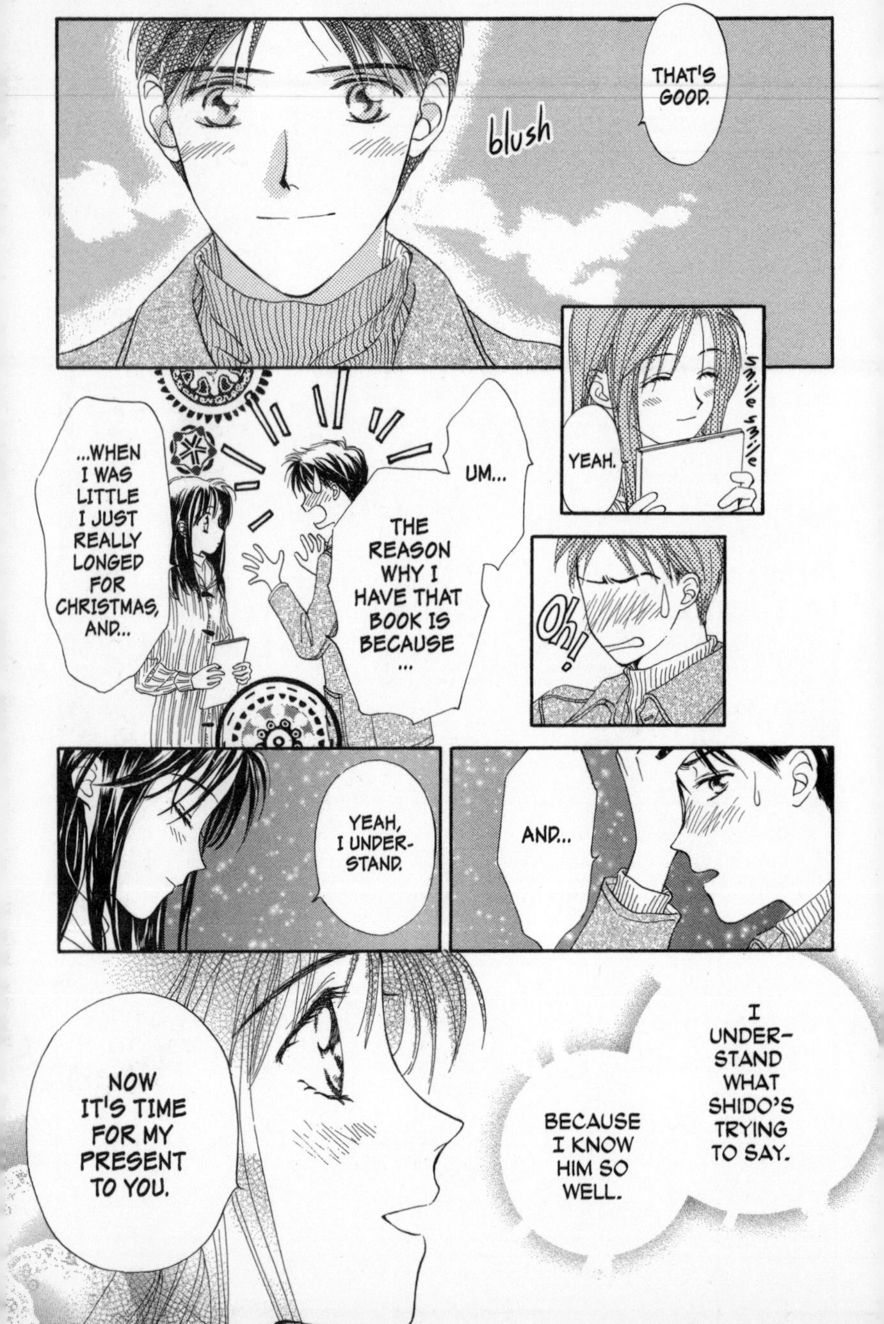
THAT'S GOOD.
blush
YEAH.
smile smile
Oh!
UM...
THE REASON WHY I HAVE THAT BOOK IS BECAUSE ...
...WHEN I WAS LITTLE I JUST REALLY LONGED FOR CHRISTMAS, AND...
AND...
YEAH, I UNDER-STAND.
I UNDER-STAND WHAT SHIDO'S TRYING TO SAY.
BECAUSE I KNOW HIM SO WELL.
NOW IT'S TIME FOR MY PRESENT TO YOU.

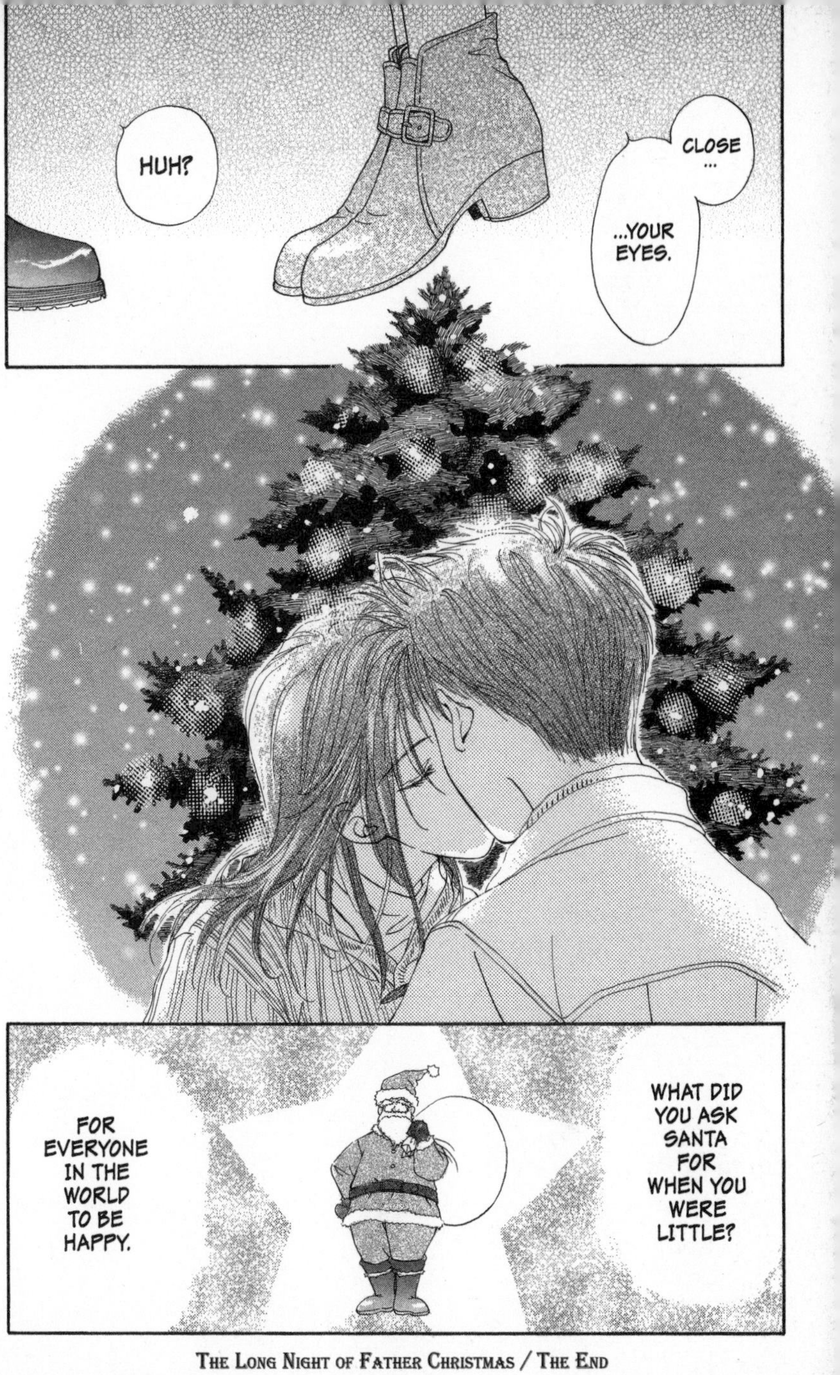
CLOSE ...
...YOUR EYES.
HUH?
WHAT DID YOU ASK SANTA FOR WHEN YOU WERE LITTLE?
FOR EVERYONE IN THE WORLD TO BE HAPPY.

The Long Night of Father Christmas / The End

Muro-
machi
Era
Sequel

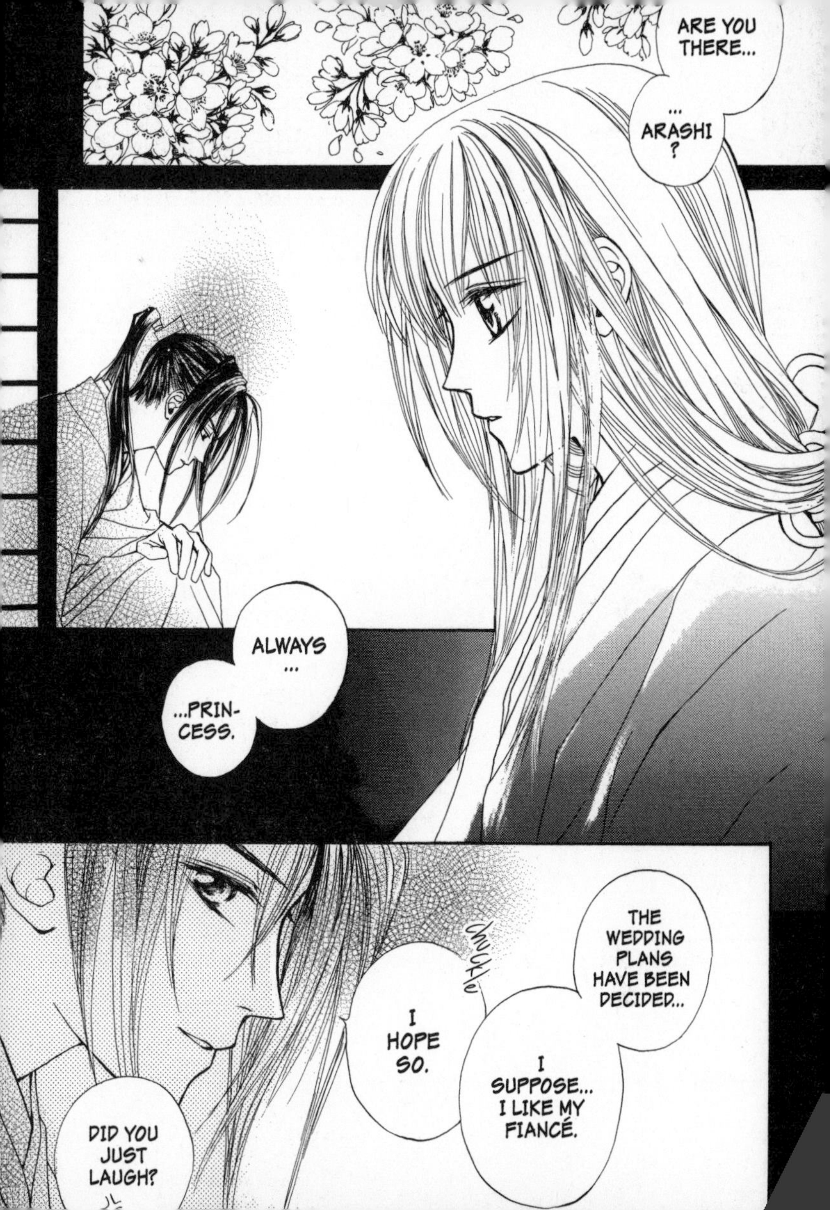
ARE YOU THERE...
...ARASHI?
ALWAYS...
...PRINCESS.
THE WEDDING PLANS HAVE BEEN DECIDED...
I SUPPOSE... I LIKE MY FIANCÉ.
chuckle
I HOPE SO.
DID YOU JUST LAUGH?

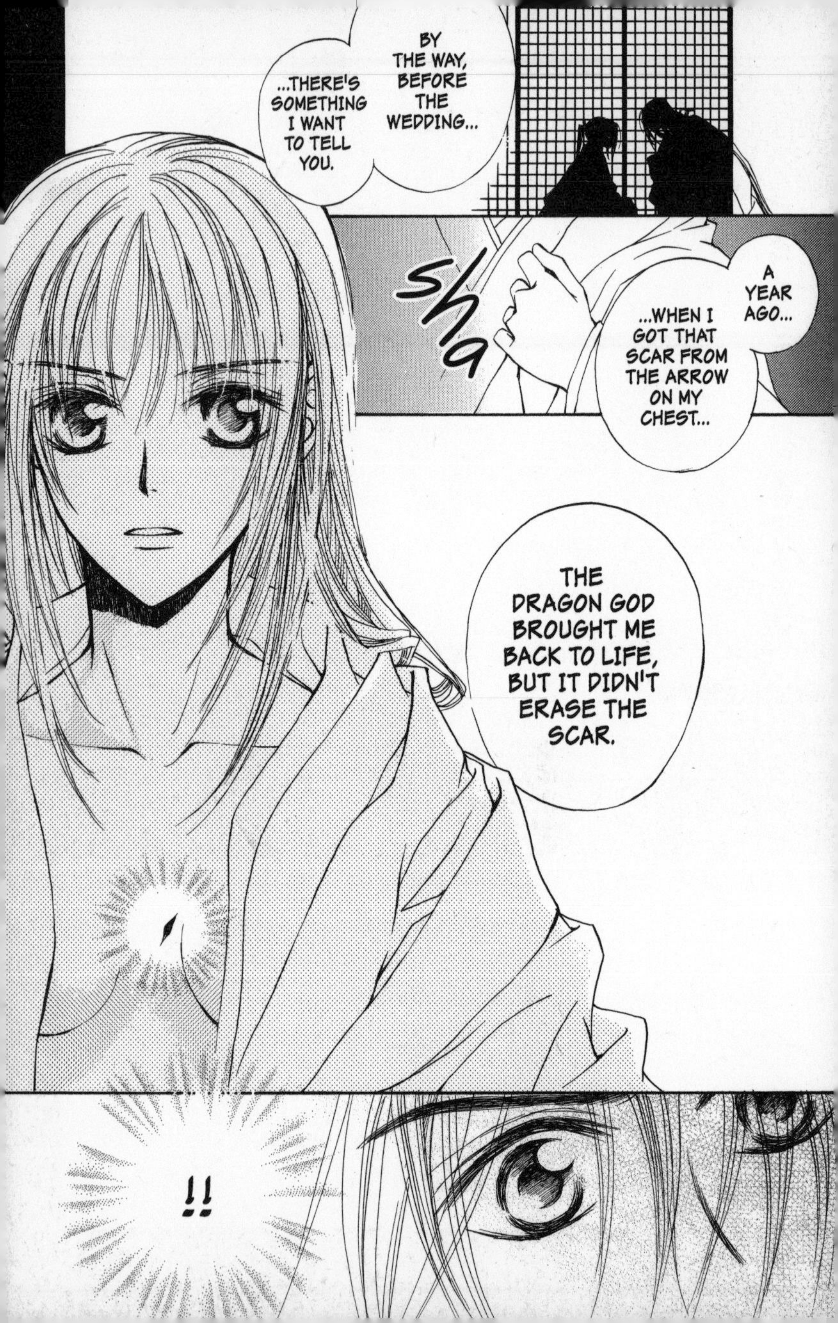
BY THE WAY, BEFORE THE WEDDING...
...THERE'S SOMETHING I WANT TO TELL YOU.
SHA
A YEAR AGO...
...WHEN I GOT THAT SCAR FROM THE ARROW ON MY CHEST...
THE DRAGON GOD BROUGHT ME BACK TO LIFE, BUT IT DIDN'T ERASE THE SCAR.
!!

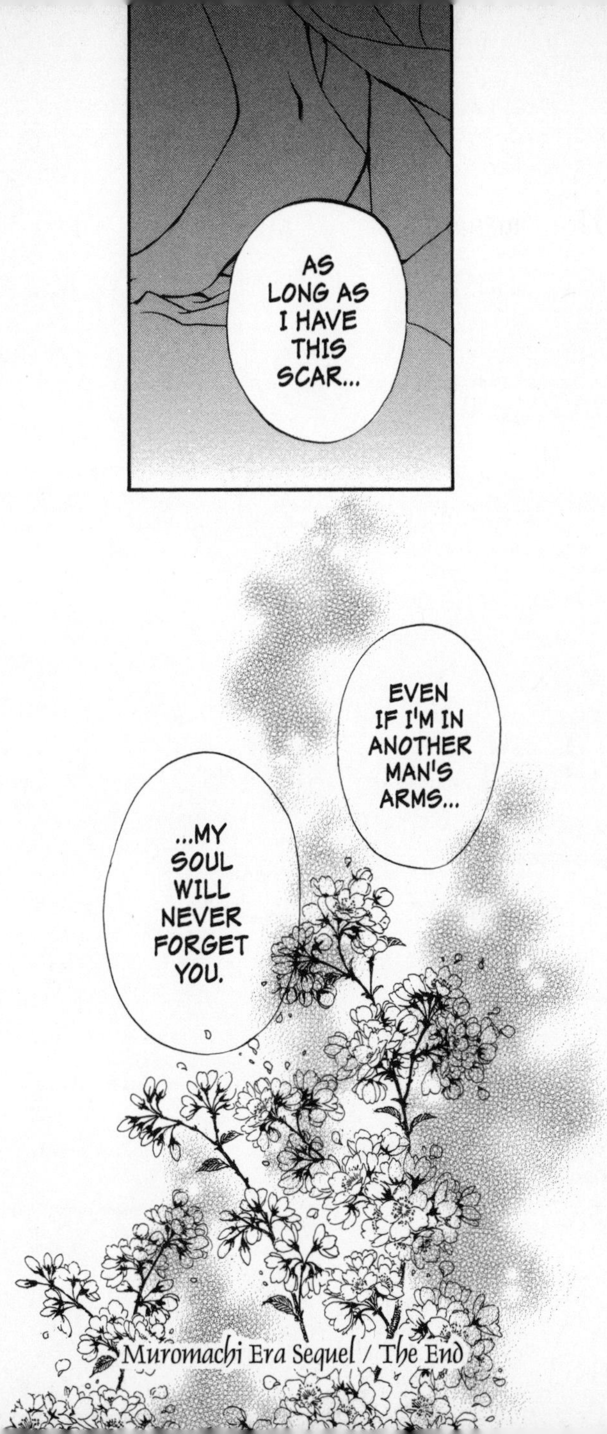
AS LONG AS I HAVE THIS SCAR...
EVEN IF I'M IN ANOTHER MAN'S ARMS...
...MY SOUL WILL NEVER FORGET YOU.
Muromachi Era Sequel / The End

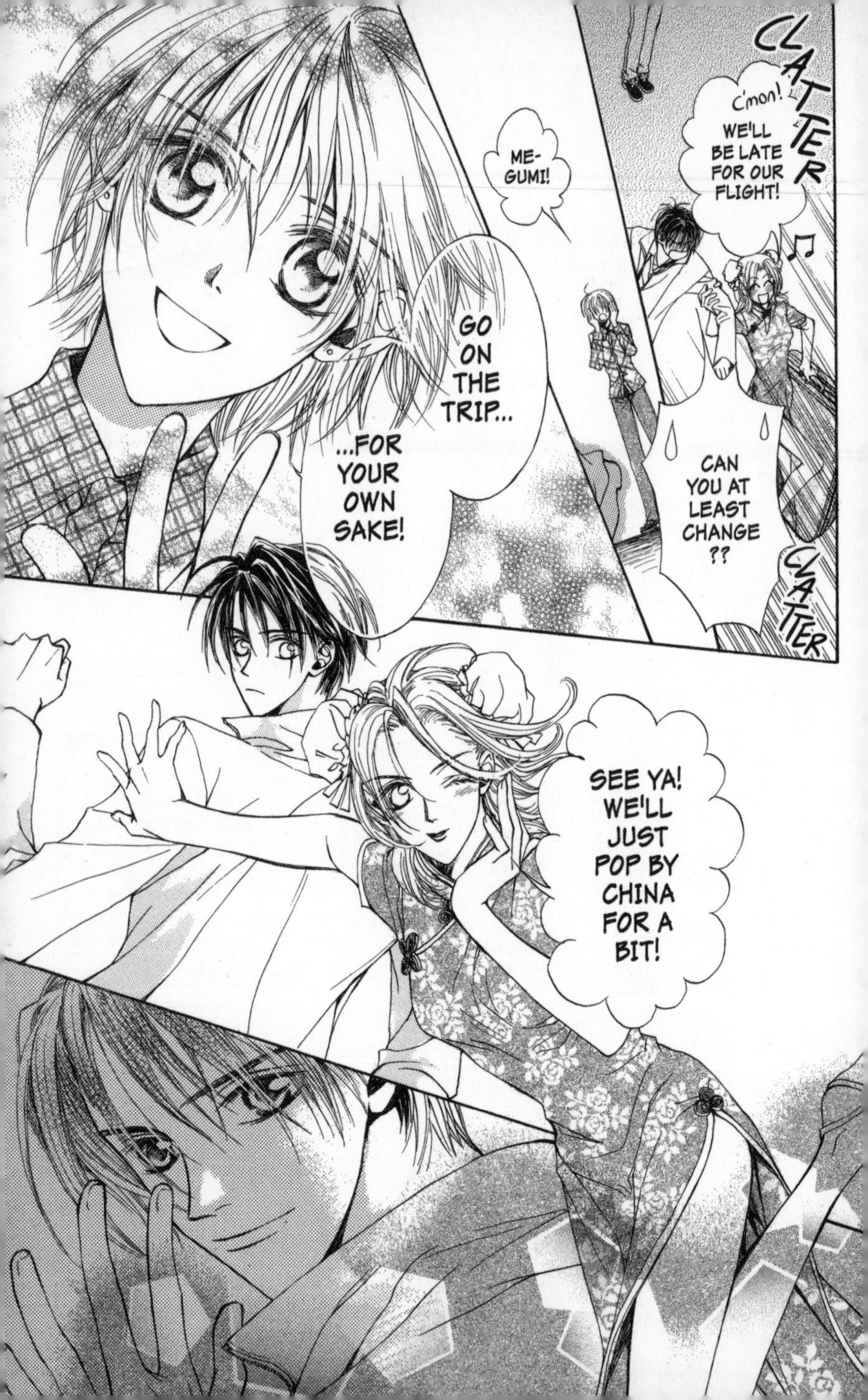
CLATTER
C'mon! WE'LL BE LATE FOR OUR FLIGHT!
CAN YOU AT LEAST CHANGE??
CLATTER
ME-GUMI!
GO ON THE TRIP...
...FOR YOUR OWN SAKE!
SEE YA! WE'LL JUST POP BY CHINA FOR A BIT!

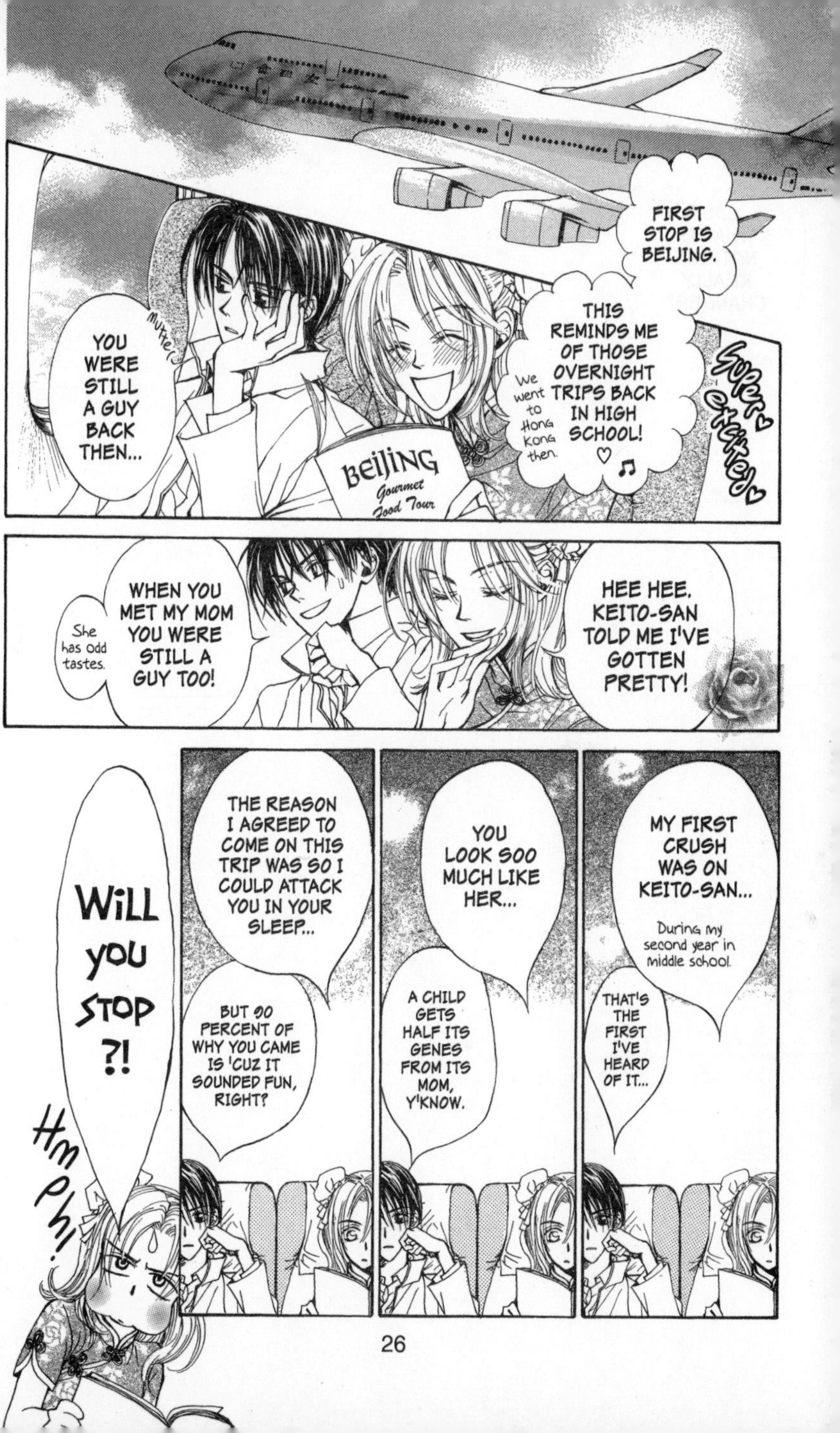
Super excited♥
FIRST STOP IS BEIJING.
THIS REMINDS ME OF THOSE OVERNIGHT TRIPS BACK IN HIGH SCHOOL! ♡ ♫
We went to Hong Kong then.
BEIJING Gourmet Food Tour
Mutter
YOU WERE STILL A GUY BACK THEN...
HEE HEE. KEITO-SAN TOLD ME I'VE GOTTEN PRETTY!
WHEN YOU MET MY MOM YOU WERE STILL A GUY TOO!
She has odd tastes.
MY FIRST CRUSH WAS ON KEITO-SAN...
During my second year in middle school.
THAT'S THE FIRST I'VE HEARD OF IT...
YOU LOOK SOO MUCH LIKE HER...
A CHILD GETS HALF ITS GENES FROM ITS MOM, Y'KNOW.
THE REASON I AGREED TO COME ON THIS TRIP WAS SO I COULD ATTACK YOU IN YOUR SLEEP...
BUT 90 PERCENT OF WHY YOU CAME IS 'CUZ IT SOUNDED FUN, RIGHT?
WILL YOU STOP?!
Hmph!

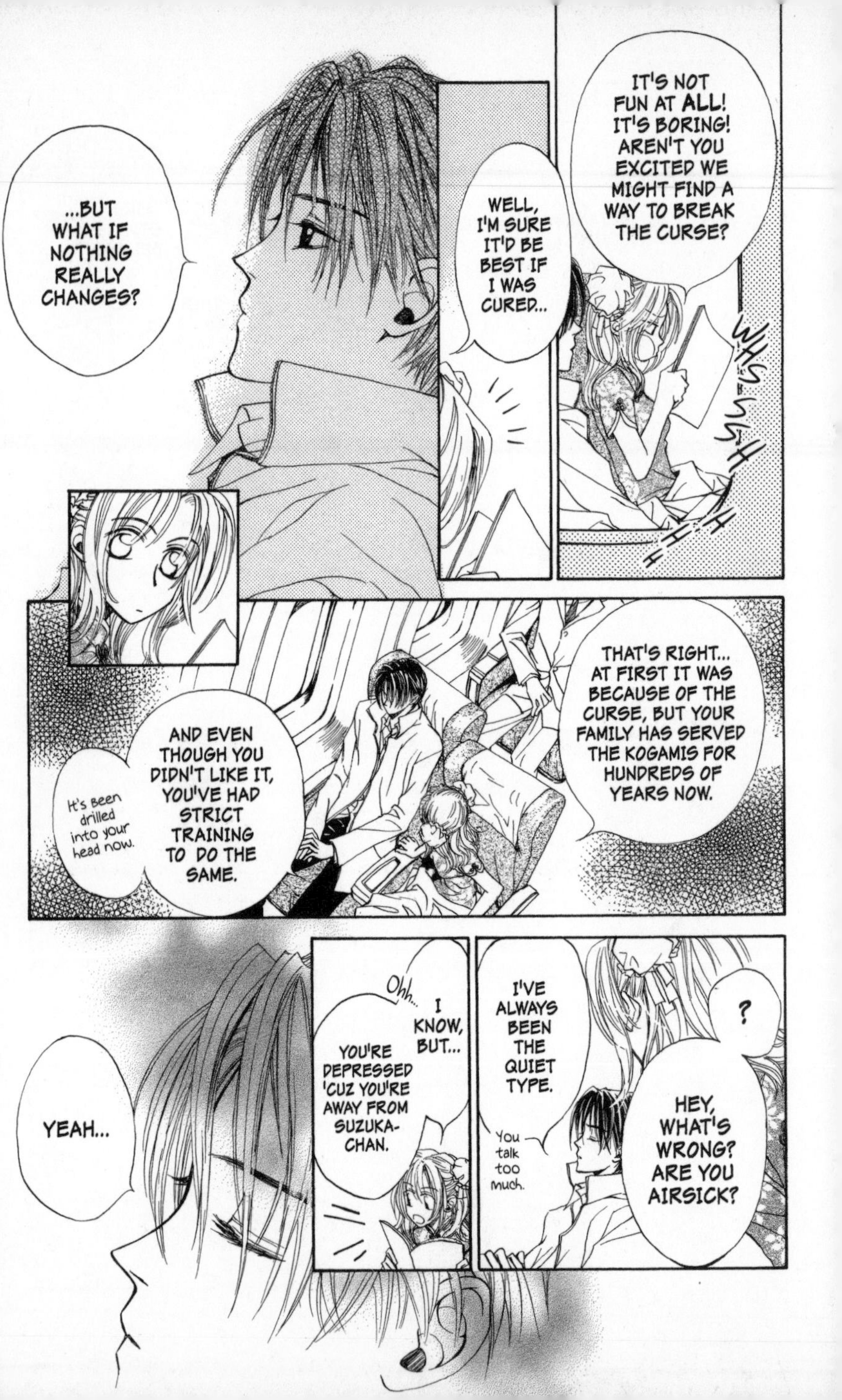
IT'S NOT FUN AT ALL! IT'S BORING! AREN'T YOU EXCITED WE MIGHT FIND A WAY TO BREAK THE CURSE?
WELL, I'M SURE IT'D BE BEST IF I WAS CURED...
...BUT WHAT IF NOTHING REALLY CHANGES?
THAT'S RIGHT... AT FIRST IT WAS BECAUSE OF THE CURSE, BUT YOUR FAMILY HAS SERVED THE KOGAMIS FOR HUNDREDS OF YEARS NOW.
AND EVEN THOUGH YOU DIDN'T LIKE IT, YOU'VE HAD STRICT TRAINING TO DO THE SAME.
It's been drilled into your head now.
?
HEY, WHAT'S WRONG? ARE YOU AIRSICK?
I'VE ALWAYS BEEN THE QUIET TYPE.
You talk too much.
I KNOW, BUT...
Ohh...
YOU'RE DEPRESSED 'CUZ YOU'RE AWAY FROM SUZUKA-CHAN.
YEAH...

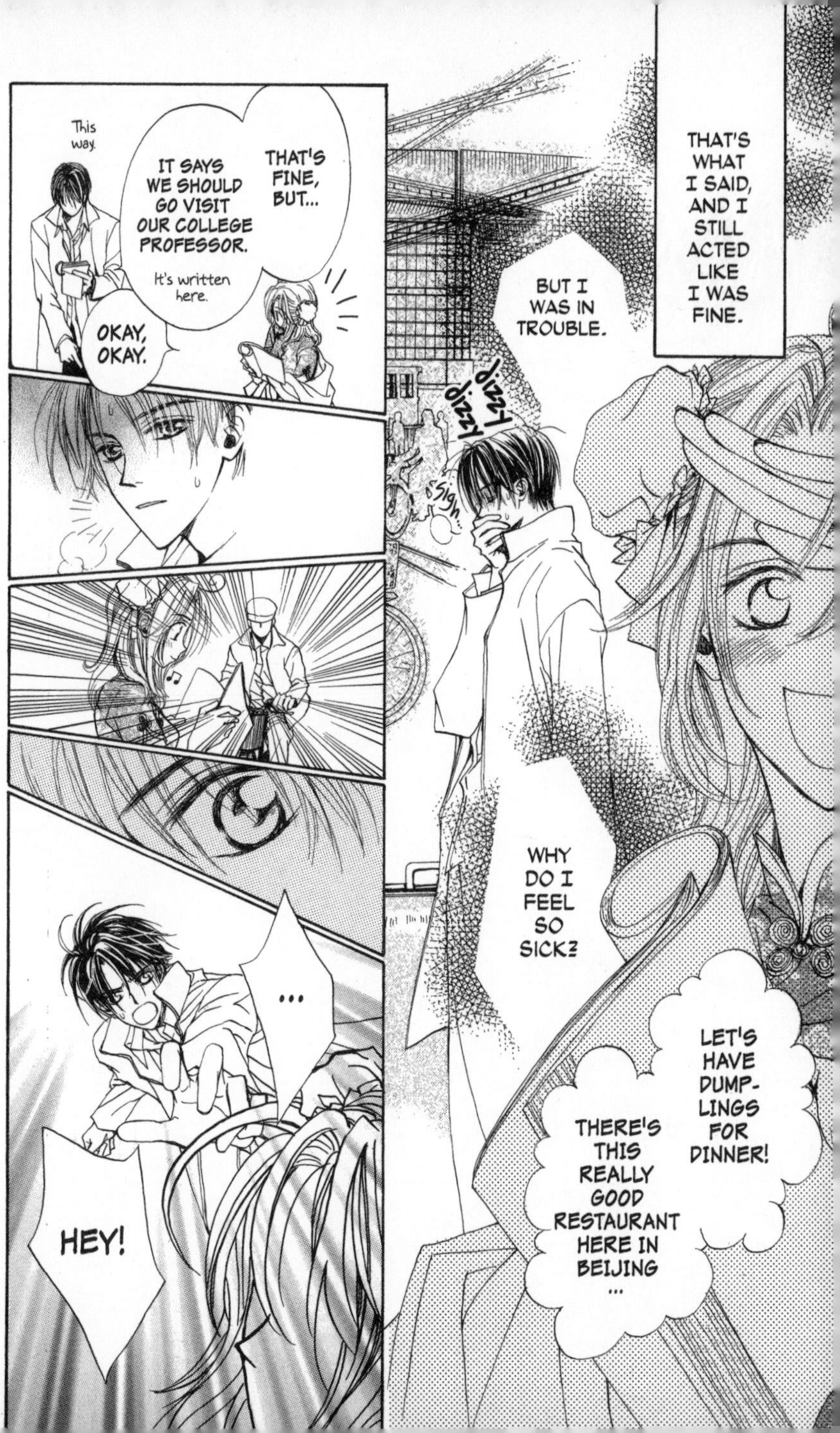
THAT'S WHAT I SAID, AND I STILL ACTED LIKE I WAS FINE.
BUT I WAS IN TROUBLE.
dizzy dizzy
Sigh...
WHY DO I FEEL SO SICK?
LET'S HAVE DUMPLINGS FOR DINNER!
THERE'S THIS REALLY GOOD RESTAURANT HERE IN BEIJING ...
THAT'S FINE, BUT...
IT SAYS WE SHOULD GO VISIT OUR COLLEGE PROFESSOR.
It's written here.
This way.
OKAY, OKAY.
...
HEY!

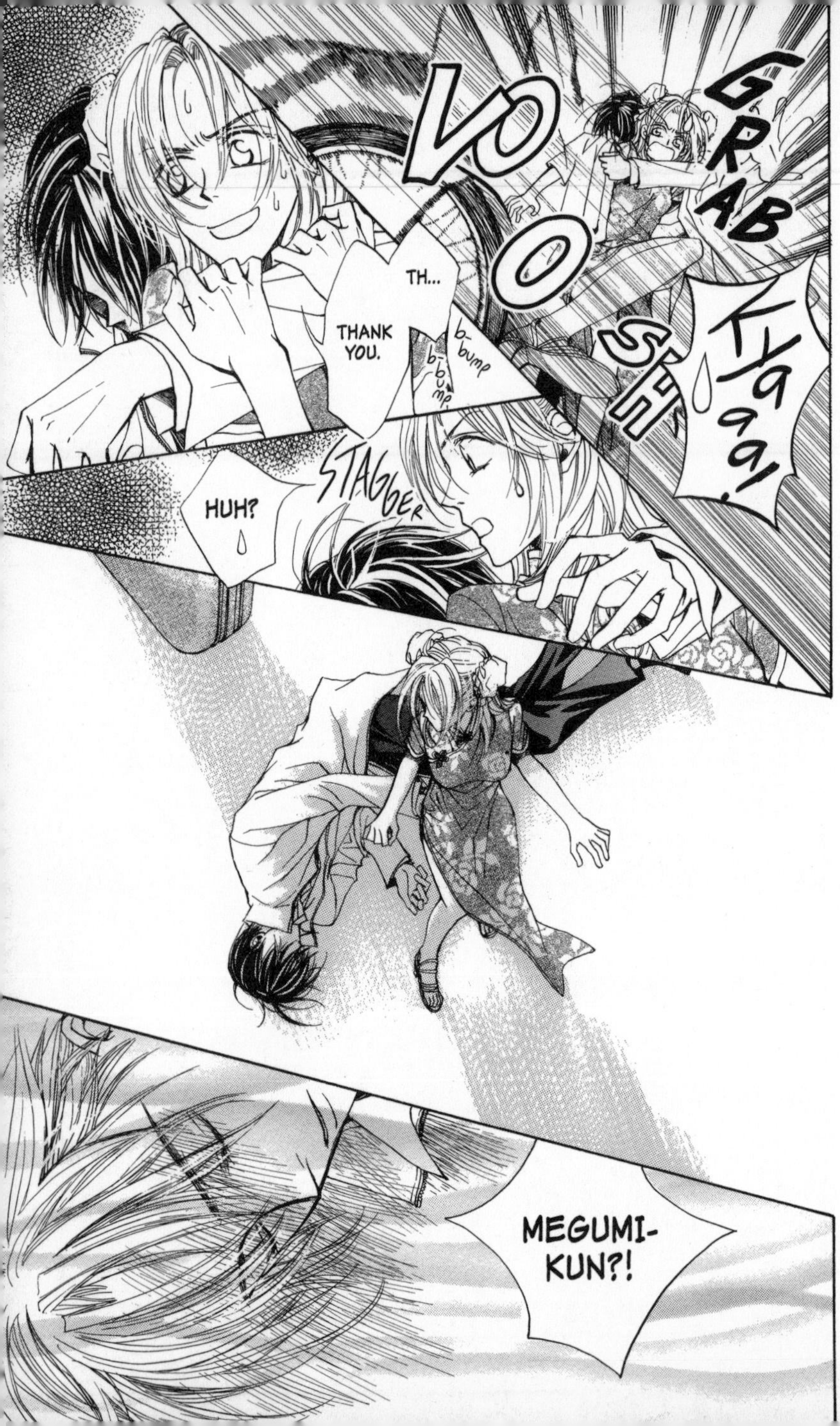
GRAB
Kyaaa!
VOOSH
TH...
THANK YOU.
b-bump
b-bump
STAGGER
HUH?
MEGUMI-KUN?!

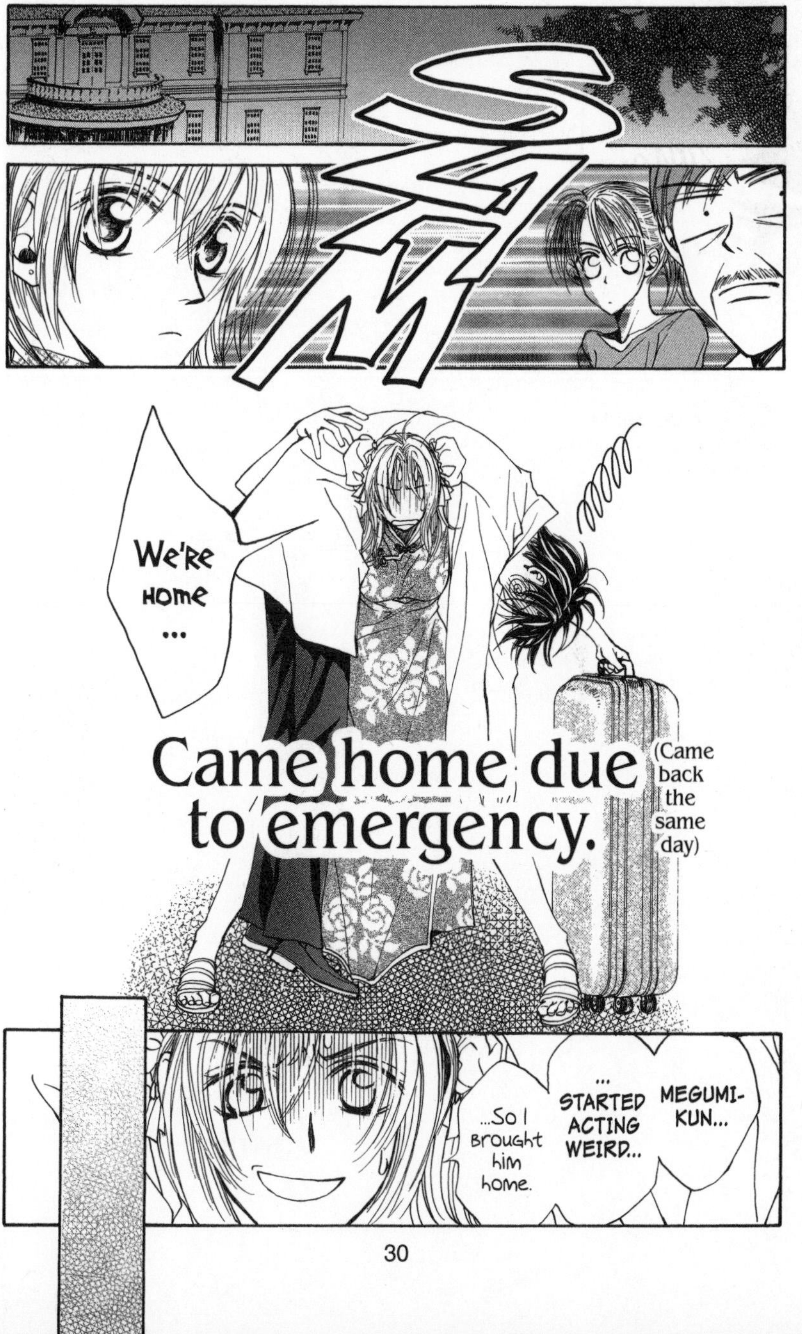
SLAM
We're home ...
Came home due to emergency.
(Came back the same day)
MEGUMI-KUN...
... STARTED ACTING WEIRD...
...So I brought him home.

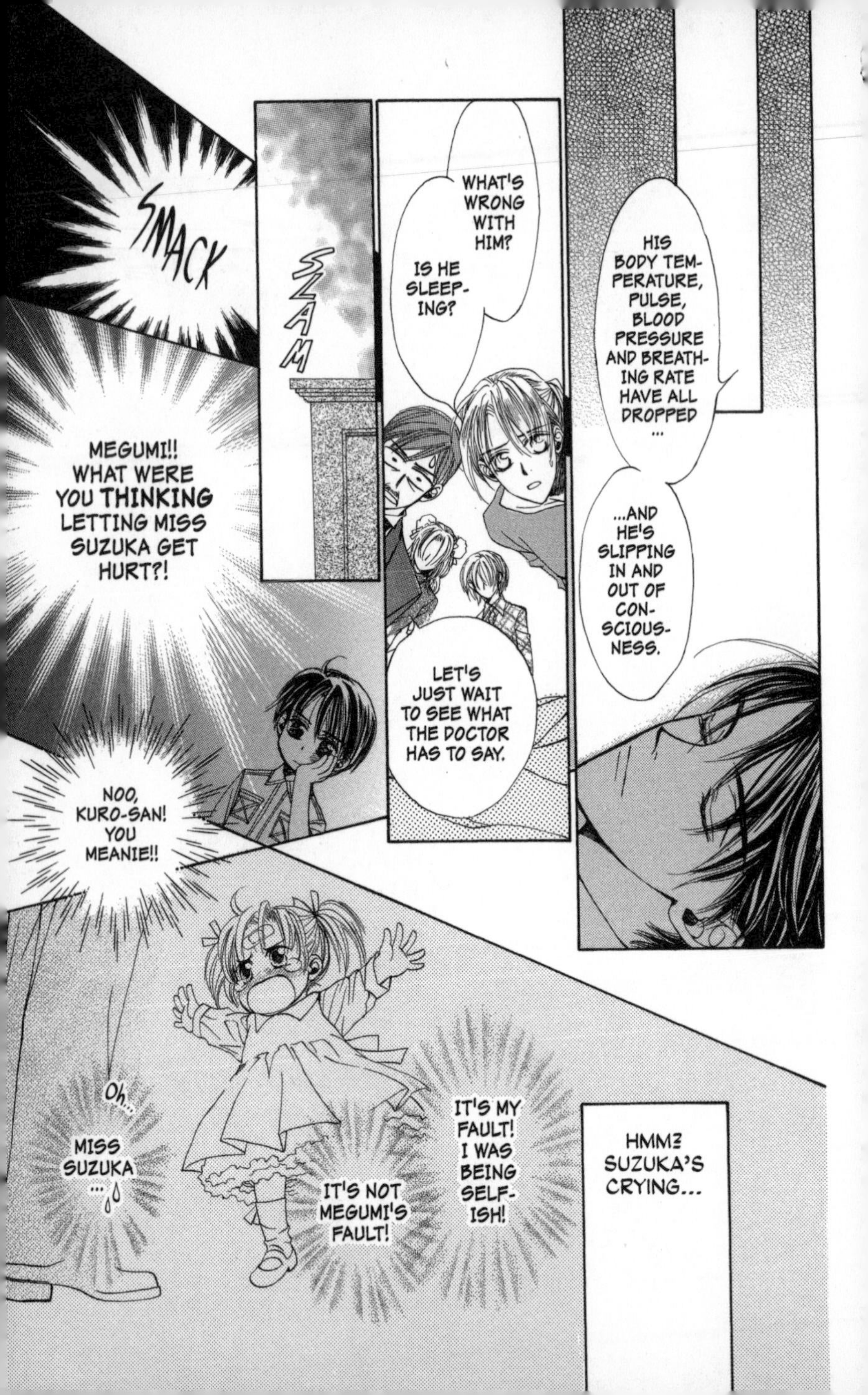
HIS BODY TEMPERATURE, PULSE, BLOOD PRESSURE AND BREATHING RATE HAVE ALL DROPPED...
...AND HE'S SLIPPING IN AND OUT OF CONSCIOUSNESS.
WHAT'S WRONG WITH HIM?
IS HE SLEEPING?
LET'S JUST WAIT TO SEE WHAT THE DOCTOR HAS TO SAY.
SLAM
SMACK
MEGUMI!! WHAT WERE YOU **THINKING** LETTING MISS SUZUKA GET HURT?!
NOO, KURO-SAN! YOU MEANIE!!
HMM? SUZUKA'S CRYING...
IT'S MY FAULT! I WAS BEING SELFISH!
IT'S NOT MEGUMI'S FAULT!
Oh...
MISS SUZUKA...

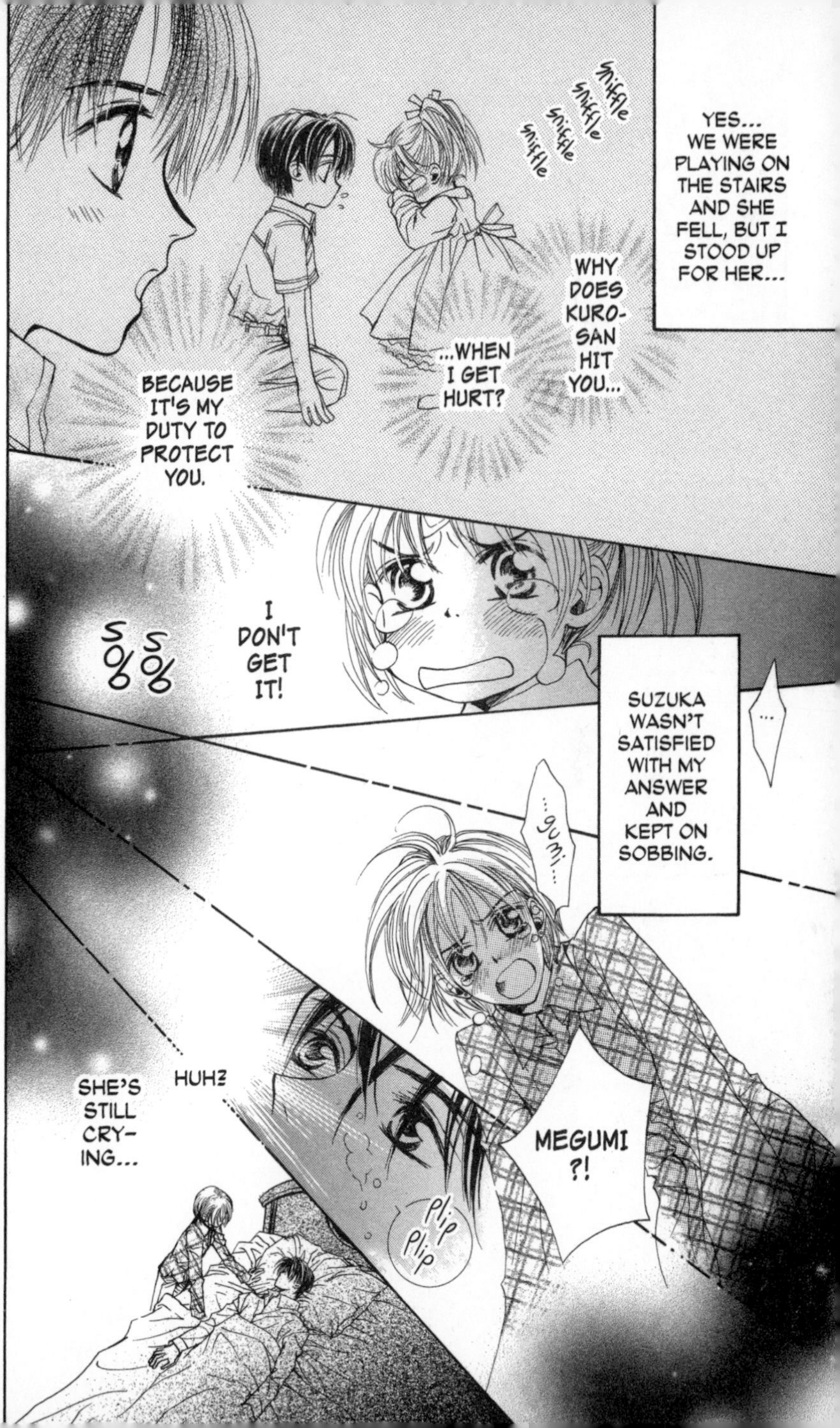

YES... WE WERE PLAYING ON THE STAIRS AND SHE FELL, BUT I STOOD UP FOR HER...
sniffle sniffle sniffle sniffle
WHY DOES KURO-SAN HIT YOU...
...WHEN I GET HURT?
BECAUSE IT'S MY DUTY TO PROTECT YOU.
I DON'T GET IT!
SOB SOB
...
SUZUKA WASN'T SATISFIED WITH MY ANSWER AND KEPT ON SOBBING.
...gumi...
MEGUMI ?!
Plip Plip
HUH?
SHE'S STILL CRY-ING...

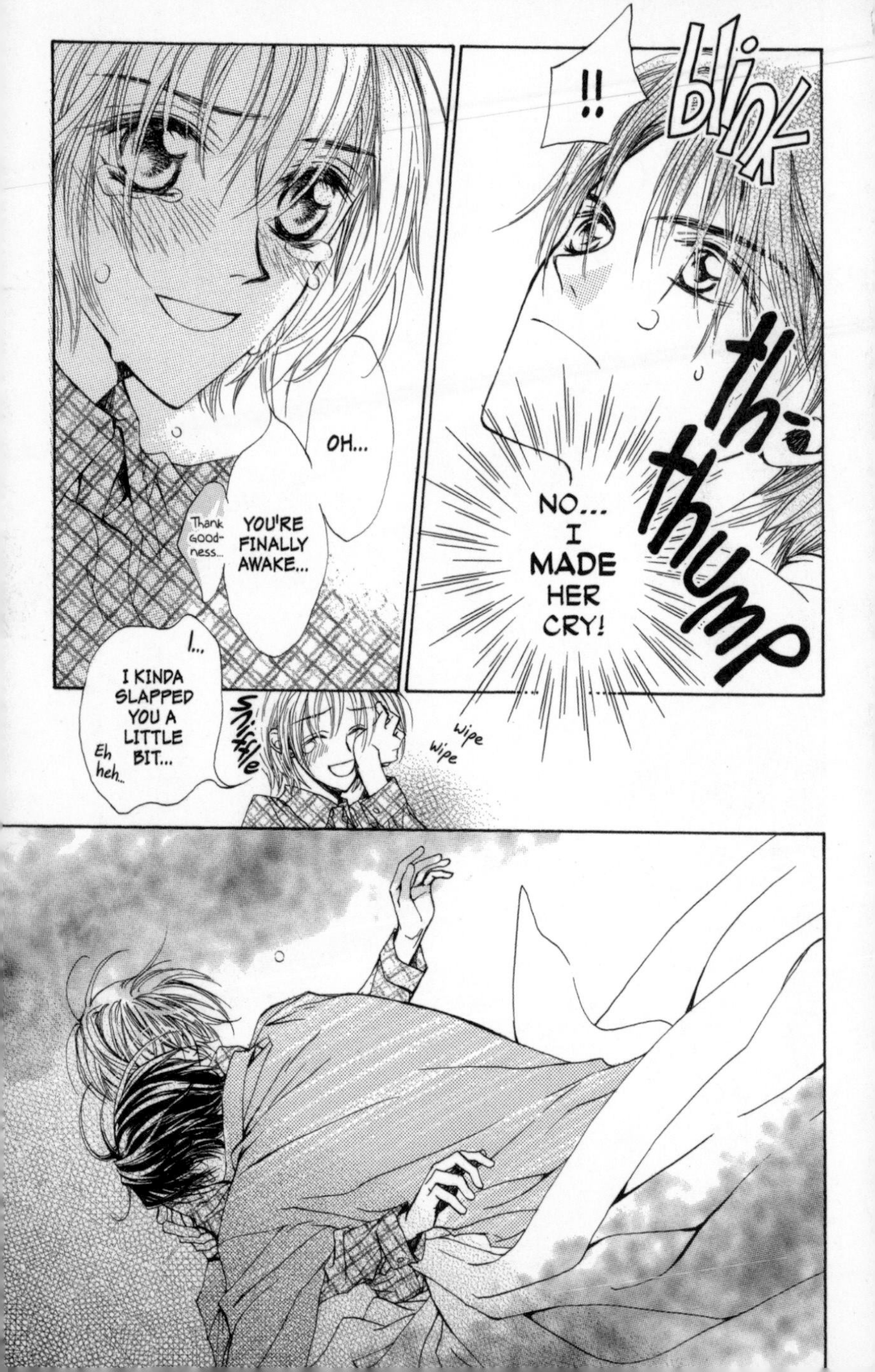
!!
blink
th-thump
NO... I MADE HER CRY!
OH...
YOU'RE FINALLY AWAKE...
Thank Good-ness...
wipe wipe
snifffle
I...
I KINDA SLAPPED YOU A LITTLE BIT...
Eh heh...

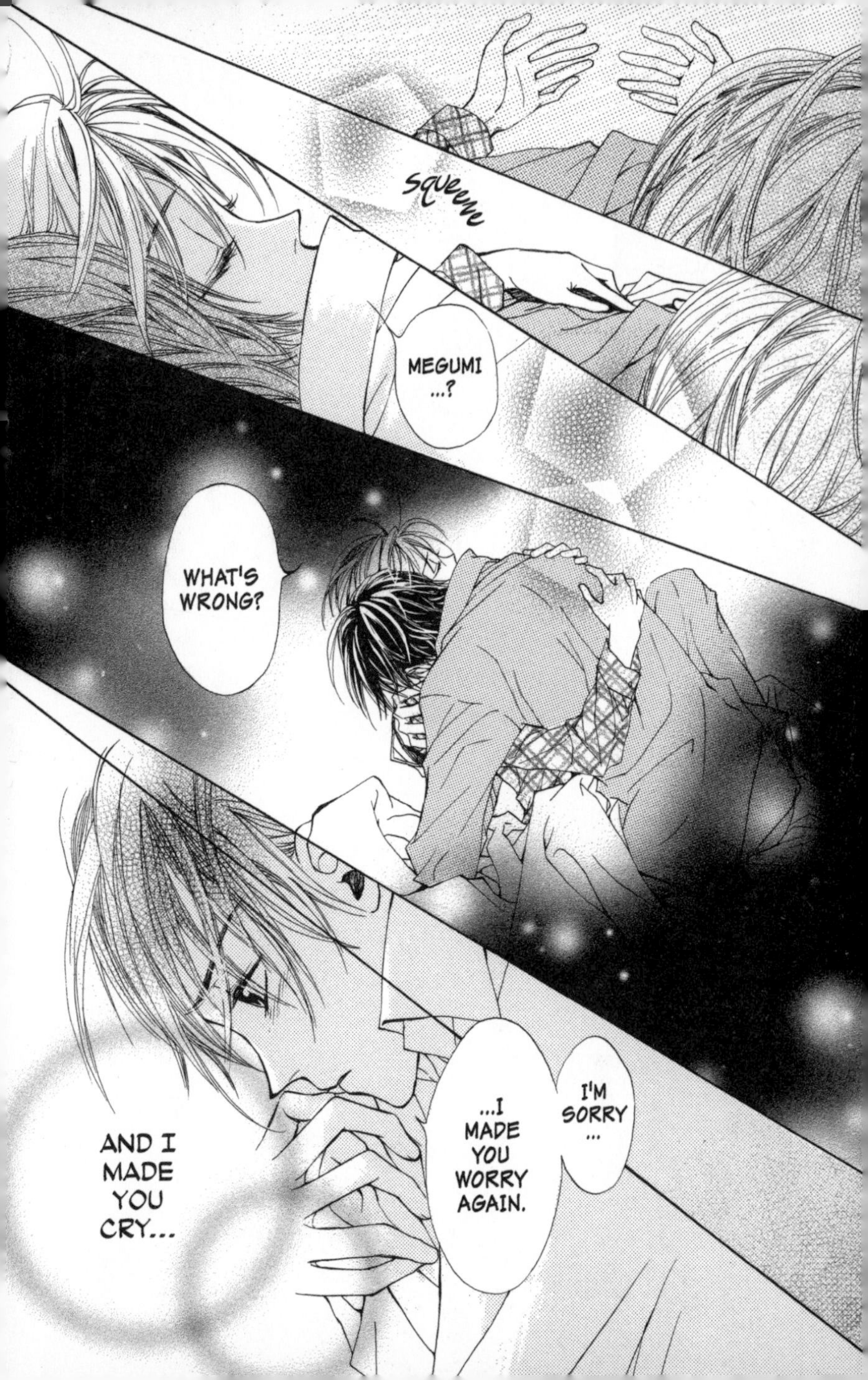
squeeeee
MEGUMI ...?
WHAT'S WRONG?
I'M SORRY ...
...I MADE YOU WORRY AGAIN.
AND I MADE YOU CRY...

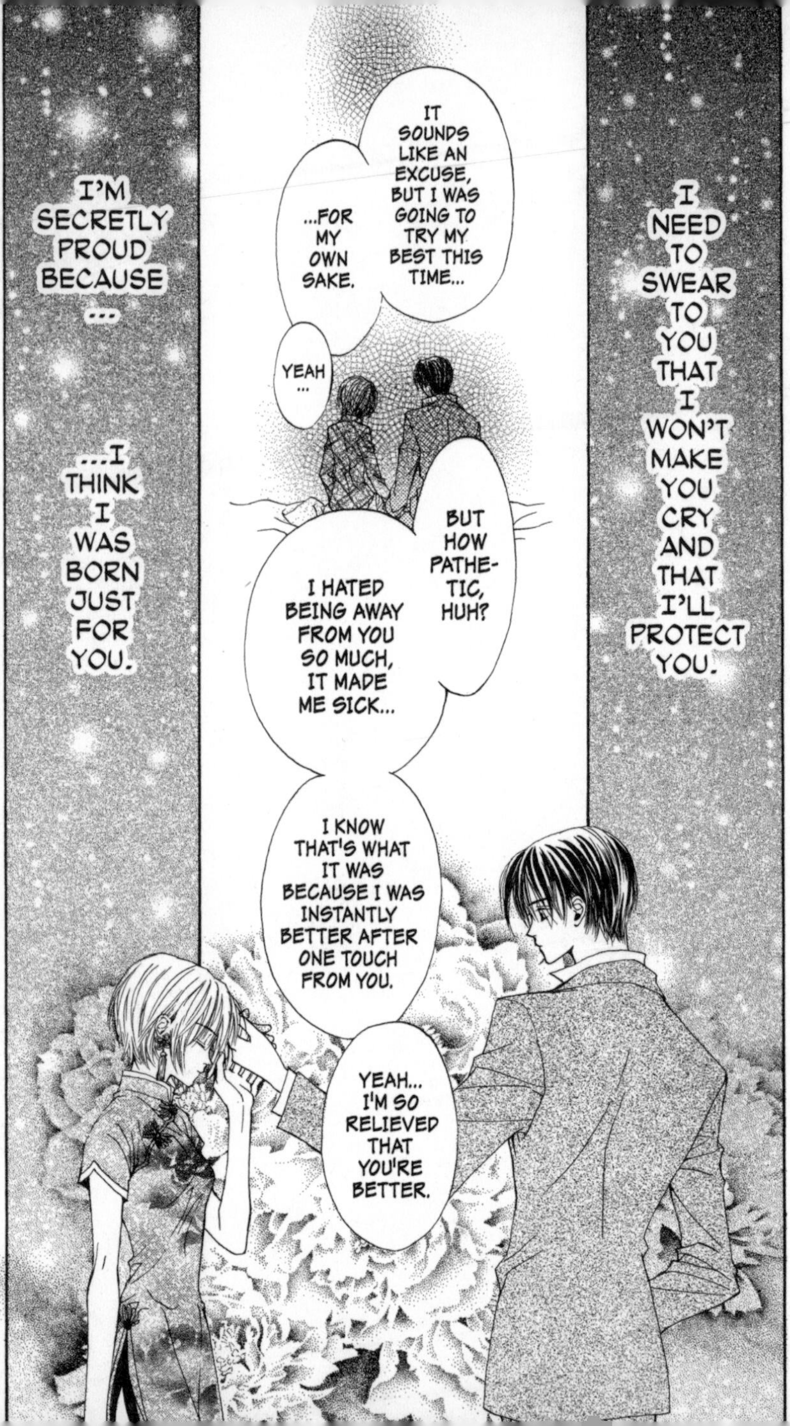
I NEED TO SWEAR TO YOU THAT I WON'T MAKE YOU CRY AND THAT I'LL PROTECT YOU.
IT SOUNDS LIKE AN EXCUSE, BUT I WAS GOING TO TRY MY BEST THIS TIME...
...FOR MY OWN SAKE.
YEAH...
BUT HOW PATHETIC, HUH?
I HATED BEING AWAY FROM YOU SO MUCH, IT MADE ME SICK...
I KNOW THAT'S WHAT IT WAS BECAUSE I WAS INSTANTLY BETTER AFTER ONE TOUCH FROM YOU.
YEAH... I'M SO RELIEVED THAT YOU'RE BETTER.
I'M SECRETLY PROUD BECAUSE...
...I THINK I WAS BORN JUST FOR YOU.

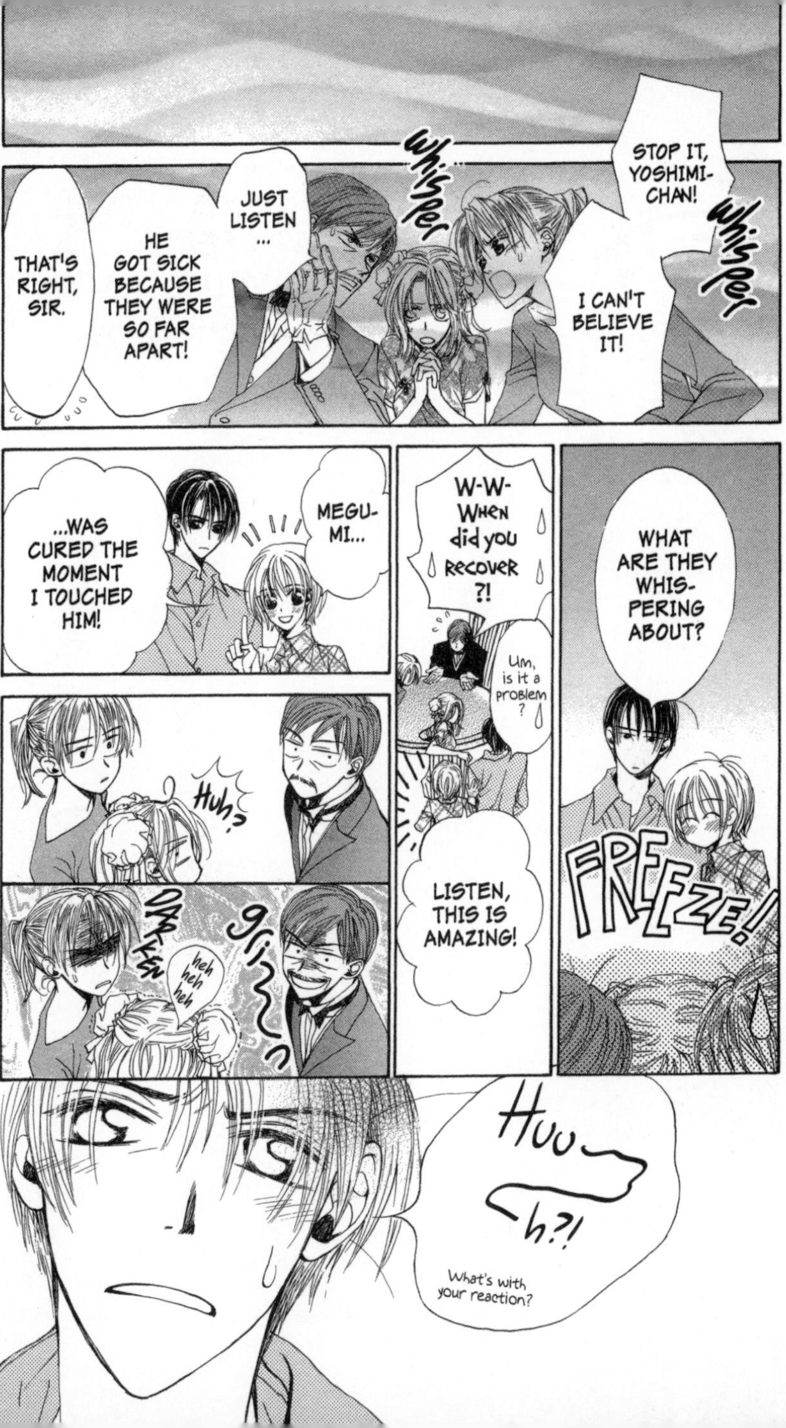
STOP IT, YOSHIMI-CHAN!
whisper
I CAN'T BELIEVE IT!
whisper...
JUST LISTEN...
HE GOT SICK BECAUSE THEY WERE SO FAR APART!
THAT'S RIGHT, SIR.
WHAT ARE THEY WHISPERING ABOUT?
FREEZE!
W-W-When did you recover?!
Um, is it a problem?
LISTEN, THIS IS AMAZING!
MEGUMI...
...WAS CURED THE MOMENT I TOUCHED HIM!
Huh?
grin
heh heh heh
DARKEN
Huuu-h?!
What's with your reaction?

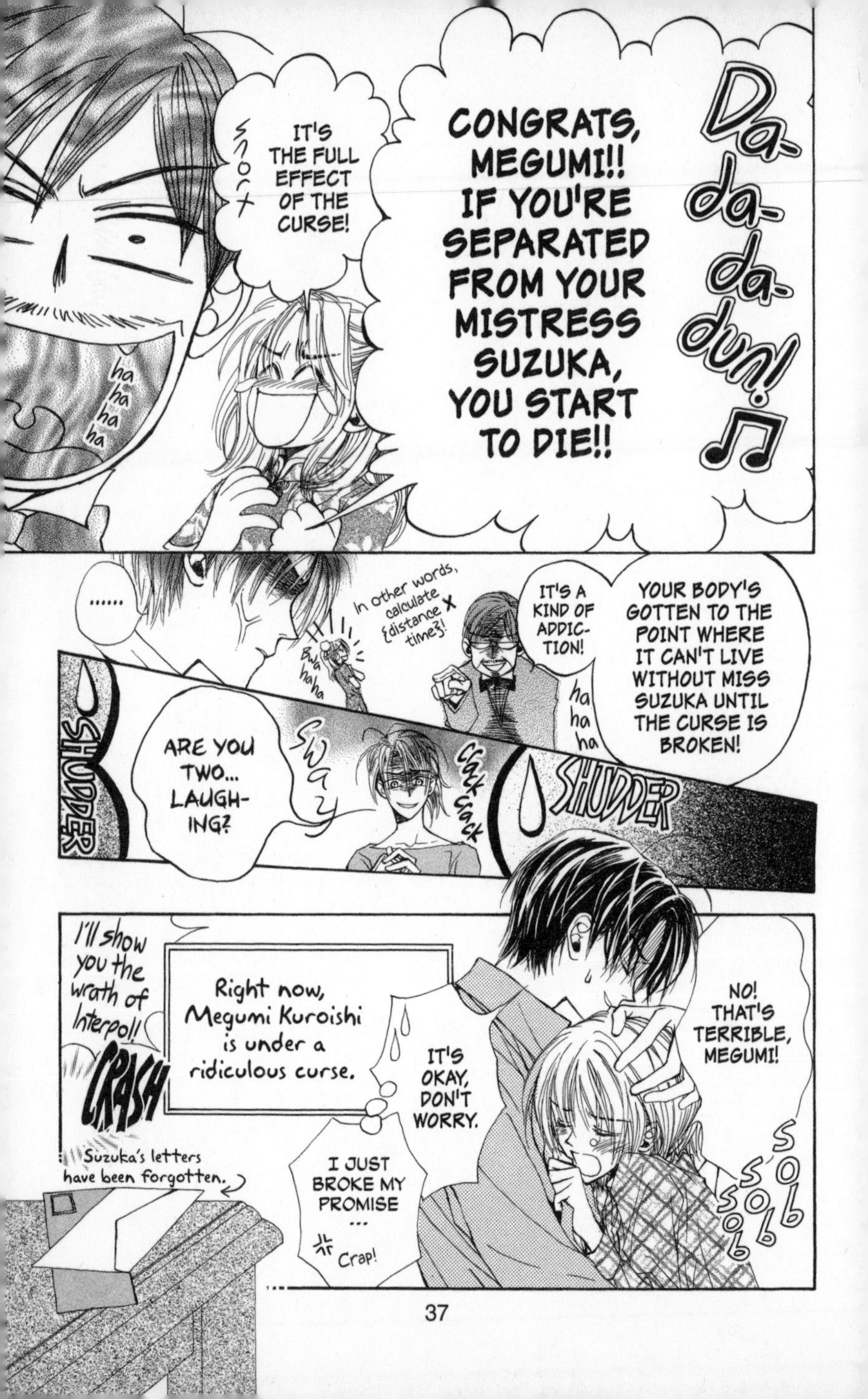
Da-da-da-dun! ♫
CONGRATS, MEGUMI!! IF YOU'RE SEPARATED FROM YOUR MISTRESS SUZUKA, YOU START TO DIE!!
snort
IT'S THE FULL EFFECT OF THE CURSE!
ha ha ha ha
YOUR BODY'S GOTTEN TO THE POINT WHERE IT CAN'T LIVE WITHOUT MISS SUZUKA UNTIL THE CURSE IS BROKEN!
IT'S A KIND OF ADDICTION!
ha ha ha
In other words, calculate {distance X time}!
Bwa haha
......
SHUDDER
clack clack
sway
ARE YOU TWO... LAUGHING?
SHUDDER
NO! THAT'S TERRIBLE, MEGUMI!
sob sob sob
IT'S OKAY, DON'T WORRY.
I JUST BROKE MY PROMISE...
Crap!
Right now, Megumi Kuroishi is under a ridiculous curse.
I'll show you the wrath of Interpol!
CRASH
Suzuka's letters have been forgotten.

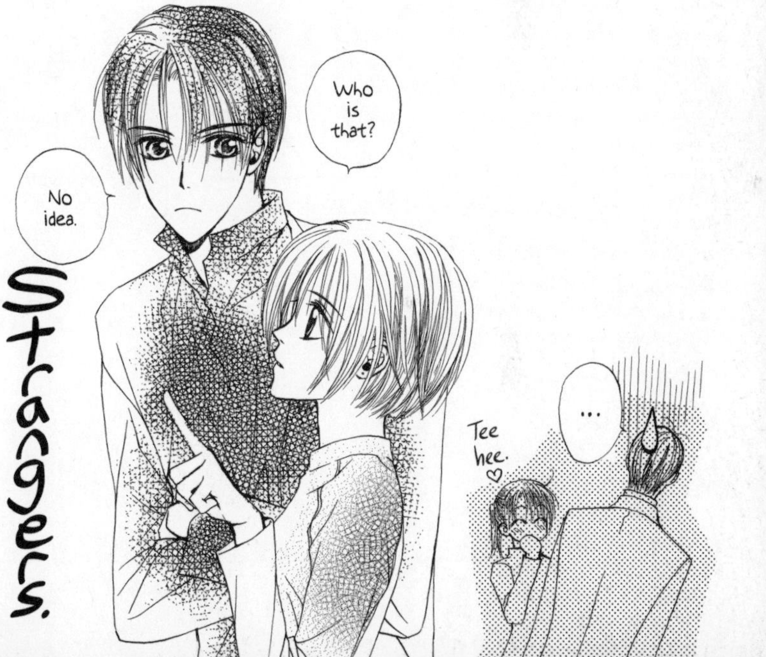
...
Tee hee. ♡
Who is that?
No idea.
Strangers.

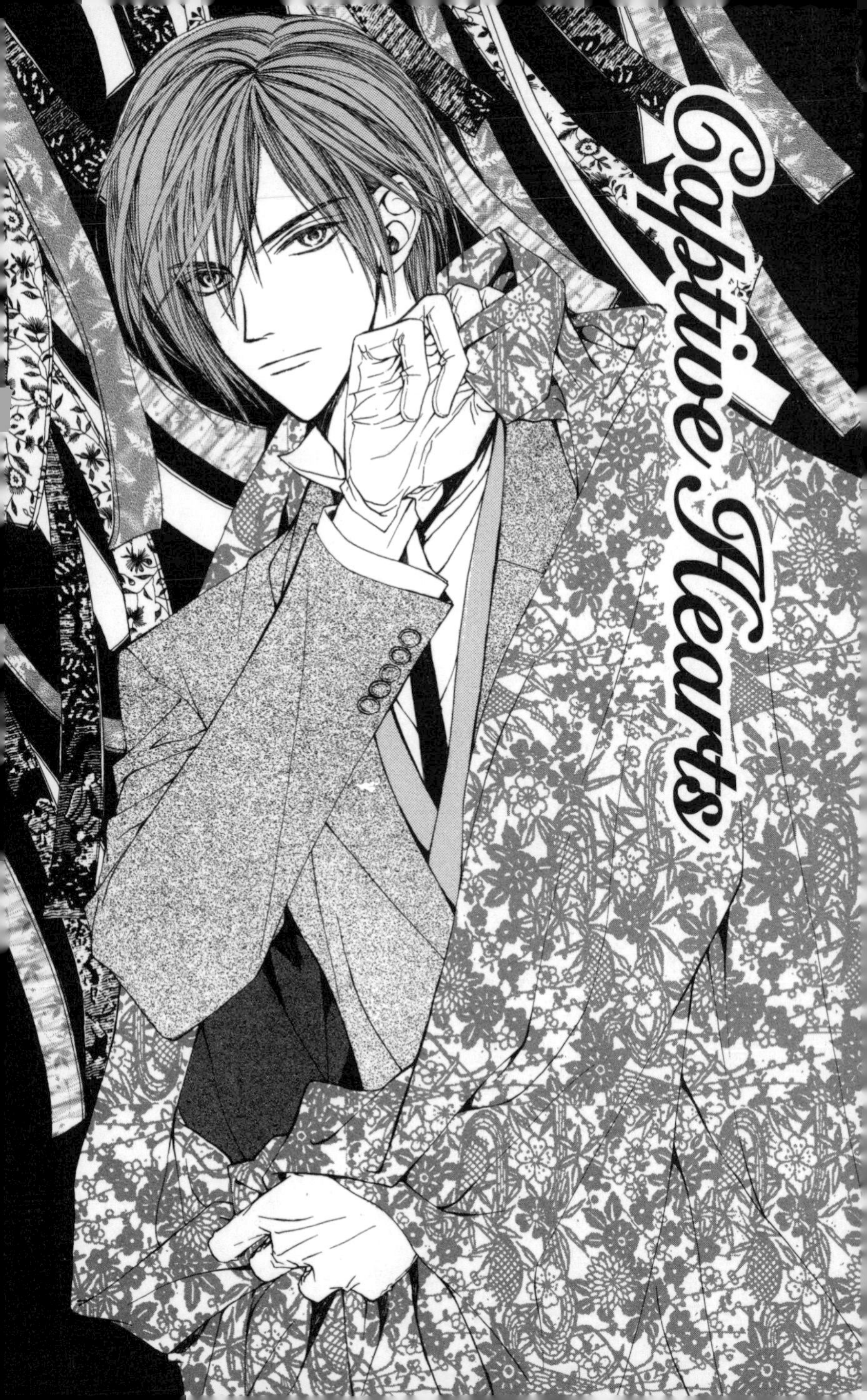
Captive Hearts

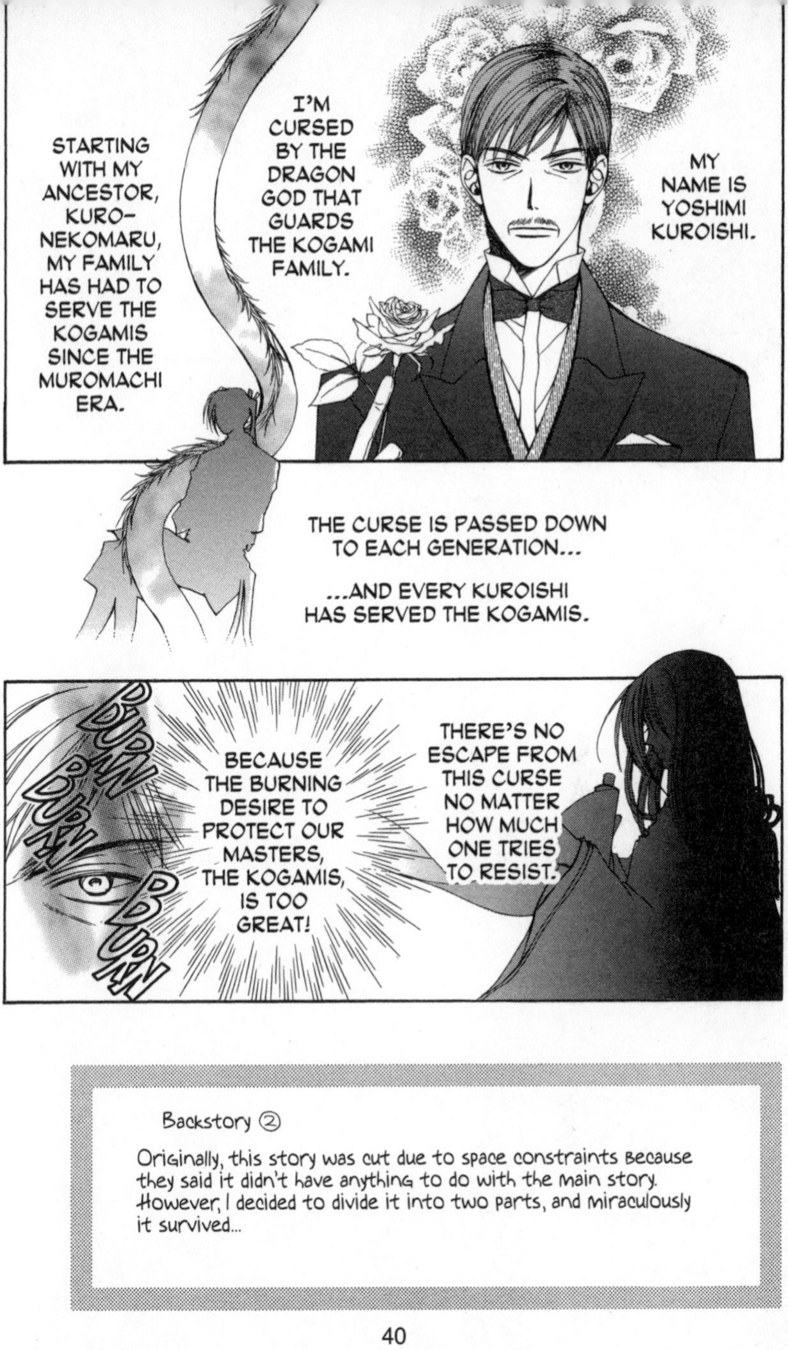
MY NAME IS YOSHIMI KUROISHI.
I'M CURSED BY THE DRAGON GOD THAT GUARDS THE KOGAMI FAMILY.
STARTING WITH MY ANCESTOR, KURO-NEKOMARU, MY FAMILY HAS HAD TO SERVE THE KOGAMIS SINCE THE MUROMACHI ERA.
THE CURSE IS PASSED DOWN TO EACH GENERATION...
...AND EVERY KUROISHI HAS SERVED THE KOGAMIS.
THERE'S NO ESCAPE FROM THIS CURSE NO MATTER HOW MUCH ONE TRIES TO RESIST.
BECAUSE THE BURNING DESIRE TO PROTECT OUR MASTERS, THE KOGAMIS, IS TOO GREAT!
BURN BURN
BURN

Backstory ②

Originally, this story was cut due to space constraints because they said it didn't have anything to do with the main story. However, I decided to divide it into two parts, and miraculously it survived...

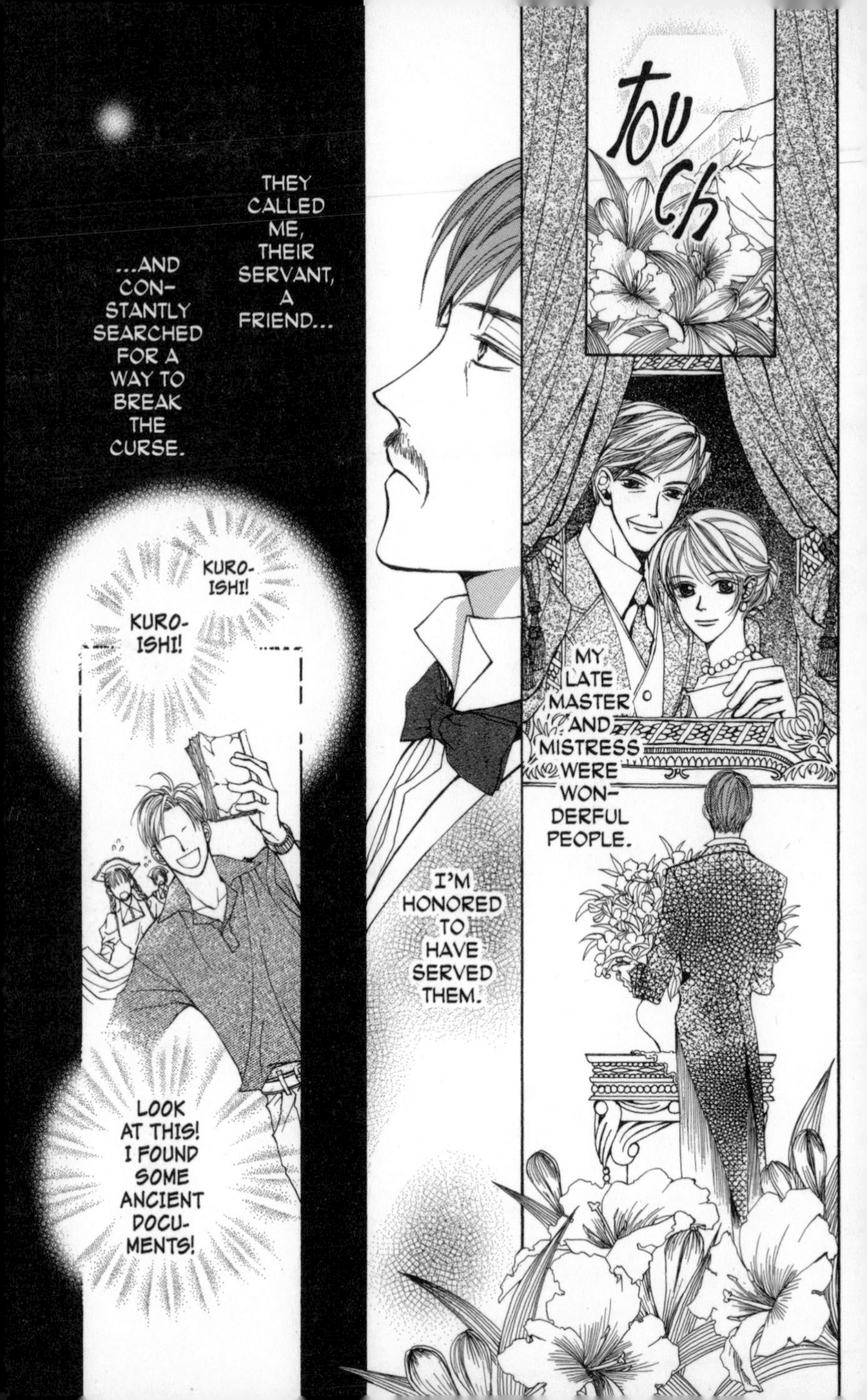
touch
MY LATE MASTER AND MISTRESS WERE WONDERFUL PEOPLE.
I'M HONORED TO HAVE SERVED THEM.
THEY CALLED ME, THEIR SERVANT, A FRIEND...
...AND CONSTANTLY SEARCHED FOR A WAY TO BREAK THE CURSE.
KURO-ISHI!
KURO-ISHI!
LOOK AT THIS! I FOUND SOME ANCIENT DOCUMENTS!

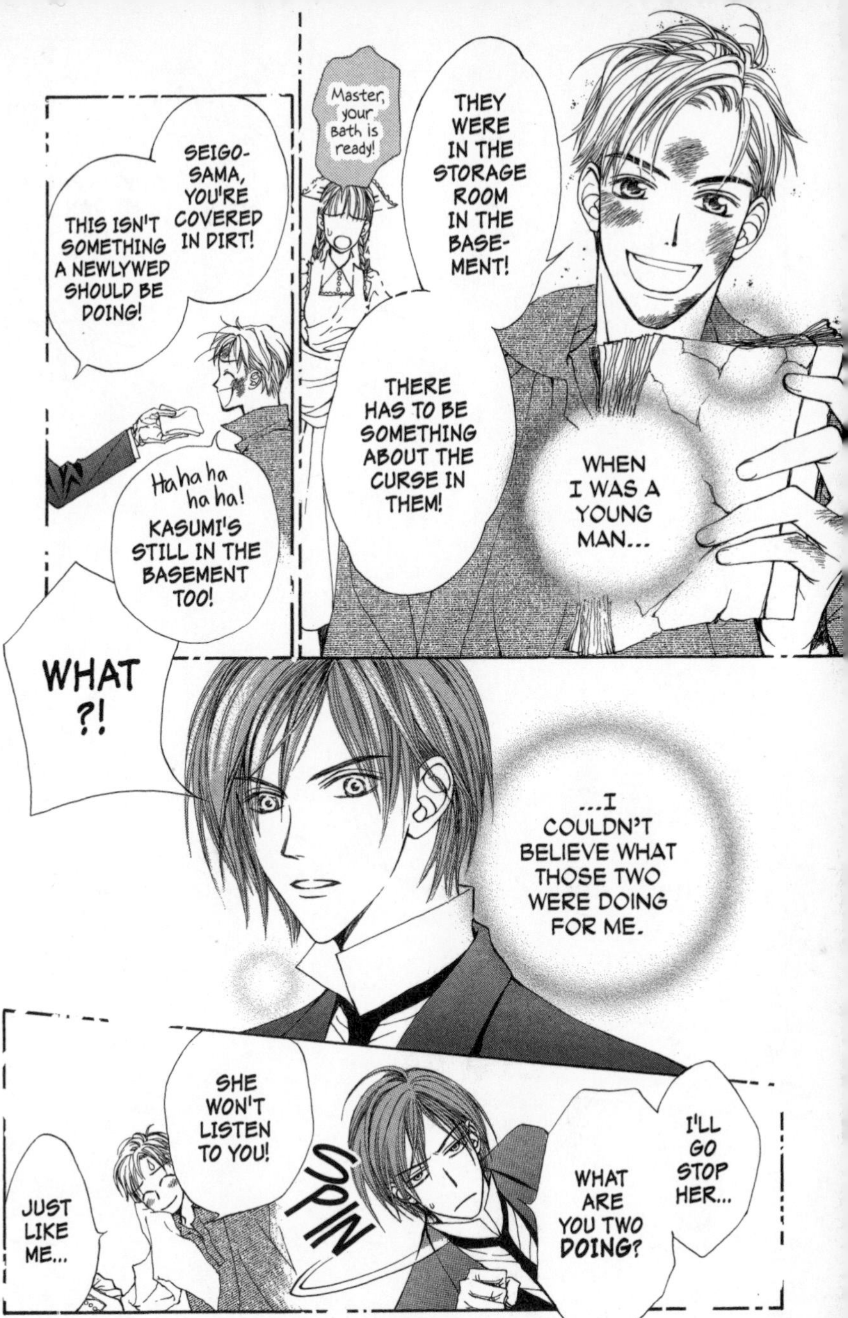

THEY WERE IN THE STORAGE ROOM IN THE BASEMENT!
Master, your Bath is ready!
THERE HAS TO BE SOMETHING ABOUT THE CURSE IN THEM!
WHEN I WAS A YOUNG MAN...
SEIGO-SAMA, YOU'RE COVERED IN DIRT!
THIS ISN'T SOMETHING A NEWLYWED SHOULD BE DOING!
Hahaha haha! KASUMI'S STILL IN THE BASEMENT TOO!
...I COULDN'T BELIEVE WHAT THOSE TWO WERE DOING FOR ME.
WHAT?!
I'LL GO STOP HER...
WHAT ARE YOU TWO DOING?
SPIN
SHE WON'T LISTEN TO YOU!
JUST LIKE ME...